To Dennis,

With Warm Regards

and Best Wishes,

4/15/2016

The U.S.-Taiwan-China Relationship in International Law and Policy

Lung-chu Chen

OXFORD
UNIVERSITY PRESS

Oxford University Press is a department of the University of Oxford. It furthers the University's objective of excellence in research, scholarship, and education by publishing worldwide.

Oxford   New York
Auckland   Cape Town   Dar es Salaam   Hong Kong   Karachi   Kuala Lumpur   Madrid
Melbourne   Mexico City   Nairobi   New Delhi   Shanghai   Taipei   Toronto

With offices in
Argentina   Austria   Brazil   Chile   Czech Republic   France   Greece   Guatemala   Hungary
Italy   Japan   Poland   Portugal   Singapore   South Korea   Switzerland   Thailand
Turkey   Ukraine   Vietnam

Oxford is a registered trademark of Oxford University Press in the UK and certain other countries.

Published in the United States of America by
Oxford University Press
198 Madison Avenue, New York, NY 10016

Library of Congress Cataloging-in-Publication Data
Names: Chen, Lung-chu, author.
Title: The U.S.-Taiwan-China relationship in international law and policy / Lung-chu Chen.
Description: New York : Oxford University Press, 2016. | Includes bibliographical references and index.
Identifiers: LCCN 2015039361 | ISBN 9780190601126 ((hardback) : alk. paper)
Subjects: LCSH: Taiwan—International status. | Taiwan—Relations—China. |
   Taiwan—Foreign relations—United States. | Taiwan—Politics and government—1945-
Classification: LCC KZ4372 .C439 2016 | DDC 327.51249073—dc23 LC record available at
http://lccn.loc.gov/2015039361

9 8 7 6 5 4 3 2 1
Printed in the United States of America on acid-free paper

Note to Readers

This publication is designed to provide accurate and authoritative information in regard to the subject matter covered. It is based upon sources believed to be accurate and reliable and is intended to be current as of the time it was written. It is sold with the understanding that the publisher is not engaged in rendering legal, accounting, or other professional services. If legal advice or other expert assistance is required, the services of a competent professional person should be sought. Also, to confirm that the information has not been affected or changed by recent developments, traditional legal research techniques should be used, including checking primary sources where appropriate.

(Based on the Declaration of Principles jointly adopted by a Committee of the American Bar Association and a Committee of Publishers and Associations.)

You may order this or any other Oxford University Press publication
by visiting the Oxford University Press website at www.oup.com

Dedicated to
My wife, Judith—and all those struggling for a free Taiwan.

Contents

About the Author

DR. LUNG-CHU CHEN is an internationally recognized scholar and Professor of Law at New York Law School, specializing in international law, human rights, the United Nations, and Taiwan. He previously served as Research Associate, Senior Research Associate, and Senior Research Scholar at Yale Law School. He was a distinguished visiting chair professor at the National Taiwan University, College of Law. He received his LL.B. with first-place honors from the National Taiwan University, his LL.M. from Northwestern University, and his LL.M. and J.S.D. from Yale University. While still a junior at the National Taiwan University, he ranked first of some four thousand participants in Taiwan's national examination for judgeship and other high governmental posts—a unique distinction in Taiwan's history.

Passionately committed to fostering a global understanding of his native land, Taiwan, and cherishing the democracy, freedom, and human rights of his adopted country, the United States, Dr. Chen is the founder and president of the New Century Institute (New York) and the Taiwan New Century Foundation (Taiwan), a dual-nation think tank dedicated to the advancement of human dignity values for Taiwan and the world community. He is charter president and honorary president of the Taiwan United Nations Alliance (TAIUNA), a board member of the Policy Sciences Center, a former president of the Taiwanese Society of International Law, and a former national policy advisor to the president of Taiwan.

Formerly he was also chairman of the section on international law of the Association of American Law Schools, a member of the executive council of the

American Society of International Law, a director of the American Society of Comparative Law, and a member of the editorial board of its journal (*American Journal of Comparative Law*). He was chief editor of *Human Rights*, published by the American Bar Association Section on Individual Rights and Responsibilities. In addition, he served as vice president and a member of the governing council of the International League for Human Rights and president of the North America Taiwanese Professors' Association. He was a principal lecturer at the International Institute of Human Rights in Strasbourg, a training center for human rights experts founded by Nobel Peace Prize winner René Cassin.

His publications include *An Introduction to Contemporary International Law: A Policy-Oriented Perspective*, 3rd Edition (New York: Oxford University Press, 2015); *Membership for Taiwan in the United Nations: Achieving Justice and Universality* (Editor) (New York: New Century Institute Press, 2007); *International Conference on a New Constitution for Taiwan, January 14, 2005* (Editor) (New York: New Century Institute, 2005); *An Introduction to Contemporary International Law: A Policy-Oriented Perspective*, 1st and 2nd Editions (New Haven and London: Yale University Press, 1989 and 2000); *Human Rights and World Public Order: The Basic Policies of an International Law of Human Dignity* (with Myres S. McDougal and Harold D. Lasswell) (New Haven and London: Yale University Press, 1980), and *Formosa, China, and the United Nations: Formosa in the World Community* (with Harold D. Lasswell) (New York: St. Martin's Press, 1967). Currently he is general editor of a series of books relating to the UN system published under the auspices of the Taiwan Center for UN Studies, a project of the Taiwan New Century Foundation. He is also editor-in-chief of *New Century Think Tank Forum*, a quarterly in Chinese published jointly by the Taiwan New Century Foundation and the New Century Institute since its inception in 1998. He was a long-time editorial commentator for Formosa Television and *The Liberty Times*.

Dr. Chen has written and edited numerous books and articles in Chinese. These include: *The Sustainable Development of Taiwan in the World: A Collection of Editorial Commentaries from the Formosa Television and the Liberty Times, 2006–2012* (Taipei: Taiwan New Century Foundation, 2012); *The Category and Practice of International Plebiscites* (Chief Editor) (Taipei: Taiwan New Century Foundation, 2011); *The Practice of Important International Plebiscites: Case Studies and Commentaries* (Chief Editor) (Taipei: Taiwan New Century Foundation, 2010); *The Specialized Agencies of the United Nations: Their Structure, Functions and Development* (Chief Editor) (Taipei: Taiwan New Century Foundation, 2009); *The United Nations: Its Structure, Functions and Development* (Chief Editor) (Taipei: Taiwan New Century Foundation, 2008); *In the Name of Taiwan: A Collection of Editorial Commentaries from the Formosa Television and the Liberty Times, 2002–2005*

(Taipei: Yuncheng Culture Publishing Co., 2007) (recipient of the Wu Yung-fu Foundation Cultural Award); *International Human Rights Law: Selected Documents and Commentaries* (Chief Editor) (Taipei: Avanguard Publishing House, 2006); *The Nation of Taiwan in the New Century: A Collection of Editorial Commentaries from the Formosa Television and from the New Century Thinktank Column of the Liberty Times, 1998–2001* (Taipei: Yuanliu Publishing Co., 2003); *The Method and Strategy for Internalizing the International Covenants on Human Rights* (Taipei: Research, Development and Evaluation Commission, The Executive Yuan, 2003); *A Study on the Strategies for International Participation by Taiwanese NGOs* (Taipei: Research, Development and Evaluation Commission, The Executive Yuan, 2002); *The New Century, the New Constitutional System: A Collection of Essays Delivered at Constitutional Symposia* (Editor) (Taipei: Angle Publishing Co., 2002); *An Introduction to Contemporary International Law* (Taipei: Angle Publishing Co., 1999); *Plebiscite and the Future of Taiwan* (Editor) (Taipei: Avanguard Press, 1999); *Selective Documents of Contemporary International Law* (General Editor) (Taipei: Avanguard Press, 1998); *Toward the Establishment and Development of a Constitutional Culture in Taiwan* (Editor) (Taipei: Avanguard Press, 1996); *The Independence and Nation-Building of Taiwan* (Taipei: Yuedan Publishing Co., 1993) (recipient of the Taiwan Pen Society Best Book Award); *The Evolution and Regression of the Legal Status of the Island Nation of Taiwan—Forty Years after the San Francisco Peace Treaty* (Taipei: Plebiscite Publishing House, 1991); *The Independence and Nation-Building of Taiwan* (New Haven, Conn.: Yale Law School, 1971).

Preface

AFTER RECEIVING A J.S.D. degree (Doctor of the Science of Law) from Yale University in 1964, I had the privilege of working as a research associate at Yale Law School and the great honor of collaborating with the noted social scientist Professor Harold D. Lasswell. The American Council of Learned Societies gave Lasswell the accolade of "master of all social sciences and pioneer in each" in recognition of his enormous contributions in integrating law and political science with sociology, psychology, and philosophy for well over three decades. In 1967, we published a policy-oriented monograph entitled *Formosa, China, and the United Nations: Formosa in the World Community*. Professor Lasswell and I wrote that the people of Taiwan, having already suffered through generations of colonial rule, were entitled to throw off the yoke of the Chinese Nationalist military occupation which, by that time, had been underway for more than twenty years. In the mid-twentieth century, we did not anticipate that the People's Republic of China (PRC) would be the stumbling block to the Taiwanese people's achievement of sovereignty. Taiwan, we wrote, belonged to neither the Republic of China (ROC) nor the PRC. We appealed to the United Nations and the world community, the United States especially, to support the Taiwanese people in their struggle for liberation, self-determination, and ultimate sovereignty, along with other formerly colonized peoples. Four years later, in 1971, I released *The Independence and Nation-Building of Taiwan* in Chinese which made me *persona non grata* with the ROC's Kuomintang (KMT) regime in Taiwan. In 1972, I collaborated with Professor W. Michael Reisman to write an article for the *Yale Law Journal* entitled "Who Owns Taiwan? A Search for International Title." The focus of our inquiry was the illegitimate rule of Chiang Kai-shek and the KMT, which had fled from mainland China in the late 1940s and undertaken a military occupation on Taiwan. By the 1970s, world opinion was quickly turning against Chiang's exiled regime. Nineteen seventy-two was the year of Richard Nixon's momentous journey to China. The previous year, the UN General Assembly, under Resolution 2758, voted to expel Chiang Kai-shek's representatives from the United Nations and to seat the PRC. One by one governments shifted diplomatic recognition away from Taipei and to Beijing. Stressing the urgency of the question, Professor Reisman and I laid out a blueprint for a plebiscite to give voice to the collective will of the Taiwanese people and to settle once and for all the island's undetermined status.

Almost fifty years since *Formosa, China, and the United Nations*, Taiwan has undergone a tremendous evolution in every respect. In 1978, President Jimmy Carter surprised the world by announcing that the United States, too, would shift diplomatic recognition from the ROC on Taiwan to the PRC on mainland China. Moreover, the U.S.-ROC Mutual Defense Treaty, in force since 1955, would be allowed to lapse. It was the first time in history the United States had cut off ties with an allied nation.

Carter's decision to derecognize the ROC was a turning point in Taiwan's history, and the decades that followed brought enormous social, political, cultural, and economic changes to the island. In 1979, the U.S. Congress passed the Taiwan Relations Act (TRA) to establish unofficial relations with the people of Taiwan and to make the continuation of defensive arms sales to Taiwan a permanent feature of U.S. policy. Furthermore, the TRA declared that the peace and security of the Asia Pacific were matters of U.S. national interest. Were it not for Congress' foresight, Taiwan may very well have been lost to Chinese aggression years ago.

After the death of Chiang Kai-shek's son, Chiang Ching-kuo, in 1988, Taiwan began a dramatic transformation from a militarily occupied territory under martial law to a vibrant democracy that embraces the values of democracy, freedom, and human rights. An even more important transformation has taken place in the cultural realm. Chiang's successor, President Lee Teng-hui, nurtured the development of a "New Taiwanese" identity that embraces Taiwan's status as an island nation of immigrants with a shared destiny. President Chen Shui-bian promised in his first inaugural address in 2000 that Taiwan would define itself in the twenty-first century as an open society and a leader in international human rights. Throughout his tenure, Chen endeavored to make Taiwan a normal, dignified member of the United Nations. The effects of this process of *Taiwanization* and democratization cannot be overstated. Nowadays the vast majority of people living in Taiwan identify themselves as Taiwanese, rather than Chinese. The younger generations have only known Taiwan as the free, democratic, and prosperous country that it is today.

As the saying goes, the more things change the more they stay the same. The question of Taiwan's status under international law has yet to be authoritatively resolved. The Taiwanese people are not represented in the United Nations. The PRC still presses its unfounded claims over Taiwan's territory—backed by the threat of force. U.S. policymakers for the most part cling to outmoded formulae of the 1970s, which, under a veil of diplomatic obfuscation, feign ignorance of the obvious change in circumstances, leaving Taiwan's predicament to fester year after year. On the domestic front, the era of President Ma Ying-jeou brought economic policies designed to increase integration with mainland China (and, according to many of his critics, increase economic dependency for Taiwan). Ma's policies were widely and loudly rejected by the Taiwanese public. Dissatisfaction with his administration's handling of cross-strait affairs gave rise to the Sunflower Movement, whose members dramatically occupied the Legislative Yuan in early 2014. The Sunflower Movement's momentum continues today as high school students protest the China-centric orientation of changes made to history textbooks as they relate to Taiwan. Through the exercise of self-determination in the most comprehensive and effective sense the people of Taiwan have demonstrated their collective desire and will to maintain their country's status as a free, independent, and sovereign state, contrary to the claims of the PRC.

This book has been a long time in the making. And with it I hope to accomplish many things. As a legal scholar, I have long documented Taiwan's development within the wider context of regional and global trends and conditions. This is the policy-oriented approach of the New Haven School of international law expounded by Professors Myres S. McDougal and Harold D. Lasswell, under whom I had the great privilege of studying at Yale Law School and with whom I had the honor of co-authoring *Human Rights and World Public Order: The Basic Policies of an International Law of Human Dignity*. This book is intended to articulate my perspective on the intersecting legal principles and power processes that shape Taiwan and international affairs generally. As a native-born Taiwanese, I have watched my nation's evolution with great eagerness and admiration. In 1993, after thirty-three years in the United States and having just been removed from the ROC's blacklist, I returned to Taiwan. At the invitation of my alma mater, the National Taiwan University, I delivered a series of three public lectures on International Law and Human Rights, the Constitutional Culture of Taiwan, and Membership for Taiwan in the United Nations. I found a people who were awakening after generations of authoritarian rule under martial law. My banned book, *The Independence and Nation-Building of Taiwan*, was released that year for the first time in Taiwan and won the Best Book honor awarded by the Taiwan Pen Society. Soon after, the Taiwan

University College of Law invited me to serve, in 1994, as a distinguished visiting chair professor in International Law, Human Rights, and the United Nations.

In 1997, with the support of private donations, I established the Taiwan New Century Foundation (TNCF), the first private think tank dedicated to the furtherance of Taiwan's domestic and international development through education. In 2000, I founded a sister organization in the United States called the New Century Institute. By this time, I was spending about half of my time in Taiwan, while teaching one semester per year at New York Law School in the United States. Together, the two think tanks promote the concepts of human dignity and human security for Taiwan and the world community through the production of original research, newspaper and television commentaries, publications, and elite legal camps. The TNCF has three major areas of publication: *The New Century Think Tank Forum*, a quarterly published in Chinese since 1998 in collaboration with the New Century Institute; the New Century Think Tank Book Series; and the Taiwan-UN Library Book Series under the auspices of the Taiwan Center for UN Studies, a project of the Foundation. Taiwan's participation in the United Nations and the World Trade Organization has received particular focus over the years.

When I visit Taiwan these days, I see a country that has changed tremendously in a very short period. A new generation of young people, who have only ever lived in a democracy, are organizing themselves and demanding to participate in decisions that will affect their lives and the well-being of their island nation. I hope this book inspires them to continue their fight and for others to join them in the broader effort to secure human security and human dignity for all. As a citizen of the United States, I take great pride in knowing that my adopted country has done so much to support the Taiwanese people in their times of need. Taiwan's evolution was underwritten in large part by U.S. policy from 1979 to the present within the framework of the TRA. The story of the TRA is at the heart of this book, together with the evolution of Taiwan statehood in international law. The chapters that follow will shine a light on this important piece of legislation, and I hope it inspires decision makers to renew their commitment to the protection of Taiwan's free and democratic society. To my knowledge, there has not been a major scholarly work concerning the TRA published for at least twenty years. This is not because it is insignificant. The TRA is a cornerstone of U.S. policy toward Taiwan and is cited frequently by policymakers, members of Congress, scholars, and others who speak on foreign relations. Lawmakers routinely offer resolutions and bills reaffirming the objectives of the TRA. More generally, the TRA represents a successful attempt by the Congress to influence U.S. foreign policy through the adoption of domestic law. The limits, and the potentials, of Congress' shared powers to shape foreign policy under the Constitution is as vital an issue today as it was in 1979.

In the concluding chapter, I return to a theme that Professor Reisman and I advocated in our article in 1972: that of a plebiscite for the people of Taiwan. A plebiscite undertaken in full view of the international community under the guidance of an appropriately empowered Plebiscite Commission would be the ideal mechanism for ascertaining the will of the Taiwanese people and charting a course for the future political development of the island. This book ends with a call for the world community to let the people of Taiwan decide their own future. Although my land of origin is Taiwan, and my adopted country the United States, the policy considerations and recommendations made in this book aim to serve the common interests of all parties concerned: not only the interests of the people of Taiwan but also those of the United States, China, the Asia Pacific, and even the world community and humankind as a whole. Like so many things, the desire of the Taiwanese people to live independently and freely has not changed. If anything it has been amplified and strengthened. And it is a desire that can be shared by all of the world's people.

DEBTS OF GRATITUDE

I am indebted to my mentors and co-authors, Myres S. McDougal and Harold D. Lasswell, who extolled the promise of an international law based on human dignity. Countless scholars, students, practitioners, and other members of the world community have benefited and will continue to benefit from their legacies as founders of the New Haven School of international law.

Throughout my nearly forty years at New York Law School, I have received much support from both the faculty and the student body. I wish to thank Dean Anthony Crowell, Associate Dean William LaPiana, as well as the colleagues who have offered their assistance and generous feedback. I am also indebted to the staff of the New York Law School library, especially Associate Dean Camille Broussard, Senior Reference Librarian Professor Michael McCarthy, and their teams. My appreciation goes to Stan Schwartz for his manifold faculty assistance. From the student body, I would like to acknowledge with thanks my research assistants, William Fenwick, Aaron Krowne, Jeffrey Liu, Sheila Munn, James Tai, Alexander Talel, and Jessie Tang for their contributions. Particular recognition goes to Nicholas Turner, who, despite being half a world away, supplied outstanding and much-needed drafting, organizational, and technical expertise via email and video conferences over many months.

I also extend a special thank you to the directors and friends of the New Century Institute for support, including Dr. Lung-Fong and Joanne Chen, Rosa Cheng, Eleanor Tyson, Samuel Cheng, and James Lin. My appreciation also goes to the staff of the Taiwan New Century Foundation for their professional assistance, notably Tony Su, Grace Huang, and Kim Chen.

At Oxford University Press, I give my gratitude to Acquisitions Editor Blake Ratcliff for his support and enthusiasm. I also wish to thank Editor-in-Chief John Louth, Editorial Assistant Alden Domizio, and the production team led by Arun Kumar Vasu, for their professionalism and expertise throughout the publication process. Their creative design for the book's cover, with its image of rocks, water, and three leaves, symbolizes the dynamic, triangular U.S.-Taiwan-China relationship and the pursuit of their common and respective interests.

Most of all, I wish to thank my dear wife Judith, our children, children-in-law, and grandchildren for their affection, patience, and enduring support. This book is for them and for people everywhere who are struggling for human dignity and human security, for a normalized State of Taiwan, and for a just and peaceful world of globalization.

Introduction

FOR A COUNTRY of its size, Taiwan has had an outsized influence on world affairs. The island nation has played an important role in the Asia Pacific for centuries owing to its location amid vital waterways. Today, Taiwan is a partner to the United States and serves as a strategic buffer for China, Japan, and other neighboring countries. The island is an economic powerhouse, an essential regional trading partner, and a model of Asian democracy. Taiwan is also the subject of a dangerous and long-running territorial dispute between the People's Republic of China (PRC) in China and the Republic of China (ROC) in Taiwan—a dispute over which the United States holds tremendous sway. Taiwan's future is a matter of great concern to every member of the world community. The resurgence of conflict across the Taiwan Strait would jeopardize the well-being of billions of people whose prosperity depends on peace and security in the Asia Pacific.

Cross-strait relations are at their highest point since the Kuomintang (KMT) fled China in 1949 after the party's defeat in the Chinese civil war. Under President Ma Ying-jeou, the ROC government has sought closer economic ties with the PRC and downplayed Taiwan's *de facto* independent status. This is a sharp contrast to the policies of Ma's predecessors, Presidents Lee Teng-hui and Chen Shui-bian, who embraced Taiwan's sovereignty. While Ma has won many admirers within the Chinese Communist Party (CCP), his popularity among his own people is at rock bottom. The emergence of Taiwan's Sunflower Movement and the KMT's major losses in island-wide elections in November 2014 demonstrated that the Taiwanese people are dissatisfied with Ma's and the KMT's attempts to foster dependency on China. At the time of this writing, the opposition Democratic Progressive Party (DPP) is poised to gain the presidency in general elections scheduled for January 2016. The DPP has historically been associated with the movement for greater national independence and normalization for Taiwan, and the shift in power will likely reinvigorate the debate over Taiwan's status under international law and the PRC's persistent claims to ownership over Taiwan. In the United States, U.S. policy in the Asia Pacific is sure to figure prominently in the upcoming 2016 presidential and congressional election season.

Interest in Taiwan's future among foreign policy experts and commentators has intensified as the PRC projects its growing military power in the region. The people of Taiwan are increasingly wary of Chinese overtures toward the island and fear losing their independence. The subject has inspired numerous U.S. congressional hearings and countless books, articles, and commentaries by scholars, legislators, think tanks, and editorialists. Many fixate on the potential for a military conflict between the United States and China. Others believe that Chinese hegemony in the region is inevitable. The purpose of this book is to give readers a fresh take on Taiwan and offer an optimistic vision based on the attainment of human dignity, human security, and self-determination. Taiwan is not a piece of property to be traded. It is home to 23 million people who have chosen to live freely and democratically. This is a fact that is often, sadly, overlooked.

Unlike books written from the perspective of geopolitical strategy, this book will appraise foreign policy decisions in terms of the common interest of the world community. The approach taken in this book is inspired by the tradition of the New Haven School of international law, which emphasizes the common interests of all of the world's peoples. These interests include shared demands for human dignity and security and the protection of human rights—bedrock norms in contemporary international law along with the principles of self-determination and the peaceful resolution of conflict. The New Haven School is a policy-oriented approach to international law. It offers a theory of how international law works and a program for applying that theory to real-life problems. This program unfolds in five stages: (1) the establishment of an observational standpoint; (2) the formulation of problems; (3) the delimitation of the focus of inquiry; (4) the explicit postulation of public order goals; and (5) the performance of intellectual tasks which include recommending policy alternatives and appraising outcomes in terms of stated goals. The author takes the position that Taiwan is an independent state (although it lacks widespread international recognition) and that the people of Taiwan should be given an opportunity to define their international status and ultimate fate once and for all through a fair and open plebiscite undertaken in full view of the world community. This book is divided into five parts which explore the central issues animating the dynamic U.S.-Taiwan-China relationship in the twenty-first century. In following the five-part sequence defined above, this analysis will give a comprehensive view of the Taiwan question in the style of the New Haven School's policy-oriented approach to international law.

Together, the five parts of this book explore the historical trends and conditioning factors underlying the geopolitical situation in the Asia Pacific and the salient international and domestic legal issues shaping U.S. policy in the region. Two of these issues receive particular attention: Taiwan's status under international law and the role of the U.S. Taiwan Relations Act (TRA) in the formulation and execution of U.S. policy toward Taiwan. The book also considers a range of possible future outcomes and makes policy recommendations for furthering shared interests. Discussions of law, while substantive, are not overly technical and are suited for interested readers of all levels. Legal issues are presented in the context of effective power, foreign policy, geography, economics, national security, and history.

Chapter 1 reviews the history of Taiwan from its ancient settlers to the military occupation of Chiang Kai-shek's ROC in the mid-1940s and the eventual decision by the United States to end diplomatic recognition in 1979. Contrary to claims by the PRC, China's control over Taiwan was historically tenuous and short-lived. The chapter describes the sequential colonization by ancient peoples, the European occupations that began in the seventeenth century, the Qing (Ch'ing) dynasty's efforts to control the island, the Japanese colonization that began in 1895, and finally the ROC's military occupation of Taiwan on behalf of the Allied Forces in 1945 and the regime's exile there after its defeat in the Chinese civil war. The chapter ends with a brief summary of U.S. policy toward Taiwan after World War II, a topic that will be explored in greater depth in later chapters.

Taiwan in the twenty-first century is home to a vibrant social and political culture that is unique to the island. Chapter 2 describes major historical events since the United States derecognized the ROC in 1979 which conditioned the distinctive political, economic, social, cultural, diplomatic, and military features of Taiwan's contemporary landscape. Of special note are the dual processes of democratization and *Taiwanization* that have propelled the country's development since the late 1980s. After thirty-eight years of authoritarian rule based on martial law under Chiang Kai-shek and his son, Chiang Ching-kuo, the people of Taiwan were free to develop and embrace a unique identity. Chapter 3 argues that the world community has a shared interest in promoting Taiwan's continued development as a normalized state. To do so would embrace the universal values of freedom, democracy, and other human rights; economic cooperation and prosperity; and the rule of law that is essential to the realization of the dual objectives of minimum and optimum world order—otherwise known as human security. The current dispute over Taiwan is at its core a question over who has the right to make decisions about the country's present and future. The New Haven School of international law encourages thinkers to identify with the whole of humankind and to clarify common interests for the world community, policy decision makers, and the individuals affected by a particular problem. In resolving questions over Taiwan's future, decision makers must always remember that it is the future of Taiwan's people that ultimately matters.

Is Taiwan a state? This seemingly easy question has aroused vigorous debate from international law scholars and commentators since the conclusion of the San Francisco Peace Treaty with Japan in 1951. Taiwan easily satisfies the traditional requirements for statehood: a permanent population, effective control over a territory, a government, and the capacity to interact with other states. Yet the realities of global power politics have kept Taiwan from being recognized as such. Taiwan has been denied the stature of a normalized state in the international community. Chapter 4 summarizes three common viewpoints on Taiwan's legal status: that Taiwan is a part of China, that Taiwan's legal status is undetermined, and that Taiwan has *de facto* independence from China. It then argues for a fourth viewpoint: the theory of the evolution of Taiwan statehood. Taiwan's status was indeed undetermined after the San Francisco Peace Treaty entered into force in 1952, but it has since evolved over more than sixty years in keeping with the country's tremendous social and political development. This viewpoint is consistent with the principle of self determination—a peremptory norm (*jus cogens*) of contemporary international law.

Chapter 5 reviews the legislative history behind the TRA and considers the constitutional questions raised by Congress' attempt to shape U.S. foreign policy. In December 1978, President Jimmy Carter surprised the nation by announcing that the United States would derecognize the ROC as the government of China in favor of the PRC while allowing the U.S.-ROC Mutual Defense Treaty to expire. Members of Congress long expected the shift but were furious at the Carter administration's refusal to consult them during negotiations. Their dissatisfaction, in part, led to the adoption of the TRA, which provided the basis for unofficial relations with the people of Taiwan. The TRA provided for the establishment of the American Institute in Taiwan (sometimes called the *de facto* U.S. embassy), committed the United States to providing defensive weapons to Taiwan, and declared that the peaceful resolution of the Taiwan question was a matter of U.S. national interest. The constitutional issues raised by the TRA are no less pertinent today than when the Act was adopted in 1979. The basis for the United States' current policy toward Taiwan can be found in the TRA and the three joint U.S.-PRC communiqués of 1972, 1979, and 1982. Under the constitution, however, the TRA is a primary source of law. The president may not adopt a new policy that contradicts the TRA's requirements. Chapter 5 will explore this and other important constitutional questions. What are the limits of the president's authority over U.S. foreign policy under the constitution? What is the appropriate role for Congress in the formulation of U.S. foreign policy? When must the president abide by the limits set by Congress? In 1979, President Carter faced stiff resistance from Congress when he announced the United States would switch diplomatic recognition from the ROC to the PRC. The TRA sprung from this clash. It stands today as a preeminent example of shared powers under the U.S. constitution.

Chapter 6 presents the major developments in the U.S.-Taiwan relationship before and after the adoption of the TRA. Although the United States initially took an ambivalent view toward Taiwan's future at the end of World War II, the outbreak of the Korean War proved the island's strategic value. Throughout the 1950s and 1960s, the United States maintained official diplomatic relations with the ROC, which was exiled on Taiwan, and ensured the island's security through a Mutual Defense Treaty. In the 1970s, countries began shifting diplomatic recognition to the PRC in China, and in 1971, the UN General Assembly voted to expel Chiang Kai-shek's representatives and to seat the PRC as the only lawful representative of China in the United Nations. In 1972, President Nixon made his historic visit to China, and in 1979 the United States recognized the PRC and ended diplomatic relations with the Chiang Ching-kuo regime in Taiwan. Congress, concerned about Taiwan's continued security, adopted the TRA, which laid the foundation for continued unofficial relations with the people of Taiwan. Chapter 6 also reviews the implementation of the TRA under successive presidential administrations and offers an appraisal of the TRA's effects on Taiwan's security and development since the 1980s.

Chapter 7 traces the development of the U.S.-China relationship. In the 1970s, the United States abandoned its policy of containment toward the PRC in favor of diplomatic engagement. This shift was dramatized by President Nixon's historic visit to China in 1972. In 1979, after President Carter's announcement, Chinese leader Deng Xiaoping made a much televised visit to the United States. Subsequent administrations would further the policy of deepening U.S.-China ties with varying levels of success. In 1982, President Reagan issued a joint U.S.-China communiqué that promised to limit U.S. arms sales to Taiwan under certain conditions. President George H. W. Bush oversaw a low point in U.S.-China relations following the Tiananmen Square massacre of June 4, 1989. Relations improved significantly under President Clinton, who struck a deal to permit China's accession to the World Trade Organization and, in a discussion with a group of Shanghai residents, gave

"Three Noes" regarding Taiwan. The Clinton administration was also confronted by the Taiwan Strait Crisis of 1995 to 1996. Under the George W. Bush administration U.S.-China relations became more cooperative following the events of September 11, 2001, while China's economic strength grew in the lead-up to the global financial crisis. During the Barack Obama administration, U.S. officials promised a strategic rebalancing (or "pivot") to the Asia Pacific amid rising tensions over territorial disputes in the East and South China Seas.

Chapter 8 considers the Taiwan-China relationship from ancient times to the contemporary era. China's control over Taiwan has historically been tenuous and short-lived. Early Chinese emperors dismissed the island as "no bigger than a ball of mud," whose inhabitants were beyond its jurisdiction and influence. Beginning in the mid-twentieth century, the PRC intensified its claims over Taiwan following Chiang Kai-shek's exile to the island. From 1945 to the 1980s, the relationship was marked by rivalry and intense hostility. A dramatic shift occurred during the era of Taiwanese presidents that began in 1988 following the death of Chiang Ching-kuo. In 1991, President Lee Teng-hui proclaimed the end of the period of Communist rebellion that had existed since the Chinese civil war. Lee, affectionately known as "Mr. Democracy," was the driving force behind Taiwan's transformation toward democracy and Taiwanization. He described Taiwan as a state and sought greater participation in the United Nations. The PRC responded belligerently to Lee's policies, testing missiles near the island during the Taiwan Strait Crisis of 1995 to 1996. Lee's presidency was also a time of greater dialogue across the strait under the auspices of Taiwan's Straits Exchange Foundation (SEF) and the PRC's Association for Relations Across the Taiwan Straits (ARATS). From 2000 to 2008, President Chen Shui-bian's Democratic Progressive Party (DPP) administration intensified the campaign for UN participation and membership. However, steps were also taken to improve ties between Taiwan and the PRC, including greater trade, travel, and communication links across the strait. Relations improved dramatically under the presidency of Ma Ying-jeou, who sought to build stronger economic ties with China. Many critics accused Ma of fostering Taiwan's economic dependency on the PRC as part of a move toward "ultimate unification." Dissatisfaction with the Ma administration culminated in the Sunflower Movement in March 2014, when demonstrators occupied the Legislative Yuan in protest of pro-PRC trade agreements. In November 2014, voters dealt a smashing defeat to Ma's KMT in the nine-in-one island-wide elections, positioning the DPP to take the presidency in January 2016 for the first time in eight years. In November 2015, Ma met with Chinese President Xi Jinping in Singapore, the first meeting between the leaders of Taiwan and China since 1949. The meeting, while historic, was widely panned, with many critics accusing Ma of undertaking a last-ditch effort to bolster his own legacy at the cost of Taiwan's sovereignty.

Taiwan's economic and strategic well-being hinges on the continuation of positive diplomacy between the United States and China. In recent decades relations between the two countries have been characterized by equal measures of stability and volatility, and the future of the relationship remains highly uncertain. Some observers speculate that we are witnessing the beginnings of a new Cold War. Others contend that the countries' shared interests are equally profound. Chapter 9 builds on the background given in Chapters 5 to 7 by examining the trends and conditioning factors shaping the interactions between the United States and China in the economic, diplomatic, ideological, and military spheres. Taiwan lives in the shadow of the U.S.-China relationship. Chapter 9 concludes by echoing calls for China to act as a "responsible stakeholder," a term popularized by Robert Zoellick, while underscoring the common interests highlighted in Chapter 3, which ought to serve as the basis for global policy in the decades to come.

The author holds throughout this book that Taiwan should continue down the path of normalized statehood in keeping with its evolution as a prosperous and free democracy in the Asia Pacific. Chapter 10 considers several developmental constructs that assist the reader in projecting likely future developments. Taiwan could indeed position itself as a normalized state, abandoning the ROC name and its antiquated constitution. Such a move would require support from the international community and would undoubtedly invoke a critical response from the PRC. To counter the PRC's influence, Taiwan could seek to fashion itself as the "Switzerland of Asia," adopting permanent neutrality in the region and acting as a buffer between other Asian states. Alternatively, it could pursue a path of "Finlandization" by which it would seek close ties with its powerful neighbor. One version of this outcome includes Taiwan's annexation by the PRC under the "one country, two systems" formula. On the other extreme, the possibility that Taiwan may someday become a part of the United States cannot be entirely dismissed. The people of Taiwan may choose to maintain the status quo, avoiding actions that would challenge the PRC's claims over the island. While this strategy has proven popular with many Taiwanese thus far, it comes at a cost as the strategic balance tilts further in the PRC's favor. Taiwan may someday find itself with few options should it fail to decisively clarify its international legal status as a normalized state.

With the U.S. pivot to Asia Pacific underway, now is an opportune time to reevaluate U.S. policy toward Taiwan. The United States is in the best position to provide the people of Taiwan with alternatives to ensure the island nation's continued prosperity, security, and democracy. Chapter 11 considers concrete measures the United States could undertake to promote Taiwan's economic growth and security, to consolidate Taiwan's democracy and human rights, and to facilitate Taiwan's participation in the international community. These measures would be consistent with the language and aims of the TRA and the three communiqués. They include re-evaluating the U.S. "One China Policy" as expressed by President Clinton, concluding a bilateral trade agreement with Taiwan, supporting Taiwan's membership in the Trans-Pacific Partnership agreement, promoting Taiwan's membership or participation in the United Nations and other international organizations, and committing to the sale of defensive arms under the TRA.

Chapter 12 concludes by proposing that Taiwan's future ought to be decided by the people of Taiwan through a plebiscite under the supervision of the international community. A plebiscite offers an ideal procedure for resolving disputes concerning territory in accordance with the wishes of the territory's inhabitants. The chapter offers a blueprint for giving voice to Taiwan's 23 million people through the establishment of a Plebiscite Commission composed of national and international stakeholders who would be charged with carrying out every phase of the plebiscite process in full view of the international community. Its responsibilities would include delimiting the key features of the plebiscite process: voter eligibility, restrictions on funding and campaigning, voting procedures, and, perhaps most important, the questions to be posed.

The book includes an appendix of key historical texts, including the TRA and the three communiqués, for the reader's convenience. Many other documents concerning the history of the U.S.-Taiwan-China relationship can be found online in the public domain and through the digitized collections of universities and libraries. The book also includes a list of suggested readings in both English and Chinese, representing a broad range of opinion. The Chinese selections include materials from governmental sources and scholars from Taiwan and China on the topics of Taiwan's international legal status and probable future developments for Taiwan. Readers who wish to learn more about Chinese and Taiwanese perspectives on these questions will discover a lively debate indeed.

The Taiwan question cannot be analyzed from the perspective of pure international law or pure politics. We must utilize all available intellectual skills to understand the situation in light of the evolving global context. The major trend in contemporary international law is that of self-determination, and any solution to the Taiwan question must comply with this principle. Should the people of Taiwan vote to continue down the path of normalized statehood, their wish would be in accordance with international law, historical trends, and contemporary political conditions. Most of all, the people of Taiwan would continue to live freely and democratically—a state of affairs made possible by the long-time support of the United States, thanks to the TRA.

Whatever the outcome, Taiwan cannot be expected to remain in perpetual limbo. The author hopes that this book will influence the perspectives of lawmakers and other decision makers whose actions are critical to the future of U.S.-Taiwan relations. The Sunflower Movement dramatized the Taiwanese people's desire and will to determine their own future free from external coercion. This outcome is the culmination of a long process of evolution and democratic development, which might not have taken place without the support of the United States. The future of Taiwan should be decided peacefully in accordance with the principle of self-determination and with the goal of securing human dignity and security for all of Taiwan's people. It bears repeating: Taiwan is more than a piece of property to be traded by powerful nations. It is home to 23 million people who live prosperously and democratically and who, as citizens of the world, are entitled to the fundamental human right to decide their own future.

I   Historical and Contemporary Facts

1   Historical Background

WHEN PORTUGUESE EXPLORERS first set eyes on the island of Taiwan in 1544, they called it *Ilha Formosa*, the beautiful island. Soon, it would prove to offer more than natural splendor. It promised strategic advantages as well. To grasp Taiwan's importance in the history of the Asia Pacific, one need only consider its geography. The island is both close to the Asia landmass and situated in the middle of several major waterways including the East China Sea, the South China Sea, and the Philippine Sea. Taiwan is separated from China by the Taiwan Strait, another major waterway which measures approximately 220 kilometers (137 miles) at its widest point and about 130 kilometers (81 miles) at its narrowest. The island has long served as a gateway to the region and as a foothold for foreign powers—among them the Netherlands, Japan, China, and the United States—which have sought to dominate the region economically and militarily over the last four and a half centuries.

I. Taiwan's Geographic Importance

All told, Taiwan's territory measures approximately 36,000 square kilometers including the island of Taiwan (also known as Formosa) and the Penghu Archipelago (also known as the Pescadores). Two volcanic islets, Green Island (Lü Dao) and Orchid Island (Lan Yu), are situated amid coral reefs to the southeast of the island of

Taiwan, as illustrated in Figure 1.1. To the northeast, in the resource-rich East China Sea, lie the Diaoyutai (known to the Chinese as the Diaoyu and to the Japanese as the Senkaku Islands). These islands are well known as the subject of a territorial dispute involving China, Japan, and Taiwan. Quemoy (Kinmen) and Matsu, two small islands off the coast of China's Fujian province, have long been considered an integral part of the China mainland, but have been under the occupation of the Republic of China (ROC) government on Taiwan since 1949. As such, the islands have a different international legal status from that of Taiwan. (Throughout this book, the term *Taiwan* also refers to the Penghu archipelago, unless otherwise noted—but not Quemoy and Matsu.)

Taiwan's geography can be roughly divided between east and west. Mountains and subtropical forests dominate the eastern two-thirds of Taiwan. The Central Mountain Range extends from the northeast to the southern tip of the island with Mount Jade (Yu Shan), Taiwan's tallest summit, reaching 3,952 meters (12,966 feet)

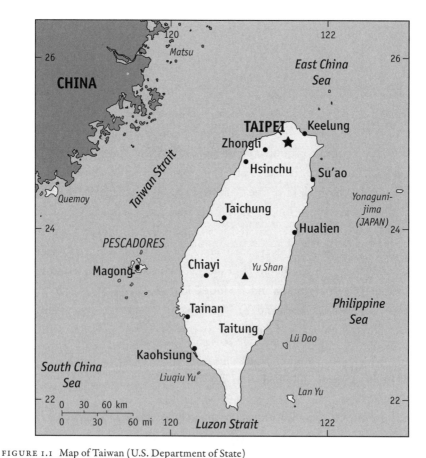

FIGURE 1.1 Map of Taiwan (U.S. Department of State)

Source: Central Intelligence Agency/*The World Factbook* (online), https://www.cia.gov/library/publications/the-world-factbook/geos/tw.html.

above sea level. Western Taiwan is characterized by rolling plains and is home to approximately 90 percent of the country's 23 million people. The western coast is among the world's most densely populated places. Taiwan's urban areas are crowded with motorways, trains, buildings, and other modern infrastructure. Its rural areas are renowned for their lush forests, hot springs, and beaches.

The realities of geography and politics are inseparable. This is as true for Taiwan as for any country, perhaps more so. In recent times, though no longer an occupied territory, Taiwan has served as an important buffer separating China from the waters of the Western Pacific Ocean, which have been patrolled by the U.S. Navy since the end of World War II. The freedom to navigate the Philippine Sea is crucial to the United States, which has stationed military personnel in Okinawa, Japan and Guam, and maintains a fleet of ships in the surrounding waters.

Taiwan's presence is also significant for its neighbors. Japan utilizes the waterways surrounding Taiwan to transport billions of dollars of goods to and from trading partners in Southeast Asia. Taiwan itself is one of the five largest importers of Japanese merchandise and one of the ten largest exporters to Japan. Taiwan also helps to shield Japan from China's attempts to assert control over the disputed Diaoyutai (Senkaku Islands). Although Japan exercises control over the islands, both Taiwan and China have advanced claims to the territory with varying degrees of intensity throughout history. Taiwan's presence moderates the threat of outright military conflict. Were China to establish military dominance over Taiwan or nearby waters, no guarantees could be made as to Japan's continued stake in the islands. Taiwan is equally crucial to South Korea, the Philippines, Vietnam, and other nations whose expanding economies depend on trade routes to and around Taiwan.

China's geostrategic interests in Taiwan are readily apparent. Like others in the region, China depends on access to the Western Pacific for the imports and exports that fuel its expanding economy. Taiwan itself is one of China's most important trading partners. On a symbolic level, China has long asserted the island to be "a renegade province." Gaining political control over Taiwan's government would decisively settle a long-running territorial dispute and further actualize the status of the People's Republic of China's (PRC) as a rising Asian power. However, as the following sections will illustrate, the PRC's territorial ambitions for Taiwan are not supported by historical facts and international law.

II. From Ancient Settlers to World War II

Given the PRC's repeated claims that Taiwan has been an integral part of China since "time immemorial," due attention must be given to Taiwan's ancient history. Historical accounts—supplemented by archaeological, linguistic, and genetic data—strongly support the theory that the first inhabitants of Taiwan were the Formosan Aborigines, who were of Austronesian heritage. Our knowledge of the island's early history owes much to the work of foreign anthropologists such as John Shepherd, Emily Martin Ahern, Myron Cohen, and others, as well as translations by historians including Leonard Blusse and Natalie Everts. Documents left by seventeenth-century Dutch missionaries and Qing dynasty scholars concerning Taiwan's indigenous peoples were enriched by anthropological and scientific studies made during the Japanese occupation of 1895 to 1945. During that time author Kobayashi Gakuji detailed the indigenous experience under Japanese colonial rule. Chinese researchers such as Lin Hui-hsiang have also made inquiries into Taiwan's indigenous history, although with a notable bias toward affirming Chinese perspectives. Professor Murray A. Rubinstein, an expert in both Taiwanese and Chinese history, has compiled numerous essays written by Taiwan experts concerning the island's historical development in his book *Taiwan: A New History*, which has been widely read and cited since its first publication in 1999.

A. TAIWAN'S FIRST INHABITANTS

Artifacts left by Taiwan's earliest inhabitants include pottery, animal remains, shell ornaments, and axe-like tools called adzes. Though the exact date of Taiwan's settlement is unknown, evidence suggests that humans were present in Taiwan since the Paleolithic Age approximately 15,000 years ago. Researchers have looked to the distribution of Austronesian languages for clues about the arrival of the early Taiwanese. The three major Austronesian languages—Formosan, Malayo-Polynesian, and Oceanic—are spoken throughout the Asia-Pacific region. Some researchers believe the earliest of the Austronesian languages emerged somewhere in Southeast Asia before spreading eastward.[1] Linguistic analyses suggest the earliest of the Austronesian speakers were living in Taiwan before 2000 BCE. Investigations by Isidore Dyen in the 1960s pinpointed Taiwan as a possible birthplace of the Austronesian language group, as the greatest number of Austronesian languages can be found there.[2] A model proposed by Robert Blust, a professor of linguistics, and Peter Bellwood, a professor of archeology, envisioned Taiwan as a stopping point en route to Southeast Asia and Oceania. Their "Out of Taiwan" theory suggested that Austronesian culture amassed on Taiwan before migrating to the islands of Southeast Asia and Oceania.[3] Austronesian languages may have evolved on Taiwan before spreading via the Philippines and the Indo-Malaysian archipelago to New Guinea and Island Melanesia and finally Polynesia and Micronesia beginning around 5000 to 2500 BCE.[4] The Out of Taiwan theory was renewed and strengthened with the publication of Peter Bellwood's article "The Austronesian Dispersal and the Origin of Languages" in 1991.[5] According to Paul Jen-Kuei Li of the Institute of Linguistics at Academia Sinica, the present-day diversity of Formosan languages points to Taiwanese antecedents.[6] Social scientist Jared Diamond has referred to Taiwan as an "express train" to Polynesia and described its role in spreading Austronesian language and culture as a "gift to the world."[7] Competing theories about the origin of Austronesian languages propose a Polynesian origin expanding through Melanesia, making Taiwan a hostland rather than a homeland for the language group. Dr. Stephen Oppenheimer's "Sundaland" or "East of Eden" theory posits that population dispersals occurred in Southeast Asia, possibly as a result of flooding, beginning at least 10,000 years ago.[8] DNA tests conducted by Taipei's Mackay Memorial Hospital in 2001 found that Taiwan's indigenous peoples were closely related to Southeast Asian populations.[9] At the same time, the study cast doubt on the existence of a connection between Taiwan's early people and the Han Chinese, China's dominant ethnic group.[10]

B. HISTORICAL CONNECTIONS BETWEEN TAIWAN AND CHINA

Historically, relations between China and Taiwan have always been intermittent and tenuous. The Chinese emperors regarded the island as an inferior like Thailand, Nepal, Burma, Vietnam, Laos, Korea, and other foreign places. Before the sixteenth century Taiwan had little contact with the China mainland and, according to imperial records, never sent tribute to China, even after the establishment of regular trading in the sixteenth century.[11] As observed by historian Emma Teng, before the Qing conquest in 1683, Taiwan was literally "off the map."[12] The first descriptions of Taiwan and its indigenous peoples were provided by Chen Di, a Chinese scholar and traveler of the Ming dynasty, in *Dong Fan Ji* ("an account of the eastern barbarians"), which he wrote after returning from an anti-Japanese piracy mission in 1603.[13] His report described Taiwan's indigenous inhabitants as lacking in the basic elements of civilization such as writing, a calendar, and Confucian propriety.[14] Late Ming and early Qing descriptions of Taiwan emphasized the island's separateness from the Chinese mainland. It was variously described as "faraway overseas," "hanging alone beyond the seas," "an isolated island surrounded by the ocean," or "far off on the edge of the oceans."[15]

Taiwan remained an obscure and isolated place with little or no Chinese settlement as late as 1600. The indigenous peoples who lived there were only sometimes visited by fishermen, pirates, and other seafarers. Official accounts of the island were few, consisting mainly of records from officials tasked with patrolling the South China coast.[16] In the late fifteenth and early sixteenth centuries, some dissident Chinese began settling in Taiwan. However, substantial Chinese migration did not begin until around 1624, spurred by Dutch colonization on the island.

C. WESTERN COLONIZATION

Taiwan in the seventeenth century saw maritime Chinese, Japanese, Spanish, English, and Dutch soldiers and traders variously seeking to settle on the island, establish commercial bases, and exploit its natural resources. Taiwan had never been formally incorporated into any political entity until the period of Dutch colonization from 1624 to 1662. The Dutch had tried but failed to conquer Portuguese-controlled Macao and China-controlled Penghu (the Pescadores). After a brief war with the Chinese that ended in 1624, the Dutch retreated to the island of Formosa (Taiwan). When the Dutch East India Company first arrived on the island, its representatives found no evidence of administration by the imperial Chinese government. The Dutch established a commercial colony on the southern coast of the island named Zeelandia, close to present-day Tainan, where they operated until 1662. The Dutch referred to the area as *Tayouan*—an indigenous word for foreigners—which eventually gave rise to the name Taiwan. In 1626, the Spanish established a settlement on the north of the island that served as a trading post and base of operations for missionaries. The Dutch were eventually able to expel their Spanish competitors with the assistance of indigenous villagers in 1642.

The Dutch used their soldiers to bring under control those villages that resisted foreign authority. In the mid-1630s a *Pax Hollandica* took hold on the island. The Dutch colonizers ruled over a population that included Han Chinese traders, merchants, fisherman, and farmers; Japanese traders; Dutch missionaries and officials; Portuguese mercenaries working for the Dutch East India Company; and a small number of African slaves.[17] Dutch colonial policies encouraged Chinese immigration to support rice and sugarcane cultivation, and large-scale migrations brought Han immigrants from Fujian. Indigenous people assisted the Dutch in maintaining law and order on the island.[18] The colony's revenues derived almost entirely from the Chinese settlers, and there was much resentment as Han farmers and laborers were required to pay taxes to the Dutch. Governor Nicholas Verburg is said to have quipped that "the Chinese are the only bees on Formosa that give honey."[19] Taiwan's indigenous population was required to pay taxes starting in 1642. In 1652, farmers and laborers, provoked by high taxes and administrative corruption, rose up against the Dutch in the Kuo Huaiyi Rebellion. Dutch forces put down the rebellion in a few days, killing several thousand.

In 1662, Dutch rule came to an end after nearly forty years when Koxinga (Cheng Cheng-kung), accompanied by remnants of the Ming dynasty, took refuge on Taiwan. Many Chinese living on the island were pleased when Koxinga's forces, consisting of hundreds of ships and more than 25,000 men, arrived on the island in April 1661.[20] By February 1662, the forces of the Dutch East India Company were defeated, and a treaty was signed to allow the Dutch to withdraw in peace. Koxinga then used the island as a base for his campaign against the newly formed Qing dynasty in China. The Qing cleared a ten-mile wide strip of coastline in present-day Fujian Province to prevent any contact with the Koxinga's loyalists, who were branded as traitors. After Koxinga's death in 1662 his son Cheng Ching became ruler of the island.

D. QING RULE OF TAIWAN (1683 TO 1895)

Qing forces managed to seize Taiwan and the Penghu islands from the Cheng family in 1683. An expedition force sent by Emperor Kang Hsi—assisted by the Dutch—defeated Cheng's soldiers and occupied the island. Following the Qing takeover, Taiwan was left mostly to its own devices. For nearly two centuries the Qing government did virtually nothing to govern or develop the island. Indigenous tribes controlled large swaths of the island and even negotiated with European powers on occasion.[21] Qing officials at court in Peking had initially planned to abandon Taiwan after defeating the rebel Cheng regime and to evacuate its Chinese population to the mainland. In the emperor's view, "[the Chinese] gain nothing by possessing [Taiwan], and it would be no loss if we did not acquire it."[22] One Qing official wrote that "Taiwan is merely a ball of mud beyond the seas, unworthy of development by China. It is full of naked and tattooed savages, who are not worth defending. It is a daily waste of imperial money for no benefit."[23] However, Qing Admiral Shi Lang was strongly opposed to giving up the island after having fought many years to gain control over it. Shi argued for Taiwan's annexation, warning that foreign powers were already coveting the island and pointing out the dangers to China's coastal security if the island were to be claimed by another nation or by pirates. Drawing from his firsthand experience, Shi described the island as a fertile and bounteous territory:

> Both mulberry and field crops can be cultivated; fish and salt spout forth from the sea; the mountains are filled with dense forests of tall trees and thick bamboo; there are sulfur, rattan, sugarcane, deerskins and all that is needed for daily living. Nothing is lacking . . . This is truly a bountifully fertile piece of land and a strategic territory.[24]

Shi's arguments persuaded the emperor to incorporate the island into the empire, thereby making Taiwan a prefecture of the Fujian province in 1684. The Qing restricted contact between China and Taiwan and limited Han immigration to the island, fearing that an influx of new settlers would create potential rebellions while upsetting the ethnic balance on the island.[25] In actuality, Taiwan was of little interest to the Chinese, except during periods of crisis. Clashes arose periodically as a result of resentment between the local population and Qing officials. According to a well-known Qing-era proverb: "Every three years a small revolt; every five years a big one."[26]

E. THE MUDAN INCIDENT OF 1871

In 1871, members of the crew of an Okinawan vessel shipwrecked on the southern coast of Taiwan and were murdered by indigenous Botan tribespeople. The ship carrying sailors from Japan's Ryukyu Islands had encountered a violent storm in the sea near the island. The area's inhabitants mistook the crew for local enemies and proceeded to behead fifty-four of them near the village of Mudan. In 1873, Japanese Foreign Minister Soejima Taneomi was appointed to lead a mission to Peking to seek reparations from the Qing government. According to a Japanese diplomatic document, the Qing ministers suggested that there were two kinds of indigenous peoples: the "ripe barbarians" who came under Qing rule and the "raw barbarians" who were beyond China's influence.[27] The ministers claimed that the Qing government could not be held responsible for the actions of the indigenous tribesmen who had murdered the Japanese crew since "they are beyond the reach of our government and culture."[28] Soejima was under the impression that the Chinese would not object to Japan's punishing the Botan for the murders.[29] In the spring of 1874, the Japanese government launched a military expedition to Taiwan to exact punitive measures. This incursion was the first time the Japanese deployed forces overseas since the Meiji Restoration. When the Chinese government received word of the expedition, it accused Japan of invading Chinese territory and violating the Sino-Japanese Friendship and Trade Treaty.

Prolonged negotiations followed, and at times, it seemed the two nations were at the brink of open war. Japanese expeditionary forces remained in Taiwan throughout the negotiations, and the Japanese negotiators claimed that China's control over Taiwan did not extend to the indigenous territory. Meanwhile, Chinese officials claimed the eastern part of Taiwan fell under its jurisdiction based on the traditional universal Chinese state system. Japanese negotiators maintained that under international law, "an effective control and administration of the territory must be enforced" for a claim of sovereignty over a territory to be recognized.[30] To this, the Chinese responded that they had no occasion to study the details of international law and would refer to the Sino-Japanese Treaty for the basis of relations between China and Japan.[31] The diplomatic gridlock ended in October 1874 following mediation efforts by Thomas F. Wade, the British minister in Peking (and co-originator of the Wade-Giles system of Chinese transliteration). The resolution was humiliating for China, which agreed to compensate Japan over the incident. In exchange, Japan agreed to recognize China's authority over the entire island of Taiwan. The event convinced the Qing of the necessity of asserting control over the overseas territory. The Qing government intensified its efforts to extend Chinese administration to Taiwan, and it took measures to incorporate the indigenous territory into the prefectural administrative system. Chinese officials aimed at "opening up the mountains and pacifying the aborigines" in order to bring Taiwan's underdeveloped central mountain belts under Han Chinese settlement.[32]

F. JAPANESE COLONIZATION (1895 TO 1945)

The Qing designated Taiwan as a province of China in 1887, with Liu Ming-ch'uan as its first provincial governor. Liu undertook a number of projects aimed at administrative modernization, fiscal reforms, infrastructure improvements, and other governance measures. This period of modernization would last only eight years before China ceded Taiwan to Japan in perpetuity under the Treaty of Shimonoseki, following the Chinese defeat in the Sino-Japanese War of 1894 to 1895. The war began as a series of skirmishes for control over Korea in the 1870s and 1880s. Japan, whose rising Meiji government was seeking a path to modernization and increased influence, began challenging the weakening Qing dynasty for control of territories near the Chinese mainland. On March 28, 1895, Japan seized the Penghu Islands and demanded the surrender of Taiwan. The next month, on April 17, 1895, China and Japan signed the Treaty of Shimonoseki. By the terms of the treaty China was to recognize the independence of Korea and give up spoils including cash reparations, and access to trading routes and ports. China agreed to cede "in perpetuity and full sovereignty" the Liaodong Peninsula and the islands of Taiwan and Penghu; to pay an indemnity of 200 million taels; and to sign a commercial treaty opening the ports of Shashi, Chongqing, Suzhou, and Hangzhou to Japanese trade.

The sudden cession and military takeover of Taiwan incited chaos among the island's inhabitants. When Penghu was seized in March 1895, rumors of the impending cession of Taiwan sparked disorder and panic that lasted for months.[33] Organized resistance by the Taiwanese to Japanese military rule complicated the handover. The Qing government avoided involvement, fearing Japanese reprisals or setbacks in negotiations over the retrocession of the Liaodong Peninsula. With no assistance forthcoming from the Qing government, the Taiwanese revolted and established the Republic of Taiwan (Formosa) in Taipei on May 23, 1895. The newly proclaimed republic would be led by Governor T'ang Ching-sung. Supporters hoped the desperate act of declaring statehood would help persuade Western powers to intervene to take possession of the island in lieu of Japan. Within a year, the republic was suppressed by an invading Japanese force in Tainan.

Taiwan was a Japanese colony for fifty years, from 1895 to 1945. It remained a Japanese territory until 1952 when the San Francisco Peace Treaty entered into force. Japanese rule all but obliterated lingering ties with China and initiated a half century of political, social, and economic development that left a permanent imprint on the culture and perspectives of the Taiwanese people. The annexation and development of Taiwan was a historic occasion for Meiji Japan, as its acquisition represented a crucial step in Japan's strategy of colonial modernization. By 1939, Taiwan's per capita value of foreign trade was thirty-nine times greater than China due to considerable efforts to develop the local economy.[34] By seizing Taiwan, Japan secured raw materials for its growing economy and appeared to gain an almost equal status with the Western powers that it sought to emulate.

As Japan's first overseas colony, Taiwan was molded into the ideal of Meiji military, economic, and administrative power. The construction of roads, power plants, electrical grids, and irrigation and the development of public health and sanitation laid the foundation for Taiwan's rapid economic development in the twentieth century. Educational reforms established a mandatory public school system and elevated literacy rates, while wealthy Taiwanese could send their sons to universities in Japan. These advances aside, the early period of Japanese colonization saw persistent civic disturbances, a series of local uprisings, and conflict with the indigenous population. While the Qing dynasty had never asserted its control beyond the western region of the island, the Japanese were determined to bring the entire island under their control. Taiwan's indigenous people were subject to aggressive pacification campaigns by the Japanese. Police misconduct, disregard of land rights, and forced labor were common.

The Japanese encouraged the Taiwanese to live like them, declaring the assimilation of the Taiwanese population as a national policy. To monitor and control the Taiwanese population without increasing the size of its police force, the Japanese government implemented a *hoko* system, requiring every Taiwanese person to register with the police as a member of a household. The system allowed the Japanese to mobilize a substantial body of compliant local elite, whose services were relied on to manage the colony. After the Japanese invasion of China in 1931, the Japanese government accelerated its efforts to indoctrinate the Taiwanese through its policy of *kominka*. War planners saw Taiwan's full assimilation as crucial to ensure the island was fully committed to Japan's nationalistic aspirations. Governors sought to "Japanize" the Taiwanese more thoroughly, banning Chinese-language sections in newspapers, removing classical Chinese from the elementary school curriculum, pressuring Taiwanese to adopt Japanese names, and recruiting locals for military service in the Japanese armed forces. Assimilationist programs sought to replace Taiwanese culture. The most drastic included the coerced conversion of Taiwanese to Japan's state religion, Shintoism.

Japanese rule over Taiwan ended in 1945, when Allied forces defeated Japan in the finale of World War II. In 1943, Chiang Kai-shek, leader of the Republic of China (ROC), met with British Prime Minister Winston Churchill and U.S. President Franklin Roosevelt in Cairo, Egypt. At these meetings, Chiang succeeded in getting some of his government's territorial aspirations included in the Cairo Declaration of December 1, 1943. As set forth in the declaration, the Allied powers intended to strip Japan of territories seized since 1914. The declaration, though not an international agreement, also specified that all territories Japan had taken from China, including Manchuria, Formosa (Taiwan), and the Pescadores (Penghu), would be ceded to the ROC. As will be explored in Chapter 4, the Cairo Declaration was legally superseded by the San Francisco Peace Treaty with Japan in 1951.

III. Taiwan after World War II

At the end of World War II, General Douglas MacArthur, the Supreme Commander of the Allied forces in the Pacific, authorized the ROC (also known as Nationalist China) to accept the surrender of Formosa from the Japanese and to undertake a military occupation on behalf of the Allied Powers that was intended to last from 1945 to 1952, when the Peace Treaty with Japan was to take effect. To the Chinese Nationalists, the opportunity to occupy Taiwan symbolized the restoration of a lost territory, and October 25, 1945, is remembered today as "Retrocession Day." It should be noted that the ROC's claims to Taiwan were as unfounded in 1945 as the claims made today by the PRC. The island had never before been an integral part of China, except for the brief period prior to the signing of the Treaty of Shimonoseki in 1895.

A. THE NATIONALIST CHINESE MILITARY OCCUPATION (1945 TO 1949)

The Taiwanese people initially welcomed the return to Chinese control under the government of the ROC. However, the occupation quickly took a turn for the worse. The new government declared Mandarin as its official language and implemented harsh cultural policies aimed at removing any trace of Japanese influence on the island. A report authored by George H. Kerr, an American diplomat stationed at the U.S. Consulate in Taipei, remarked that the "disillusionment after one month is apparent and, though there is an atmosphere of watchful waiting, a deep ground swell of resentment and reaction is developing."[35] Meanwhile, the occupiers portrayed the Taiwanese as disloyal because of their Japanese ways and complained that the Taiwanese knew little of China or its culture. The Chinese Nationalist occupation was initially overseen by Governor Chen Yi, a close confidant of Chiang Kai-shek. His administration was characterized by rampant political corruption and bribery, administrative incompetence, and repressive policies. Chen's policy of "Necessary State Socialism" saw local industries monopolized and placed under Kuomintang (KMT) control, while raw materials and equipment were expropriated and shipped to China. The new Chinese Nationalist administration oversaw a rapid deterioration in the island's economy. It became apparent that these new rulers were ill-equipped to govern a society that had modernized under the Japanese. The Taiwanese viewed many of the Chinese newcomers as carpetbaggers bent on exploiting the territory. "Out went the [Japanese] dogs, in came the [Chinese] pigs," became a popular saying. The meaning was: Whereas a dog would at least keep guard over a house, a pig simply takes without giving anything in return.

The uprising of February 28, 1947—known today as the 228 Incident—dramatized the frustrations caused by the Chinese occupation. The incident began when police officers arrested and beat a woman caught selling contraband cigarettes. When the officers demanded that the woman hand over the cigarettes, she refused, reportedly saying, "If you confiscate everything, I will not be able to eat. At least let me have my money and the cigarettes provided by the Monopoly Bureau."[36] One of the police officers struck the woman on the head with the butt of his pistol. An angry crowd quickly gathered to confront the police, and an officer fired his weapon into the mob, killing a bystander. As news of the incident spread, scores of Taiwanese congregated at the Taipei Police Bureau demanding that the guilty police officers be handed over to them or severely punished. Groups took to the streets shouting slogans and urging Taiwan's 6 million people to rebel.[37] On March 7, 1947, a group of Taiwanese citizens issued a list of thirty-two demands for reforms targeting corruption and promoting equal treatment of the local population.

The Chinese authorities responded brutally, suppressing the demonstrations and killing thousands of Taiwanese in the process. On March 8, Chinese Nationalist reinforcements arrived from China with orders from Chiang Kai-shek to reassert control no matter what. Governor Chen Yi declared martial law throughout the island and forbade the protest activities. The occupation forces seized, tortured, and massacred an estimated twenty thousand Taiwanese, wiping out an entire generation of leaders from all walks of life, among them educators, students, lawyers, doctors, landlords, journalists, and politicians. Taiwanese resistance was quickly and brutally crushed. At the time of the massacre, Kerr witnessed firsthand many of the atrocities. He sharply criticized the Chinese Nationalist regime in his book *Formosa Betrayed*. The 228 Incident was a wake-up call for Taiwanese who naively believed the Chinese

Nationalists had come to liberate them from the Japanese. Disillusionment with their so-called Chinese "brothers and sisters" quickly gave way to a growing sense of Taiwanese identity and solidarity, like other newly emancipated colonial peoples. The Taiwanese realized they must have their own country and their own government to survive. The local elite who managed to live through the crackdown and suppression sought refuge abroad or went underground to commence their struggle for self-determination and independence for Taiwan. This was the beginning of the Taiwan Independence Movement.

The 228 Incident was followed by the era of "White Terror" during which thousands were arrested, tortured, imprisoned, and murdered, or simply disappeared, well into the 1970s. The KMT regime sought to eradicate and suppress the Taiwanese people's rising consciousness and demands for self-determination. Restrictions on civil society would grow under the Chinese Nationalists, and martial law was employed to justify violations and deprivations of fundamental freedoms and human rights. In May 1948, the government promulgated the Temporary Provisions Effective During the Period of Mobilization for Suppression of the Communist Rebellion, overriding many provisions embodied in the 1946 ROC Constitution. The "temporary" provisions were used to consolidate control and to minimize dissent from both Communist sympathizers and activists seeking self-determination and independence for the island. Under KMT rule, the mere mention of the 228 Incident was a taboo and a crime, not unlike the 1989 Tiananmen Square massacre, which is largely unspoken of in China today. It wasn't until 1995 that Taiwanese President Lee Teng-hui would publicly address the 228 Incident and its aftermath and offer an apology to the victims and their families on behalf of the Taiwanese government. Today, a monument stands in Taipei commemorating the incident. February 28 is now remembered as Peace Memorial Day.

B. THE NATIONALIST CHINESE IN EXILE (1949 TO 1987)

By 1947, the Chinese Nationalists were engaged in a bloody civil war with the Chinese Communists led by Mao Zedong (Tse-tung). In early 1947, the Nationalist government unilaterally and arbitrarily declared Taiwan to be one of the thirty-five provinces of the Republic of China, an act in violation of the Allied accords and general international law. In January 1949, as the civil war worsened, Chiang Kai-shek resigned his presidency. Soon after, the Communists seized power and, on October 1, 1949, Mao declared the founding of the People's Republic of China (PRC) on the China mainland. Defeated, Chiang and more than one million of his supporters sought refuge on Taiwan. There, Chiang proclaimed the re-establishment of the Republic of China (ROC) in Taipei (an exile government), declaring on May

19, 1949, a permanent state of martial law on the island, which would last for thirty-eight years, until June 1987.

On March 1, 1950, Chiang named himself president of the ROC on Taiwan and appointed representatives of the KMT to various positions in the new government. For the next four decades, the KMT regime, through the ROC government on Taiwan, carried on the fight against the Chinese Communists. Under martial law, the state criminalized political speech perceived as subversive or critical of government policy. The Taiwan Garrison Command was tasked with suppressing activities posing a challenge the KMT's monopoly of power. Taiwanese who challenged the government risked being sentenced to concentration camps or even death.

As of October 1949, the ROC government's controlled territory had been reduced from the entire Chinese mainland to an exiled island of some 8 million people, consisting of Taiwanese and mainland refugees, accounting for about 85 percent and 15 percent of the population, respectively. However, the exiled ROC regime continued to claim sovereignty over all of China and its population of roughly 500 million. As representation in the KMT government was apportioned by the origin of the population, the 85 percent of the population who were Taiwanese were allotted just 3 percent of the legislative seats on the island, while KMT members who fled from China were given 97 percent of the seats to represent their so-called "lost" constituencies on the China mainland, now under the PRC's communist rule.

C. U.S. POLICY TOWARD TAIWAN AFTER WORLD WAR II

The United States' actions in late 1949 and early 1950 made it clear that U.S. leaders had no desire to become involved in the Chinese civil war. On January 5, 1950, several months after the Communists' victory, President Truman issued a statement announcing the United States would not interfere in the cross-strait conflict. Nor did the United States offer military aid to Chiang's forces on Taiwan. Truman was forced to reverse his position two days after the outbreak of the Korean War, on June 25, 1950. Military planners suddenly found it necessary to seek the "neutralization of Formosa" as part of an overall U.S. strategy in Asia. Truman dispatched the Seventh Fleet to deter hostilities between the ROC and the PRC. Henceforth, Taiwan would be under the military protection of the United States. The United States began providing economic and military aid to the ROC regime and established the U.S. Military Assistance and Advisory Group in Taiwan. The 1948 Temporary Provisions Effective During the Period of Mobilization for Suppression of the Communist Rebellion gave Chiang Kai-shek practically unlimited power, and he used the provisions as a basis for martial law on Taiwan, even in the absence of a Communist uprising on the island. With support from the United States, which then recognized the ROC as the only lawful government of China, the KMT military occupation of Taiwan would persist until the late 1980s.

In his State of the Union address in 1953, President Dwight Eisenhower proclaimed that the Seventh Fleet would no longer be "employed to shield Communist China" from the ROC.[38] Nevertheless, the Chinese Nationalists never undertook a large-scale invasion of China. Instead, in 1954, the PRC initiated its own artillery attacks on offshore islands held by the ROC (Quemoy and Matsu and other small islands). The crisis spurred the United States and the ROC to sign a mutual defense treaty in December 1954, whereby the United States committed itself to the defense of Taiwan (Formosa) and the Pescadores (Penghu) and "such other territories as may be determined by mutual agreement."[39] The conclusion of the Mutual Defense Treaty in 1954, which entered into effect in 1955, protected Taiwan from an invasion by the PRC. On January 29, 1955, before the ratification of the treaty, Congress passed the Formosa Resolution, which authorized the president to deploy U.S. armed forces "as he deems necessary for the specific purpose of securing and protecting Formosa and the Pescadores against armed attack," including "the securing and protection of such related positions and territories of that area now in friendly hands."[40]

During the late 1960s, Henry Kissinger, the presidential assistant for national security affairs, and other members of the Nixon administration began laying the groundwork for negotiations with the PRC over normalizing relations. In 1971, Kissinger made a secret trip to the PRC as the administration began to take steps to end its policy of isolation against the PRC. Meanwhile in the United Nations, the PRC was assembling a bloc of friendly nations to support its bid to replace the ROC as China's representative in the General Assembly and the Security Council. Since 1945, Chiang Kai-shek's ROC regime had clung to its seat in the United Nations, where it claimed to represent the whole of China in the international community, even while exiled in Taiwan without any control over the China mainland.

On October 25, 1971, the General Assembly adopted Resolution 2758, acting to "restore all its rights to the People's Republic of China and to recognize the representatives of its Government as the only lawful representatives of China to the United Nations and to expel forthwith the representatives of Chiang Kai-shek from the place which they unlawfully occupy at the United Nations and in all the organizations related to it."[41] Before the vote, the United States campaigned to preserve the ROC's seat in the General Assembly and to allow both countries to hold UN seats. But the effort was in vain, as Chiang stubbornly insisted that "patriots and traitors cannot coexist." Events progressed rapidly over the next two years. In December 1971, Kissinger declared in a news conference that "[t]he ultimate disposition, the ultimate relationship of Taiwan to the People's Republic of China should be settled by direct negotiations between Taiwan and the People's Republic of China."[42]

Shortly after, Nixon announced a "journey for peace" to China in February of 1972.[43] On February 9, 1972, President Nixon announced in his "The State of the World" message that "[t]he ultimate relationship between Taiwan and the mainland is not a matter for the United States to decide. A peaceful resolution of this problem by the parties would do much to reduce tension in the Far East. We are not, however, urging either party to follow any particular course."[44] On February 28, the United States and the PRC issued the Joint Communiqué of the United States of America and the People's Republic of China (also known as the Shanghai Communiqué), in which the United States acknowledged (but did not recognize) that "all Chinese on either side of the Taiwan Strait maintain there is but one China and that Taiwan is a part of China." After Nixon's resignation, and several years of continued U.S.-PRC negotiations, on December 15, 1978, President Jimmy Carter revealed that the United States would formally recognize the PRC as the sole legal government of China and permit the expiration of the U.S.-ROC Mutual Defense Treaty. The United States would cease to recognize the ROC government as of January 1, 1979. Carter's announcement was accompanied by the text of the Joint Communiqué on the Establishment of Diplomatic Relations (the Second Communiqué) in which the United States again acknowledged the Chinese position regarding Taiwan without recognizing it as such.

D. THE TAIWAN RELATIONS ACT (1979)

Carter's announcement, which will be explored in depth in Chapter 5, marked the end of the United States' alliance with the ROC that had existed since World War II. However, derecognition did not mean a complete severing of ties. The joint U.S.-China communiqué of 1978 which announced the establishment of diplomatic relations stated that the people of the United States would maintain cultural, commercial, and other unofficial relations with the people of Taiwan. On January 29, 1979, twenty-eight days after the United States terminated diplomatic relations with the ROC, Senator Frank Church introduced Senate bill S.245, titled the Taiwan Enabling Act. On the same day, Representative Clement Zablocki introduced H.R. 1614, a companion bill to S.245, in the House of Representatives. The Act provided a basic legal framework for the United States to maintain commercial, cultural, and other ties with the people of Taiwan on an unofficial basis. The bill, renamed the Taiwan Relations Act (TRA), received overwhelming bipartisan support and passed by a vote of 339 to 50 in the House on March 28, 1979, and 85 to 4 in the Senate on March 29, 1979. On April 10, 1979, President Carter signed the TRA into law.[45]

The TRA establishes several critical expectations for U.S. policy concerning Taiwan and the Asia Pacific generally. As stated in Section 2(a), the TRA's purpose is to "help maintain peace, security, and stability in the Western Pacific; and to pro-mote the foreign policy of the United States by authorizing the continuation of commercial, cultural, and other relations between the people of the United States and the people on Taiwan." The TRA declares that the "peace and stability in the area are in the political, security, and economic interests of the United States, and are matters of international concern." The law further states that "the United States decision to establish diplomatic relations with the People's Republic of China rested upon the expectation that the future of Taiwan would be determined by peaceful means."[46]

Section 3 of the TRA authorizes the United States to "provide Taiwan with arms of a defensive character." This provision has served as the basis for U.S. arms sales to Taiwan since 1979. Under the TRA, it is U.S. policy to remain able "to resist any resort to force or other forms of coercion that would jeopardize the security, or the social or economic system, of the people on Taiwan."[47] The TRA does not commit the United States to military action, as was the case under the U.S.-ROC Mutual Defense Treaty. However, the TRA has long been recognized as a functional equiva-lent of the Mutual Defense Treaty.

The TRA makes certain that U.S. laws in force before 1979 continue to apply to Taiwan regardless of its diplomatic status. Examples include laws that refer or relate to foreign countries, nations, states, governments, or similar entities or laws govern-ing programs, transactions, or relations with them; rights or obligations in contracts and debts under U.S. laws; Taiwan's treatment for the purposes of the Immigration and Nationality Act; and Taiwan's standing in U.S. courts.

To address the risk that Taiwan could be ostracized from the international com-munity, the TRA states that "nothing in the [TRA] may be construed as a basis for supporting the exclusion or expulsion of Taiwan from continued membership in any international financial institution or any other international organization."[48] The provision does not impose on the United States an affirmative obligation to sup-port Taiwan's participation in international organizations. However it implies that the United States will not actively discourage Taiwan from joining them.

Though U.S.-Taiwan relations are of an informal nature, the United States must still perform certain governmental functions in Taiwan, such as rendering consular services to American citizens on the island. In recognition of this need, the TRA provides for the establishment of the American Institute in Taiwan (AIT). The AIT is a nonprofit organization incorporated under the laws of the District of Columbia and is commonly referred to as the *de facto* U.S. embassy in Taiwan. The AIT's main functions include conducting programs, transactions, and other relations autho-rized by the president or any agency of the U.S. government. Simultaneously, the TRA confers on the AIT the ability to enter into and enforce agreements and transactions on behalf of the United States subject to the authorization of the president or a U.S. government agency. The AIT offers a range of services both to Taiwanese and U.S. citizens designed to "preserve and promote extensive, close, and friendly commercial, cultural, and other relations between the people of the United States and the people of Taiwan." Today there are a total of four AIT offices, including a headquarters in Arlington, Virginia, a principal branch office in Taipei, and two smaller branch offices in the cities of Kaohsiung and Taichung. A new, modernized facility is scheduled to open in the Neihu District of Taipei in late 2015.

Nineteen seventy-nine was a watershed year for Taiwan's contemporary development. The decades that followed brought enormous social, political, cultural, and economic changes to the island. This evolution was underwritten in large part by U.S. policy within the framework of the TRA. With support from the United States, Taiwan transitioned from a militarily occupied territory under martial law to a vibrant democratic society that embraces the values of democracy, freedom, and human rights. Chapter 2 focuses on the major events after 1979 which have shaped, and continue to shape, Taiwan's contemporary landscape.

Notes

1. *See, e.g.*, Malcolm Ross, *The Integrity of the Austronesian Language Family: From Taiwan to Oceania, in* PAST HUMAN MIGRATIONS IN EAST ASIA: MATCHING ARCHAEOLOGY, LINGUISTICS AND GENETICS 161–81 (Alicia Sanchez-Mazas et al. eds. 2008).

2. *See* Michael Stainton, *The Politics of Taiwan Aboriginal Origins, in* TAIWAN: A NEW HISTORY 27–44 (Murray A. Rubinstein ed., 2015).

3. Peter Bellwood, *Formosan Prehistory and Austronesian Dispersal, in* AUSTRONESIAN TAIWAN: LINGUISTICS, HISTORY, ETHNOLOGY, PREHISTORY 337–65 (David Blundell ed., 2009).

4. Ross, *supra* note 1, at 173.

5. Peter Bellwood, *The Austronesian Dispersal and the Origin of Languages*, SCI. AM. 88–93 (July 1991).

6. Paul Jen-Kuei Li, *The Great Diversity of Formosan Languages*, 9 LANGUAGE & LINGUISTICS 523–46 (2008).

7. Jared M. Diamond, *Express Train to Polynesia*, 336 NATURE 307–08 (1988); Jared M. Diamond, *Taiwan's Gift to the World*, 403 NATURE 709–10 (2000).

8. *See* STEPHEN OPPENHEIMER, EDEN IN THE EAST: THE DROWNED CONTINENT OF SOUTHEAST ASIA (1999).

9. Jean Trejaut et al., *Traces of Archaic Mitochondrial Lineages Persist in Austronesian-Speaking Formosan Populations*, 3 PLoS BIOL. e247 (2005).

10. See Marie Lin et al., *The Origin of Minnan and Hakka, the So-called "Taiwanese," Inferred by HLA Study*, 57 TISSUE ANTIGENS 192–99 (2001).

11. *See* EMMA JINHUA TENG, TAIWAN'S IMAGINED GEOGRAPHY: CHINESE COLONIAL TRAVEL WRITING AND PICTURES 1683–1895, at 38 (2004).

12. *Id.* at 45.

13. *See* Tonio Andrade, How Taiwan Became Chinese: Dutch, Spanish, and Han Colonization in the Seventeenth Century 3 (2008). For an English translation of Chen Di's Dong Fan Ji, *see* Laurence Thompson, *The Earliest Chinese Eyewitness Accounts of the Formosan Aborigines*, 23 Monumenta Serica: J. Oriental Stud. 163–204 (1964).

14. Teng, *supra* note 11, at 63.

15. *Id.* at 38.

16. *See, e.g.*, John E. Wills Jr., *The Seventeenth-Century Transformation: Taiwan Under the Dutch and the Cheng Regime*, *in* Taiwan: A New History 84–106 (Murray A. Rubinstein ed., 2015).

17. *See* Melissa J. Brown, Is Taiwan Chinese? The Impact of Culture, Power, and Migration on Changing Identities 37 (2004).

18. *Id.* at 36.

19. Andrade, *supra* note 13, ch. 8.

20. Wills, *supra* note 16, at 95.

21. *See* Lung-chu Chen & W. Michael Reisman, *Who Owns Taiwan: A Search for International Title*, 81 Yale L.J. 599, 609 (1972).

22. Teng, *supra* note 11, at 34.

23. *Id.* at 2.

24. *Id.* at 35.

25. John Robert Shepherd, *The Island Frontier of the Ch'ing, 1684–1780*, *in* Taiwan: A New History 107, 108–09 (Murray A. Rubinstein ed., 2015).

26. Chen & Reisman, *supra* note 21, at 609 n.32; *citing* Office of Economic Research, Bank of Taiwan, Ch'ing-tai Tai-wan min-pien-shih yen-chu: A Study on the History of Taiwan Rebellions during the Ch'ing Dynasty (1970).

27. *See* Nagao Ariga, *Diplomacy*, *in* Japan by the Japanese 142, 162–63 (Alfred Stead ed., 1904).

28. *Id.* at 163.

29. *Id.*

30. Sophia Su-Fei Yen, Taiwan in China's Foreign Relations, 1836–1874, at 251 (1965).

31. *Id.* at 271.

32. Robert Gardella, *From Treaty Ports to Provincial Status, 1860–1894*, *in* Taiwan: A New History 164 (Murray A. Rubinstein ed., 2015).

33. *See* Harry J. Lamley, *Taiwan Under Japanese Rule, 1895–1945: The Vicissitudes of Colonialism*, *in* Taiwan: A New History 201 (Murray A. Rubinstein ed., 2015).

34. Chen & Reisman, *supra* note 21, at 611.

35. Zehan Lai et al., A Tragic Beginning: The Taiwan Uprising of February 28, 1947, at 93 (1991), *citing* Formosa: Internal Affairs, 1945–1949, Reel I, Enclosure no. 232 (Jan 28, 1946), p. I (report by Lt. George H. Kerr, Nov. 23, 1945).

36. *Id.* at 103.

37. *Id.* at 107.

38. Dwight D. Eisenhower, Annual Message to the Congress on the State of the Union, Feb. 2, 1953, *available at* http://www.presidency.ucsb.edu/ws/?pid=9829.

39. Mutual Defense Treaty Between the United States of America and the Republic of China 6.1 U.S.T. 433 (1955), TIAS 3178.

40. H.J. Res. 159, 69 Stat. 7 (Jan. 29, 1955).

41. UN General Assembly, "Resolution 2758, A/RES/2758 (XXVI)," Oct. 25, 1971.

42. N.Y. TIMES, Dec. 2, 1971, at 19, col. 1.

43. Richard Nixon, Remarks to the Nation Announcing Acceptance of an Invitation to Visit the People's Republic of China, July 15, 1971, *available at* http://www.presidency.ucsb.edu/ws/?pid=3079.

44. Richard Nixon, Third Annual Report to the Congress on United States Foreign Policy, Feb. 9, 1972, *available at* http://www.presidency.ucsb.edu/ws/?pid=3736.

45. Taiwan Relations Act, Pub. L. 96–8, 93 Stat. 14 (Apr. 10, 1979); 22 U.S.C. §3301 et seq.

46. 22 U.S.C. §3301(b)(3); §3302.

47. *Id.* at §3301(b)(6).

48. *Id.* at §3303(d).

2 Taiwan's Contemporary Landscape

THIS CHAPTER WILL trace Taiwan's distinctive political, economic, social, cultural, and strategic development since the United States derecognized the Republic of China (ROC) government in 1979. The approach taken will be familiar to practitioners and students of the New Haven School of international law. In the New Haven School's tradition, the effects of global and regional legal and power processes can be described and appraised in terms of eight value categories: power, wealth, skill, well-being, enlightenment, respect, rectitude, and affection. The categories, which are described in greater detail in the sections that follow, are strongly interrelated and interdependent, and the contents of each category are overlapping. They offer a convenient framework for making a comparative analysis of legal systems, institutions, and time periods. Political elites routinely promote and adopt recommendations aimed at the production and redistribution of these values in accordance with the rules of their respective political systems and constitutional frameworks. Civil society organizations, individual citizens, outside authorities, and other stakeholders may participate in, reinforce, and challenge governmental decision processes at both the national and international levels. The resulting public order is dynamic and subject to change. Every government—those of Taiwan, China, and the United States included—is conditioned by the evolving demands and expectations of their peoples. Their performance is subject to appraisal from a multitude of quarters: constituents, political commentators, scholars, foreign elites, and many others.

Taiwan's contemporary development, like that of all countries, has been strongly influenced by external factors as well. The effects of global power processes on domestic outcomes cannot be exaggerated. This is especially true in the case of Taiwan, a small nation long caught in a tug-of-war between larger powers. The New Haven School describes international law as a global process of authoritative decision through which the members of the world community identify, clarify, and secure their common interests. This legal process of authoritative decision does not operate in a vacuum, but within regional and global processes of effective power. That is to say, one cannot fully understand international law without coming to grips with politics. Within the earth-space arena, participants, both states and nonstate actors, vie for access to authoritative arenas and control over resources for the advancement of their interests. Between states, the tools of national policy are the military, diplomatic, ideological (information and cultural), and economic instruments. Their use is conditioned by the perspectives of elites within the respective territorial communities, which may be global in nature or parochial. These instruments may be deployed singularly or in tandem with many degrees of intensity and coordination. This chapter will consider the interplay of the four instruments of policy in relation to Taiwan and their effects on the island's internal and external development. And it will begin to take stock of each of the eight values listed above as they relate to the island's political (power), economic (wealth, skill, and well-being), social (enlightenment and respect), and cultural (rectitude and affection) landscapes.

I. From Authoritarian Rule to Democracy

In the terminology of the New Haven School of international law, power refers to the making and influencing of community decisions. In Taiwan, the development of democratic institutions has ensured that the country's people are able to participate broadly in decisions affecting every aspect of society. Taiwan is home to numerous political parties with platforms representing the concerns and priorities of various constituencies. Power is distributed among national, county, and city-level governments, with many prominent figures having spent time in local politics before ascending to the national stage. This is a far cry from the situation for much of the twentieth century, when the Kuomintang (KMT) regime held a monopoly of power over the island.

The ROC constitution dates to December 1946 and was adopted by the KMT government in China before its exile to Taiwan. The constitution took effect on Taiwan later that year following the creation of the Taiwan Provincial Government.

Taiwan's government is a representative democracy with five branches: the Executive Yuan, the Legislative Yuan, the Judicial Yuan, the Examination Yuan, and the Control Yuan. The ROC president, who is directly elected by the people, serves as the head of state and appoints a premier to manage the country's various ministries. The 113 members of the Legislative Yuan are elected for four-year terms. The three-tiered judiciary includes a Supreme Court, appellate courts, and district courts with the power to hear both civil and criminal cases. The Judicial Yuan oversees the court system, and its fifteen-member Council of Grand Justices (Constitutional Court) is responsible for interpreting the constitution. The Examination Yuan is responsible for administering the country's civil service, while the Control Yuan monitors and investigates the other branches of government and exercises the power of audit. The island's local governmental system includes six special municipalities, three provincial cities, and thirteen counties. It is worth noting that the governmental organs in place today were established during the Chinese civil war at a time when the ROC governed the whole of China. In April 1948, many of the constitution's provisions were suspended with the adoption of the Temporary Provisions Effective During the Period of Communist Rebellion, which consolidated power in the executive and eliminated term limits for the president and the vice president. When the KMT was exiled to Taiwan, it continued to maintain its claim to govern the whole of China. To sustain this myth, the ROC government retained its constitution. It soon became a tool for denying equal representation to the Taiwanese people, who were severely underrepresented in the Legislative Yuan in favor of exiled Chinese Nationalists. Constitutional amendments adopted in 1991 terminated the Temporary Provisions and authorized free elections in Taiwan. Since then, the constitution has been revised several times, most recently in 2005. Direct elections for the president and other officials were adopted in 1992. The Legislative Yuan gained the power of impeachment in 1997. The 2005 amendments disbanded the National Assembly, a remnant of the ROC government in China, and provided for the ratification of constitutional changes by popular referendum.

After Chiang Kai-shek's death in 1975, his son and heir, Chiang Ching-kuo, took over as KMT Party chairman before being elected to the presidency by the National Assembly in 1978. Chiang Ching-kuo had been a prominent figure in his own right, having served as head of the Nationalist government in Shanghai during the Chinese civil war. As a young man, he spent twelve years living in Russia, where he received a political education among the Communist elite and married a Belarusian woman, Faina Vakhreva (known in Chinese as Faina Chiang Fang-liang). In the early 1950s, he led the KMT's efforts to root out corruption in the ROC government. Later, as the head of the ROC's secret police, Chiang Ching-kuo earned a reputation for cracking down on the KMT's enemies, among them political dissidents and communists.

The U.S. decision to derecognize the ROC government was a diplomatic blow for the aging Chiang Ching-kuo regime. But for the Taiwanese people, it was a remarkable turning point. Within a decade of President Carter's announcement, pressures from inside and outside of Taiwan forced the ROC to abandon many of its oppressive policies based on martial law. Taiwan's increasing international isolation combined with U.S. lobbying convinced Chiang Ching-kuo's government to give space to the country's democratic opposition movement in the late 1970s and early 1980s. The KMT permitted more Taiwanese elites to join its ranks, and ordinary citizens could vote for legislative representatives for the first time—although the scope of the elections and campaigning were sharply curtailed. During this period, a loosely knit political faction known as the *tangwai* (*dangwai*) (literally "those outside the party") began making overt demands for political reform. Chiang Ching-kuo initially responded by calling for the arrests of the movement's leaders and the blacklisting of academics who were critical of his regime. One year after President Carter's announcement, the Kaohsiung Incident (also known as the Formosa Incident) brought the issue to a head. The leaders of the *tangwai*, who were also contributors to the pro-democracy *Formosa Magazine*, were preparing to stage a rally in Kaohsiung to commemorate International Human Rights Day on December 10, 1979. Thousands of supporters gathering outside a political organizing office were met by a brutal crackdown from KMT forces. The assault ended with the arrest of dozens of well-known opposition leaders, who were summarily imprisoned or tried on charges of subversion. Organizers and participants were arrested and jailed. Eight of the group's leaders were tried in military court on charges of sedition—which carried a possible death sentence—and were given lengthy prison sentences. Dozens more faced civil trials, including members of the Presbyterian Church who were accused of sheltering one of the protest organizers.

Among the defendants were individuals who would eventually rise to prominence as leaders in Taiwanese culture, politics, and international diplomacy. They included future Vice President Annette Lu Hsiu-lien, future DPP Chairmen Lin Yi-hsiung and Shih Ming-te, and future mayor of Kaohsiung Chen Chu, as well as their attorneys who included future President Chen Shui-bian, future Premier Frank Hsieh Chang-ting, and future DPP Chairman Su Tseng-chang. The trials were followed closely by human rights organizations, such as the International League for Human Rights, and Western media, and the U.S. Congress held a number of hearings on the human rights situation in Taiwan throughout the late 1970s and early 1980s. Many in the United States shared Taiwan's democratic aspirations, and allies in many Western governments placed significant pressure on the KMT regime. With the strong support of Taiwanese activists at home and abroad, U.S. policymakers pushed the KMT regime to end its authoritarian abuses and to embark on long-sought democratic reforms.

By the end of his life, Chiang Ching-kuo had refashioned his identity, no longer as a Chinese in exile, but as a Taiwanese. He cemented this legacy in 1984 when he appointed Lee Teng-hui, a Taiwan-born politician and former mayor of Taipei as his vice president. Lee would succeed to the presidency upon Chiang's death in 1988. In 1985, Chiang approved a package of initiatives aimed at suppressing corruption within the government and opening additional executive and legislative offices to Taiwanese. The government lifted the ban on opposition parties and ended media censorship. Surprising many, Chiang allowed the formation of the Democratic Progressive Party (DPP) on September 28, 1986. Less than a year later, on July 14, 1987, Chiang proclaimed the end of the thirty-eight-year martial law in Taiwan.

A. LEE TENG-HUI, "MR. DEMOCRACY"

Lee Teng-hui became Taiwan's first native-born president following Chiang Ching-kuo's death in 1988. Lee, who was born a Japanese citizen under colonial rule, earned his Ph.D. in agricultural economics from Cornell University in 1968. The reform process that had begun during Chiang Ching-kuo's final years accelerated under Lee. Measures included the termination of the Period of National Mobilization for Suppression of the Communist Rebellion in April 1991; a National Assembly election at the end of 1991 (the same year, aging KMT members of the Taiwan legislature, who were elected in China in 1947, were finally forced into retirement); a legislative election at the end of 1992 that allotted seats in accordance with the Taiwanese population; popular elections for Taiwan provincial governor and city mayors; the first direct presidential election in March 1996 (with Lee winning a second term); and the transfer of political power from the KMT to the DPP after the election of Chen Shui-bian as president in May 2000.

During Lee's term, the Taiwanization of the KMT accelerated also. Mainland Chinese no longer exclusively dominated the top echelons of the party and government. Lee embarked on efforts to reconcile the ethnic divide and to emphasize the "new" KMT commitment to the island. Under his administration, the ROC ended its claims to the China mainland and Mongolia, formally apologized to the victims of the 228 Incident, and constructed a large memorial in the center of Taipei to commemorate the tragedy. In the late 1990s, Lee strove to form the basis for a new national Taiwanese identity. He promoted the concept of a "new Taiwanese" identity embracing international influences. His approach proved popular across the political spectrum.

In 1990, widespread public discontent with the KMT led to a six-day student protest called the Wild Lily movement. President Lee responded by calling for a National Affairs Conference to be held from June to July that year. The conference welcomed attendees from both the KMT and the DPP, as well as former political prisoners, to discuss options for political reforms around five topics: parliamentary reform, presidential elections, amending the 1946 constitution, the nature and elections of local governments, and relations between Taiwan and China. It was the first time in the country's history that dialogue on such subjects had been held in the open, let alone with an invitation from the government.

Beginning in 1990, Lee launched a series of constitutional reforms. On April 22, 1991, he proclaimed the end of the Period of National Mobilization for the Suppression of Chinese Communist Rebellion, thereby giving tacit recognition to the People's Republic of China (PRC) government's jurisdiction in China and unilaterally declaring an end to the Chinese civil war. From 1991 to 2000, legislators made several revisions to the ROC constitution, adopting ten amendments in April 1991. A complete re-election of all Congressional representatives (members of the National Assembly and Legislature) took place from 1991 to 1992. The election of a new, 327-seat National Assembly took place in 1991, and the election of a new, 161-seat Legislative Yuan followed in 1992. The legislative seats were finally allotted in accordance with the actual population of Taiwan, giving the Taiwanese people full representation for the first time since the ROC's exile to Taiwan. At the same time, National Assembly members' terms were reduced from six years to four years. Nineteen ninety-two was also the last year the National Assembly was responsible for electing the ROC president. In 1996, President Lee carried Taiwan's first-ever direct presidential election, ending fifty years of undemocratic rule by the KMT.

Under Lee's administration, the 1990s saw definite, albeit cautious, steps toward a rapprochement in Taiwan-China relations. On February 19, the ROC's Mainland Affairs Council established the "nongovernmental" Straits Exchange Foundation (SEF) as the country's representative in dealings with the PRC, acknowledging "the complex and unique nature of relations across the Taiwan Strait."[1] In December, the PRC reciprocated with the establishment of the Association for Relations Across the Taiwan Straits (ARATS). Although both the SEF and the ARATS are referred to as nongovernmental, in actuality the governments of China and Taiwan exercise a large degree of control over the organizations, which receive funding and employ former government personnel. In practice, the entities allow the PRC and the ROC to avoid the appearance of government-to-government contacts while having a mechanism for carrying out cross-strait interactions. In October 1992, representatives of the SEF and the ARATS met in Hong Kong for the first time for a "practical meeting" on certificate registration and registered mail exchanges. It was this meeting that gave rise to the controversy over the so-called "1992 Consensus." There is no official record from the meeting. However, PRC attendees stated that the two sides agreed that there was "one China," which includes Taiwan, but that the two sides disagreed as to which government, the ROC or the PRC, was its legitimate government. In 2000, Su Chi, Minister of the Mainland Affairs Council of the Executive Yuan, fabricated the term "1992 Consensus," stating that the agreement was implied during the summit to build trust between the KMT and the Chinese Communist Party (CCP).[2] President Lee repeatedly denied that any such agreement had been struck. The 1992 Consensus would become a key symbol of the Ma Ying-jeou administration, which sought common ground for establishing closer ties with the PRC. Nowadays, however, the PRC uses the 1992 Consensus as a code word for its One China Principle. It takes the term to mean that there is one China, with no room for respective interpretations. Chinese officials have even stated that Taiwan's acceptance of the 1992 Consensus is a precondition for the continuation of peaceful cross-strait relations.

In an interview with German radio network *Deutsche Welle* in 1999, President Lee stated that the reforms carried out under his leadership had redefined the ROC and PRC relationship as a "special state-to-state relationship." Lee, who gave his interview just prior to the 2000 presidential election, saw his popularity skyrocket to 87 percent as Taiwanese citizens applauded his two-state vision. The PRC reacted negatively to Lee's statements, casting them as a ploy to strengthen Taiwan's negotiating stance ahead of a planned visit to the island by China's top negotiator with Taiwan. The visit was subsequently canceled. Following Lee's declaration of the two-state policy, China responded by publishing a white paper on "The One China Principle and the Taiwan Issue" before Taiwan's polling day. The paper asserted that Taiwan was an inalienable part of China and that inevitably "the total reunification of China will be achieved through the joint efforts of the entire Chinese people . . . on both sides of the Taiwan Straits and those living overseas."[3]

II. Contemporary Politics in Taiwan

Taiwan's relationship to the PRC is the defining issue in modern Taiwanese politics, with the country's political parties divided between the Pan-Blue and Pan-Green camps. The Pan-Blue Coalition includes the KMT as well as smaller parties such as the People First Party and New Party. The Pan-Green Coalition includes the Democratic Progressive Party (DPP) and Taiwan Solidarity Union. The KMT's platform has evolved since the 1980s from a focus on retaking China to seeking closer economic ties with the PRC. The KMT maintains that there is "one China" and that Taiwan is a part of China. Some of its members argue for eventual unification between the ROC and PRC governments. On the contrary, the DPP supports Taiwan's continued development as an independent state. In 1999, the DPP adopted the "Resolution on Taiwan's Future" at its eighth annual assembly. The resolution declared the party's position that "Taiwan is a sovereign and independent country" and that any changes in the country's status must be decided by a plebiscite.[4] The Resolution rejected the PRC's One China Principle while calling for bilateral engagement with China and greater participation for Taiwan in the international community. Some DPP members support revising the ROC constitution to reflect Taiwan's current status, including ending the ROC's claims to govern the whole of China, as embodied in the constitution.

A. CHEN SHUI-BIAN

Taiwan's transition to democracy was made complete in 2000 with the election of the DPP's Chen Shui-bian as president. Born to an impoverished family in southern Taiwan in 1951, Chen excelled at the National Taiwan University, College of Law, before rising to prominence for his courageous defense of activists arrested following the Kaohsiung Incident of 1979. He served on the Taipei City Council in the early 1980s and then as a DPP member of the Legislative Yuan. He was the first popularly elected mayor of Taipei City in twenty-seven years, as well as the first DPP candidate to win such a position. Although he lost the Taipei mayoral bid for a second term to Ma Ying-jeou in 1998, he would begin campaigning for the presidency soon after. Chen and his running mate, Annette Lu, won the 2000 election with 39.3 percent of the vote in a close race against the KMT's Lien Chan and Independent James Soong.

On May 20, 2000, President Chen delivered his inaugural address enumerating his "Four Noes and One Shall Not" pledge: So long as the PRC did not use military force against Taiwan, there would be no declaring of independence, no changing of the national title, no incorporating of the "state-to-state theory" in the ROC constitution; and no promotion of a referendum to change the status quo on independence or unification.[5] Chen described his vision for Taiwan as a country respecting and dedicated to the protection and fulfillment of human rights. In October 2003, he received the Human Rights Award from the International League for Human Rights. Past honorees include Nelson Mandela, Kim Dae-jung, Elie Wiesel, and Mary Robinson, among other luminaries. Chen was greeted by more than twelve hundred attendees at the award ceremony in the Grand Ballroom of the Waldorf-Astoria Hotel in New York City, which was covered by national and international media.

Chen's policy of "one country on each side" emphasized the distinct status of the PRC and the ROC. However, throughout his administration, gradual steps were taken to re-establish direct contact with China. Beginning in 2001, the administration worked to build the "Little Three Links," allowing registered residents of Quemoy and Matsu islands to visit China directly. In 2003, Taiwanese carriers were given permission to charter indirect flights for travelers between Taiwan and China. This led to limited direct flights beginning in 2005. The administration also lifted the fifty-year direct trade and investment ban between Taiwan and China.

The Chen administration inherited a largely KMT bureaucracy along with a KMT-dominated legislature, which significantly curtailed the new president's power. At the same time, PRC leaders showed little interest in developing high-level contacts with Chen's government. Nevertheless, he managed to take several important unilateral steps to buttress cross-strait ties even while taking a strong stance in favor of Taiwan independence. In 2002, Chen gave a speech at the annual meeting of the World Federation of Taiwanese Associations in which he stated that the PRC and Taiwan were "each one country on each side of the [Taiwan] strait."[6] And in 2004, he proposed that Taiwan should reform the ROC constitution, an act the PRC considered provocative, as it could strengthen the legal basis for Taiwan's statehood claim.[7]

Chen won a second term in a tightly contested election in 2004. On March 19, the day before the election, Chen and Vice President Annette Lu were the targets of an assassination attempt while campaigning in the city of Tainan. Chen and Lu were standing in the back of an open car when assailants fired two shots, striking Chen in the abdomen and Lu in the right knee. Chen and Lu won re-election by less than 30,000 votes, with 50.11 percent of the popular vote.

Chen's second term was characterized by heightened tensions with the KMT domestically and the PRC internationally. Chen softened his position on holding a referendum for Taiwan independence, stating that any such move should be undertaken through normal constitutional processes, which would require considerable KMT support. During his second term, Chen attended the funeral of Pope John Paul II at the Vatican, becoming the first sitting ROC president to visit Europe. In September 2005, the U.S. State Department permitted Chen to stop for one day in Miami, Florida, where he met (by teleconference) with members of the Congressional Human Rights Caucus. The Caucus awarded Chen with its Human Rights Award for his work to promote democracy and human rights in Taiwan. In 2006, Chen canceled a visit to the United States when U.S. officials rejected his request for a layover within the lower-forty-eight states. Instead, Chen was offered a fueling stop in Alaska, which he refused. Chen's second term as president ended in scandal after allegations of corruption were made against him and family members, include his wife Wu Shu-chen. In 2009, he was sentenced to twenty years in prison after a trial on charges of embezzlement and bribery. Some of Chen's supporters argued that the charges were a form of political persecution, accusing President Ma of interfering with the proceedings after he declassified documents related to government expenses in order to aid prosecutors.[8] The former president's incarceration was also blamed for his rapidly declining health. In January 2015, prison authorities granted Chen parole to seek medical treatment for what was reported as neural degeneration.

B. MA YING-JEOU

Ma Ying-jeou became Taiwan's third democratically elected president in 2008 following a two-year stint as chairman of the KMT. Ma earned a bachelor's degree from the National Taiwan University, College of Law, and degrees from New York University and Harvard Law School. As a young man, Ma worked as an English-language interpreter for Chiang Ching-kuo. He served as Justice Minister and Mayor of Taipei before rising to the chairmanship of the KMT in 2005. After announcing his candidacy for presidency, Ma embarked on an island-wide campaign, biking through towns and villages and living among the people. The campaign became known as Ma's "Long Stay."

During his campaign for re-election in 2012, Ma sought to maintain the cross-strait status quo under the "Three Noes" policy—no unification, no independence and no use of force—while leveraging the purported 1992 Consensus to promote cross-strait relations.[9] DPP presidential candidate Tsai Ing-wen, former chairwoman of the DPP, refused to acknowledge the existence of the so-called consensus, instead advocating for a "Taiwan consensus." Tsai said the term was meant to describe a local democratic process that excluded no outcomes.[10] Tsai's China policy was based on the theme of "reserving the right to disagree while seeking harmony and seeking agreement in a spirit of conciliation."[11] The PRC warned that a win by the DPP candidate could threaten the peaceful development of cross-strait ties.[12] Millions of mainland Chinese avidly followed the campaign between Ma and Tsai. Notably, China's Xinhua news agency omitted the words "democracy" and "president" from its coverage, portraying the contest as a local election.[13]

Ma took the presidency in 2008 in a landslide victory with a total of 7.65 million ballots, or 58.5 percent of the vote. In his first inaugural address entitled "Taiwan's Renaissance," Ma promised to lead the ROC in overcoming Taiwan's domestic and overseas challenges.[14] He pledged to ease regulatory restrictions to strengthen Taiwan's economic competitiveness and to encourage domestic firms to establish a strong home base in Taiwan while networking throughout the Asia Pacific and globally. As elaborated in Chapter 8, relations between Taiwan and the PRC advanced rapidly under the Ma administration. The administration's willingness to put aside the question of independence to focus on economic matters initially made Ma an asset, and PRC leaders hoped to lock in changes that would further integrate the two countries' economies. In the first three months of his presidency, Ma's government introduced direct charter flights between China and Taiwan, opened the country to Chinese tourists, and removed restrictions on investment and stock purchases. Under Ma, the SEF and the ARATS were brought out of dormancy to take up negotiations that would culminate in more than twenty cross-strait agreements, including the 2010 Economic Cooperation Framework Agreement (ECFA). Ma took credit for developing cross-strait relations by avoiding difficult political question in favor of promoting mutually beneficial economic policies.[15] But Many Taiwanese voiced their concern that the president was eroding the country's sovereignty in the process. Ma argued that characterizing Taiwan and the PRC as "two areas," rather than "state to state" or "one country on each side," allowed the two sides to overlook questions of sovereignty that threatened to undermine relations.[16] His characterization of an "area-to-area relationship" drew vocal opposition from DPP representatives and others who feared Ma was hinting at a basis for unification. Ma's China-centric leanings grew more pronounced when he declined to pursue Taiwan's bid for UN participation or membership for the first time in seventeen years.

When Ma took office in 2008, the KMT was in the midst of a political comeback in Taiwan. The party secured landslide victories in both the presidential and legislative elections, and Ma enjoyed tremendous popularity among the Taiwanese people. But the honeymoon period did not last long. Over the course of his administration, Ma's popularity fell due to the weakening economy, rising consumer prices, and concerns over his handling of cross-strait relations. Ma's commitment to democratic reforms was also questioned. Above all, throughout his administration, Ma has been accused of adopting policies designed to deliberately foster Taiwan's economic dependence on the PRC. His administration began pushing for the ECFA with the PRC shortly after taking office in 2008. The ECFA, which went into effect in September 2010, was intended to relax trade restrictions on both sides of the strait. Ma claimed that Taiwan's adoption of the ECFA would attract foreign investors and smooth the way for free-trade agreements with the United States and the Association of Southeast Asian Nations (ASEAN). While the ECFA has succeeded in fostering increased economic activity between Taiwan and China, the benefits of increased trade have not accrued equally to all segments of society. A 2011 report commissioned by the Research, Development and Evaluation Commission of Taiwan's Executive Yuan found that "[p]eople who possess large amounts of capital appeared to reap benefits from the [ECFA], while those on the lower end of the economic scale absorbed the costs."[17]

In 2012, Ma won re-election with 51.6 percent of the vote. Nearly 75 percent of eligible voters participated in the 2012 election, according to the Central Election Commission. More than two hundred thousand Taiwanese citizens residing in China flew home to take part in the vote, most of them taking direct flights introduced during the Ma administration. Speaking on the importance of the 2012 election, former American Institute in Taiwan Director Richard C. Bush stated that "[t]he true message of this election is that people in Taiwan are anxious about the future, and Beijing would be wise to note this division."[18] In August 2012, shortly after Ma won his second term, the SEF and the ARATS signed the Cross-Strait Bilateral Investment Protection and Promotion Agreement that established a mechanism for resolving trade and investment disputes. In June 2013, the two sides signed the Cross-Strait Service Trade Agreement (CSSTA), which would allow exchanges in banking, healthcare, transportation, travel, communications, and construction, and permit cross-strait investment by citizens from both countries. Critics immediately raised alarms over the lack of transparency during the negotiations for the CSSTA and criticized the Ma administration for throwing open the doors to Chinese interests without securing protections for Taiwan's ongoing sovereignty or national security. According to some critics, under President Ma, Taiwan has become in effect an undefended island, allowing hostile PRC agents unfettered access. In the Legislative Yuan, opposition lawmakers demanded a close review of the agreement over the KMT's push for a hasty ratification. In June 2013, the KMT and DPP agreed to a process for a clause-by-clause review. In September, the parties agreed to hold public hearings to consult academics, business leaders, and nongovernmental organizations regarding the potential impact of the CSSTA.

In March 2014, in violation of the agreed procedures, KMT lawmakers attempted to force the CSSTA through the legislature, sparking immediate protests. On the evening of March 18, hundreds of protestors stormed the Legislative Yuan building in Taipei and occupied the legislative floor. A group of about three hundred students, academics, and civic leaders barricaded themselves inside. Thus began the Sunflower Movement. The protesters demanded that the president and KMT lawmakers reinstate the clause-by-clause review process agreed to the year before in addition to the passage of legislation to monitor all cross-strait agreements. At a press conference on March 23, Ma reaffirmed his support for the CSSTA and urged its passage.[19] A massive rally on March 30 saw hundreds of thousands of people take to the streets of Taipei in support of the occupiers' demands. Solidarity protests were held in major cities around the world, including New York, London, and Paris. The occupation of the Legislative Yuan ended peacefully on April 10 after KMT Legislative Speaker Wang Jin-pyng pledged to enact legislation to monitor cross-strait legislation before reviewing the CSSTA. Ma, claiming he had no knowledge of Wang's promise, again called for the quick ratification of the CSSTA.[20]

The occupation of the legislative floor by the Sunflower Movement was unprecedented in Taiwan's history. Dozens of civic and nongovernmental organizations participated in the protests against the CSSTA. The movement sparked a passionate interest among the island's younger generation in protecting their country's future.

It also highlighted the failure of the major parties to meet the public's expectations. Constant legislative gridlock has been a hallmark of the Taiwanese legislature in recent years. And the Ma administration's approach to the CSSTA negotiations and subsequent ratification reminded some of the bad old days of authoritarian rule. The Sunflower Movement's momentum continues today as high school students protest the China-centric orientation of changes made to history textbooks as they relate to Taiwan. Demonstrators expressed outrage at the Ministry of Education for its "black box" procedures and lack of transparency. The high school students' protests have earned the moniker "the small Sunflower Movement."

III. Taiwan's Economic Landscape

Aside from the shaping and sharing of power, as elaborated above, human beings engage in activities directed at the attainment of other cherished values such as wealth, skill, well-being, enlightenment, respect, rectitude, and affection. This section considers the first three of these values as they relate to Taiwan's dynamic economic landscape. The term *wealth* refers to activities aimed at the production, distribution, and consumption of goods and services, as well as the control over resources. *Skill* is the acquisition and exercise of individual and collective capabilities in the context of vocations, professions, and the arts. Skill, when applied to resources in the form of professional competency, contributes to a society's economic development and elevates individuals. In this sense skill is a value that is used to obtain other desired values, among them wealth, power, and affection. However, an individual's talents may also be exercised in the pursuit of entertainment or personal fulfillment. The ability to select, acquire, and deploy learned skills is an important component of the ideology of the free market. *Well-being* broadly encompasses the concepts of safety, health, and comfort. The term comprises many subjective and objective dimensions. For the individual, well-being may be measured in the quality of one's life and in bodily fitness. At the community level well-being may be considered through aggregate measures of disease, debilitation, life expectancy, and other factors. Without a doubt, well-being is strongly correlated to the attainment and exercise of other cherished values such as skill, affection, rectitude, and wealth.

Over the course of several decades Taiwan has evolved from a largely agricultural economy to one of the most advanced manufacturing centers in the world. For much of the twentieth century, it enjoyed one of the highest standards of living of any Asian nation. Columnist Thomas Friedman once wrote that his favorite country in the world, besides the United States, is Taiwan. Friedman recalled telling his friends in Taiwan: "You're the luckiest people in the world . . . You have no oil, no iron ore, no forests, no diamonds, no gold, just a few small deposits of coal and natural gas—and because of that you developed the habits and culture of honing your people's skills, which turns out to be the most valuable and the only truly renewable resource in the world today."[21] Indeed, the people of Taiwan have made the most of their country's strategic location, and today Taiwan is among the region's most important economies thanks to its high-tech and specialized services sectors. According to a January 2014 report from the Brookings Institution, Taiwan's gross domestic product (GDP) has grown 4.5 percent on average since 1992.[22] This period of rapid industrialization became known as the "Taiwan miracle," and Taiwan was soon counted among the four "Asian Tigers," alongside South Korea, Singapore, and Hong Kong. Real per capita income grew from USD 9,116 to USD 19,762 between 1992 and 2012, while international trade swelled from approximately USD 180 billion to more than 650 billion.[23] Taiwan is among the top twenty-five most popular economies for foreign investment in the world.

The *economic instrument* may be used to facilitate or restrict the movement of capital, goods, and services between nation states. It affects the production, conservation, distribution, and consumption of wealth and other values such as power, enlightenment, and well-being. The economic instrument may be used by a community of states acting in coordination through regional or international governmental organizations for their collective benefit or by individual states singularly to acquire wealth, facilitate relations, or as a sanctioning measure. In this regard, Taiwan's foreign policy is closely tied to the island's economic welfare, and trade has long served as the cornerstone of the Taiwanese economy. The Taiwan Strait is one of the world's busiest transportation routes, playing host to hundreds of commercial vessels and civilian aircraft each day. Taiwan's trade hubs include Kaohsiung, a major regional hub port, Chilung (Keelung), Hualian, and Taichung. Its largest trading partners include China (including Hong Kong), the United States, and Japan. In 2012, Taiwan's total trade amounted to about USD 549.8 billion (of which USD 288.2 billion was from exports and USD 261.6 billion was from imports).

Taiwan's economy has become increasingly reliant on regional trading partners. More than 85 percent of Taiwan's exports are consumed by just fifteen trading partners, eleven of which are located in the Pacific. Meanwhile, Taiwan's total share of global trade volumes has fallen by 30 percent since 2000.[24] In 2008, China surpassed the United States to become Taiwan's largest trading partner, with USD 105.4 billion in total bilateral trade. Trade with the United States now accounts for less than 10 percent of Taiwan's total foreign trade. Since the early 2000s, Taiwan's trade with ASEAN member economies has grown from approximately USD 500 million to more than USD 6 billion annually. With the exception of the ECFA, Taiwan does not participate in any major regional trade pacts, and it lacks bilateral treaties with several of its largest trading partners. It has signed bilateral investment treaties with twenty-four nations (only fifteen of which are currently in force). Taiwan has signed free trade agreements with only eight other countries.

As Friedman remarked, Taiwan's natural resources may be scarce, but the island has no shortage of human capital. The country has sought to develop its people through a variety of policies, particularly in education. Taiwan first implemented a nine-year national educational system under the Compulsory School Attendance Act in 1968. Between 1980 and 2010, illiteracy on the island diminished from around 10 percent to 2 percent. Today, roughly 45 percent of the Taiwanese workforce possesses some higher education, with roughly 320,000 students graduating from colleges, universities, and other institutions each year. The number of Taiwanese with Ph.D.s increased from 13,000 to 33,000 between 1999 and 2009. The number of research personnel for every thousand employees in Taiwan grew from 1.3 in 1985 to 6.7 in 2009. Taiwan consistently ranks among the top-twenty countries for number of scientific papers published annually. Taiwan's National Cheng Kung University, National Taiwan University, and National Chiao Tung University are ranked among the top universities worldwide for publications in the fields of science, computers, and engineering.

Taiwan also possesses one of the world's most entrepreneurial societies. Taiwan ranks thirteenth in terms of research and development expenditures, according to the IMD's World Competitiveness Yearbook 2014. The island's three largest science parks in Hsinchu, Central Taiwan, and Southern Taiwan together produce nearly NTD 2.16 trillion annually (USD 70.3 billion). Investment in research and development has allowed Taiwan to become a leader in information technology manufacturing. In 2010, Taiwan was a top-three global supplier of thirty-five key industrial products, and the world's number one supplier of twenty-one key products, among them motherboards, notebook computers, navigation devices, and optical discs. Taiwan ranked sixth in the world on Economist Intelligence Unit's 2009 to 2013 Global Innovation Index, trailing only behind the likes of Japan, Switzerland, Finland, Germany, and the United States.

From a public health standpoint, Taiwan is one of the healthiest countries in Asia. The country has achieved close to 99 percent enrollment in the compulsory National Health Insurance program since its inception in 1995. The system, which is financed through shared deductions by employers and employee subsidies, allows participants to choose among any doctor or hospital on the island. Healthcare now accounts for roughly 6 percent of Taiwan's GDP. The system is administered electronically through a unified record system, which gives every patient access to his or her health records via an identification card. Thanks to this paperless system, Taiwan's health system boasts some of the lowest administrative costs in the world. Taiwan's universal health insurance has become a showcase for others to study and emulate.[25]

IV. Taiwan's Social and Cultural Landscape

The value of *respect* corresponds to the freedom of choice, equality, and recognition. Respect, when afforded to members of a society, ensures that individuals and groups may participate equally in institutions and are able to express distinctive identities without fear of reprisal. The term respect is closely related to popular conceptions of human rights and carries both political and nonpolitical connotations. The concept of respect includes the recognition and protection of cultural identities, as well as the ability of the individual to contribute to the common good. *Enlightenment* refers to the gathering, processing, and dissemination of information and knowledge. It concerns the freedom of the press and individuals' access to formal institutions of learning, as well as the right to make personal inquiries beyond the limits of received knowledge. It refers not only to formal training of skills but also enlightenment for the sake of enlightenment. *Rectitude* concerns acts involved in the formation and application of norms of responsible conduct. In most societies the word is associated with the concepts of ethics, morality, justice, fairness, and religion or other traditional institutions. As a social value, rectitude, when invoked and applied to facts, designates people or things as embodying the good, however conceived. One aspect of rectitude is religion; however, rectitude in its fullest extent embraces all legal and nonlegal conceptions of appropriate conduct. The value of *affection* embraces the need for intimacy, friendship, loyalty, and the enjoyment of positive sentiments between individuals and groups. The desire to secure and maintain the affections of others strongly influences human behavior and motivates the pursuit of many other values. Affection between individuals, embodied in the concepts of friendship and love, is expressed through the bonds of families and interpersonal relationships. Affection held at the community level can contribute to the development of peaceful relations between groups. An absence of affection or the presence of negative sentiment may lead to violence between individuals and groups whose perspectives prove to be irreconcilable.

Like the United States, Taiwan is largely a nation of immigrants. Long before Portuguese sailors spotted *Ilha Formosa*, Austronesian tribes—ancestors of Taiwan's indigenous peoples—made their home on the island. During the seventeenth and eighteenth centuries, Dutch and Spanish colonists, joined by an influx of Han Chinese settlers, reshaped the island and its culture. This period was followed by fifty years of Japanese rule from 1895 until 1945, during which the local population was encouraged to assimilate into the Japanese culture. By 1945, when the Chinese Nationalists undertook their military occupation on Taiwan, the Taiwanese people had more or less adopted Japanese culture and language. The ROC quickly sought to

Sinicize the people and imposed a Chinese national culture on the island. Mandarin was decreed as the official national language and was the only language to be used in official affairs, in schools, on radio, and on television. Japanese as well as Taiwanese languages were banned. Some dialects such as Hoklo and Hakka survived and continued to be widely used among Taiwanese in private settings. Under the KMT, textbooks took on a distinctly China-centric ideology. Streets were renamed to reflect Chinese Nationalist and Confucian concepts and values. President Chen Shui-bian famously renamed the Chiang Kai-shek Memorial Hall to the National Taiwan Democracy Memorial Hall during his government's Name Rectification Campaign of 2005. The campaign sought to remove terms such as "China" or "Chinese" from the names of many institutions, including some private companies. Many of Chen's efforts were reversed under President Ma, who quickly reverted the Taiwan Democracy Memorial Hall and other entities to their former names.

In reality cultural identifications between the peoples of China and Taiwan are attenuated. The majority of ethnic Chinese living in Taiwan today are descendants of immigrants who came from the Southern Fujian province at the end of the seventeenth century, a time when the government of China had little influence on Taiwan. As a result, most of their descendants on the island consider themselves Taiwanese, not Chinese, and identify the island uniquely as their homeland. Intermarriage over the years has further blurred the distinctions between groups and led to a greater sense of Taiwanese-ness, particularly among second- and third-generation citizens. The number of people who identify as Taiwanese has increased from about 17.5 percent in 1992, to more than 60 percent in 2015, according to a survey by National Chengchi University.[26] The number identifying as Chinese-only dropped from about 25 percent in 1992 to 3.5 percent in 2015.[27] A poll released by *The Liberty Times* in September 2015 found that almost 65 percent of respondents in Taiwan believed that Taiwan and China were independent sovereign nations.[28] A survey conducted in November 2015 by the Taiwan Brain Trust, a policy think tank, found that an astounding 82 percent of young people between the ages of twenty and twenty-nine, and 61.4 percent of all survey takers, believed that Taiwan should become an independent state. Ninety-eight percent of young people identified as Taiwanese, according to the survey. An editorial in *The Taipei Times* commented on the findings:

> The message young Taiwanese have for the nation's leaders and for the rest of the world is simple: We were born and raised in an independent state that we identify as "Taiwan"—regardless of how many foreign nations recognize its sovereignty—and its name is not the Republic of China (ROC), Chinese Taipei or any other appellation forcefully assigned to it.[29]

Today's Taiwan is also home to a vibrant popular culture. Taiwanese television shows, singers, and actors have as many fans in China and Hong Kong as they do at home (if not more). Their appeal is not limited to the Chinese-speaking world. Many Taiwanese celebrities are also well known globally. They include Nobel laureate Yuan T. Lee, filmmaker Ang Lee, female golfer Yani Tseng, fashion designer Jason Wu, and merchant-philanthropist Chen Shu-chu. Just to name a few. Their accomplishments are all the more remarkable considering the restrictions against freethinking and individual expression during the Chinese Nationalist occupation.

The term *rectitude* embraces all concepts of ethics, morality, religion, and any related institutional practices. It touches on the ideas of freedom of religion, high moral standards, fairness, and justice. Many belief systems coexist in Taiwan, among them Buddhism, Taoism, Confucianism, Islam, folk religions, ancestor worship, Christianity, and atheism. Taoism is China's native religion and was brought to Taiwan by Chinese immigrants in the seventeenth century. Its practice was suppressed during the period of Japanese colonial occupation. Today, the Taiwanese population is approximately 93 percent Buddhist and Taoist, 4.5 percent Christian, and 2.5 percent "other," including Muslim. Christianity first arrived in Taiwan when Spanish and Dutch missionaries introduced Catholicism and Presbyterianism in the seventeenth century and has played a significant role in the island's political development. Most contemporary Christians in Taiwan tend to be well-educated members of the middle or upper classes. Some commentators have attributed the United States' support of the Chinese Nationalists, in part, to the fact that Chiang Kai-shek and his wife, Madame Chiang Kai-shek, were Christian. Former President Lee Teng-hui is also Christian.

In traditional Taiwanese culture, the family was "the center of existence" and consisted of multiple generations living under one roof, headed by a senior male member. When Taiwan was an agricultural society, larger families provided higher labor productivity. As in other parts of the world, the dual processes of industrialization and urbanization have led to transformations in the Taiwanese family structure, and the nuclear family model is increasingly favored. Today, the Taiwanese people live a thoroughly modern existence, with traditional modes of living increasingly rare, especially within the country's urban centers. Modern Taiwanese society is also home to an increasing number of multiethnic and divided families. In addition to the many expatriates who come to Taiwan on professional work visas, many foreign workers from the Philippines and other Southeast Asian countries are earning livings as caregivers and domestic helpers, many of whom eventually settle down with local Taiwanese partners. Meanwhile, the introduction of air travel has made it easier for professionals to travel back and forth between Taiwan and China for the purpose of doing business. Hundreds of thousands of Taiwanese are currently living and working in China, with some estimates as high as 850,000. While some have settled down, many of them choose to return to Taiwan regularly. A peculiar result of this trend has been increasing reports of unfaithful spouses maintaining romantic relationships on both sides of the strait. The practice has given rise to the popular term *bao er nai* (keeping a mistress).

V. Taiwan's Diplomatic and Defense Landscape

A. TAIWAN'S DIPLOMATIC LANDSCAPE

The *diplomatic instrument* generally is concerned with communications between elites of various nations. It is the most commonly used of all policy instruments and is often the channel through which elites exchange signals of expectations and intentions. Diplomatic communication can be carried out through formal utterances, spoken or written, or by deeds, openly or secretly, and may be transmitted directly between nations or through intermediaries. Diplomacy may be carried out in a variety of forums, from the sidelines of international conferences to the private residences of ambassadors to the open stages of electronic media. Closely related is the *ideological* (cultural) instrument. Unlike the diplomatic instrument, the ideological instrument is directed toward the interests of a wide audience. It may be deployed in a variety of forums in order to mobilize public opinion or to reinforce individual identifications and loyalties. The ideological instrument when used constructively is a tool of enlightenment. However it also carries the potential to be used as a tool of misinformation. For this reason it is imperative for individuals to have access to and the right to share a broad range of information comprising both official and nonofficial sources.

Taiwan's diplomatic presence in the international community has declined significantly since the early 1970s. The number of countries that maintain formal diplomatic relations with Taiwan has fallen from more than one hundred during the first half of the twentieth century to today's total of twenty-one countries (plus the Holy See). Taiwan's participation in international organizations has likewise been curtailed. The ROC is no longer a member of the United Nations, and Taiwan has been blocked by the PRC from joining other organizations for which statehood is a requirement for membership. Taiwanese officials are restricted in their ability to travel internationally on diplomatic missions and to interact with high-ranking officials from foreign governments.

While its formal diplomatic relations are limited, Taiwan carries out unofficial relations with most countries via *de facto* embassies and consulates such as the Taipei Economic and Cultural Representative Office in the United States. In substance, unofficial relations are very much the same as normal diplomatic relations. The United States has closer relations with Taiwan than it has with some countries with which it maintains formal diplomacy. The American Institute in Taiwan (AIT) acts as the United States' *de facto* embassy in Taiwan, and the United States and Taiwan have entered into more than two hundred agreements through the AIT. Moreover, in today's world, state-to-state diplomacy revolves in large part around the economy, trade, and investment. In this sense, Taiwan is able to engage in substantive and meaningful exchanges with other countries. The barrier preventing Taiwan from engaging in normal relations with most other countries is the PRC, which adamantly opposes Taiwan's participation in international arrangements, whether bilateral or multilateral. Notwithstanding this challenge, Taiwan participates in about thirty intergovernmental organizations (IGOs) and related groups. These include the Asian Development Bank, the World Trade Organization (as the "Separate Customs Territory of Taiwan, Penghu, Kinmen and Matsu"), and the Asia-Pacific Economic Cooperation forum (as "Chinese Taipei"— a degrading name the country is forced to use for its national Olympic Committee and in the World Health Assembly). Additionally, Taiwan has observer status or membership in about twenty other IGOs and subsidiary bodies.[30]

Taiwan's relations with its regional neighbors are generally positive. Even though Japan formally switched its diplomatic recognition from Taipei to Beijing in 1972, relations between Japan and Taiwan have remained friendly. A 2010 survey by Japan's *de facto* embassy in Taipei revealed that more than half of Taiwanese respondents chose Japan as their favorite country, and 62 percent described Japan as a "closely-related" country. In 2001, the Japanese government permitted former Taiwanese president Lee Teng-hui to seek medical treatment in Japan against protests from the PRC. Japan provided aid and disaster relief to Taiwan after the 1999 Jiji earthquake and Typhoon Morakot in 2009. Likewise, in the wake of the earthquake and tsunami that struck Japan in 2011, Taiwan donated more money than any other country, with contributions totaling upward of USD 260 million. According to Japanese magazine *Shukan Shincho*, Taiwan's generosity demonstrated that the two countries were "true friends."[31]

Relations between Taiwan and China have evolved rapidly under President Ma, who has taken a notably conciliatory tone toward the PRC in contrast to his predecessors. Unlike Lee Teng-hui's "state-to-state relations" and Chen Shui-bian's "one country on each side" formulations, Ma has defined the relationship between China and Taiwan as a special relationship between "two areas" within one state. Ma endorsed the so-called 1992 Consensus and the "Three Noes" (no unification, no independence, and no use of force) as a basis for engaging in relations with China. Ma characterized his approach as "flexible diplomacy," which makes cooperation a central element of cross-strait diplomacy, arguing that his approach would permit the PRC and the ROC to arrive at a *modus vivendi* in diplomatic relations. Ma's strategy is well in line with the proposal made by Chinese President Hu Jintao in 2008 to seek "fair and reasonable arrangements on Taiwan's participation in international organizations . . . through pragmatic consultation between [Taiwan and the PRC]."[32] Taiwan did gain observer status at the 2009 World Health Assembly and signed several bilateral agreements with Asia Pacific nations. But critics contend that requiring China's assent to participate in international forums is both humiliating and degrading to Taiwan's sovereign authority. Others warn that the "diplomatic truce" between Taiwan and the PRC could not be maintained because Ma's approach depended on the PRC's acquiescence for its effectiveness. Indeed, the PRC has threatened boycotts against organizations that referred to Taiwan by name, as opposed to "Taiwan, China," "Taipei, China," "Taiwan Province of China," or "Taiwan Province of the PRC." Take, for example, the PRC's resistance to efforts by Taiwan to join the UN Framework Convention on Climate Change and the International Civil Aviation Organization (ICAO).

B. TAIWAN'S DEFENSE LANDSCAPE

In the New Haven School's analytical framework, the *military instrument* concerns the use of organized violence to compel compliance with expectations of conduct, whether on behalf of the world community, a coalition of nations, or a singular state. Employed constructively for collective security, the military instrument can be vital to the maintenance of minimum world order. Indeed, the UN Charter embodies the notion of collective defense. All nations, even the United States, require alliances in this era of collective security. Used coercively, the military instrument can destroy conditions necessary for the attainment of shared values and fundamentally undermine relations between states and their peoples, as well as world order generally.

Unfortunately, warfare has been commonplace in Asia for much of recorded history. The history of China itself is punctuated by periods of intense violence dividing periods of political calm. The twentieth century saw vicious civil and interstate conflicts throughout the Pacific that left virtually no country unscathed. The remnants of war are highly visible today. They can be seen in the neutralized zone between North Korea and South Korea, in the monuments celebrating Hanoi's victory over Saigon, and at the tourist centers that welcome Chinese visitors to the abandoned ROC barracks and tunnels of Quemoy. While much of Asia today enjoys relative peace and rising economic prosperity, disputes over islands in the East and South China Seas and other territories threaten to unleash new conflicts that could hurl the region into chaos once again.

During World War II, the United States actively supported Chiang Kai-shek's ROC forces, which had been battling the Japanese since the start of the Second

Sino-Japanese War in 1937. Support began to waver near the end of the war, as the United States sought to roll back its commitments in the Pacific and bring home its war-weary troops. After the ROC government fled to Taiwan in 1949, President Truman opted to "let the dust settle," accepting the possibility that Communist forces would overrun the ROC on the island. Truman's policy was quickly reversed with the outbreak of the Korean War in 1950. Truman declared Taiwan a neutral territory and sent the Seventh Fleet to patrol the Taiwan Strait. In Taiwan, Chiang Kai-shek saw the opportunity to consolidate power and prepare the ROC military for an eventual reconquest of China.

Chiang Kai-shek's hand was strengthened with the election of President Eisenhower. Upon taking office in 1953, Eisenhower ended the U.S. policy of neutralizing the Taiwan Strait. Chiang Kai-shek responded by deploying forces to the ROC-controlled islands of Quemoy and Matsu close to the Chinese mainland. The First Taiwan Strait Crisis began the next year in September 1954 when the PRC launched artillery attacks on the islands. The attack led the United States to adopt a Mutual Defense Treaty with the ROC in 1954, which provided for the defense of Formosa and the Pescadores and "such other territories as may be determined by mutual agreement." Although the ROC had fortified Quemoy and Matsu with more than 70,000 troops, the islands were intentionally omitted from the treaty. U.S. officials worried that a small conflict over Quemoy and Matsu could trigger a large-scale war. Skirmishes between the PRC and the ROC continued through early 1955. In January 1955, the U.S. Congress passed the Formosa Resolution, authorizing the president to deploy U.S. armed forces "as he deems necessary for the specific purpose of securing and protecting Formosa and the Pescadores against armed attack," including "the securing and protection of such related positions and territories of that area now in friendly hands."[33] Later that year, the United States established the Taiwan Defense Command (also known as the Formosa Liaison Center) in Taipei to support U.S. commitments to Taiwan under the Mutual Defense Treaty. The United States extended its commitment to Quemoy and Matsu following the Second Taiwan Strait Crisis in 1958. On August 23, the PRC launched fresh attacks on Quemoy in an effort to overtake the island. With military support from the United States, the ROC was able to achieve a stalemate, and the PRC reverted to a policy of "ceremonial" shelling of Quemoy on odd days of the month. The ROC in turn shelled the Chinese mainland on even days. The alternating exchange of fire, which lasted until 1979, symbolized the continued existence of the "civil war" between the Communist and Nationalist regimes. At the same time, the ROC's continuing occupation of Quemoy and Matsu supported its symbolic claim to the whole of China.

In December 1978, the United States extended diplomatic recognition to the PRC and derecognized the ROC as the government of China. On April 10, 1979, the United States enacted the Taiwan Relations Act establishing informal relations with the people of Taiwan and making it the policy of the United States to provide sufficient weapons to Taiwan to ensure the island's defense. Sixteen days later, the Taiwan Defense Command ended its mission as a result of the expiration of the Mutual Defense Treaty. The history of U.S. arms sales to Taiwan after 1979 is explored in greater depth in Chapter 6.

In an absolute sense, Taiwan has a formidable, modern military force. Taiwan's military comprises an army, navy, air force, marine corps, and military police force. The military commands more than 240,000 active-duty service personnel (1.37 million including reservists, compared to the PRC's 2.1 million), more than 300 amphibious assault ships, 230 helicopters, 3,500 tanks and armored vehicles, 360 fighter aircraft, and 26 warships. Strategically, Taiwan has abandoned Chiang Kai-shek's objective of reconquering China, permitting the creation of a more efficient and more defensive-focused military force. It has shifted from an "area-control" strategy focused on the Taiwan Strait to an "area-denial" strategy aimed at preventing control over the island by the PRC or other powers.

Historically, the military was effectively a branch of the KMT. In 2002, the military was reorganized under civilian political control, with the president as Supreme Commander and the Chief of General Staff reporting to the Minister of National Defense. The new arrangement also made the military explicitly nonpartisan and non-ideological. These changes were part of the country's overall transition from military occupation. Taiwanese lawmakers are also taking steps to end compulsory military service, which will leave Taiwan with an all-volunteer army for the first time in its history.

On the other side of the Taiwan Strait, the People's Liberation Army (PLA) has been rapidly modernizing, increasing military spending by double-digit percentages every year since the mid-1990s. The PRC is focused on steadily strengthening the country's offensive capabilities in the air, on the sea, in space, and in cyberspace. One of its objectives is to ensure supremacy over the Taiwan Strait and dominance over Taiwan. The PRC has obtained significant weaponry that could be used in an attack on Taiwan, including more than 1,600 short-range ballistic and cruise missiles aimed at the island—a constant threat of the use of force that is in violation of the UN Charter. This is widely considered to be the highest concentration of missiles deployed anywhere on Earth. The accuracy of these missiles has improved dramatically since the 1980s. As Mark Stokes, executive director of the Project 2049 Institute, remarked in testimony to the U.S.-China Economic and Security Review Commission, "every citizen on Taiwan lives within seven minutes of destruction, and they know that."[34]

Meanwhile, the gap between national defense budgets is widening. The PRC's military budget is now about twenty-one times that of Taiwan's.[35] The PRC's military spending is second only to the United States. As of 2014, the PLA had about 2,100 fighter planes to Taiwan's 330. The PLA navy consisted of 280 ships, including more than 50 destroyers and frigates and 1 aircraft carrier, in addition to 60 submarines. In 2007, the PLA commissioned three Yuzhao amphibious transport docks. These enormous ships are each capable of carrying up to 4 hovercraft, 20 amphibious armored vehicles, 800 troops, and at least 4 helicopters. The PLA's ground forces consist of more than 11,000 tanks and armored vehicles and 1.6 million deployed troops. The PRC has about half a dozen nuclear submarines, including five attack submarines. Its JIN-class submarines are capable of carrying nuclear missiles with a range of roughly 4,500 miles. The PRC is also determined on building an aircraft carrier fleet to support its naval ambitions.

Taiwan has strived to maintain an adequate defensive military capacity; however, the goal has proven increasingly difficult in the face of economic and political challenges. In the past, Taiwan had ample capacity to engage in self defense. But the equilibrium has been disrupted by China's rise and the expansion of its military budget. Taiwan's own defense budget fell from about 3.8 percent of GDP to 2 percent of GDP between 1994 and 2014. The nominal amount remained flat at around USD 10 billion. Both the KMT and DPP have pledged to raise defense spending to 3 percent of GDP, a target that has so far gone unmet. Spending during the first six years of the Ma administration averaged about 2.2 percent of GDP. Nevertheless, Taiwan's defense spending amounts to about 16 percent of the national budget—a high level compared to many advanced economies, but far less than the 24 percent reported in 1994.[36]

The U.S. and ROC militaries engage in numerous areas of exchange. The U.S. Air Force has provided training to Taiwanese pilots at Luke Air Force Base, Arizona, since 1997 as part of Taiwan's acquisition of F-16 A/B fighters. A 2005 U.S. Department of Defense assessment found that the Taiwanese pilots "performed brilliantly."[37] The two countries also engage in officer exchanges at multiple levels. For example, the Pacific Command's Asia-Pacific Center for Security Studies has accepted Taiwanese officers since 2002. High-ranking Taiwanese generals and defense ministers regularly attend defense conferences and meetings in the United States. In March 2002, ROC Defense Minister Tang Yiau-ming attended a defense conference in Florida, where he met U.S. Deputy Secretary of Defense Paul Wolfowitz, becoming the first Taiwanese defense minister to do so since 1979. The same year, Deputy Defense Minister Kang Ning-hsiang attended meetings inside the Pentagon, another first since 1979. In 2005, General Lee Tien-yu was the first Chief of General Staff to visit the United States since 1998. Since 1997, the U.S. Department of Defense has hosted closed-door talks with Taiwan national security officials at least annually in Monterey, California (the "Monterey Talks"). The summits include discussions on intermilitary coordination and how best to provide for Taiwan's defense. U.S. teams visit Taiwan periodically to evaluate specific aspects of the country's defensive capabilities. In 2002, the countries established a crisis hotline and have discussed joint undersea monitoring for Chinese submarines.

The United States has supported Taiwan in developing technology to enhance the island's command and control structure. Since the 1990s, the United States has provided advanced computer technologies to increase the island's defensive coordination. The most well known of these efforts is the Po Sheng program involving the deployment of a Lockheed Martin–developed communications network to support missile defense and other functions. In 2011, the program made headlines when a Taiwanese-American citizen, Kuo Tai-sheng, was arrested for espionage after passing classified information about the program to a Chinese official.

Taiwan has succeeded in developing a local weapons industry, and more than half of the island's hardware is "made in Taiwan."[38] Among its accomplishments was the development of the F-CK-1 Ching-kuo fighter jet. The ROC government launched the F-CK-1 program after the Reagan administration canceled the sale of U.S. F-20/FX jets in 1982. The program relied extensively on U.S. contractors such as General Dynamics, who transferred know-how and expertise to local producers. The F-CK-1 program was intended to produce hundreds of jets for Taiwan's air force, but budget constraints meant that only 131 jets were produced between 1990 and 1999. Taiwan has also developed various munitions, including missiles such as the Tien Chien ("Sky Sword"), which is comparable to the U.S. AIM-9 Sidewinder and AIM-120 AMRAAM short- and medium-range missiles. Both were developed by Taiwan's Chungshan Institute of Science and Technology and were first deployed on the F-CK-1 fighter jets. The Sky Swords are also being deployed by Taiwan's navy to replace 1970s-era U.S. missiles, which will extend the firing range of the navy's frigates from 10 kilometers (km) to 100 km. More recently Taiwan has developed the Hsiung Feng 2E land-attack cruise missile with a reported range of 600 km. The military has reportedly deployed about three hundred of the missiles since 2012.

The development of Taiwan's navy is critical in order to ensure the island's ability to defend itself against an invasion by sea. Among the most important assets are submarines, which would permit the ROC navy to patrol the Taiwan Strait. Taiwan currently has just four submarines, two of which are used only for training purposes due to their age. Attempts to acquire additional submarines from the United States stalled during the George W. Bush administration. Taiwan is now seeking to develop indigenous diesel-electric submarines to counter the PRC's growing fleet. In late 2014, the navy took delivery of the Tuo Jiang, a 500-ton stealth corvette. The advanced ships—known as "carrier killers"—are capable of traveling at speeds of up to 40 knots and can fire supersonic missiles.

Taiwan has in the past worked on domestic nuclear weapons development. In 1967, Taiwan started a civilian nuclear program under its Institute for Nuclear Energy Research. The program was secretly a dual-purpose program and was eventually revealed by the International Atomic Energy Agency. The ROC dismantled the program in 1976 in response to U.S. pressure. However, a second secret nuclear program was begun thereafter. The program was revealed by defector Colonel Chang Hsien-yi in 1987, leading once again to the halting of Taiwan's nuclear development program. After the Third Taiwan Strait Crisis from 1995 to 1996, President Lee Teng-hui proposed restarting the program, but quickly backed down under intense international criticism. Today, Taiwan voluntarily adheres to the Treaty on Non-proliferation of Nuclear Weapons (NPT), even though it is not a UN member.

As will be elaborated in later chapters, the military assistance provided under the Taiwan Relations Act has been successful in deterring Chinese aggression toward Taiwan and has contributed to peace and security in the Asia Pacific. Yet Taiwan's national defense continues to focus on the threat posed by the PRC. Although cross-strait tensions have fallen markedly over the past decade, the PRC has never renounced the use of force in its quest for unification with Taiwan. In 2005, following President Chen's election to a second term, the National People's Congress passed the "Anti-Secession Law," which codified for the first time the PRC's intention to use force in the case of a declaration of independence by Taiwan. Regional conflicts over the East China Sea, South China Sea, and Diaoyutai (Senkaku Islands) have also grown into potential military flashpoints involving the PRC and other countries, including Japan. China's recent provocative behavior, including the reclamation of land around coral reefs and construction of offshore military facilities, has created high anxiety in Taiwan and elsewhere.

Notes

1. Straits Exchange Foundation, History of the SEF, http://www.sef.org.tw/ct.asp? xItem=48843&CtNode=3987&mp=300.

2. *See* Chris Wang, *KMT beyond "1992 Consensus": DPP*, TAIPEI TIMES, July 26, 2013, *available at* http://www.taipeitimes.com/News/taiwan/archives/2013/07/26/2003568197.

3. Taiwan Affairs Office of the State Council PRC, The One-China Principle and the Taiwan Issue, Feb. 21, 2000, *available at* http://www.gwytb.gov.cn/en/Special/WhitePapers/201103/t20110316_1789217.htm.

4. Democratic Progressive Party, 1999 Resolution Regarding Taiwan's Future, Dec. 2, 1999, *available at* http://english.dpp.org.tw/1999-resolution-regarding-taiwans-future/.

5. Office of the President of the Republic of China (Taiwan), President Chen's Inaugural Address, May 20, 2000, *available at* http://english.president.gov.tw/Default.aspx?tabid=491&itemid=18907&rmid=2355&size=100.

6. *President Chen: "One Country on Each Side" Our Own Taiwanese Road*, 102 TAIWAN COMMUNIQUÉ 1 (2002), *available at* http://www.taiwandc.org/twcom/tc102-int.pdf.

7. *Chen Vows Constitutional Reform*, BBC NEWS, Mar. 30, 2004, *available at* http://news.bbc.co.uk/2/hi/asia-pacific/3581407.stm.

8. *Taiwan President Sued for Declassifying Controversial Documents*, TREND NEWS AGENCY, Aug. 8, 2008, *available at* http://en.trend.az/world/other/1265205.html.

9. Raju Gopalakrishnan & Jonathan Standing, *Taiwan Says Yes to Ma Re-election and His "Three No's,"* REUTERS, Jan. 14, 2012, *available at* http://www.reuters.com/article/2012/01/14/us-taiwan-election-ma-idUSTRE80D0ID20120114.

10. Chris Wang, *Presidential Election: DPP Presidential Candidate Tsai Ing-wen's Election Platform*, TAIPEI TIMES, Jan. 9, 2012, *available at* http://www.taipeitimes.com/News/taiwan/archives/2012/01/09/2003522803.

11. *Id.*

12. Andrew Jacobs, *President of Taiwan Is Re-elected, a Result That Is Likely to Please China*, N.Y. TIMES, Jan. 14, 2012, *available at* http://www.nytimes.com/2012/01/15/world/asia/taiwan-presidential-election.html.

13. Andrew Jacobs, *Taiwan Election Stirs Hopes Among Chinese for Democracy*, N.Y. TIMES, Jan. 16, 2012, *available at* http://www.nytimes.com/2012/01/17/world/asia/taiwan-vote-stirs-chinese-hopes-for-democracy.html.

14. Ma Ying-jeou, Taiwan's Renaissance: Inaugural Address, May 20, 2008, *available at* http://english.president.gov.tw/Portals/4/images/PresidentOffice/AboutPresident/pdf/section1.pdf.

15. William Wan, *Taiwan's President, Ma Ying-jeou, Plans to Expand Relations with China*, WASH. POST, Oct. 24, 2013, *available at* http://www.washingtonpost.com/world/taiwans-president-ma-ying-jeou-plans-to-expand-relations-with-china/2013/10/24/0e38bb7e-3cbd-11e3-b6a9-da62c264f40e_story.html.

16. *Ma Clarifies "Two Areas," Reaffirms Non-denial*, CHINA POST, Oct. 25, 2008, *available at* http://www.chinapost.com.tw/taiwan/china-taiwan-relations/2008/10/25/180363/Ma-clarifies.htm.

17. Su Yung-yao, *ECFA Benefiting Wealthy: Report*, TAIPEI TIMES, Mar. 27, 2011, *available at* http://www.taipeitimes.com/News/front/archives/2011/03/27/2003499218.

18. Jacobs, *supra* note 13.

19. Ben Blanchard, *Taiwan Leader Says Protest-Hit China Trade Pact Vital*, REUTERS, Mar. 23, 2014, *available at* http://www.reuters.com/article/2014/03/23/us-taiwan-protests-idUSBREA2M0322014032.

20. *Ma Calls for Early Passage of Services Pact Despite Wang's Pledge*, FOCUS TAIWAN, Apr. 4, 2014, *available at* http://focustaiwan.tw/news/aipl/201404060009.aspx.

21. Thomas L. Friedman, *Pass the Books. Hold the Oil*, N.Y. TIMES, Mar. 10, 2012, *available at* http://www.nytimes.com/2012/03/11/opinion/sunday/friedman-pass-the-books-hold-the-oil.html.

22. Joshua Meltzer, *Taiwan's Economic Opportunities and Challenges and the Importance of the Trans-Pacific Partnership*, Brookings Institute, East Asia Policy Paper Series (Jan. 2014), *available at* http://www.brookings.edu/research/papers/2013/09/30-taiwan-trans-pacific-partnership-meltzer#_ftnref4.

23. *Id.*

24. *Id.*

25. *See, e.g.*, Tsung-Mei Cheng, *Taiwan's Health Care System: The Next 20 Years*, Brookings Institution (May 2015), *available at* http://www.brookings.edu/research/opinions/2015/05/14-taiwan-national-healthcare-cheng.

26. Tseng Wei-chen & Chen Wei-han, *"Taiwanese" Identity Hits Record Level*, Taipei Times, Jan. 26, 2015, *available at* http://www.taipeitimes.com/News/front/archives/2015/01/26/2003610092.

27. *Id.*

28. Chung li-hua & Jake Chung, *Poll: 64.97% Say Taiwan Is Independent*, Taipei Times, Sept. 25, 2015, *available at* http://www.taipeitimes.com/News/taiwan/archives/2015/09/25/2003628550.

29. *Editorial: "Why Fear the T-Word"?*, Taipei Times, Nov. 20, 2015, *available at* http://www.taipeitimes.com/News/editorials/archives/2015/11/20/2003632875.

30. *See, e.g.*, Republic of China (Taiwan) Ministry of Foreign Affairs, International Organizations, http://www.taiwan.gov.tw/ct.asp?xItem=27190&ctNode=1922&mp=1001.

31. *Taiwan Gives Most in World to Japan*, Taipei Times, Apr. 17, 2011, *available at* http://www.taipeitimes.com/News/taiwan/archives/2011/04/17/2003500974.

32. Press Release: President Hu Jintao Offered New Proposals on Further Promoting Cross-Straits Peaceful Development, Embassy of the People's Republic of China in the United States, Dec. 31, 2008, *available at* http://www.china-embassy.org/eng/zt/999999999/t530289.htm.

33. H.J. Res. 159, 69 Stat. 7 (Jan. 29, 1955).

34. Testimony of Mark Stokes before the U.S. House of Representatives, U.S.-China Economic and Security Review Commission (Mar. 10, 2010), *available at* http://www.dtic.mil/cgi-bin/GetTRDoc?AD=ADA524332.

35. Rich Chang, *MND Report Highlights Threat of PRC*, Taipei Times, July 20, 2011, *available at* http://www.taipeitimes.com/News/front/archives/2011/07/20/2003508663.

36. *See, e.g.*, Craig Murray, *Taiwan's Declining Defense Spending Could Jeopardize Military Preparedness*, U.S.-China Economic and Security Review Commission, Staff Research Background (June 11, 2013), *available at* http://www.uscc.gov/sites/default/files/Research/Taiwan%E2%80%99s%20Declining%20Defense%20Spending%20Could%20Jeopardize%20Military%20Preparedness_Staff%20Research%20Backgrounder.pdf.

37. Shirley A. Kan, Taiwan: Major U.S. Arms Sales Since 1990, Congressional Research Service, at 2 (2014), *available at* https://www.fas.org/sgp/crs/weapons/RL30957.pdf.

38. *See* Joseph Yeh, *Taiwan Mulls Contingency After F-5 Jets Retire in 2019*, China Post, May 7, 2013, *available at* http://www.chinapost.com.tw/taiwan/national/national-news/2013/05/07/377978/Taiwan-mulls.htm.

II Articulation of Goals and Policy Considerations

3 Clarification of Common Interests

I. A Policy-Oriented Approach to International Law and World Affairs

The New Haven School is a policy-oriented approach to international law and world affairs.[1] It encourages scholars, policymakers, legal practitioners, counselors, and other thinkers to identify with the whole of humankind and to clarify the common interests of the world community as well as the particular groups and individuals affected by a legal problem. The first step in this approach is to be clear about one's own observational standpoint. Making this standpoint explicit is to engage in the task of self-scrutiny, whereby the observer strives to be as objective as possible and to minimize, as much as humanly possible, parochial or personal biases (an exercise that ought to be undertaken by scholars of all stripes). The author of this book was born in Taiwan (in those days Taiwanese were Japanese citizens before the end of World War II) and received his elementary, secondary, university, and legal training in Taiwan before coming to the United States for graduate studies. At Yale University he studied under, and co-authored with, Professors Myres S. McDougal and Harold D. Lasswell, the architects of the New Haven School of international law, whose teachings have influenced generations of legal scholars and practitioners. Although the author's land of origin is Taiwan, and his adopted country the United States, the policy considerations and recommendations made in this book aim to serve not only the interests of the people of Taiwan but also those of the United States, China, the Asia-Pacific region, and the world community as a whole. Our thinking about international legal problems—even the most intractable ones—must be balanced by a regard for the universal principles of human dignity and human security.

The task of clarifying common interests is a vital part of problem solving under international law because prescriptions that do not satisfy the needs of the people concerned are unlikely to endure, especially in an international legal system without a centralized authority in which responsibility for the enforcement of norms is largely distributed among nation-states. At the highest and most inclusive level, common interests lead us to the ultimate goals which the New Haven School terms "minimum and optimum world order." Minimum world order refers to the minimization of unauthorized coercion and violence—that is, maintaining international peace and security. Optimum world order refers to the maximization of human values—respect, power, enlightenment, well-being, wealth, skill, affection, and rectitude. Put another way, optimum world order calls for enhancing international cooperation in political, economic, social, cultural, human rights, and humanitarian spheres. Together, minimum world order and optimum world order encompass what is commonly termed "human security," a concept held in high regard universally.

The twin goals of achieving minimum world order and fostering optimum world order are most eloquently projected in the Charter of the United Nations. The Charter is regarded by many as the "constitution" of the world community and the fundamental law of all humankind in the globalized world. Charter provisions that speak to minimum world order include Chapter I (Purposes and Principles), in particular Articles 1 and 2, and Chapter VII (Threats to the Peace, Breaches of the Peace, and Acts of Aggression). Provisions especially relevant to the goal of promoting optimum world order are Chapter IX (International Economic and Social Cooperation), in particular Articles 55 and 56. The UN Charter obligates member states to carry out the Charter's purposes and principles. Among them are to:

1) settle their international disputes by peaceful means in such a manner that international peace and security, and justice, are not endangered;

2) refrain in their international relations from the threat or use of force against the territorial integrity or political independence of any state, or in any other manner inconsistent with the Purposes of the UN;

3) give the UN every assistance in any action it takes in accordance with the present Charter;

4) ensure that states which are not Members of the UN act in accordance with [UN] Principles so far as may be necessary for the maintenance of international peace and security.[2]

The dispute between China and Taiwan is at its core a question about sovereignty: the right to make decisions about a territory and the destiny of its people. How should the world community go about resolving the debate? The Charter makes the responsibilities of UN members loud and clear: peace and security are paramount. That is to say, members must not threaten or use force to violate the territorial integrity or political independence of any state. Indeed, this rule increasingly applies even where a dispute is purely domestic in nature—which is not the case for Taiwan, as will be further elaborated below.

The following sections will illustrate the principles of minimum and optimum world order as they relate to Taiwan in five areas of common concern: peace and security; freedom, democracy, and human rights; the rule of law; economic development; and international cooperation. The New Haven School of international law is unique in its emphasis on the role of effective power processes in the formulation and maintenance of policy goals, in addition to processes of authoritative decision making. The discussions that follow will consider each of the five areas within their global contexts and the geostrategic considerations relevant to their attainment.

A. PEACE AND SECURITY

The necessity of maintaining peace and security in the Asia Pacific is beyond dispute. The region plays a critical role in the global economy, and its welfare is a focus of policymakers around the globe, especially in the United States. The U.S. government has consistently demonstrated—through both executive and legislative actions—that maintaining stability in Asia is among its top foreign policy objectives. The Taiwan Relations Act (TRA) of 1979 declares that peace and stability are "in the political, security, and economic interests of the United States, and are matters of international concern." More recently, President Obama has stated that the United States was "stepping up [its] commitment to the entire Asia-Pacific region." This rebalancing (or "pivot") toward the Asia Pacific has shown that U.S. policymakers do not intend to abandon the country's long-standing leadership role in the region.

For East Asia's three largest economies—Japan, the People's Republic of China (PRC), and the Republic of Korea (ROK)—maintaining peace and security in the region is essential in two ways. First, given their geographic proximity, any cross-strait conflict between Taiwan and China would hamper the use of the waterways around Taiwan and the Taiwan Strait for all of the surrounding countries. Second, the growing interconnectedness of the Chinese, Japanese, Korean, and Taiwanese economies creates a powerful incentive for maintaining good relations. This was explicitly recognized in the Joint Statement for Tripartite Partnership at the Japan–PRC–ROK Trilateral Summit in December 2008. The summit was the first time these nations had met to discuss and promote trilateral cooperation. In a Japan-PRC-ROK joint statement issued in October 2009, the three countries agreed to "promote peace, stability and prosperity [in] Asia."[3] Specifically, the parties agreed to "strengthen cooperation so as to promote development of regional and sub-regional cooperation of various mechanisms ... and continue to work through peaceful means to pursue the denuclearization of the Korean Peninsula ... so as to safeguard peace and stability in Northeast Asia, and thereby to build an Asia of peace, harmony, openness and prosperity."[4] Though the joint statement does not mention Taiwan by name, its language implies an understanding among the parties that a peaceful resolution to the Taiwan question would also be in the shared interests of all.

Taiwan's welfare is also central to the maintenance of peace and stability globally. It is undeniable that in today's world, conflicts in a particular region can no longer be localized, but tend to generate far-reaching impacts. Take for example the Arab Spring, which began in Tunisia and sparked a movement across the Middle East and North Africa and whose reverberations are being felt to this day. What began as iso-lated demonstrations soon led to the fall of several governments. The resulting civil war in Libya became a matter of international concern calling for an intervention by the United Nations, France, the United States, the United Kingdom, and other NATO members. As of 2015, battles continue to rage in Syria, Iraq, and Yemen. No community or territory is "an island onto itself." This observation is doubly true in the case of Taiwan. It is frightening to imagine the centrifugal and destructive forces that would be unleashed were a regional conflict to develop in the Taiwan Strait. There is little chance such a conflict could be contained without spreading to places near and far whose stability is conditioned by events in Asia. Nor is it likely that global powers could avoid being pulled into such a conflict, as they have been in North Africa and the Middle East. The UN Charter emphatically states that the United Nations exists to maintain international peace and security, and to that end, in the words of Article 1, "to take effective collective measures for the prevention and removal of threats to the peace, and for the suppression of acts of aggression or other breaches of the peace, and to bring about by peaceful means, and in confor-mity with the principles of justice and international law, adjustment or settlement of international disputes or situations which might lead to a breach of the peace." It is the responsibility of the world community to uphold these principles and to do everything in its power to ensure that peace and security are maintained in the Asia Pacific.

B. UNIVERSAL VALUES OF FREEDOM, DEMOCRACY, AND OTHER HUMAN RIGHTS

Now more than ever, human beings—and human dignity—are at the center of international law. While the United Nations was established on the "sovereign equality of states," "we the peoples of the United Nations" are equally paramount. Thanks to rapid advances in technologies, individuals can play an increasingly significant role in international affairs. In an era of ubiquitous communication and physical mobility, it is now possible for individuals, as well as states and international organizations, to participate in and exert influence over global decision processes, both formally and informally. This sea change has broadened expectations for what international law can achieve. International law, once state-centered, is now increasingly a people-centered jurisprudence. Moreover, human beings are no longer content to be passive recipients of fiats from domestic power elites. With a growing awareness of world conditions, individuals are demanding the protection of their fundamental human rights and the fulfillment of cherished values. This trend is evidenced by the increasing acceptance of the concept of states' "responsibility to protect." Where states were once inviolate as a matter of international law, today national sovereignty can only be justified and sustained when elites take seriously their responsibility to protect basic rights. When national elites engage in deliberate and gross violations of human rights, they may be held individually and criminally accountable in the court of world opinion and in authoritative forums such as the International Criminal Court (ICC). The establishment of the ICC, though challenged by some, represented a remarkable moment in the contemporary human rights movement and a testament to the world community's commitment to human dignity.

The rising demands and expectations of peoples around the world for protection and fulfillment of human rights have found authoritative expression in the UN Charter and a host of international agreements. The importance of human dignity was embraced by the United Nations from the very beginning in the preamble to the Charter, as well as Articles 1(3), 55 and 56. The Charter's preamble, speaking on behalf of the peoples of the United Nations, reaffirms the "faith in fundamental human rights, in the dignity and worth of the human person, in the equal rights of men and women and of nations large and small." Article 1(3) makes the protection of human rights a goal equal to that of maintaining international peace and security. The article states that it is the United Nations' purpose "to achieve international co-operation in solving international problems of an economic, social, cultural, or humanitarian character, and in promoting and encouraging respect for human rights and for fundamental freedoms for all without distinction as to race, sex, language, or religion." Article 55 provides that:

> With a view to the creation of conditions of stability and well-being which are necessary for peaceful and friendly relations among nations based on respect for the principle of equal rights and self-determination of peoples, the United Nations shall promote:
> a) higher standards of living, full employment, and conditions of economic and social progress and development;
> b) solutions of international economic, social, health, and related problems; and international cultural and educational cooperation; and
> c) universal respect for, and observance of, human rights and fundamental freedoms for all without distinction as to race, sex, language, or religion.

Article 56 requires that "all Members pledge themselves to take joint and separate action in co-operation with the Organization for the achievement of the purposes set forth" above.

In keeping with the letter and spirit of the UN Charter, a dynamic global bill of human rights has emerged and is undergoing continual renewal and development. This global bill of rights goes beyond what is commonly known as the "International Bill of Human Rights," which consists of the Universal Declaration of Human Rights, International Covenant on Civil and Political Rights, and International Covenant on Economic, Social and Cultural Rights. It includes a host of other human rights treaties and ancillary declarations, resolutions, and judicial decisions covering a wide range of values—from "first-generation" civil and political rights to "second-generation" economic, social, and cultural rights and to "third-generation" human solidarity rights. These third-generation rights affect the very survival, prosperity, and well-being of humanity in general and include, among others, the right to peace, the right to self-determination, the right to development, and the right to a healthy environment. The achievement of human solidarity rights, by their nature, requires joint efforts at every level of the community. Some misconstrue human rights to only include freedom and democracy for the individual. But the concept of human rights is not so confined. It is, in reality, an evolving concept shaped and shared via the collective political emancipation and participation of all people.[5]

As explained in Chapter 2, in the terminology of the New Haven School the scope of cherished values embraced by the concept of human rights can be conveniently categorized and summarized as: respect (freedom of choice, equality, and recognition), power (making and influencing community decisions), enlightenment (gathering, processing, and disseminating information and knowledge), well-being (safety, health, and comfort), wealth (production, distribution, and consumption of goods and services; control of resources), skill (acquisition and exercise of capabilities in vocations, professions, and the arts), affection (intimacy, friendship, loyalty, and positive sentiments), and rectitude (participation in forming and applying norms of responsible conduct). The sum of these value categories is termed human security. The quest for human rights is itself a quest for dignity and security for all individual persons and for humankind as a whole.

The concept of human rights is by no means a recent invention. In the American tradition, the imperative of recognizing and protecting the people's inalienable rights was given concrete expression in the Declaration of Independence, which, in Thomas Jefferson's immortal words, proclaimed that "all men are created equal." In 1863, President Abraham Lincoln eulogized the soldiers who fought and died at Gettysburg for the ideal of a "government of the people, by the people, for the people." Eighty-five years later, the Universal Declaration of Human Rights, in Article 21, would affirm that "everyone has the right to take part in the government of his country. . . . The will of the people shall be the basis of the authority of government." Lincoln's conception of democracy remains as refreshing and relevant for the twenty-first century as it was in the nineteenth.

The continued progression toward greater protection of human rights can be observed in the pronouncements of successive U.S. presidents who have linked the American heritage with the wider, global struggle for human dignity in the twentieth century. On January 6, 1941, Franklin D. Roosevelt, an architect of the UN system, addressed the U.S. Congress with a vision of a world order based on four essential freedoms: the freedom of speech and expression, the freedom to freely worship, the freedom from want in terms of economic development, and the freedom from fear of the physical aggression of war. During the 1950s, in the midst of the Cold War and toward the end of the Korean War, President Eisenhower focused on maintaining peace as a method of advancing human rights. He declared that "we seek peace, knowing that peace is the climate of freedom . . . that peace may be the only climate possible for human life itself."[6] In the 1960s, the West's devotion to the principles of individual freedom and democracy stood in stark contrast to the unabashed deprivation of human rights under Communism. In the words of John F. Kennedy, in his June 11, 1963, civil rights address, "the rights of every man are diminished when the rights of one man are threatened."[7] In the 1970s, President Carter championed human rights and democracy and made promoting them an integral part of his administration. He declared that "human rights is the soul of our foreign policy, because human rights is the very soul of our sense of nationhood."[8] In the 2000s, the drive for freedom and democracy continued to animate U.S. foreign policy and formed a cornerstone of the global war on terrorism. "America is a Nation with a mission," President George W. Bush said in his 2004 State of the Union address. "[T]hat mission comes from our most basic beliefs . . . we have no desire to dominate, no ambitions of empire . . .

our aim is a democratic peace—a peace founded upon the dignity and rights of every man and woman."[9] Later that year he spoke to the UN General Assembly, declaring that "peaceful nations must stand for the advance of democracy . . . No other system of government has done more to protect minorities, to secure the rights of labor, to raise the status of women or to channel human energy to the pursuits of peace."[10] In 2015, speaking on the fiftieth anniversary of a historic American civil rights march in Selma, Alabama, President Obama declared:

That's what makes [Americans] unique, and cements our reputation as a beacon of opportunity. Young people behind the Iron Curtain would see Selma and eventually tear down a wall. Young people in Soweto would hear Bobby Kennedy talk about ripples of hope and eventually banish the scourge of apartheid. Young people in Burma went to prison rather than submit to military rule. From the streets of Tunis to the Maidan in Ukraine, this generation of young people can draw strength from this place, where the powerless could change the world's greatest superpower, and push their leaders to expand the boundaries of freedom.[11]

Ultimately, the advancement of human rights is aimed at allowing the free will of the people to prevail through the collective exercise of speech and assembly, the free exercise of religion, the attainment of universal suffrage for all, and the maintenance of the rule of law in every arena, whether domestic or international. These are not solely American concepts. Former UN Secretary-General Kofi Annan, in reporting to the General Assembly on the Millennium Development Goals in 2005, stated, in words echoing Roosevelt:

Larger freedom implies that men and women everywhere have the right to be governed by their own consent, under law, in a society where all individuals can, without discrimination or retribution, speak, worship and associate freely. They must also be free from want—so that the death sentences of extreme poverty and infectious disease are lifted from their lives—and free from fear— so that their lives and livelihoods are not ripped apart by violence and war. Indeed, all people have the right to security and to development.[12]

Ten years later, in October 2015, Zeid Ra'ad Al Hussein, UN High Commissioner for Human Rights, declared before the General Assembly's Third Committee:

The turmoil and crises that the international community faces clearly demonstrate the disasters that may occur when human rights are neglected and ground down. . . . . The right to express dissent or criticism. The right to peaceful assembly. Freedom from torture and ill-treatment. The right to decent public services, such as education and health-care. The right to development. The right to fair trial, under an impartial rule of law. Freedom from any form of discrimination. The peaceful resolution of disputes, and in the case of conflict, due protection for civilians and protected locations stipulated by international law. These are the factors that will generate durable solutions to turmoil.[13]

In the context of Taiwan, and the world community as a whole, these successive statements concerning the desire for human rights do not represent only the aspirations of the American people. They are applicable to all of humankind.

C. RULE OF LAW

A closely related concept is the rule of law. The rule of law encompasses both the prescription of a norm and its enforcement. A norm, in the words of the Security Council, is "a principle of governance in which all persons, institutions and entities, public and private, including the State itself, are accountable to laws that are publicly promulgated, equally enforced and independently adjudicated, and which are consistent with international human rights norms and standards."[14] Enforcement refers to "measures to ensure adherence to the principles of supremacy of law, equality before the law, accountability to the law, fairness in the application of the law, separation of powers, participation in decision-making, legal certainty, avoidance of arbitrariness and procedural and legal transparency."[15] The UN mandate is conspicuous about the fact that no state, no matter how rich or powerful, is above the rule of law. More important, no nation or individual ought to be held to be unworthy of the protections promised to every citizen under international law. Accordingly, the world community should embrace a robust scheme ensuring that no nation is able to shirk these bedrock principles without regard to the shared expectations and projections embodied in the UN Charter.

Even the United States and China, both powers to be reckoned with, are subject to the same standards. In October 2015, President Obama and South Korean President Park Geun-hye held a joint press conference in which President Obama remarked on China's role in the Asia community. He said: "We want to see China's peaceful rise. . . . We want to be working with them to uphold international norms and rules of the road. . . . And we don't want to see those rules of the road weakening, or some countries taking advantage because they're larger." Indeed, all UN members must ensure that the principles of the UN Charter are upheld at every juncture. Secretary-General Ban Ki-moon encapsulated this mission in remarks made at New York Law School in October 2011, when he said: "The United Nations stands with all those seeking to build societies where nobody is above the law and where laws are publicly promulgated, equally enforced and consistent with human rights."[16] The permanent members of the Security Council are especially bound to this duty, owing to their central role in the maintenance of the UN system—making China's perpetual threat of the use of force against Taiwan a particularly egregious violation of the UN Charter.

D. ECONOMIC DEVELOPMENT

Though a "barren rock in a typhoon-laden sea with no natural resources to live off of,"[17] Taiwan is a paradigm of prosperous development. It has tremendous economic power and, despite its small geographic size, is a major participant in international trade. Taiwan is a significant trading partner to nations including the United States, China, and Japan. In 2013, Taiwan ranked twentieth in the world for exports of merchandise and eighteenth for imports among the members of the World Trade Organization, ranking ahead of major economies such as Australia, Brazil, and Switzerland.[18] All countries that rely on Taiwan for trade have a shared interest in safeguarding its prosperity.

Nurturing economic cooperation and productive competition has become a primary objective for the world community as technological advances over the last century have made it possible to conduct international trade more economically and efficiently. These goals are embodied in the charters of international organizations including the World Trade Organization (WTO) as well as bilateral and multilateral agreements devoted to promoting trade. The WTO, with over one hundred fifty members, was created to reduce obstacles to international trade to promote economic growth globally.[19] Some countries have taken these efforts further by signing treaties creating unified regional markets. For example, the European Union's consolidated treaty declares that one of its objectives is to "promote economic . . . cohesion, and solidarity among Member States . . . and to establish an economic and monetary union whose currency is the euro."[20] There are countless other forums with similar purposes. They include the Group of Twenty Finance Ministers and Central Bank Governors (G-20), the Asia-Pacific Economic Cooperation (APEC), and the North American Free Trade Agreement (NAFTA). Noncooperation in economic matters, on the other hand, can lead to disruptions in cross-border business and trade. The facilitation of economic cooperation and competition is as much a concern for the world community as any other shared goal.

The rise of international organizations dedicated to the task of economic coordination evidences the rapid and fundamental shift in economic patterns that is leading the world to unprecedented integration and interdependency. Often termed globalization, this shift refers to the increasing interdependence of the world's economies that has resulted from increasing trade in goods and services and the opening of borders.[21] Advancements in science and technologies have contributed greatly to the trend by lowering barriers to transportation and communication. Moreover, economic globalization is an ongoing process. Market forces and technological improvements will lead to continued integration. Nowhere are the fruits of this progression more obvious than in Taiwan. The Taiwanese economy is intertwined with the economies of other nations. It can only be expected that this dependency will increase in years to come.

E. INTERNATIONAL COOPERATION TOWARD MINIMUM AND OPTIMUM WORLD ORDER

The common interests of humankind are embraced in the concepts of minimum world order and optimum world order. Minimum world order seeks to minimize unauthorized coercion and violence, namely, to secure international peace and security. Optimum world order seeks to foster the widest possible shaping and sharing of values through international cooperation in all value sectors. The concepts of minimum world order and optimum world order are distinct, but closely linked. Without minimum world order, demanded values could not be securely and optimally shaped and shared. Conversely, minimum world order cannot be maintained so long as individuals are denied the ability and opportunity to participate in the shaping and sharing of all widely demanded values. In everyday terms, this means striving to resolve differences through international cooperation and to spread the benefits of material prosperity and the protection of human rights and fundamental freedoms everywhere in the world.

The international legal system of today, which was built in the wake of the Second World War and endured through the east-west divisions of the Cold War, does have its shortcomings and imperfections. But it is the only system that we have. Since the end of the Cold War, global effective power processes have transitioned from unipolarity to multipolarity. Challenges to the existing system of world order based on the UN Charter have multiplied. The rapid tempo of changes generated by the universalization of science-based technologies in information, communication, and all other spheres have brought home vividly the realities of global interdependencies and have sharpened people's perception of such interdependencies. To abandon today's system, however imperfect, would be to return to an international environment modeled on the jungle in which naked power prevails over shared principles and foresight. If we did not have the United Nations, we would have to invent something like it to have any hope of striving for a global order of human dignity and human security. Planet Earth is becoming ever more interconnected and complicated. In this context, the quest for common interests is imperative in dealing with problems in international law and global affairs. International cooperation is essential in achieving minimum and optimum world order—and with it human dignity and human security—for all humankind both individually and collectively.

For Taiwan, the aforementioned international legal principles matter and are given concrete expression in the continuing quest for peace and security; freedom, democracy, and human rights; the rule of law; and economic prosperity—goals that are deeply entwined within the common interests of the world community. These concepts are not abstract. They manifest themselves in every facet of the dynamic U.S.-Taiwan-China relationship.

II. Taiwan's International Legal Status Is a Matter of International Concern

Taiwan's international legal status is a matter of international concern, not a Chinese internal affair subject to the PRC's domestic jurisdiction. An important function of international law is to permit external decision makers to intercede in matters that would otherwise be regarded as internal to a particular state. The common interests of the world community necessitate allocating competences between international authorities and the governments of the various territories, even in a world that is divided into geographic units. As such, the concept of *international concern* has undergone a continuing expansion in scope over time, while the concept of *domestic jurisdiction*, as embodied in Article 2(7), has correspondingly diminished, thanks to the acceleration of interactions and interdependencies among the world's peoples.

Events occurring within the territorial boundaries of a particular state may have effects that extend beyond the territory. In these cases, the world community can make and apply law in the defense of the common interests of the peoples affected. The trend toward the expansion of international concern can be seen by the scope of subjects handled by various UN organs. The United Nations has exercised its authority to deal with a wide range of matters extending to every value sector of community life. The comprehensive list includes matters of peace and security (including peacekeeping operations and arms control); matters of decolonization and self-determination (including trust territories and non-self-governing territories); territorial disputes; emergency humanitarian assistance; questions regarding the form of government of a state; international cooperation in economic, social, and cultural spheres; human rights matters; and the making and application of international law. It will inevitably grow as the international community responds to the challenges of an increasingly globalized and interdependent world.

Contrast this to the notion of state sovereignty, under which states have long enjoyed exclusive competence, insulating internal elites from external scrutiny. Sovereignty, as made popular by Jean Bodin in the sixteenth century, was somewhat fitting in an era of absolute monarchs. However, it is not at all apt to describe state authority in the contemporary epoch of popular sovereignty (authority in the people) and growing interdependences. The critical question confronting decision makers who represent the larger community of humankind is how best to relate inclusive claims to the fundamental policies of the community. In the words of the Permanent Court of International Justice in the *Tunis-Morocco* case of 1923: "The question whether a certain matter is or is not solely within the domestic jurisdiction of a State is an essentially relative question; it depends upon the development of international relations."[22] That is to say, determining whether a matter is of international concern depends not only on the facts of a case but also the context of world conditions and relevant policies. In practice, the United Nations is fully competent to discuss or debate any matter without doing violence to the mandate of Article 2(7) not "to intervene in matters which are essentially within the domestic jurisdiction of any state." As to the prescribing function, no limit on the United Nations' authority to legislate has been easily identifiable. The General Assembly's activities encompass practically every aspect of human life.

As the dynamics of global interdependence accelerate and peoples' perceptions of their interdependence deepen, matters having transnational ramifications will fall more easily into the compass of inclusive competence. Individual states rarely succeed, even by invoking the plea of domestic jurisdiction, in precluding interventions when transnational impacts are clearly generated. When particular events engender significant impacts, the world community can be expected to internationalize jurisdiction and to authorize appropriate action. In light of the foregoing discussion, China's unceasing threat toward Taiwan in the name of domestic jurisdiction exemplifies an abuse of the concept of domestic jurisdiction. The PRC has sought to justify its stance by claiming that Taiwan is "part of China" and that the issue is "an internal affair of China." These claims can be rejected out of hand and are totally unfounded. In addition, the PRC's threat to use missiles and other forms of violence against Taiwan to compel unification (annexation) is clearly a lawless act in violation of the UN Charter.

As will be explored in Chapter 4, Taiwan is, in fact, a sovereign, independent state and not a part of China. For more than sixty-five years since its founding in 1949, the PRC never exerted effective control over Taiwan for a single day. The PRC's introduction of an antisecession law designed to harass and intimidate the people of Taiwan, its military actions during the Third Taiwan Strait Crisis of 1995 to 1996, on the eve of Taiwan's first direct presidential election, and its unceasing military threat against Taiwan, which includes the targeting of more than sixteen hundred missiles, endanger peace and security in the Asia Pacific and constitute threats and breaches of the peace in violation of the UN Charter. Given these facts, it would be wrong to concede that Chinese military threats toward Taiwan are simply a matter of China's "core interests" under its domestic jurisdiction. China's actions encroach upon the right of the Taiwanese people to democratic self-governance and self-determination and are at odds with Taiwan's status as an independent state and the conditions of peace and security. Furthermore, controversies over Taiwan's sovereignty and international legal status involve an interpretation of international agreements, such as the San Francisco Peace Treaty with Japan, and the application of universal principles, such as the right of self-determination, to the country's 23 million inhabitants. Hence, Taiwan's status falls squarely within the scope of international concern.

III. Why Taiwan Matters

In June 2011, the House of Representatives' Committee on Foreign Affairs used the phrase "Why Taiwan Matters" as the title of its two-day hearings concerning the United States' Taiwan policy. Professor Shelley Rigger wrote an excellent book by the same name. And the phrase has appeared in numerous headlines in magazines, journals, and newspapers since. "Why Taiwan Matters" is not a question, but a statement. Though geographically small, Taiwan matters to the United States and China, and to the rest of the world community in many big ways.

First and foremost, Taiwan matters because its people matter. Taiwan is home to more than 23 million human beings—roughly equal to the population of Australia. In considering Taiwan's status and future, the welfare of the Taiwanese people should be a major concern of decision makers around the globe. Moreover, the Taiwanese people's desire to govern themselves democratically should be respected and safeguarded. The island's progression from authoritarian rule based on martial law to a progressive democracy since the late 1980s is a testament to its peoples' embrace of the fundamental freedoms enshrined in the Charter of the United Nations and related human rights instruments, especially the principle of self-determination. Historically, the path to freedom and democracy has not been easy. This makes Taiwan's peaceful political transformation especially remarkable. During the thirty-eight-year period of martial law, Taiwan experienced the wholesale and systematic suppression and deprivation of human rights. The government actively punished political dissidents with prison terms and even death sentences. Then, in 1987, an executive decision ended martial law, paving the way for the first presidential election by the people of Taiwan in 1996. A peaceful transfer of executive power followed, and a second election was held in 2000. Taiwan's democratic transformation should serve as a model for other peoples seeking greater freedom, democracy, and human rights in the new century. Taiwan's future as a modern democratic state in Asia should be nurtured and cherished.

Taiwan matters because it is geopolitically significant and serves as an important buffer state in the region. For the United States, Taiwan is a lynchpin for foreign policy in the Western Pacific and essential for access to key waterways. For neighboring Japan, Taiwan matters because it means continued stability necessary for sea trade with the nations of Southeast Asia. In this regard, Taiwan has an important role to play in the expanding Pacific security alliance that includes Japan, Australia, the United States, and other countries. In 2015, President Ma Ying-jeou made headlines for his proposal for a South China Sea Peace Initiative that would encourage the joint development of regional waterways and resources as a way to defuse tensions over unresolved territorial claims. For China, Taiwan matters because it is the subject of a long-standing territorial dispute between the PRC and the ROC governments and a focal point for China's growing regional and global power. To the PRC, Taiwan represents an opportunity to disrupt U.S. hegemony in the Pacific and secure influence over strategically important trade routes. Similarly, Taiwan matters because maintaining peace and stability in the Asia Pacific is a responsibility shared by the global community. Not only is maintaining international peace and security an express mandate in the UN Charter, it is also a declared policy objective of the United States, Japan, Korea, and China—relevant actors in any discussion of the Asia Pacific. It follows that questions about Taiwan's future should be resolved in line with these principles, and not by force or political expediency.

Taiwan matters because economic globalization has made the world's economies interdependent and interconnected like never before. One need only consider the havoc wreaked by recent economic crises in Asia, the United States, and Greece to appreciate this fact. Market downturns in even a relatively small country can have massive implications for the global economy. Or take for example the 1999 Jiji earthquake (also called the "921 earthquake"), which cut off electricity to many semiconductor factories on Taiwan. The interruption disrupted the global supply chains for high-tech products, resulting in financial losses for manufacturers around the world. Taiwan is a major trading partner to many countries and among the world's largest economies. It is not an exaggeration to say that its continued prosperity is essential to other nations. In the most general sense, Taiwan's economic output forms part of a larger flow of goods and services that powers the increasingly globalized world economy, employing billions of people. Taiwan's manufacturers also play an important role in building the global information society. Taiwanese companies produce countless motherboards, memory chips, displays, and other high-tech components that are integral to the world's communication infrastructure. Private corporations, groups, and individuals depend on Taiwan for its innovative technologies. Foxconn, which is based in Tucheng, Taiwan, has operations spanning six continents and produces upwards of 40 percent of the world's consumer electronics. Its products include the Blackberry, iPhone, iPad, and other well-known gadgets.

Finally, Taiwan matters because safeguarding its democracy is critical in maintaining an optimum world order rooted in the centrality of human beings and the rule of law. Contemporary Taiwan is a hopeful symbol for human rights and fundamental freedoms in the Asia Pacific and elsewhere. These concepts represent more than domestic preferences—they express the shared aspirations of the world's people. Policymakers in the United States and elsewhere should help Taiwan maximize its visibility in the international community, where it may serve as a beacon for people everywhere aspiring to have democracy. What is good for the people of Taiwan should be, and in fact is, good for the world community.

Chapter 4 will depict the Taiwanese people's struggle to actualize these principles in their decades-long quest for self-determination. The first articles of both the International Covenant on Civil and Political Rights and the International Covenant on Economic, Social and Cultural Rights affirm: "All peoples have the right of self-determination. By virtue of that right they freely determine their political status and freely pursue their economic, social and cultural development." Under different conditions Taiwan may have followed the same path as many de-colonized states in the years following World War II. Indeed, without the complexities introduced by the Chinese civil war, and the ROC's subsequent exile to Taiwan, it would be easy to picture Taiwan as a free and independent state today. But the realities of global power processes have forestalled such a development. Today the people of Taiwan find themselves in a state of limbo, and the promises of the international covenants remain unfulfilled. The solution to the Taiwan question cannot naively ignore the realities of global power politics. Neither can it ignore the principles embodied in the UN Charter and its supporting instruments. What is needed is a solution that harmonizes the aspirations of the Taiwanese people with the relevant international concerns. The outcome must be peaceful, and it must be carried out in a way that is consistent with the purposes and principles of the UN Charter and international law. What is clear is that Taiwan cannot stay in limbo forever. After seventy years since the end of World War II, the time has come for policymakers to address the reality of Taiwan's status as an independent state.

Notes

1. For a comprehensive treatment of the New Haven School of international law, *see* LUNG-CHU CHEN, AN INTRODUCTION TO CONTEMPORARY INTERNATIONAL LAW: A POLICY-ORIENTED PERSPECTIVE 3D ED. (2015).

2. UN Charter ch. I, art. 2.

3. Joint Statement on the Tenth Anniversary of Trilateral Cooperation among the People's Republic of China, Japan, and the Republic of Korea, *available at* http://www.mofa.go.jp/region/asia-paci/jck/meet0910/joint-1.pdf.

4. *Id.*

5. Myres S. McDougal & Lung-chu Chen, *Symposium on the Future of Human Rights in the World Legal Order/Introduction: Human Rights and Jurisprudence*, 9 HOFSTRA L. REV. 2 (1981). For a comprehensive study of the concept of human rights, *see* MYRES S. McDOUGAL, HAROLD D. LASSWELL, & LUNG-CHU CHEN, HUMAN RIGHTS AND WORLD PUBLIC ORDER: THE BASIC POLICIES OF AN INTERNATIONAL LAW OF HUMAN DIGNITY (1980).

6. Dwight D. Eisenhower, Second Inaugural Address, Jan. 21, 1957, *available at* http://avalon.law.yale.edu/20th_century/eisen2.asp.

7. John. F. Kennedy, Report to the American People on Civil Rights, June 11, 1963, *available at* http://www.jfklibrary.org/Asset-Viewer/LH8F_0Mzvoe6Ro1yEm74Ng.aspx.

8. Jimmy Carter, Universal Declaration of Human Rights Remarks at a White House Meeting Commemorating the 30th Anniversary of the Declaration's Signing, Dec. 6, 1978, *available at* http://www.presidency.ucsb.edu/ws/?pid=30264.

9. George W. Bush, Address Before a Joint Session of the Congress on the State of the Union, Jan. 20, 2004, *available at* http://www.presidency.ucsb.edu/ws/index.php?pid=29646.

10. George W. Bush, Remarks to the United Nations General Assembly in New York City, Sept. 21, 2004, *available at* http://www.presidency.ucsb.edu/ws/index.php?pid=72758&st=&st1=.

11. News Release: Remarks by the President at the 50th Anniversary of the Selma to Montgomery Marches, The White House, Mar. 7, 2015, *available at* https://www.whitehouse.gov/the-press-office/2015/03/07/remarks-president-50th-anniversary-selma-montgomery-marches.

12. Secretary-General, In larger freedom: towards development, security and human rights for all, para. 15, A/59/2005, Mar. 11, 2005, *available at* http://daccess-dds-ny.un.org/doc/UNDOC/GEN/N05/270/78/PDF/N0527078.pdf?OpenElement.

13. Statement by Mr. Zeid Ra'ad Al Hussein, United Nations High Commissioner for Human Rights, at the plenary of the Third Committee, at the 70th session of the United Nations General Assembly, Oct. 21, 2015, *available at* http://www.ohchr.org/EN/NewsEvents/Pages/DisplayNews.aspx?NewsID=16627&LangID=E#sthash.RIlkE8xo.dpuf.

14. United Nations Security Council, Report of the Secretary-General on the Rule of Law and Transitional Justice in Conflict and Post-Conflict Societies, S/2004/616 (Aug. 23, 2004), *available at* http://daccess-dds-ny.un.org/doc/UNDOC/GEN/N04/395/29/PDF/N0439529.pdf.

15. *Id.*

16. Secretary-General's Remarks at the 2011-2012 Otto L. Walter Lecture at New York Law School, Oct. 4, 2011, *available at* http://www.un.org/sg/statements/index.asp?nid=5589.

17. Thomas L. Friedman, *Pass the Books. Hold the Oil*, N.Y. TIMES, Mar. 10, 2012, *available at* http://www.nytimes.com/2012/03/11/opinion/sunday/friedman-pass-the-books-hold-the-oil.html.

18. *See* WORLD TRADE ORGANIZATION, INTERNATIONAL TRADE STATISTICS at 26 (2014), *available at* https://www.wto.org/english/res_e/statis_e/its2014_e/its2014_e.pdf.

19. World Trade Organization, Overview, https://www.wto.org/english/thewto_e/whatis_e/wto_dg_stat_e.htm.

20. European Union, The Founding Principles of the Union, http://europa.eu/scadplus/constitution/objectives_en.htm.

21. *See, e.g.*, Shangquan Gao, *Economic Globalization: Trends, Risks and Risk Prevention*, CDP Background Paper No. 1 (2000), *available at* http://www.un.org/en/development/desa/policy/cdp/cdp_background_papers/bp2000_1.pdf.

22. Advisory Opinion on the Tunis and Morocco Nationality Decrees, Ser, B. No. 4, at 24 (1923).

4 | The Evolution of Taiwan Statehood

IS TAIWAN A state? This seemingly straightforward question has aroused vigorous debate from international law scholars and other commentators since the adoption of the San Francisco Peace Treaty with Japan in 1951. The word *state* denotes a territorially organized community having achieved special status and privileges under international law. Since the rise of the nation-state system in the seventeenth century, states have played a predominant role in international law and in the global process of decision making. To this day states remain the basic political unit in international affairs and the major participants in the international legal order. The inhabitants of a state are held to possess sovereignty—the right to make decisions concerning their territory. Except in limited circumstances, these decisions are immune from outside challenge. Achieving statehood is a cherished dream for many of the world's peoples, one for which countless men and women have fought and died throughout history. In the twentieth century, the number of states multiplied greatly thanks to the disintegration of empires and the transformation of ex-colonies into independent states. Membership in the United Nations increased from the original 51 in 1945 to 193 by 2015.

As illustrated in Chapters 1 and 2, Taiwan's social and political history is anything but simple. And despite passionate arguments from all sides, an international consensus on Taiwan's legal status has yet to emerge. For the people of Taiwan, the consequences of this stalemate are significant. Statehood is a prerequisite for membership in many important international organizations, including the United Nations. As it stands, Taiwan is prevented from meaningfully participating in such forums, depriving its 23 million people of an opportunity to effectively advocate for their interests as equal participants on the world stage. More troubling, however, is the threat facing Taiwan from governments such as the People's Republic of China that wish to exploit its predicament for geostrategic gain. Without a firm answer on the question of statehood, Taiwan risks increasing marginalization—a frightening outcome in a world where interconnectedness and prosperity are so tightly intertwined.

I. Differing Viewpoints

The debate over Taiwan's statehood has given rise to a plethora of viewpoints embracing a full range of possible outcomes. On the one extreme are those who argue that Taiwan is a part of China (the so-called "renegade province"). This view calls for the unification of Taiwan with the Chinese state in order to align perceived legal and political realities. On the other extreme are those who argue unequivocally that Taiwan is a full-fledged state, and has been since the end of World War II. This viewpoint calls for permitting Taiwan to conduct its affairs without interference as becoming of any independent state. Between these poles exist numerous other positions exhibiting varying degrees of nuance.

As with all legal problems, the first step in resolving the Taiwan question is to identify the governing rules and principles. Then, facts must be deemed relevant or irrelevant to the analysis and weighted according to their importance. In practice, proponents may unconsciously or consciously interpret the facts to suit their preferred outcomes. As explained in Chapter 3, the New Haven School counsels against this tendency, encouraging scholars to view legal and policy questions comprehensively in the context of an ongoing process of authoritative decision and controlling practice, with outcomes appraised in terms of minimum and optimum world order. Within this framework questions are resolved in light of the most broadly held principles with regard to the inclusive interests of the world community.

The four viewpoints illustrated below represent the opinions most commonly advanced regarding Taiwan statehood. The first of these viewpoints, which may be placed on one extreme of the continuum, holds that international law regards Taiwan as a part of China. The second, which occupies the middle ground, suggests that Taiwan's legal status is undetermined, and has been since the conclusion of the San Francisco Peace Treaty with Japan in 1951, which entered into force in 1952. The third argues that Taiwan is a state for all intents and purposes; however, geopolitical constrains have kept it from fully expressing itself as such. That is to say, Taiwan has *de facto*, but not *de jure*, independence. The fourth and final viewpoint, which is advanced by the author, holds that Taiwan already fulfills the criteria for statehood under contemporary international law, even if its status lacks sufficient formal recognition. As proponents of the second viewpoint have observed, Taiwan's legal status was left unresolved after the conclusion of the San Francisco Peace Treaty. But international law is not static. Scholars must continually reappraise their conclusions in light of changing world conditions. What was true in 1951 may not be true today, and it would be foolish to hold fast to viewpoints that are based on outdated facts or opinions. Furthermore, the framers of the UN Charter—known to many as the "world's constitution"—believed that people ought to determine their own destiny openly and freely in full view of the world community. This is the principle of self-determination. Implicit in this principle is the idea that a people's collective status may emerge and evolve over time. Any debate about Taiwan's statehood that does not incorporate the principle of self-determination would present a very incomplete picture indeed.

It must not be forgotten that Taiwan is home to 23 million people who have been engaged in a decades-long political transformation. This democratization and Taiwanization cannot be ignored in the final analysis. The principle of self-determination must be given its due weight. The onus is on the opponents of Taiwanese statehood to show why the people of Taiwan should not be allowed to have ultimate control over their shared destiny—and if so, how this outcome is consistent with contemporary international law. Opponents of Taiwanese statehood must explain why it is just or legal to continue to treat Taiwan like a fossil, frozen in the same predicament for more than half a century.

The following sections illustrate commonly held positions on the issue of Taiwan's status under international law. The author's own view, that Taiwan has evolved into a state through the practice of effective self-determination, will be described in the second part of this chapter. For the reader's convenience, a list of Suggested Readings in Chinese is provided at the end of the book reflecting a range of contemporary viewpoints on Taiwan's international status.

A. TAIWAN AS A PART OF CHINA

The People's Republic of China (PRC) asserts that Taiwan and China have comprised one country "since time immemorial," and that international law supports this claim today. By and large, proponents of this view denounce the Treaty of Shimonoseki under which China ceded Taiwan to Japan in perpetuity in 1895. They also look for support in interpretations of historical documents such as the Cairo

Declaration, the Potsdam Proclamation, and UN General Assembly Resolution 2758. PRC leaders pointed to the Truman administration's initial desire to let events in the Taiwan Strait take their course as evidence that the United States conceded to China's claims over Taiwan. They viewed Truman's decision to neutralize the Taiwan Strait at the onset of the Korean War as an act of treachery and a betrayal of American promises made during World War II.

As recalled in Chapter 1, the Cairo Declaration of 1943 proclaimed that "all the territories Japan has stolen from the Chinese, such as Manchuria, Formosa, and the Pescadores, shall be restored to the Republic of China." In 1945, Article 8 of the Potsdam Proclamation reaffirmed these commitments. The Republic of China (ROC), the controlling government on the Chinese mainland at that time, eagerly accepted Japan's surrender of its overseas territories under the direction of General Douglas MacArthur at the end of World War II. Therefore, proponents argue, it must follow that Taiwan belonged to the ROC and that the ROC continued as the legitimate government of Taiwan (indeed, the whole of China) following its exile to the island during the Chinese civil war in 1949.

The PRC puts its own spin on this tale. It insists that Taiwan is an inalienable part of the Chinese nation. Therefore, when the PRC seized control of China from the ROC its claim to Taiwan was thusly secured. As the ROC's successor, the PRC maintains that it has assumed all rights and claims to Taiwan. The PRC points to UN Resolution 2758, which expelled Chiang Kai-shek's representatives from the United Nations and named the PRC China's sole legal representative in the United Nations, for proof of an international consensus on this viewpoint. However, it should be noted that the resolution makes no mention of Taiwan and never purported to settle the question of Taiwan's international legal status. The PRC outlined its position on Taiwan's status in two white papers issued in 1993 and 2000. The first, entitled "The Taiwan Question and Reunification of China," levels a series of accusations against the U.S. government going back to the Truman administration. According to the white paper, the United States supported the Kuomintang (KMT) in prosecuting a civil war against the Chinese Communist Party (CCP) and engaging in a policy of "isolation and containment of New China."[1] Moreover, the white paper asserts that after the establishment of diplomatic relations in 1979 the U.S. government undermined the terms of the Second Communiqué, which announced the establishment of diplomatic relations, with the passage of the Taiwan Relations Act. The white paper then incorrectly construes the Third Communiqué, which states the Reagan administration's position on defensive arms sales to Taiwan, as an agreement negotiated with the U.S. government (as elaborated in Chapter 5, the communiqué is not a binding agreement) and asserts that the United States violated the communiqué through continued arms sales to

Taiwan. The white paper calls for a resolution of the cross-strait conflict through the adoption of a "one country, two systems" framework incorporating Taiwan and China. It concludes by clarifying the PRC's position on a number of topics including Taiwan's diplomatic relations, Taiwan's participation in international organizations, and continued arms sales to Taiwan. Seven years later, the PRC's Taiwan Affairs Office and Information Office of the State Council released a white paper entitled "The One-China Principle and the Taiwan Issue" in which it reiterated the premises of the first white paper and urged Taiwan to join Hong Kong and Macau as part of the Chinese nation. The second white paper, relying heavily on historical assertions, appeals to a desire for unity among the Chinese people under the banner of One China. The white paper warns that the issue cannot be "postponed indefinitely."[2] The PRC's contentions have been flatly rejected in Taiwan. A 2006 position paper issued by the Executive Yuan's Mainland Affairs Council during President Chen Shui-bian's second term in response to remarks made by then-candidate Ma Ying-jeou, declares in its opening sentence that "the Republic of China is an independent sovereign country."[3]

Even within Taiwan, there is a minority that insists that Taiwan is a renegade province of China because it has yet to make a formal declaration of its independence. Supporters of this view believe that the ROC was a branch of the PRC government and that the ROC operated as a government-in-exile in Taiwan. The absence of an official declaration of Taiwan's independence and an official renunciation of the ROC system (which exists today in name only) is taken as a concession that Taiwan is a part of China. Supporters of this position argue that Taiwan has achieved, at most, "governmental recognition," but not "state recognition."

Influential professor James Crawford, now a judge on the International Court of Justice, discusses the issue at length in *The Creation of States in International Law*.[4] Crawford is considered one of the most preeminent scholars on the subject of the creation of states under international law. In addition to outlining the customary requirements for statehood recognized in the Montevideo Convention on the Rights and Duties of States (people, territory, government, and the capacity to enter into relations with other states), Professor Crawford adds a fifth requirement: The government of the territory in question must unequivocally declare itself to be a sovereign state. Crawford begins his argument by considering the possible effects of the Japanese renunciation of Taiwan in the San Francisco Peace Treaty. For this purpose, Crawford assumes that Taiwan was not a state at that time. As such, Crawford continues, there existed three possible conclusions as to Taiwan's territorial status. The first, which Crawford quickly rejects, was that Taiwan had been returned to China by 1949, either as a result of the Chinese pronouncement to abrogate the Treaty of Shimonoseki or as a result of the transfer of administrative authority to the ROC.

Crawford correctly rejects this argument, as Taiwan's legal status was not changed by either event, consistent with principles of both customary and contemporary international law. Taiwan's legal status continued to be that of a Japanese territory until Japan renounced its interest in the San Francisco Peace Treaty, which took effect in 1952.

Nevertheless, Crawford concludes that Taiwan not only failed to achieve statehood at any point but also somehow was a part of China. Crawford reaches this conclusion based on the circumstances surrounding the Japanese relinquishment of Taiwan following World War II. He gives considerable weight to the intentions expressed in the Cairo Declaration and Potsdam Proclamation. Moreover, he emphasizes the occupation of Taiwan by a recognized government of China (the ROC). Crawford argues that the effect of the San Francisco Peace Treaty was to return sovereignty over Taiwan to China, regardless of which government, the PRC or the ROC, benefited. Crawford recognizes that "[a]s a mode of transfer this may be unique," but went on to argue that it is more likely than the alternative, namely that the Japanese renunciation had the effect of making Taiwan a condominium of the forty-eight Allied powers that were parties to the San Francisco Peace Treaty. Crawford points to three "difficulties" that lead him to this conclusion:

1. If by 1952 the ROC had lost its claim to being the legitimate government of China, then ceding Taiwan to the ROC would have breached the terms of the peace agreement and would have constituted an intervention in the Chinese civil war.

2. If Taiwan became a part of China in 1952, then the American patrolling of the Strait of Taiwan (following the outbreak of the Korean War) would have constituted an intervention in the Chinese civil war and an attempted encroachment on China's territorial integrity.

3. "Claims to statehood are not to be inferred from statements or actions short of explicit declaration; and in the apparent absence of any claim to secede the status of Taiwan can only be that of a part of the state of China under separate administration."[5]

The first two problems can be easily settled. Both depend upon Crawford's assumption that Taiwan became a part of China in 1952. If one does not assume that Taiwan became a part of China in 1952—and one cannot assume this given the deliberate omission of China as the beneficiary state in the San Francisco Peace Treaty—neither of these problems arises. The third problem Crawford identifies— the lack of a formal declaration of independence, which Crawford views as "determinative" on the issue of Taiwanese statehood—is somewhat more difficult, but not impossible, to resolve. Assuming for the sake of argument that such a requirement exists, the response, in short, is that Taiwan has indeed asserted, usually implicitly, but at times expressly, that it is a separate state and is not a part of China. To require a more explicit declaration of independence is to ignore the reality on the ground—that is, China's ongoing threat to respond with military force to any such declaration. Crawford's interpretation falls short because it ignores the possibility that Japan's renunciation left Taiwan's international legal status undetermined. Crawford recognizes this as a potential explanation and indeed recognized that it was the view taken by both the United Kingdom and the United States in the years following the Peace Treaty, but he offered no counterargument as to why this was not the case. Rather, he rejects it implicitly, by simply asserting that circumstances surrounding the Japanese renunciation had the effect of returning Taiwan to China.

In his analysis, Professor Crawford gives little credence to the San Francisco Peace Treaty's effect on the undetermined nature of Taiwan's legal status. As to the fifth requirement, Crawford concludes that "Taiwan is not a state because it still has not unequivocally asserted its separation from China and is not recognized as a State distinct from China." In reaching his conclusion, Crawford highlights a 1999 interview by President Lee, where Lee described a special state-to-state relationship with China. However, Crawford conspicuously overlooks the more provocative remarks of President Chen Shui-bian, who said in 2002, "Taiwan and China are each one country on each side of the Taiwan Strait." Even more significant was President Chen's decision in 2007—a year after the publication of Crawford's second edition—to submit a UN membership application on behalf of Taiwan. Chen's move was tantamount to a "declaration of independence" on the international stage.

Professor Brad R. Roth offers another critique of Crawford's position, in which he observes that the question of Taiwan statehood is fundamentally one of recognition. With reference to the Montevideo Convention, Roth writes:

> If statehood were an "objective" matter and recognition merely "declaratory," the case for Taiwan's statehood would be overwhelming. For over half a century, the Taipei government has independently maintained effective control over a "permanent population" within a "defined territory.[6]

Noting that Crawford cites no authority for his claim that Taiwan must explicitly declare its statehood, Roth argues that "the true test of statehood lies in international actors' tacit attribution, *vel non*, of rights, powers, obligations, and immunities that international law ascribes uniquely to states."[7] In the case of Taiwan, Roth notes that a multitude of states, including the United States, maintain extensive formal or informal relations with Taiwan, despite the PRC's protestations, which may imply a tacit recognition of Taiwan statehood. He concludes:

> The case for attributing to Taiwan the full range of rights, powers, obligations, and immunities attendant to statehood improves the more that Taipei can establish external relationships beyond the permissible confines of mere *de facto* recognition and inconsistent with the PRC assertions of sovereign prerogative over Taiwan's external affairs.[8]

Whatever its form, the "Taiwan is a part of China" theory can be soundly rejected. There are at least four reasons. First, history shows that China has never exercised effective control over Taiwan for long periods of time. As explored in Chapter 1, Taiwan's indigenous peoples arrived thousands of years before the Han Chinese. The islands fell to Dutch and Spanish colonial settlers in the early 1600s, followed by the arrival of exiles led by Koxinga (Cheng Cheng-kung) in the late 1600s. The Qing dynasty nominally claimed Taiwan in 1683, but never established effective control or governance over the territory. The Qing waited until 1887 to make Taiwan an official province, only to cede the island in perpetuity to Japan in the Treaty of Shimonoseki eight years later. Taiwan existed as a Japanese colony for the next fifty years. At the end of World War II, Chiang Kai-shek's Chinese Nationalists undertook a military occupation on behalf of the Allied Powers pursuant to General Douglas MacArthur's instructions. The Chinese Nationalists then took refuge on Taiwan in 1949 after their defeat by the CCP in the Chinese civil war and remained there as an illegitimate government in exile. In point of fact, Taiwan's political connection to modern China is *de minimis* at best. Its historical connection to the contemporary PRC government is plainly nonexistent.

Second, the Cairo and Potsdam declarations, though provocative in their conclusions, are not authoritative under international law. The declarations outlined the intentions of the United States, the United Kingdom, and the ROC for territories held by Japan after the conclusion of the war. Notably, Japan was not a party to these discussions. As a matter of both contract and treaty law, the declarations were inoperable in effecting territorial transfers at the time of their drafting. Furthermore, the subsequent San Francisco Peace Treaty between the Allied Powers and Japan effectively overrode the prior declarations. As noted in prior chapters, Japan renounced its "right, claim, and title" over Taiwan (Formosa) and the Penghu Islands (Pescadores) in the San Francisco Peace Treaty. The Treaty of Taipei between Japan and the ROC followed a similar formula. Since the treaties conspicuously left out *to whom* the title of Taiwan should be delivered, the ROC (or any state for that matter) could not claim that it was the intended beneficiary of Taiwan's title. (Indeed, the ROC government repeatedly asked to be named the beneficiary state in the Treaty of Taipei, but Japan refused.) The treaties simply made no such specification. Furthermore, as stated above, the wartime declarations adopted before the San Francisco Peace Treaty in 1951 and the Treaty of Taipei in 1952 were insufficient to give the ROC a colorable claim to Taiwan. The policy considerations behind this were described by the author in *An Introduction to Contemporary International Law: A Policy-Oriented Perspective*:

> A peace treaty is commonly regarded as an authoritative expression of the shared expectations of both victorious and defeated powers following the formal termination of a state of "hostility." . . . Expectations expressed amid hostility are generally dictated by military expediency and necessity for victory. Other relevant policy considerations tend to disappear or to receive scant attention. The commitments made under the emergency conditions of wartime offer, at best, a precarious foundation for future order; they are most likely to lead to the disruption of public order sooner or later. . . . This explains the importance attached to the role of the "peace treaty" under traditional international law. A primary function of such an instrument is to ascertain unequivocally the shared expectations of the parties, especially the defeated powers, concerning any change of territory. Territorial clauses are particularly well drafted in order to prevent subsequent claims of ambiguity; any transfer of territory is prescribed in no uncertain terms.[9]

Third, the PRC did not inherit Taiwan from the ROC as a result of its victory in the Chinese civil war. At the end of World War II, General MacArthur directed Chiang to occupy Taiwan as a trustee on behalf of the Allied Powers, but stopped short of giving the ROC sovereignty over the island. Even when the Chinese Nationalists took refuge in Taiwan after their defeat in the civil war, they could not have claimed Taiwan lawfully—that right belonged to the Allied Powers.

Fourth, General Assembly Resolution 2758, which recognized the PRC as the only legal government of China, did not go so far as to recognize that Taiwan was an integral part of China. UN Resolution 2758 expelled Chiang Kai-shek's representatives from the United Nations, denying the ROC the right to sit in the General Assembly and the Security Council or to represent the interests of the people of China in the United Nations. Resolution 2758 did not mention Taiwan whatsoever or address the issue of whether the ROC or the PRC government could adequately represent the interests of Taiwan, nor did it state that the ROC's expulsion from the United Nations gave the PRC title over the island.

In 2007, Taiwan submitted a new application for membership to the United Nations under the name Taiwan, rather than the Republic of China. UN Secretary-General Ban Ki-moon returned the application without transmitting it to the Security Council for consideration, citing Resolution 2758 as a basis for his decision. He remarked, in keeping with the PRC's claims, that the PRC was the sole legal representative of China at the United Nations and that Taiwan was an integral part of China. The United States and Japan protested Ban's interpretation, contending instead that the effect of UN Resolution 2758, by its terms, was limited solely to the question of China's representation in the United Nations, having nothing to do with Taiwan.

B. TAIWAN'S STATUS REMAINS UNDETERMINED SINCE
THE SAN FRANCISCO PEACE TREATY OF 1951

The second viewpoint suggests that Taiwan's status remains undetermined. This could be for one or more of the following reasons: Taiwan is still under the exiled ROC regime's military occupation; the United States, as principal victor over Japan during World War II, holds sovereignty over Taiwan; or the Taiwanese people have sovereignty over Taiwan, but Taiwan is not yet a state.

Among proponents of this second viewpoint are the "strict conformists" who believe that the transfer of a territory can only be effectuated by the solemn signing of a peace treaty in the most formal of settings. This line of reasoning goes as such. In 1895, the Qing government signed the Treaty of Shimonoseki, in which it ceded Taiwan to Japan "in perpetuity and full sovereignty." This was the status quo until the end of World War II. The San Francisco Peace Treaty complicated matters. Since the treaty did not specify a recipient state to which the right, title, and claim of Taiwan would be delivered, neither the ROC nor the PRC was the beneficiary of Japan's surrender. To this point, the UK government was on record stating that "[u]nder the peace treaty of April, 1952, Japan formally renounced all right, title, and claim to Formosa and the Pescadores; but again this did not operate as a transfer to Chinese sovereignty, whether to the People's Republic of China or to the Chinese Nationalist authorities. Formosa and the Pescadores are therefore, in the view of Her Majesty's Government, territory the *de jure* sovereignty over which is uncertain or undetermined."[10]

According to the treaty's *travaux preparatoires*, a consensus existed among the states present at the San Francisco Peace Conference that, while temporarily undetermined, Taiwan's legal status would be resolved at a later time. Specifically, this resolution would be made in accordance with the principles of peaceful settlement of disputes and self-determination, ideas that had recently been enshrined in the UN Charter. While a plebiscite would have been an ideal tool for such a decision, internal and external conditions prevented Taiwan from holding a plebiscite during the subsequent decades. Noting such, proponents of the second view maintain that Taiwan's legal status remained undetermined.

The United States and Japan are among the nations whose official positions on the Taiwan issue incorporate this reasoning. Both countries adhere to a "One China Policy." The United States, for example, recognizes the PRC as the only lawful government of China. But as to the PRC's sovereignty claim over Taiwan, the United States defers to the prescription of the San Francisco Peace Treaty, in which Japan renounced all right, title, and claim to Taiwan without naming a beneficiary state. That is to say, Taiwan's international legal status has remained undetermined since 1952, when the San Francisco Peace Treaty entered into effect. This One China Policy is not to be confused with the PRC's "One China Principle," which holds that there is but one China and that Taiwan is a part of China—while the U.S. One China Policy accepts that the PRC is the only lawful government of China, the United States merely acknowledges the PRC's territorial claim to Taiwan, without ever assenting to it.

Assuming, for argument's sake, that the second viewpoint is correct and that Taiwan's status remains undetermined, who is best suited to claim sovereignty over Taiwan?

A position held by many Taiwanese is that sovereignty belongs to the people of Taiwan. Acknowledging that Taiwan's status was left undetermined after the conclusion of the San Francisco Peace Treaty, proponents maintain that it is up to the people of Taiwan to resolve this question. Ideally their wishes will be expressed and ultimately secured according to an internationally supervised plebiscite on Taiwan's continued existence as a normalized independent state. Regardless of the method, Taiwan's people should be the ultimate decision makers about the future of their country. This is the essence of self-determination.

Another view maintains that the United States, as the principal victorious power in the Far East, has residual sovereignty over Taiwan. As described in Chapter 10, this viewpoint formed the basis of the plaintiffs' argument in *Lin v. United States*, a U.S. federal court case filed in 2000. The plaintiffs, who were residents of Taiwan, had attempted several times to secure U.S. passports from the American Institute in Taiwan, but were denied and blocked from submitting future applications. In their complaint, the plaintiffs argued that they were, along with all residents of Taiwan, U.S. nationals. (Former President Chen would later use a version of this argument in an appeal to the U.S. Court of Appeals for the Armed Forces in 2009 following his arrest on corruption charges.[11]) Those who prefer this theory believe the ROC government on Taiwan always was, and continues to be, a regime-in-exile that illegally usurped power on Taiwan. The island's legal status is construed as an unincorporated territory of the United States under military administration. The reasoning behind this view is as follows. First, Taiwan became a territory of Japan under the Treaty of Shimonoseki in 1895, signed just a year after the Qing government lost the First Sino-Japanese War. In 1945, the United States won the war with Japan. As the principal victor and occupying power after World War II, the United States had the authority to dispose of Japanese territories whose status remained undetermined and to appoint a subordinate occupying power. Accordingly, Chiang Kai-shek's ROC government accepted Japan's surrender on behalf of the Allied Powers, and undertook military occupation and administration on Taiwan. After the war, the San Francisco Peace Treaty effectuated Japan's renunciation of its right, title, and claim over Taiwan. On the other hand, the United States, as principal occupying power, never formally renounced its own claim to Taiwan. Consequently, it is argued, the United States retains a residual sovereign claim to Taiwan. In effect, the island remains under military administration as an unincorporated territory of the United States.

It follows that Taiwan's international legal status should have been resolved by the countries that were the Allied Nations, most likely in consultation with the United Nations. However, a series of unfortunate events intervened to prevent the Allied Nations from resolving the Taiwan question. These included the military occupation of Taiwan in 1945 and the ROC's appropriation of Taiwan as a government-in-exile, followed shortly after by the eruption of the Korean War. During this period, wartime alliances quickly shifted. The hostilities undermined conditions necessary for a peaceful resolution of the issues left open by the San Francisco Peace Treaty. In short, Taiwan is looked at as a piece of "unfinished business" from World War II.

The foregoing viewpoints run counter to the course of U.S. actions since the end of the war. Though the United States arguably may have held residual sovereignty over Taiwan by virtue of its status as principal victor over Japan during World War II, it never exercised its right. On the contrary, U.S. actions after World War II suggested an intention to relinquish claims over Taiwan. For instance, in approving the 1954 Mutual Defense Treaty with the ROC, the U.S. Senate declared in a committee report that "nothing . . . in the treaty shall be construed as affecting or modifying the legal status or the sovereignty of the territories to which it applies."[12] This was a view held by Secretary of State John Foster Dulles among others. Such language supports the view that Taiwan's statehood remained undetermined and that the United States did not consider itself the beneficiary of Japan's renunciation of its interest in Taiwan. Further, the Taiwan Relations Act of 1979 stated that "whenever the laws of the United States refer or relate to foreign countries, nations, states, governments, or similar entities, such terms shall include and such laws shall apply with respect to Taiwan."[13] Though not an official renunciation of its right as principal victor, this provision effectively deems Taiwan to be a state for the purpose of carrying out U.S. laws, at least in practice.

C. TAIWAN HAS *DE FACTO* BUT NOT *DE JURE* INDEPENDENCE

The third viewpoint goes a step further to hold that Taiwan is a sovereign state in practice, but owing to its lack of international recognition, it holds *de facto* and not *de jure* status. Japan ceded its right, title, and claim to Taiwan in the San Francisco Peace Treaty, but failed to designate a beneficiary state. Though the ROC did legally occupy Taiwan on behalf of the Allied Powers in 1945, its presence also did not amount to a granting of sovereignty. Accordingly, some have characterized Taiwan as a "newborn state." The newborn-state theory minimizes ancient historical connections between Taiwan and China. Instead, it depicts Taiwan as a new country born after the Second World War, inheriting its status from neither the ROC nor the PRC. This approach places importance on Taiwan's success as an independent political entity between 1949 and 1990. Further, it maintains that Taiwan has satisfied the conditions for statehood as described in the Montevideo Convention (people, territory, government, and ability to conduct diplomatic relations).

This viewpoint is popular among many Western scholars. Variations of it can be found in an excellent volume edited by Jean-Marie Henckaerts entitled *The International Status of Taiwan in the New World Order*, featuring essays by attendees (including the author) of a conference on Taiwan's international status hosted by the Center for United Nations Law at the University of Brussels in 1995.[14] Proponents of the third viewpoint observe that the Taiwanese government today is self-sustaining and assumes full control over its territories. It is, for all intents and purposes, a *de facto* state. However, the PRC has made it exceedingly difficult for Taiwan to establish diplomatic relations with other countries. China's actions to isolate Taiwan politically include threatening a boycott against any country that establishes diplomatic relations with Taiwan. China has also exerted pressure to prevent Taiwan from joining international organizations where statehood is a requirement, such as the United Nations—and even those where statehood is not a requirement, such as the World Trade Organization. Despite these obstacles, some commentators propose that Taiwan should continue its pursuit of *de jure* statehood by abandoning the ROC name and campaigning for UN membership under the name Taiwan.

II. From Undetermined to Determined: The Theory of Taiwan's Evolution from a Militarily Occupied Territory to a State

The author advances a fourth viewpoint. This viewpoint accepts the premise that Taiwan's status was undetermined following the conclusion of the San Francisco Peace Treaty. However, it diverges from the perspectives described above by proposing that international legal status is not a static concept and that Taiwan's legal status has evolved from undetermined to determined over the course of several decades. This is the evolutionary theory of Taiwan statehood. This theory also accepts as true the premise that Taiwan belonged to neither the ROC nor the PRC when the San Francisco Peace Treaty took effect in 1952. From 1952 to 1987, Taiwan suffered under the ROC's unlawful military occupation, as sustained by authoritarian rule of perpetual martial law. In 1987, martial law was lifted. This was shortly followed by the death of Chiang Ching-kuo in January 1988. Succeeding him as president was Lee Teng-hui, Chiang's vice president and the first Taiwanese to hold the office of president. It was at this point that the Taiwanese people commenced a political, economic, social, and cultural transformation. Important events in this evolution included the government's recognition of the end of the Period of Communist Rebellion, the election of new and representative members to the Legislative Yuan, democratic presidential elections by the Taiwanese people, the adoption of new protections for human rights, and numerous successful transfers of executive power. Post-authoritarian Taiwan has emerged as a model democracy in Asia. The evolutionary theory holds that this transformation has brought Taiwan into alignment with the concept of modern statehood via effective self-determination. To elaborate on this progression, the following sections will explore the concept of territorial changes under contemporary international law in theory and in practice, and the four distinctive stages of the evolution of Taiwan's statehood.

A. CONTEMPORARY INTERNATIONAL LAW ON TERRITORIAL CHANGES

Three bedrock principles of contemporary international law are especially relevant to the discussion of territorial change as it relates to Taiwan: intertemporality, nonuse of force, and self-determination. First, intertemporality recognizes that the application of international law is contextual. That is to say, situations must be resolved in accordance with the relevant law in force at the time of the events in question. For example, in analyzing the effects of the Treaty of Shimonoseki, one would refer to international law as it existed in 1895. Contemporary international law, which finds its origins in the UN Charter, would be of no avail. On the other hand, disputes arising after the Second World War would be resolved by referring to contemporary legal principles.

Second, international law under the UN Charter is premised on the nonuse of force. Historically, international law placed few prohibitions on the use of force between states. Countries could conquer and seize territories and make war in order to assert sovereignty over foreign lands. To the contrary, the UN Charter expressly banned such practices. It radically altered expectations for the conduct of international relations by mandating the peaceful settlement of disputes and forbidding the threat and use of force.

Third, questions about territorial control are fundamentally about the rights and well-being of the people living therein. Accordingly, decisions about a territory must respect the will of the people. This is the principle of self-determination. As the UN Charter clearly dictates, respect for peoples' desires is the most important principle guiding the transfer of territories. As Judge Hardy Dillard of the International Court of Justice succinctly remarked, "it is for the people to determine the destiny of the territory and not the territory the destiny of the people."[15] Self-determination is the driving force behind the proliferation of new states. It is also an important part of the overall demand for freedom in our world. It is about the demand of human beings to form groups and to identify with groups that can best promote the pursuit of cherished values. The concept of self-determination crystallized at the end of World War I under the leadership of President Woodrow Wilson, who declared in 1917: "No peace can last, or ought to last, which does not recognize and accept the principle that governments derive all their just powers from the consent of the governed, and that no right anywhere exists to hand people about from sovereignty to sovereignty as if they were property." The UN Charter elevated the concept of self-determination, honoring its universal appeal rooted in the concepts of human dignity and human rights. A major purpose of the United Nations, according to Article 1(2) of the Charter, is to "develop friendly relations among nations based on respect for the principle of equal rights and self-determination of peoples, and to take other appropriate measures to strengthen universal peace." Both the International Covenant on Civil and Political Rights and the International Covenant on Economic, Social and Cultural Rights afford a prominent place to the principle of self-determination. In identical words, the covenants proclaim in their first articles that "[a]ll peoples have the right of self-determination. By virtue of that right they freely determine their political status and freely pursue their economic, social and cultural development."

The "will of the people" (as enunciated in Article 21[3] of the Universal Declaration of Human Rights) is the standard of authority of any legitimate government under international law. This is a question of procedure, not of outcome. Whether the choice in a particular case is independence or something else matters less than whether the choice is made genuinely and freely by the people concerned. If the freedom of choice of the people is sustained, the policy objective of self-determination is fulfilled. Viewing UN practice as a whole, questions of self-determination turn on the following three factors: the prospect of the territory or peoples concerned becoming a viable state; the present stage of advancement toward self-government;

and the effect of granting or refusing the exercise of self-determination in terms of regional and international peace, the effectuation of authoritative governmental processes and human rights, and impacts on all regional and global value processes. It is considered essential that the people directly concerned have a reasonable prospect of becoming a viable entity—politically, economically, and so on—in this increasingly interdependent world. The test, from the perspective of the New Haven School of international law, for determining whether to grant or reject a demand for self-determination is whether granting or rejecting the demands of a group would move the existing situation closer to the goal values of human dignity and human security, considering in particular the aggregate value consequences for the group directly concerned and the larger communities affected.[16] That is to say, self-determination should be viewed in the context of interdetermination. The basic question is whether separation or unification would best promote security for the people concerned and facilitate effective shaping and sharing of power and of all the other values.

When does a territorial community earn the right to call itself a state and thus act as a full-fledged member of the world community? For many scholars, the answer lies in the practice of recognition. The term *recognition* refers to the act of one state signifying that it is willing to accept another territorial community as a diplomatic partner with all the rights and privileges that follow. A wide consensus exists that the minimum conditions of statehood are those outlined in the Montevideo Convention: people, territory, government, and the capacity to enter into relations with other states. Scholars disagree, however, on the modalities for applying these criteria to concrete cases. The declaratory theory of recognition holds that statehood is automatic upon the objective existence of the requisite conditions. This is the approach prescribed in the Montevideo Convention. The constitutive theory on the other hand maintains that the essential ingredient is the formal recognition of other states. In practice, the act of recognition often lies somewhere between the two theories. The declaratory theory, in its search for objective pronouncements, is limited by subjective disagreements between observers. Determining whether a government is capable of interacting with others is particularly challenging in this regard. By contrast, adherents of the constitutive theory cannot escape the need to satisfy underlying legal and factual precepts. In theory and in practice, a distinction is often made between *de jure* and *de facto* recognition. Generally speaking, when a government is recognized as *de facto*, its effective control is also recognized, at least for the present moment. However, if a government is deemed *de jure*, its control over a territory is viewed as permanent. *De facto* recognition is often regarded as a prelude to *de jure* recognition, and the distinction is often blurred, while the act of granting recognition may be implicit or explicit in nature.

B. TAIWAN'S EVOLUTION TO STATEHOOD UNDER INTERNATIONAL LAW: FOUR DISTINCTIVE STAGES

Taiwan's evolution to statehood can be understood as taking place in four distinctive stages. From 1895 to 1945, Taiwan was a colony under Japanese rule, as China ceded the territory to Japan in perpetuity under the Treaty of Shimonoseki. In the second stage, from 1945 to 1952, Chiang Kai-shek's ROC forces carried out a military occupation on Taiwan on behalf of the Allied Powers, acting under the authority granted to them by General Douglas MacArthur, Supreme Commander for the Allied Powers in the Far East. After the entry into force of the San Francisco Peace Treaty and the Treaty of Taipei in 1952, Taiwan's legal status remained undetermined. The third stage was the longest and covered the period between 1952 and 1987. The ROC continued its military occupation on the island unlawfully following its defeat in the Chinese civil war. The ROC leadership fled to Taiwan and established a government in exile there while claiming to be the government of the whole of China. For more than three decades, Chiang Kai-shek and his son, Chiang Ching-kuo, maintained their authoritarian rule based on martial law and carried out systematic and wholesale human rights deprivations and abuses against the Taiwanese people. The voice of the Taiwanese people was silenced. The island's legal status remained undetermined.

The fourth stage of Taiwan's evolution, from 1988 to the present, took place following the end of martial law and the death of Chiang Ching-kuo. President Lee Teng-hui, a native-born Taiwanese, inspired a dramatic transformation on the island and started a process of democratization and Taiwanization. During this period the Taiwanese people voted in their first open presidential election, the Legislative Yuan became representative of Taiwan's population, executive power was peacefully transferred to the Democratic Progressive Party—and then back to the Kuomintang—and Taiwan's people embraced the fundamental freedoms of expression and democratic participation. The fourth stage of Taiwan's evolution represents effective self-determination as a continuous process. It was during this period that Taiwan's status shifted from undetermined to determined.

1. From 1895 to 1945: Taiwan Was a Territory and Colony of Japan

In 1895, representatives of the Qing dynasty and Japan signed the Treaty of Shimonoseki. The treaty called for China to cede sovereignty over Taiwan to Japan in perpetuity. According to international law at the time, this was a legally valid transfer; thus, Taiwan officially became a territory of Japan. Both the Chinese Nationalists and the Chinese Communists have argued that ownership of Taiwan devolved to China in 1941 as a result of its declaration of war against Japan in which it renounced prior treaties between the two countries. However, their unilateral repudiation of the Treaty of Shimonoseki did not effectively change Taiwan's legal status. It is a well-established principle under contemporary international law that one party cannot unilaterally terminate a dispositive treaty involving the transfer of a territory.

2. From 1945 to 1952: The ROC Undertook a Military Occupation on Behalf of the Allied Powers

After the Second World War, Taiwan was a Japanese territory under military occupation by the Allied Powers. Pursuant to General Order No. 1 by General MacArthur, Supreme Commander for the Allied Powers, Chiang Kai-shek and his ROC forces were tasked with accepting the Japanese surrender on Taiwan and overseeing the military occupation of the island. The ROC's presence on Taiwan during this period did not amount to ownership or sovereign rule. In October 1949, the Chinese Communists established the People's Republic of China in Beijing. Chiang Kai-shek and his ROC forces fled to Taiwan and undertook what would become thirty-eight years of authoritarian rule under martial law. In 1949, as a matter of international law, Taiwan was still a territory of Japan; hence, Chiang's Nationalists were a regime in exile there. When the San Francisco Peace Treaty came into force in 1952, Taiwan's international legal status was undetermined. In April 1952, the ROC government and the Japanese government signed the Treaty of Taipei, in which Japan relinquished Taiwan in accordance with the San Francisco Peace Treaty but remained silent on whether the ROC was the beneficiary state. Accordingly, the Treaty of Taipei did not change Taiwan's status; Taiwan belonged neither to the ROC, nor the PRC. At the time, both the ROC and the PRC insisted that Taiwan was a part of China, as proclaimed in the Cairo Declaration and affirmed in the Potsdam Proclamation. However, under international law, terms defining the cession and transfer of territories after the end of a war must be provided for in a peace treaty between the victors and the defeated. Moreover, a treaty supersedes any wartime declarations or proclamations. Therefore, the Cairo Declaration and the Potsdam Proclamation were rendered ineffective under international law because they were superseded by the San Francisco Peace Treaty, if they had any legal effect at all. As observed above, peace treaties, for good reason, are given higher authority than statements made during the frenzy of war, particularly in matters concerning territorial changes.

3. From 1952 to 1987: The ROC Was a Regime in Exile that Engaged in an Illegal Military Occupation of Taiwan

In 1952, the year the San Francisco Peace Treaty took effect, the ROC regime continued with its military occupation on Taiwan. During this era, the Chiang Kai-shek regime engaged in the wholesale and systematic deprivations of fundamental freedoms and abuses of human rights. The continued military occupation of Taiwan exceeded the mandate given to the ROC by General MacArthur after the Japanese surrender. The ROC's rule, as sustained by perpetual martial law, was illegal and illegitimate and persisted without the consent of the Taiwanese people.

The United Nations grappled with Taiwan's situation as early as the 1950s. At the time, Chiang's ROC held a seat at the United Nations. Ultimately, in October 1971, UN General Assembly Resolution 2758 declared that the PRC, not the ROC, was the only lawful representative of China in the United Nations. The resolution did not indicate the General Assembly's views on whether Taiwan was a part of China. While the resolution dispelled the myth that the ROC represented the whole of China, it also contributed to Taiwan's status as an international orphan. Taiwan could not become a member of the United Nations, nor could it meaningfully participate in any international organization under the UN system. Countries that previously had diplomatic relations with the ROC shifted their allegiances to the PRC. The Taiwanese people became increasingly isolated. This trend accelerated after the United States and the PRC established diplomatic relations in January 1979.

As its international isolation grew, the ROC government became increasingly oppressive internally. Early on, Chiang Kai-shek took steps to manipulate the electoral process, stacking the National Assembly with exiled members of the KMT and ensuring that he and his son, Chiang Ching-kuo, would hold the presidency without term limits. The National Assembly's primary responsibility was to elect and recall the president and vice president and to amend the constitution. Other branches of Taiwan's central government (the Executive Yuan, the Legislative Yuan, the Examination Yuan, the Control Yuan, and the Judicial Yuan) were occupied largely by exiled KMT cronies who were not subject to elections in Taiwan. These bodies represented nearly the entirety of the ROC government that had been imported wholesale from the Chinese mainland.

Chiang Kai-shek and his son, Chiang Ching-kuo, knew their exiled political bodies did not have the consent of the people and lacked legitimacy to govern Taiwan. Only when necessary to ease political tensions did the Chiangs offer the Taiwanese people a sliver of token democracy. In the 1950s and the 1960s, the people of Taiwan could participate only in local-level elections. By the end of 1972, the government made additional legislative seats available for elections at the national level. In reality, however, these seats constituted only a small percentage of the National Assembly and of the Legislative Yuan, and promised little political impact. The two Chiangs recruited Taiwanese-born politicians to win public support for their political agenda only when needed.

The ROC military regime deprived the people of Taiwan of basic freedoms and human rights, including the freedoms of thought and expression and the rights of association and assembly. Nevertheless, activists waged a ceaseless battle for their fundamental human rights both at home and abroad. After the Kaohsiung Incident of December 10, 1979, democratization took on greater urgency. Policymakers in the United States as well as Taiwanese activists at home and abroad placed significant pressure on the KMT regime, pushing it to end its authoritarian abuses and to embark on long-sought democratic reforms. With a social landscape ripe for reform, a rival political party, the Democratic Progressive Party (DPP), took root in 1986 and pressured the KMT to lift martial law the following year.

4. From 1988 to the Present: Taiwan Achieved Effective Self-Determination of the People and Evolved into a Sovereign and Independent State

Taiwan's "Silent Revolution" began with the succession of Lee Teng-hui to the presidency after the death of Chiang Ching-kuo in 1988. Under Lee's administration, the people of Taiwan worked openly toward the goals of greater democracy, freedom, and human rights, staging mass protests, public speaking events, demonstrations, petitions, and other activities that were dangerously taboo under the previous regime. The Wild Lily movement in March 1990 saw more than three hundred thousand college students demonstrate in favor of democratic reforms including the dissolution of the National Assembly, the convening of a National Affairs Conference, and the outlining of a schedule for political reforms. Lee's government responded not by cracking down but by accelerating changes. The months that followed brought new elections for the National Assembly, the release of political prisoners, the repeal of ordinances that punished political activism, and the amendment of the criminal law—permitting blacklisted Taiwanese to return home from overseas. In 1991, President Lee declared the termination of the Temporary Provisions Effective During the Period of Communist Rebellion. Between 1991 and 1992, members of both the National Assembly and Legislative Yuan were subject to re-election, as a result of a ruling by the Council of Grand Justices. This had the effect of removing aging legislators who were elected prior to the KMT's arrival on Taiwan and who purported to represent constituencies on the Chinese mainland. In 1996, the people of Taiwan participated in their first-ever direct presidential election. The country was at last able to distance itself from the Chiangs' authoritarian rule and to move closer to achieving freedom and democracy.

In 2000, Taiwan held its second direct presidential election and elected the DPP's Chen Shui-bian as president. His victory, and the peaceful transfer of power that followed, marked the end of fifty-five years of KMT rule on Taiwan. During his eight-year administration, President Chen pressed for Taiwanese statehood, publicly characterized the Taiwan-China relationship as "one country on each side of the Taiwan Strait," and advocated for a national referendum on Taiwan's membership in the United Nations. In 2007, Chen submitted an application for UN membership. In doing so, the president implicitly declared that Taiwan was an independent, sovereign, and peace-loving nation that possessed the ability and willingness to carry out the purposes, principles, and obligations of the UN Charter. The move was tantamount to a "declaration of independence" addressed to all humankind.

In 2008, the people of Taiwan elected the KMT's Ma Ying-jeou to the presidency, undertaking yet another peaceful transfer of executive power—the second in Taiwan's modern history. The fifth direct presidential election held in 2012 brought another human rights milestone when a female candidate, Tsai Ing-wen, ran a nearly successful campaign for president. The emergence of Tsai Ing-wen as a political star, and overwhelming 2016 presidential favorite, not only represented the DPP's continued relevance but also the growing acceptance of women in politics.

C. EFFECTIVE SELF-DETERMINATION

Applying the facts to the aforementioned principles, Taiwan's qualification for statehood is best understood in the context of an ongoing process of evolution propelled by the desire of the Taiwanese people for self-determination and democracy. Unlike in bygone eras, international law no longer conceives of territories as mere pieces of property to be traded or conquered. To the contrary, in today's world, human beings are properly held to be at the center of international law. Even in the absence of a declaration of independence, Taiwan ought to be recognized as a *de jure* state because its people have achieved effective self-determination. Over the course of twenty years, the Taiwanese have held regular presidential and legislative elections and built, through their collective will and action, fully mature democratic institutions and practices.

When the international legal status of a territory is in dispute, a UN-sponsored plebiscite provides an ideal means of resolving the dispute peacefully. But a plebiscite is not the only way of achieving self-determination. All of the inhabitants of a disputed territory, through collective effort and nation building, can express their emphatic desire for self-determination. Such a cumulative expression of popular will over time can be more powerful and persuasive than a one-time vote or even a declaration of independence. This is self-determination in action.

In the case of Taiwan, there can be no doubt that the Taiwanese people have exercised their right to freely determine their political status and pursue their own path of economic, social, and cultural development. In effect, a perpetual plebiscite, not just a one-shot ratification, has been in progress. Through this exercise, Taiwan has evolved from a territory with an undetermined legal status to a state, both sovereign and independent. Taiwan's sovereignty belongs to neither the ROC, the PRC, nor the United States, but rather rests with the people of Taiwan. This is the very essence of popular sovereignty in the contemporary era.

The transfer of a territory is not a property transaction; a transfer affects the human rights, the well-being, and even the survival of the territory's inhabitants. Over decades, endowed with their inherent sovereignty, the people of Taiwan have worked together day in and day out to redefine their own political status and to develop their distinctive political, economic, social, and cultural system. The significance of the above milestones cannot be overstated. Taiwan's remarkable transformation must be taken into account if we are to arrive at a satisfactory answer to the question of statehood. It is the collective expression of political will that truly distinguishes today's Taiwan from life under the ROC's authoritarian rule—and from China. Taiwan is Taiwan, and China is China, and there are stark contrasts between these two separate states. There is no need for Taiwan to make a formal declaration of independence in the manner of the American Declaration of Independence. That Taiwan exists as an independent, sovereign state is a reality that must be embraced.

Notes

1. Taiwan Affairs Office & Information Office of the State Council, The Taiwan Question and Reunification of China, Aug. 1993, *available at* http://www.china.org.cn/english/taiwan/7953.htm.

2. Taiwan Affairs Office & Information Office of the State Council, The One-China Principle and the Taiwan Issue, Feb. 2000, *available at* http://www.china.org.cn/english/taiwan/7956.htm.

3. Republic of China, Mainland Affairs Council, The Government's Position Paper on Ma Ying-jeou's Stance about "Taiwan's Pledge of Not Seeking Independence in Exchange for China's Commitment of Not Using Force against Taiwan," Nov. 3, 2006, *available at* http://www.mac.gov.tw/ct.asp?xItem=50718&ctNode=5913&mp=3.

4. JAMES CRAWFORD, THE CREATION OF STATES IN INTERNATIONAL LAW 2D ED. (2006).

5. *Id.* at 209.

6. Brad R. Roth, *The Entity that Dare Not Speak Its Name: Unrecognized Taiwan as a Right-Bearer in the International Legal Order*, 91 E. ASIA L. R. 91, 98 (2009).

7. *Id.* at 97.

8. *Id.* at 122.

9. LUNG-CHU CHEN, AN INTRODUCTION TO CONTEMPORARY INTERNATIONAL LAW: A POLICY-ORIENTED PERSPECTIVE, 3D ED. at 155 (2015).

10. Great Britain, Parliamentary Debate (Hansard), House of Commons, Official Report, Vol. 536: col. 159 (written answers) (Feb. 4, 1955); LUNG-CHU CHEN & HAROLD D. LASSWELL,

FORMOSA, CHINA, AND THE UNITED NATIONS: FORMOSA IN THE WORLD COMMUNITY 92 (1967).

11. *See* Chinmei Sung & Janet Ong, *Jailed Taiwan Ex-President Chen Sues in the U.S.*, BLOOMBERG, Sept. 24, 2009, *available at* http://www.bloomberg.com/apps/news?pid=newsa rchive&sid=aIMgLeoCrU78.

12. *See* RICHARD C. BUSH, AT CROSS PURPOSES: U.S.-TAIWAN RELATIONS SINCE 1942, at 99 (2015).

13. 22 U.S.C. §3303(b)(1).

14. JEAN-MARIE HENCKAERTS, ED. THE INTERNATIONAL STATUS OF TAIWAN IN THE NEW WORLD ORDER: LEGAL AND POLITICAL CONSIDERATIONS (1996).

15. *Western Sahara*, Separate Opinion of Judge Dillard, I.C.J. Reports 1975 at 122.

16. CHEN, *supra* note 9, at 38.

5 U.S. Constitutional Issues Concerning the Taiwan Relations Act

I. President Carter's Announcement

At 9:00 p.m. on December 15, 1978, President Jimmy Carter addressed the American people live by radio and television from the White House Oval Office. In a surprise announcement, Carter revealed that the United States would normalize relations with the People's Republic of China (PRC) effective January 1, 1979, and, as a consequence, would derecognize the Republic of China (ROC) on Taiwan. "I would like to read a joint communiqué," the president began, "which is being simultaneously issued in Peking at this very moment by the leaders of the People's Republic of China."[1] He then recited the text of the "Joint Communiqué on the Establishment of Diplomatic Relations between the United States of America and the People's Republic of China" (the Second Joint Communiqué). It stated:

> The United States of America and the People's Republic of China have agreed to recognize each other and to establish diplomatic relations as of January 1, 1979.
>
> The United States of America recognizes the Government of the People's Republic of China as the sole legal Government of China. Within this context,

the people of the United States will maintain cultural, commercial, and other unofficial relations with the people of Taiwan.

The United States of America and the People's Republic of China reaffirm the principles agreed on by the two sides in the Shanghai Communiqué and emphasize once again that:

Both wish to reduce the danger of international military conflict.

Neither should seek hegemony in the Asia-Pacific region or in any other region of the world and each is opposed to efforts by any other country or group of countries to establish such hegemony.

Neither is prepared to negotiate on behalf of any third party or to enter into agreements or understandings with the other directed at other states.

The Government of the United States of America acknowledges the Chinese position that there is but one China and Taiwan is part of China.

Both believe that normalization of Sino-American relations is not only in the interest of the Chinese and American peoples but also contributes to the cause of peace in Asia and the world.

The United States of America and the People's Republic of China will exchange Ambassadors and establish Embassies on March 1, 1979.[2]

After reading the text of the communiqué, the president offered several reasons in favor of normalization, which he said would be "of great long-term benefit to the peoples of both our country and China and . . . to all the peoples of the world." Normalization would promote stability in Asia and bring the United States into closer contact with the PRC and its many citizens, he said. As for the fate of Taiwan, the president remarked:

. . . I wish also tonight to convey a special message to the people of Taiwan— I have already communicated with the leaders in Taiwan—with whom the American people have had and will have extensive, close, and friendly relations. This is important between our two peoples.

As the United States asserted in the Shanghai Communiqué of 1972, issued on President Nixon's historic visit, we will continue to have an interest in the peaceful resolution of the Taiwan issue. I have paid special attention to ensuring that normalization of relations between our country and the People's Republic will not jeopardize the well being of the people of Taiwan. The people of our country will maintain our current commercial, cultural, trade, and other relations with Taiwan through nongovernmental means. Many other countries in the world are already successfully doing this.[3]

Carter added that members of his administration "have already begun to inform our allies and other nations and the Members of the Congress of the details of our intended action." To careful listeners, the implication that Congress had yet to be fully informed was sure to underscore the surprise nature of the announcement and drive home that this was a unilateral move by the executive. That is not to say that Congress or the American people were unprepared for normalization with the PRC or even that they opposed the development in principle. Normalization had been widely expected in Washington as early as 1971, when Henry Kissinger made his secret visit to China. By 1979, normalization was an accepted element of the Democratic Party agenda. And lawmakers on both sides of the aisle were on record as supporting deepening relations with the PRC under the right conditions. After all, it was diplomatically and strategically unwise not to have relations with a country as populous and geographically significant as China, as Richard Nixon had argued in his famous 1967 essay for *Foreign Affairs*. Nevertheless, the timing of Carter's announcement, and the abrupt manner of the reversal of the U.S. position toward the ROC, came as a shock to many. Journalist Ted Koppel, reporting that evening for ABC News, summarized the mood in the capital when he remarked that Carter's announcement "was the logical consequence of the Nixon mission [to build relations with China], but somehow no one expected it quite this soon."[4]

Carter followed his televised announcement by issuing a written statement regarding the terms of normalization. The PRC issued its own statement. Both documents reflected the centrality of the Taiwan question during negotiations. However, the U.S. statement, while outlining specific measures toward unofficial relations with Taiwan, was markedly ambiguous as to the long-term prospects for the island. The PRC on the other hand clearly envisioned an eventual unification between itself and Taiwan. The U.S. stated the following expectations:

> On that same date, January 1, 1979, the United States of America will notify Taiwan that it is terminating diplomatic relations and that the Mutual Defense Treaty between the United States and the Republic of China is being terminated in accordance with the provisions of the Treaty.
>
> The United States also states that it will be withdrawing its remaining military personnel from Taiwan within four months.
>
> In the future, the American people and the people of Taiwan will maintain commercial, cultural, and other relations without official government representation and without diplomatic relations.
>
> The Administration will seek adjustments to our laws and regulations to permit the maintenance of commercial, cultural, and other non-governmental relationships in the new circumstances that will exist after normalization.

The United States is confident that the people of Taiwan face a peaceful and prosperous future. The United States continues to have an interest in the peaceful resolution of the Taiwan issue and expects that the Taiwan issue will be settled peacefully by the Chinese themselves.[5]

In contrast, the PRC stated the following:

As of January 1, 1979, the People's Republic of China and the United States of America recognize each other and establish diplomatic relations, thereby ending the prolonged abnormal relationship between them. This is a historic event in Sino-U.S. relations.

As is known to all, the Government of the People's Republic of China is the sole legal government of China and Taiwan is a part of China. The question of Taiwan was the crucial issue obstructing the normalization of relations between China and the United States. It has now been resolved between the two countries in the spirit of the Shanghai Communiqué and through their joint efforts, thus enabling the normalization of the relations so ardently desired by the people of the two countries. As for the way of bringing Taiwan back to the embrace of the motherland and reunifying the country, it is entirely China's internal affair.

At the invitation of the U.S. Government, Teng Hsiao-ping, Vice Premier of the State Council of the People's Republic of China, will pay an official visit to the United States in January 1979, with a view to further promoting the friendship between the two peoples and good relations between the two countries.[6]

The U.S. statement reflected three commitments agreed upon with the PRC in late 1978. First, the United States agreed to derecognize the ROC government on Taiwan as the lawful government of China. Second, it agreed to terminate the Mutual Defense Treaty of 1954. It is worth noting that the United States would allow the agreement to expire one year after giving notice to the ROC, as permitted in the treaty's Article X.[7] The administration revealed that PRC negotiators had at first insisted that the United States abrogate the treaty immediately, but their demand was refused by the White House. Third, the United States would withdraw its remaining troops from Taiwan. While the statement noted that the United States would maintain unofficial relations with Taiwan, it made no mention of security guarantees for the island. Furthermore, Carter expressed the hope that the Taiwan question would be settled peacefully between the Chinese people on both sides of the Taiwan Strait. As to this point, the PRC promised not to contradict Carter publicly, although Chinese negotiators steadfastly refused to rule out the possibility of using force, as they claimed that the Taiwan matter was an internal affair.

The PRC leadership made great use of the rhetorical ground that had been ceded by the United States in the two Communiqués, asserting that the Taiwan question had been settled insofar as the United States was concerned and insisting that Taiwan was, and would remain, an internal affair. What should be kept in mind is that the statements represented each country's views of the outcome of the negotiations. By all accounts the statements are comprehensive as to the details of the negotiations. However, as will be discussed later in the chapter, the documents were not formal agreements, were not signed, and were not intended to be construed as treaties. Each merely represented the preferred interpretation of the two sides as to the terms of normalization and expectations for the resolution of open issues. While the statements evidenced a common understanding of many facts, there are significant points that were left unsettled. The discrepancies between the two statements foreshadowed conflicts that would emerge in the coming years, as each seized on the statements' ambiguities to advocate for its own interests, with the PRC often accusing the United States of abandoning their shared understanding—assuming that one ever existed.

At 9:30 p.m., following his announcement, Carter held a briefing with members of the press, in which he referred to the decision as a "long-awaited development in international diplomacy," but he acknowledged the concerns held by members of Congress about the termination of the ROC Mutual Defense Treaty and the feasibility of maintaining cultural, commercial, and other informal ties with the people of Taiwan.[8] Carter said he expected there would be some members of Congress who would have preferred to maintain the status quo, but he felt that most of lawmakers' concerns would be addressed by the legislation he was preparing to implement the transition. When asked about the expected response in Taiwan, Carter replied, "I doubt if there will be massive applause in Taiwan." But he assured journalists that the administration would "do everything we can to assure the Taiwanese that we put at top—as one of the top priorities in our own relationships with the People's Republic and them—that the well-being of the people of Taiwan will not be damaged."

Indeed, Carter was correct that the news would be unwelcome in Taiwan. The derecognition of the ROC and the accompanying termination of the Mutual Defense Treaty marked the first time in history that the U.S. government had derecognized an allied country. Adding to this perceived insult was the unilateral and secretive manner in which the White House communicated the news to the public, to lawmakers, and to ROC leaders. According to reports, U.S. Ambassador to the ROC Leonard Unger was pulled away from a holiday ball in Taipei to receive a sudden telephone call from the State Department. Officials informed him that

President Carter would announce derecognition imminently. Hurrying from the ball, Unger convinced ROC aides to awaken President Chiang Ching-kuo in the early morning hours in Taipei. He delivered the news to Chiang himself shortly before Carter's televised announcement.[9]

A. HISTORY OF THE NEGOTIATIONS OVER U.S.-PRC DIPLOMATIC RELATIONS

Given the manner in which the Carter administration communicated its decision to Chiang Ching-kuo, it goes without saying that the ROC's perspectives were not highly sought after by the White House. Indeed, according to later reports, Carter insisted on making a surprise announcement to head off the ROC's powerful U.S. lobby, which may have been able to persuade Congress to help delay the change in recognition. Such behavior, whatever the political calculations behind it, gave the impression that the United States viewed Taiwan as an inconvenience, or worse, as a mere token to be played in negotiations with the PRC. In either scenario, it does not seem unreasonable that many in Congress and the public would question the administration's commitment to the island's security following Carter's announcement.

In September 1978, having anticipated the White House's intentions, Congress passed the Dole-Stone Amendment to the International Security Assistance Act of 1978 concerning the Mutual Defense Treaty with the ROC. The Amendment, which Carter signed as part of the Act, stated it was "the sense of the Congress that there should be prior consultation between the Congress and the Executive Branch on any proposed policy changes affecting the continuation in force of the Mutual Defense Treaty of 1954."[10] Not only had Carter neglected to consult with Congress on the proposed termination of the treaty, the administration had even declined to inform members of Congress on the impending announcement, except for a few select members who, like Chiang Ching-kuo, were given scarcely more than a few hours warning. Senator Dennis DeConcini of Arizona revealed that members of the Senate Foreign Relations Committee and select other members of Congress were "called in by the President 3 hours before his broadcast. We were notified, not consulted. We were told what the administration's decision was."[11]

Carter was not entirely to blame for this impression. His approach was emblematic of the executive's conduct during negotiations with the PRC since the early 1970s. When President Nixon announced his 1972 visit to China, he remarked that the trip would present an opportunity to discuss "the normalization of relations between the two countries."[12] Though the objective was well known, the Nixon administration conducted the negotiations in high secrecy, with the White House sometimes keeping its own State Department in the dark, creating friction even within the executive branch.[13] Little changed during the Ford administration from 1974 to 1977. When Carter entered office in 1977, he was determined to finish the job his predecessors started, and perhaps saw little opportunity or need to act transparently.

Some in the administration felt that Congress was exceeding its authority in attempting to regulate the president's use of his foreign affairs powers.[14] From the executive's perspective, Congress was overstepping its constitutional role in demanding a seat at the table in discussions over normalization. The founding fathers assigned responsibility for foreign affairs to the executive precisely to allow the president to operate independently and discretely in sensitive diplomatic matters. Subjecting the normalization process to congressional oversight would have jeopardized the White House's ability to reach an understanding with the PRC amid a host of delicate topics. Furthermore, some in the administration believed that Congress' dramatic response to the normalization announcement was less about policy and more about the desire to project congressional power following the unpopular events of the Vietnam War and the Watergate scandal that had ended the Nixon presidency.

By late 1978, Carter estimated that the United States had obtained enough concessions from the PRC to undertake normalization without undermining U.S. interests. For the United States, one of the key objectives of normalizing relations with the PRC was to establish an important counterweight to the Soviet Union, whose border with China stretched approximately 2,650 miles. The Sino-Soviet split that developed in the 1970s provided the ideal opportunity to nurture a strategic alliance with the PRC, which proponents argued would have the added benefit of stabilizing Asia regionally and checking Soviet expansion.[15] For the PRC, establishing stable relations with the industrialized West was essential to its plans to modernize its economy following the disaster of the Cultural Revolution and the post–Mao Zedong era.

The first milestone in the road toward normalization was the issuance of the Shanghai Communiqué in 1972, in which the United States acknowledged the Chinese view that "there is but one China and that Taiwan is a part of China." The United States also assented to a gradual withdrawal of U.S. troops on the island. These gestures were sufficient to move the conversation forward, and Kissinger proposed in 1973 that the United States could normalize relations "along the Japanese formula."[16] By this he referred to the approach to normalization taken by the Japanese in 1972, in which Tokyo formally recognized the PRC, while maintaining unofficial instrumentalities in Taiwan. Congress boosted the effort on April 20, 1973, when lawmakers approved the establishment of semidiplomatic relations with the PRC under S. 1315, which extended diplomatic privileges and immunities to the PRC's liaison offices in the United States.

Had Nixon remained in office, it is possible that diplomatic relations with the PRC would have been achieved during his administration. But there is no telling what form such a decision would have taken in the political climate of the early 1970s. In addition to demanding the withdrawal of troops, the PRC insisted that the United States terminate relations with the ROC and immediately abrogate the Mutual Defense Treaty. According to insiders, President Nixon was willing to accept these terms in exchange for a pledge from the PRC that it would seek a peaceful resolution to the Taiwan matter. After taking office in 1974, Gerald Ford attempted to continue the negotiations; however, he was rebuffed as the PRC took a more hardnosed approach to the discussions. Once again the PRC restated its three conditions: derecognition of the ROC government, abrogation of the Mutual Defense Treaty, and the removal of U.S. military personnel from Taiwan. It refused to forego the use of force against Taiwan.

Under Carter, Secretary of State Cyrus Vance again outlined the U.S. position toward Taiwan, but the Chinese simply reiterated their three conditions.[17] In principle, the White House was prepared to accept the Chinese conditions with certain modifications. The United States was willing to derecognize the ROC, with some administration officials conceding that it was no longer possible to adhere to the fiction that the government on Taiwan somehow maintained a legitimate claim to the whole of China. Removing U.S. military personnel also was an acceptable condition, as military exigencies in the Pacific had changed significantly since the end of the Korean War, and maintaining a forward military presence on Taiwan was no longer needed in the eyes of U.S. military planners. As to the Mutual Defense Treaty, however, the administration was not willing to abrogate the agreement, instead insisting that the treaty would be allowed to expire according to its own terms.

Carter's principal aims were to achieve normalization while protecting U.S. interests on Taiwan and making provisions for Taiwan's security. To this end, the United States expected that it would, like Japan and many other countries, continue commercial, cultural, and other relations with Taiwan and maintain an unofficial presence on the island after derecognizing the ROC government. To discourage attacks from outside powers, particularly the PRC, the United States would continue selling defensive arms to Taiwan. Finally, U.S. negotiators restated that the PRC should adopt a peaceful approach to cross-strait relations.

In 1978, Chinese negotiators initially stated they would not accept a unilateral U.S. declaration of support for Taiwan's security nor continued weapons sales to Taiwan. However, in late 1978, PRC intermediaries signaled their governments' willingness to settle the matter, and negotiations entered into high gear. The United States softened its position, by expressing via National Security Advisor Zbigniew Brzezinski, a hope, not a demand, that the Taiwan question would be resolved peacefully. Carter then authorized Leonard Woodcock, Chief of the U.S. Liaison Office in China, to begin negotiations on normalization.[18] The Chinese maintained their position that the resolution of the Taiwan question was an internal affair there-fore permitting force. However, in December, Vice Premier Deng Xiaoping[19] stated that the Chinese government would "take note" of Carter's suggestion, providing a tacit acceptance of the condition, without overtly endorsing it.[20] Secretary of State Warren Christopher later argued to the Senate that "making the statement with the other party agreeing not to contradict it has great significance in international law as well as for the two parties involved."[21] PRC negotiators also agreed that the United States would terminate the Mutual Defense Treaty under Article X, providing the ROC with one year's notice, rather than abrogating the treaty outright. The PRC also accepted the fact that the United States would continue to make defensive arms sales to Taiwan after derecognizing its government.

II. Enactment of the Taiwan Relations Act

In his written statement on U.S.-PRC diplomatic relations, Carter promised "adjust-ments to [U.S.] laws and regulations to permit the maintenance of commercial, cul-tural, and other non-governmental relationships" with Taiwan. The first step came on December 30, 1978, when the president issued a memorandum to all executive depart-ments and agencies instructing them on how to conduct relations with the "People on Taiwan."[22] The memorandum directed executive staff to continue to engage with counterparts on Taiwan and to continue to apply laws and regulations to Taiwan, as if it were a foreign state. The memorandum identified a then unnamed "unoffi-cial instrumentality" (what would be the American Institute in Taiwan) that would carry out programs, transactions, and other relations with Taiwan. The memoran-dum largely negated the practical effects of derecognizing the ROC, while permitting Congress time to devise a legislative solution for maintaining unofficial relations.[23]

On January 29, 1979, the White House submitted the text of a bill called the Taiwan Enabling Act, which provided a legal basis for maintaining unofficial rela-tions with Taiwan. Congress was underwhelmed by the proposal. As Representative Lester Wolff of New York later wrote, "[w]e were not satisfied with Carter's ver-sion, which we felt too weak a statement to fulfill the need of the people of Taiwan who did not want to come under Communist domination."[24] Wolff, working with Senator Alan Cranston of California and others formulated a new bill that would ultimately be passed as the Taiwan Relations Act (TRA).

Lawmakers who wanted the United States to give more support to Taiwan had the American people on their side. A poll conducted in mid-1978 found that two-thirds of Americans did not want the United States to derecognize the ROC, and the same number wished to maintain the Mutual Defense Treaty.[25] By January

1979, a month after the normalization decision became public, nearly 50 percent of Americans were still opposed to recognizing the PRC if it meant undermining the security of allied Taiwan.[26] The concerns raised by the public and members of Congress went far beyond the perceived mistreatment of Taiwan arising from the executive branch's dealings with the PRC. Setting aside the question of which entity should be recognized as the government of China, many observers were greatly concerned that the president's sudden move and dismissiveness toward the ROC would send the wrong signal that the United States was not committed to its international alliances. These fears were heightened after the U.S. withdrawal from Vietnam.

The dissatisfaction of the Taiwan people was evident when Warren Christopher visited Taipei on December 27, 1978, shortly after Carter's announcement. An unruly crowd surrounded Christopher's motorcade, hurling eggs and breaking a window in the ambassador's car. As for the ROC itself, officials on Taiwan were insulted by the United States' sudden disengagement and initially refused to cooperate on establishing a framework for unofficial relations. Finally, the White House issued an ultimatum in late January urging Taipei to reach an agreement on nongovernmental relations by February 10, 1979, or risk "a complete rupture in U.S.-ROC ties."[27]

Domestically, the administration set a March 1, 1979, deadline for Congress to pass the Taiwan Enabling Act. Some lawmakers were furious that the president expected Congress to hold hearings, debate the specifics of the bill, and secure its passage within just four weeks. Simultaneously, Carter threatened to veto any bill that contradicted the conditions agreed upon with the PRC.[28] Deadlines or no deadlines, the ninety-sixth Congress was not going to let the executive branch dictate all of the terms. While the president may possess most of the foreign affairs powers, Congress holds sway over domestic legislation, which was precisely where Carter needed reform to support unofficial relations with Taiwan. In just a matter of weeks, Congress pushed its legislative authority to the limits and reshaped U.S. foreign policy in the process. In doing so, lawmakers reminded the White House and the American public that the Constitution with its checks and balances does not give absolute authority to any one branch.

Responsibility for the bill fell to the powerful Senate Committee on Foreign Relations, whose members included Committee Chairman Frank Church (Idaho) and Senators Claiborne Pell (Rhode Island), George McGovern (South Dakota), Joe Biden (Delaware), John Glenn (Ohio), Richard Stone (Florida), Paul Sarbanes (Maryland), Edmund Muskie (Maine), Edward Zorinsky (Nebraska), Jacob Javits (New York), Charles Percy (Illinois), Howard Baker (Tennessee), Jesse Helms (North Carolina), S. I. Hayakawa (California), and Richard Lugar (Indiana). Despite one of the snowiest Februaries on record in Washington, D.C., the Committee held six sessions of hearings on the bill between February 5 and 22, 1979, featuring more than twenty-five witnesses including fellow members of Congress, academics, businesspeople, military experts, and advocates for Taiwanese independence. Senator Church famously set the tone for the hearings in his opening statement when he called the president's bill "woefully inadequate to the task, ambiguous in language, and uncertain in tone."[29]

Heated rhetoric aside, the hearing transcripts reveal that lawmakers were nearly uniform in their approval of normalization with the PRC in principle. As Committee Chairman Church stated, "President Carter's action in extending U.S. diplomatic recognition to the People's Republic as the legal government of China gives long overdue acknowledgment of one of the central realities of Asian affairs, the existence of the government which actually exercises jurisdiction over the most populous and second largest nation on Earth."[30] But deep resentment existed over the executive's handling of negotiations and the perception that the ROC was being left without adequate assurances for its security or for the interests of U.S. businesses there. Additionally, with the exception of Senator Barry Goldwater and his supporters, witnesses believed the president had acted within his constitutional authority in terminating the Mutual Defense Treaty according to its terms. The committee was left with the task of balancing U.S. and Taiwanese interests while respecting the boundaries of the executive's agreement with the PRC, thereby establishing a firm basis for continued unofficial relations without jeopardizing normalization. As Church put it, "it is not for us to decide Taiwan's ultimate destiny. However, the United States does have an important interest that this issue be resolved peacefully and in [a] manner that takes into account the will of the people of Taiwan."[31] Church added, "the task of embracing China without deserting Taiwan will require a high order of diplomatic skill and legislative ingenuity."[32] Indeed, that is what Congress delivered.

The committee members and witnesses were consistent in how they articulated Congress's mission. Senator Glenn put the committee's task this way:

> I would prefer the simplest kind of agreement and to give the President reasonable latitude, quite wide latitude as a matter of fact, to make normalization work. Now that we have made this jump, I would like to get behind it and make it work. I would like the security guarantees that I think we could have gotten for Taiwan set apart from recognition. That is water over the dam. Let's make normalization work, still maintaining a moral commitment to see that there is no bloodshed in the area.[33]

Robert A. Scalapino, Director of the Institute for East Asian Studies at the University of California at Berkeley, and a noted expert on Taiwan, also commented on the challenge before Congress. The use of force and defensive arms sales "could easily become a bone of contention between Peking and Washington in the future, particularly if Congress does not speak on this matter with firmness and clarity," Scalapino warned. "It is my belief that if Congress were to fail to act or if it were to pass a weak resolution that leaves our position ambiguous, far from laying the ground for a good United States-People's Republic of China relation, it would provide the basis for future miscalculation and controversy."[34] Ralph N. Clough, a fellow with the Woodrow Wilson International Center for Scholars, testified as to the desired policy outcome of the committee's work. He presciently said:

> [A] delicate balance is called for in furthering relations with Peking and Taipei—enough support for Taiwan to insure that the use of force against the island would entail high political and military costs for the People's Republic of China, and enough momentum in the expansion of Washington/Peking relations to cause both countries to value highly the contribution made by the relationship to their broad global objectives. Managed successfully, such a policy would enable Washington and Peking to continue to keep the unresolved Taiwan problem on the back burner.
>
> So long as the possibility of reunifying Taiwan and the mainland is not foreclosed, Peking can probably live with a separate Taiwan for years to come, just as it appears to be willing to continue to live with a separate Hong Kong.[35]

Clough testified that although Taiwan was severely limited after losing its seat in the United Nations and diplomatic relations with most other countries, it nevertheless managed to succeed economically by maintaining trading relationships around the world. The PRC was willing to permit Taiwan to operate independently, but would not renounce the use of force, which would remove an incentive for ROC officials to engage with the PRC in discussions of possible future unification. "Recognizing that economic or military pressures are not practicable options at the present time, PRC leaders have launched a campaign of conciliatory proposals, offering to trade with Taiwan, open postal services, and encourage travel back and forth," he observed.[36]

The Carter administration feared that Congress would upset the agreement reached with the PRC by insisting on measures that exceeded the administration's intentions in the Second Communiqué. The president warned that he would veto any bill that he found inconsistent with the terms of the normalization agreement. Deputy Secretary of State Warren Christopher represented the executive branch during the hearings. He argued that the agreement itself was sufficient to protect Taiwan because the PRC was unlikely to use violence against its neighbor, as the

PRC relied heavily on good relations with the United States and other Western nations to support its modernization. "Such a sharp reversal of policy would, in our view, appear to be highly unlikely," Christopher stated.[37] He indicated two general boundaries for Congress in regard to the threat of a presidential veto: giving Taiwan relations an "official" character and re-establishing the Mutual Defense Treaty. He explained that the executive was unable to persuade China to renounce the use of force against Taiwan, stating that, as during the lead up to the adoption of the communiqué, "the sovereignty issue was a barrier to an explicit renunciation of the use of force. That particular background pervaded the recent discussion."[38] However, the PRC did agree not to contradict an expectation expressed by the United States that the matter would be resolved peacefully. Carter made this statement as part of his announcement on December 15. The administration invited Congress to make its own statement hoping for a peaceful resolution, provided it did not undermine the agreement reached with the PRC.

Secretary of Defense Harold Brown buttressed Christopher's viewpoint when he stated that the Sino-Soviet split relieved the United States of having to maintain forces in Taiwan, while shifting the PRC's attention to its border with the USSR. A large part of the administration's theory was based on political constraints, as the PRC depended heavily on the industrialized democracies to facilitate its modernization. Brown indicated that military planners believed the PRC was unlikely to use force against Taiwan for reasons that included its limited military capabilities and the likelihood of diplomatic blowback. Based on this assessment, the executive chose to make no arms sales to Taiwan in 1979 because the United States did not want to give the impression it was "loading up" Taiwan before normalization. Furthermore, Brown said, U.S. military planners assessed that the PRC was unlikely to attack Taiwan, so providing arms was not necessary at that time. Leonard Unger, former ambassador to the Republic of China, echoed the assessment, stating there was "no near-term threat of military attack" against the ROC.[39]

Day two of the hearings featured impassioned testimony by Senator Barry Goldwater, an outspoken critic of Carter's normalization decision. In principle, Goldwater agreed with the intent of the Taiwan Enabling Act. "My objection is to the method, not the purpose," he said, because it does not provide for "continued Government-to-Government contacts."[40] He wanted the text to recognize "the people and government of Taiwan" and to provide full diplomatic immunities to officials. He also wanted a full defensive commitment, including arms sales.[41] He further asserted that there is an "advise and consent power of the Senate in the termination of treaties" and that to permit Carter to terminate the treaty without congressional advice would be "fast traveling down the road to a dictator." Goldwater referred to an 1856 report by the Foreign Affairs Committee that suggested that when a treaty reserves a right to the parties to terminate the treaty, "such discretion resides in the President and Senate."[42]

Goldwater and the State Department submitted dueling memoranda to the committee on the subject of the shared powers of Congress and the president in terminating treaties. Goldwater argued that the Mutual Defense Treaty used the word "party," which referred to the "sovereign authority of the Nation who is empowered to perform the act for the country." He said to understand the meaning of that provision required consulting the Constitution and that the Constitution says it is a shared power. Goldwater noted that while there were precedents (weak, in his opinion) of presidents unilaterally terminating treaties (examples which, he mused, may have been unconstitutional), there was stronger precedent for Congress giving its authorization for the termination of treaties. "Just as the President alone cannot repeal a statute, I believe that he cannot repeal a treaty," Goldwater said.[43] In a letter to Goldwater, Eugene Rostow, former Under Secretary of State and former dean of Yale Law School, said that "[t]he assurances of the President and of the redoubtable Mr. Teng [of China] are not a sufficient basis for a nation's security."[44] Rostow stated: "For us to terminate the American security treaty with Taiwan does not advance the common interest in stability and peace. On the contrary, it creates doubt and uncertainty throughout the world about the credibility of our security commitments, the only cement of the world political system."[45]

The hearings provided many lively and memorable moments as Senators took turns haranguing the Carter administration and underscoring issues they felt were being overlooked in the rush to establish diplomatic relations with the PRC. There were several lighthearted exchanges, including those between the Senators and Herbert Hansell, legal advisor to the Department of State, who struggled at times to articulate how the AIT would act as a suitable counterparty on behalf of the U.S. government. Hansell and Stone debated over how to identify a governing authority on Taiwan, and the pair seemed unable to agree that "the people of Taiwan" could be defined with adequate precision to carry out the Act's purpose. Senator Stone quipped that "obviously if the Defense Department of the United States were to consider selling a destroyer to the people of Taiwan, they would not want to sell it to the zoning board of Taipei."[46] Senator Bob Dole shared his characteristic humor in opposing the "shotgun method" by which the administration was pushing for congressional action. "There is a gun to our head and one to the head of Taiwan and they say there is a deadline," Dole remarked.[47]

The committee delved into many technical aspects of the president's proposed legislation, paying particular attention to the legal requirements for the AIT and measures needed to protect U.S. business interests in Taiwan as well as Taiwanese assets in the United States. Committee members variously referred to the proposal for the American Institute as the "institute approach" or "the Japanese formula." The AIT was modeled on the approach taken by the Japanese in 1972, when Tokyo terminated diplomatic relations with the ROC but maintained informal relations through a nongovernmental instrumentality on the island. Unlike the Japanese approach, the United States intended to maintain certain existing governmental arrangements through the AIT, whereas the Japanese ended all government-to-government agreements. As Javits said, Japan's handling of the issue was "useful as a precedent," but "an American formula" was needed "to take account of the legal and constitutional differences between Japan and the United States and the responsibility of the United States to the people of Taiwan."[48] Unger reported that Taiwan maintained informal, nongovernmental relations with more than one hundred countries and formal diplomatic relations with twenty. "The arrangements which the administration has proposed, through the creation of the American Institute and in this bill, are more elaborate and more detailed than those of any other country that presently maintains these nonofficial relations," he said.[49]

The committee spent relatively little time discussing Taiwan's legal status under international law. Victor Li, a professor of law at Stanford University, was one of the few witnesses to testify on the issue and argued in favor of recognizing Taiwan as a juridical person (as opposed to recognizing the PRC as the ROC's successor state). According to Li, "the need to obtain the People's Republic of China's consent, even if only implied, for continued dealings with Taiwan constantly places the United States on the defensive."[50] Li acknowledged that one reason the ROC did not give up the fiction that it was the government of the whole of China was that there were about fifteen hundred legislators in the National Assembly purporting to represent districts in mainland China. Giving up the claim to the mainland would undermine their positions. Li said adopting a position of ambiguity toward the Taiwan question would be expedient in the short term for the United States, but would likely create problems down the road. The United States would harm Taiwan by recognizing the PRC as a successor state, while granting Taiwan *de facto* recognition would antagonize the PRC. In his words: "This policy of intentional ambiguity may be difficult to maintain for an indeterminate time. In the years to come I suspect that we will see many situations where the PRC would attempt to assert its position as the successor. Each instance would set a precedent for future dealings."[51] Li suggested that the administration should clarify what theory it was adopting behind the Taiwan Enabling Act (i.e., that Taiwan was a *de facto* legal entity) in order to clarify questions around its status. As to Taiwan's international legal status, the committee ultimately concluded that addressing the matter was unnecessary because the bill dealt not with international law, but with Taiwan's treatment under U.S. domestic law.

In all, Congress added provisions to the president's bill that addressed five areas of concern. The revised TRA declared that peace and security in the Western Pacific were matters of U.S. interest. It memorialized Congress' expectation that the Taiwan question must be resolved peacefully. It specified that nonpeaceful actions, which would include boycotts and embargoes, would be viewed as a threat to regional peace. Taiwan would be provided with enough weapons to maintain its self-defense capability. Moreover, the United States would maintain the capacity to resist any resort to force or other forms of coercion that would jeopardize the security, or the social or economic system, of the people on Taiwan.

Additionally, Congress modified the administration's bill to protect the interests of U.S. businesses in Taiwan. U.S. investors would continue to receive guarantees from the Overseas Private Investment Council, although Taiwan's per capita income surpassed the program's ordinary maximum. The TRA also clarified that the term *Taiwan* would include the governing authorities on the island and provided that the Taiwan government could sue and be sued in U.S. courts and that Taiwan's assets in the United States would not be affected by the loss of diplomatic recognition. Other provisions specified treatment under the Immigration and Nationality Act and provided for privileges for staff members of the Coordination Council for North American Affairs, the counterpart to the AIT. Finally, Congress affirmed that U.S. derecognition of the ROC should not serve as the basis for excluding Taiwan from membership in international organizations.

Reflecting Congress's interest in seeing the law faithfully executed, the TRA requires the president to inform Congress promptly of any threat to Taiwan's security. Agreements reached by the AIT would be subject to existing notification and approval procedures in keeping with the Case-Zablocki Act, and the president would be required to report to Congress on any regulations implemented under the TRA. The Secretary of State was required to make regular reports to Congress on the status of U.S.-Taiwan relations for two years after the Act's passage. The House Foreign Affairs and Senate Foreign Relations committees would be tasked with overseeing the TRA's implementation.

The TRA received overwhelming bipartisan support and passed by a vote of 339 to 50 in the House on March 28, 1979, and 85 to 4 in the Senate on March 29, 1979. Carter signed the Act into law on April 10, 1979. On July 6, 1979, three months after signing the TRA into law, the Carter administration sent the following note to the PRC:

The United States shall comply with various understandings reached with the People's Republic of China on establishing diplomatic relations ... The Taiwan Relations Act finally adopted by the Congress does not comply with the wishes of the [U.S.] government in every detail; however, it provides full discretionary authority to the President in dealing with [difficult] situations and enables the President to implement this Act in a manner fully consistent with the normalization formula. It is on that basis that the President signed this bill and made it law. The United States Government has ensured that the language used in this Act will not impair the understanding reached with your government or compel our government to take action deviating from such understanding.[52]

III. Congressional and Executive Powers in Foreign Affairs

Support for the Taiwan Relations Act (TRA) among members of Congress remains strong to this day, as evidenced by the passage of resolutions affirming the TRA's objectives. Professor Robert Sutter, an expert in U.S. foreign policy and Asia, has proposed three reasons for Taiwan's continued relevance for members of Congress. First, Taiwan remains an important economic power in the Asia Pacific and is an important U.S. trading partner. Second, Taiwanese officials have focused on effective lobbying efforts to educate Congress on Taiwan affairs. Third, the TRA provides Congress with a unique influence over U.S. foreign policy in contrast to areas where the president's power is relatively unchallenged.[53] The author would add a fourth reason to this list: that members of Congress admire Taiwan and its people for their commitment to democracy and for the values of human rights and freedom shared between the people of Taiwan and the United States. The TRA is a symbol of this common bond.

Congress enacted the TRA pursuant to its powers under Article I of the Constitution, which authorizes the legislative branch to enact federal statutes in accordance with certain enumerated purposes. These include raising taxes, regulating commerce, and making laws that are necessary and proper for carrying out constitutional objectives. By drawing on its Article I powers, Congress was on firm constitutional ground in passing the TRA. Although supporters of a strong executive may question the extent to which Congress should participate in foreign policy making, there is no question about the legitimacy of the TRA's provisions under the Constitution. Responsibility for carrying out the TRA's lies with the president. It is here where constitutional issues may arise in practice. To what extent may the president alter U.S. policy toward Taiwan within the framework established by the TRA? This issue was raised forcefully in August 1982, when President Reagan accepted the Third Communiqué, which projected a gradual reduction in U.S. arms sales to Taiwan. The communiqué stated:

> . . . the United States Government states that it does not seek to carry out a long-term policy of arms sales to Taiwan, that its arms sales to Taiwan will not

exceed, either in qualitative or in quantitative terms, the level of those supplied in recent years since the establishment of diplomatic relations between the United States and China, and that it intends gradually to reduce its sale of arms to Taiwan, leading, over a period of time, to a final resolution.[54]

On its face, this statement appears to contradict Section 2 of the TRA, which establishes that it is U.S. policy to "provide Taiwan with arms of a defensive character." The TRA does not mandate arms sales, but it also does not empower the president to cease providing defensive arms to Taiwan, as implied in the Third Communiqué. Noting this discrepancy, Congress immediately summoned administration officials to Capitol Hill for another set of hearings in August and September 1982. Underscoring the constitutional nature of the inquiry, the hearings included two sessions before the Senate Judiciary Committee's Subcommittee on Separation of Powers. In his opening statement, Senator John P. East said that the newly issued communiqué raised "a serious problem of separation of power" and that the TRA and the newly issued communiqué "appear to be in conflict, very serious conflict."[55] On August 17, the day the Third Communiqué was issued, John H. Holdridge, the Department of State's Assistant Secretary for the Bureau of East Asian and Pacific Affairs, appeared before the Senate Foreign Relations Committee to defend the administration. In opening the Foreign Affairs hearing, Senator Church was firm that the executive's new "policy statement cannot change a public law." He affirmed that lawmakers "must assure that Taiwan's legitimate defense needs are met as the Taiwan Relations Act requires of us."[56]

Holdridge insisted that the communiqué was consistent with the requirements of the TRA because, as he emphasized, the TRA required that Taiwan receive sufficient weapons to meet its self-defense needs. Provided that the PRC maintained a peaceful posture toward Taiwan, it followed that those needs would be minimized, requiring fewer arms sales. As the PRC had stated that its fundamental policy was to achieve a peaceful outcome to the Taiwan question, the administration saw it fit to respond in kind. Holdridge underlined that the word *fundamental* should be read with emphasis, as the word implied a long-term view on the part of the PRC. If, however, the PRC were to act belligerently, the expectations of the communiqué would be invalidated. He noted that the United States had refused to end arms sales to Taiwan in 1978, despite the PRC's insistence, but that normalization had proceeded anyway. At that time, the Chinese reserved the right to raise the issue again, which they had done with President Reagan. Holdridge warned that failing to address the PRC's concerns regarding continuing arms sales would have led to a deterioration in the relationship. In the administration's view, the Third Communiqué represented an application of the principles embodied in the TRA to the facts on the ground in 1982. For this reason, Holdridge argued, the communiqué did not challenge the TRA's primacy as a basis for U.S. policy toward Taiwan.

Importantly, Holdridge clarified that from the administration's perspective, the Third Communiqué was "not a treaty or an agreement but a statement of future U.S. policy."[57] As detailed later in this chapter, a document's format, and its signatories' intentions, are critical factors in determining whether a country has adopted an enforceable commitment under both domestic and international law.

A. TREATY MAKING UNDER THE U.S. CONSTITUTION

U.S. law provides three modalities for making international agreements: treaties, congressional-executive agreements, and sole executive agreements. Each mode is binding under international law. Of the three, the treaty-making power, which is entrusted to the executive branch, is the only method of concluding international agreements expressly recognized under the Constitution. The subject of a treaty may properly include any aspect of that sovereign power, subject only to constitutional limitations. As the sole representative of the United States in foreign affairs, the president appoints and supervises the officials who negotiate agreements with other countries. Any treaty thereby concluded, may be submitted by the president to the Senate. If the Senate approves the treaty by a two-thirds vote, the president then ratifies it, and the treaty becomes binding on the United States.

Concluding treaties through the Article II process has several constitutional consequences. The Constitution expressly provides that treaties concluded in this manner are the supreme law of the land, binding not only on the federal government but on the states as well. Additionally, the judicial branch of the federal government has the express power to review cases and controversies that arise under treaties so concluded, and Congress can implement and enforce treaty obligations through the passage of "necessary and proper" domestic legislation. The Supreme Court has held that treaties and federal legislation may have equal constitutional status—they are, with certain restrictions, both the supreme law of the land. As such, a valid legislative act by Congress can also modify, amend, or terminate a treaty, even though every effort is generally made to reconcile inconsistencies between congressional legislation and existing treaties.

Although the Constitution provides the method by which treaties are established, it is silent as to which branch of government has the power to terminate treaties and international agreements. This silence formed the centerpiece of Senator Goldwater's challenge to the termination of the Mutual Defense Treaty with the ROC in the case *Goldwater v. Carter*. On December 22, 1978, Senator Goldwater, supported by several other members of Congress, filed suit in the U.S. District Court of Columbia seeking declarative and injunctive relief to bar the termination of the U.S.-ROC Mutual Defense Treaty of 1954.[58] The plaintiffs contended that President Carter's unilateral act of terminating the defense treaty violated their constitutional right to be consulted and to vote on the treaty's termination. The federal district court ruled in favor of the plaintiffs, finding that the president had exceeded his authority because "treaty termination generally is a shared power, which cannot be exercised by the President acting alone."[59] However, the U.S. Court of Appeals for the District of Columbia reversed and held that "the President did not exceed his authority when he took action to withdraw from the treaty, without the consent of the Senate or other legislative concurrences."[60] (Interestingly, Senator Goldwater said that he would have voted to accept the proposed termination of the treaty had President Carter formally presented it before Congress.)[61] After the Court of Appeals decision, Senator Goldwater filed a petition for certiorari with the Supreme Court, which the Court granted on December 13, 1979.

As Goldwater observed, from time to time, the Senate Foreign Relations Committee has taken the position that the termination of treaties required joint action by the president and the Senate or Congress.[62] Yet, the legal question of whether the president can unilaterally terminate a treaty has never been authoritatively settled. Actual instances involving treaty termination have varied considerably. For instance, treaties have been terminated by the president in accordance with their terms pursuant to congressional action; terminated by the president pursuant to Senate resolutions; and terminated by the president with or without notification to, and approval by, both houses of Congress.[63] The courts, in exercising judicial review, could in theory, settle the issue by defining one or more constitutional mechanisms for treaty termination. However, the Supreme Court, without opinion, ordered the lower court to dismiss the case. Four Justices concurred, finding that the issue of whether the president could terminate a treaty without congressional approval was a nonjusticiable political question because it involved the president's authority in the conduct of foreign affairs and the extent to which Congress could check presidential action. Justice Brennan accepted the political doctrine argument but rejected the majority's interpretation of the political doctrine, declining to review the decision to terminate the treaty because it turned on the president's sole power to recognize foreign governments. Only Justice Powell rejected the political question premise entirely. He concurred in the judgment because he believed the question was not ripe, as Congress had not adopted legislation contrary to the president's decision. Nonetheless, he suggested that if Congress had adopted a conflicting law, the Court could have settled the conflict by exercising its power to interpret the Constitution.[64] To date no such action has taken place, and there have been no other major Supreme Court rulings on treaty termination.

B. THE TRA AND THE THREE COMMUNIQUÉS

Not all international agreements are concluded under the Article II process. These other types are generally referred to as *executive agreements* and are concluded by the executive branch without Senate confirmation. Executive agreements are binding under the U.S. Constitution, but have a lower legal status than treaties. They can be further distinguished from political statements or other proclamations made by the president which are nonbinding under domestic law. It is likely that the executive branch viewed the three communiqués as less than executive agreements at the time of their adoption. For example, pursuant to the Case-Zablocki Act of 1973, the Department of State is required to transmit executive agreements to Congress to permit the Senate to distinguish between agreements that fall under an existing treaty or statute.[65] Since none of the three joint communiqués were ever officially reported to Congress, including the two adopted after 1973, the executive must have viewed them as falling short of executive agreements.[66] Furthermore, according to a study prepared by the Congressional Research Service (CRS) for the Senate Committee on Foreign Relations, "joint statements of intent are not binding agreements unless . . . the parties intend to be legally bound," with "substance and not the title [being] dispositive."[67] In other words, joint communiqués are, by default, nonbinding statements, absent evidence to the contrary. The question, then, is: Did the United States and China intend to be bound under international law by their joint communiqués in 1972, 1978, and 1982?

The CRS report summarizes the features of a binding international agreement as: evidencing an intention by the parties for the instrument to be legally binding under international law; dealing with significant matters; clearly and specifically describing the legal obligations of the parties; and possessing a form indicating an intention to conclude a treaty—although the substance of the instrument rather than the form is the governing factor.[68] The agreement in question must meet all four requirements in order for it to be binding on the parties.

There is a two-step analysis for inferring the first element, that the United States and China intended the communiqués to be binding. First, a determination must be made based on facts and circumstances that the parties intended to enter into a binding agreement of a legal nature. Second, the agreement must be subject to international law.[69] The following paragraphs will consider these requirements as they apply to the three communiqués.

The Shanghai Communiqué of 1972 was the first of the three joint statements adopted by the United States and China concerning the normalization of relations. Applying the foregoing concepts, it does not appear that the countries intended the Shanghai Communiqué to be legally binding. First, there was no express provision included in the communiqué that would clearly indicate the parties' intention to be bound. Second, the communiqué revealed that the leaders of both countries were taking the opportunity to review "the international situation in which important changes and great upheavals are taking place and expounded their respective positions and attitudes" in the joint statement.[70] This strongly suggests the Shanghai Communiqué was merely a provisional exercise, permitting both parties to "present candidly to one another their views on a variety of issues."[71] The format adopted in the communiqué, by which each side would state their positions separately and agree only to general principles, supports this interpretation.

Similarly, the Second Communiqué does not contain express language stating that it will be binding on the parties involved. Thus, intent, if any, must be inferred from its words and phrases. The United States and China agreed to establish diplomatic relations as of January 1, 1979, and agreed to recognize the PRC as the legal government of China. This seems to suggest an intent to be bound. However, foreign affairs decisions concerning diplomacy and recognition of a government are often subject to change—as the seasoned negotiators would have been aware—thus it is unlikely that both parties intended the language to bind them irrevocably and indefinitely. Additionally, the language found in the Second Communiqué is largely inconsistent with that which typically connotes an obligation. Sentences such as "both wish to reduce" and "both believe" are discretionary and simply do not demand future performance. Accordingly, the communiqué, at best, reflects a desire on the part of the United States and China to establish diplomatic relations, but is not legally binding to the extent that either can rely on it with certainty.

The Third Communiqué, like its predecessors, lacked language that would expressly indicate the parties wanted to strike a legally binding deal. The communiqué reaffirmed the principles agreed to by both sides in the Shanghai Communiqué and the Second Communiqué, addressed the issue of U.S. arms sales to Taiwan, and repeated the formula by which the two sides stated their individual positions. However, absent evidence of an intention to be bound, those statements would be confined to the political and moral realms, without legal effect. Hence, on its face, the Third Communiqué does not amount to a legally binding agreement. This interpretation was buttressed by Holdridge's testimony to Congress following its adoption, which emphasized the discretionary nature of U.S. arms sales. It was further strengthened by the revelations of Reagan's Six Assurances and his secret memorandum, which will be discussed in Chapter 6.

The second prong of the four-part analysis requires that the agreement itself must deal with significant matters. The Shanghai Communiqué memorialized President Nixon's visit to China and leaders' plans to normalize relations. Additionally, the United States and China stated positions on other concrete issues such as Taiwan,

Korea, and maintaining peace and security in Asia. The Second Communiqué marked the establishment of official diplomatic relations between the United States and China, while the Third Communiqué addressed U.S. arms sales to Taiwan. General statements regarding diplomacy, though not quantifiable, are certainly significant and cannot be considered trivial. Accordingly, the Shanghai Communiqué, the Second Communiqué, and the Third Communiqué collectively, and individually, deal with significant matters.

The third prong of the analysis demands evidence that the agreement clearly lay out the obligations of the signatories so that a neutral observer can infer that the parties intended to be bound by their terms.[72] In other words, diplomatic statements that are not specific as to the parties' legal obligations are not legally binding.[73] Excluding provisions summarizing Nixon's visit to China and those concerning general policy statements on international affairs, the Shanghai Communiqué did not discuss legal obligations precisely and with specificity. Only two provisions in the Shanghai Communiqué addressed Taiwan, with one stating the Chinese position and the other that of the United States. With such a cursory treatment, the parties could not have "assented" to one another's positions. Had they done so, a single provision would have been drafted to encapsulate their collective understanding. Furthermore, the two-provision approach only highlighted the differences between the U.S. and Chinese positions. Since the terms had not been properly agreed to, the provisions in question could only be considered policy statements, each unique to its side, and not legally binding obligations on either.

In the Second Communiqué, there is a single provision addressing U.S.-Taiwan relations, which states that the United States "acknowledges the Chinese position that there is but one China and Taiwan is part of China."[74] This appeared to be a precise description of an international diplomatic undertaking. That is, that the United States would hold to a certain view on Taiwan. However, it did not amount to a legal obligation for two reasons: First, the provision failed to mandate adherence to the position, through the use of an operative term such as "shall." Second, there is no indication that the United States desired (or would ever desire) to bind itself to a diplomatic position indefinitely, as changes in political landscape and surrounding circumstances may require reevaluation in the future. This certainly would have been the case in the dynamic international environment of the Cold War era.

The Third Communiqué was largely an attempt to ease tensions between the United States and China over U.S. arms sales to Taiwan. In the communiqué, the United States and China provided their respective views on Taiwan. Then, the United States declared that it did not seek to carry out a long-term policy of arms sales to Taiwan. The provision addressed the anticipated duration of arms sales and the quality and quantity of such sales. The phrase "does not seek," however, would imply that the commitment was merely discretionary—to create an obligation would require stronger language, for example, something along the lines of "*shall not* carry out a long-term policy of arm sales to Taiwan." Accordingly, the language concerning the length of such sales could not be binding under international law. With respect to the quality and quantity of sales, the provision states that the United States would not exceed the level of arms sales to Taiwan attained since 1979. The stronger term *will* implies that the parties likely intended to create a strong expectation. The ending of the provision, wherein the United States indicated it would gradually reduce arms sales to Taiwan, reinforced the previous part, in which the United States agreed that it did not seek to carry out a long-term Taiwan arms sales policy. Viewing this provision in its entirety, only the part concerning quality and quantity could reasonably be construed as a binding obligation. However, Reagan's Six Assurances to Taiwan and his secret memorandum undermine this conclusion. Nevertheless, this argument is ultimately moot because only one party to the agreement assented to the provision. That is to say, it only presented the United States' perspective, not China's. As the next provision stated, "the two Governments will make every effort to adopt measures and create conditions conducive to the thorough settlement of this issue,"[75] which signified future collaborations would be necessary to define a course of action.

The fourth prong of the analysis requires that the form of the documents must signify that the parties intended to reach an agreement.[76] Indicia of this intention would include, for example, a title incorporating the word *agreement*, the inclusion of "final clauses, signature blocks, entry into force dates, and dispute settlement provisions," and having the negotiations done by diplomats.[77] While all three communiqués were adopted after extensive negotiations by experienced diplomats from both sides, the documents are widely referred to not as treaties but as joint statements. As noted above, the communiqués did not represent a shared agreement between the United States and China. Rather, they speak to the differing, but sometimes overlapping, perspectives held by the two sides on the same issues and their willingness to engage in further diplomatic relations notwithstanding certain disagreements. The communiqués make no provision for dispute resolution and refer to no other body of law, as might be expected of a formal treaty. The issue therefore shifts to whether the parties intended to be bound, irrespective of the form of the agreement. As the foregoing analysis has suggested, the communiqués' provisions lacked intention and specificity. Consequently, the form and general content of all three documents would tend toward the conclusion that they were not intended as legally binding international agreements.

Even if the joint communiqués were mere political obligations, lacking legally binding effects, the parties may still expect the commitments implied by the documents to be honored. In point of fact, neither the United States nor the PRC has extricated itself from the political undertakings embodied in the communiqués.[78] However, that is not sufficient to make the documents legal in nature. A country's fidelity to its political commitments is (more often than not) desirable. And in cases where a country chooses not to follow through with its political commitments, it should anticipate a negative response, likely designed to discourage future defections, even in the absence of a legally binding agreement.[79]

As for the communiqués status under U.S. law, even if the joint communiqués were construed as executive agreements, their legal authority would likely be limited. An executive agreement is an agreement between the United States and another country signed by the heads of both states.[80] An executive agreement carries with it an authority that supersedes conflicting state laws and policies but not federal legislations.[81] Generally, executive agreements fall into one of two categories: congressional-executive agreements and sole executive agreements.[82] Congressional-executive agreements may be concluded by the president prior to submission to Congress, or adopted by the president subject to congressional legislation requiring or authorizing the president to conclude an agreement.[83] Because they have congressional approval, agreements of these types may carry the same force as treaties.[84] Alternatively, sole executive agreements, also known as presidential agreements, rely solely on the president's foreign affairs powers and do not require congressional approval.[85]

Even if, for the sake of argument, the joint communiqués were considered executive agreements, well-established constitutional principles require the TRA to supersede them. The president has broad plenary authority concerning foreign affairs.[86] Thus, it is within the president's authority to issue joint communiqués pursuant to the executive's enumerated powers. But an action taken solely by the president would not preempt an existing federal law or be granted greater authority than a congressional-executive agreement or treaty. As many commentators have observed, such power would risk creating an "imperial president," with the authority to issue sole executive agreements without limitations. Congress would be powerless to keep the president in check under such circumstances. Thankfully, our constitutional system, with its balancing of powers, does not permit such an outcome. In 2015, the Supreme Court reaffirmed this principle in *Zivotofsky v. Kerry*, a case concerning the president's authority over foreign affairs. Justice Kennedy, writing for the majority, observed that "[t]he Executive is not free from the ordinary controls and checks of Congress merely because foreign affairs are at issue."[87] While the Court decided in favor of the Department of State in the case, holding that the president has certain broad authority in foreign affairs that cannot be contravened by a congressional act, it is clear that there are limits to the president's power that must always be borne in mind.

C. CONCLUSION: THE TRA IS THE LAW OF THE LAND

In the TRA, Congress declared that maintaining peace and stability in the Asia Pacific is in the national interest of the United States and is a matter of international concern. In the Third Communiqué, the United States reiterated that it had "no intention of infringing on Chinese sovereignty and territorial integrity, or interfering in China's internal affairs, or pursuing a policy of 'two Chinas' or 'one China, one Taiwan.'"[88] Though the two provisions appear to conflict—the TRA provided that affairs in the region were matters of U.S. and international interest, while the communiqué implied that Taiwan was a domestic Chinese issue—the provisions can be read consistently. The communiqués implied that the United States preferred that Taiwan and China sort out their territorial disputes through cross-strait dialogue over time. Hence, in Reagan's Six Assurances to Taiwan, which were sent to the ROC government at the same time as the Third Communiqué (see Chapter 6), the president insisted that the United States would not "play any mediation role between Taipei and Beijing," that it had not "altered its position regarding sovereignty over Taiwan," and that it would not "exert pressure on Taiwan to negotiate with the PRC."[89] However, if the Taiwan dispute escalated to a point where it compromised regional peace and stability, it would be incumbent upon the United States to intervene.

With respect to arms sales, Section 2 of the TRA requires the United States to make available to Taiwan defensive articles in a quantity necessary to maintain sufficient self-defense capabilities. The Third Communiqué seemed to undermine the TRA's provisions by stating that the United States did not seek to carry out a long-term policy of arms sales to Taiwan. However, Reagan's Six Assurances stated that the United States would not set an end date for arms sales to Taiwan. Additionally, the Six Assurances clarified that the United States would not hold prior consultations with the PRC on arms sales. Furthermore, Reagan's secret memorandum explained that the volume of U.S. arms sales to Taiwan was contingent on the continuation of peaceful cross-strait relations.

Congress enacted the TRA in 1979 to fill the gap left by the termination of the U.S.-ROC Mutual Defense Treaty of 1954 and the termination of diplomatic relations between the United States and the ROC. Some commenters have erroneously described the TRA and the three communiqués as coequal sources of authority governing U.S. policy toward Taiwan. In fact, under the Constitution, the TRA is superior to the communiqués. Communiqués are policy statements which are neither treaties nor executive agreements and lack the assent of Congress.[90] Should the president's actions concerning Taiwan ever come into conflict with the TRA, the TRA—as the law of the land—should prevail.

Notes

1. Jimmy Carter, Address to the Nation on Diplomatic Relations Between the United States and the People's Republic of China, Dec. 15, 1978, *available at* http://www.presidency.ucsb.edu/ws/?pid=30308.

2. Joint Communiqué of the United States of America and the People's Republic of China, Jan. 1, 1979, *available at* http://www.taiwandocuments.org/communique02.htm.

3. Carter, *supra* note 1.

4. *The China Decision*, ABC News, Dec. 15, 1978, *available at* http://abcnews.go.com/Archives/video/dec-15-1978-china-decision-12365666.

5. Jimmy Carter, Diplomatic Relations Between the United States and the People's Republic of China United States Statement, Dec. 15, 1978, *available at* http://www.presidency.ucsb.edu/ws/index.php?pid=30309&st=China&st1=.

6. People's Republic of China Statement Accompanying the Joint Communiqué on the Establishment of Diplomatic Relations between the United States and the PRC, Dec. 15, 1978, *in* Selected Documents, 5 Md. J. Int'l L. 109 (1979), *available at* http://digitalcommons.law.umaryland.edu/mjil/vol5/iss1/17.

7. Mutual Defense Treaty between the United States of America and the Republic of China, 6 U.S.T. 433; T.I.A.S. No. 3178.

8. Jimmy Carter, Diplomatic Relations Between the United States and the People's Republic of China Remarks at a White House Briefing Following the Address to the Nation, Dec. 15, 1978, *available at* http://www.presidency.ucsb.edu/ws/index.php?pid=30310.

9. *See* Association for Diplomatic Studies and Training, Foreign Affairs Oral History Project, Interview with Neal Donnelly, Dec. 11, 2001, *available at* http://lcweb2.loc.gov/service/mss/mfdip/2007%20txt%20files/2007don01.txt.

10. International Security Assistance Act of 1978, Public Law 95-384, § 26, Sept. 26, 1978.

11. *Taiwan: Hearings before the Committee on Foreign Relations,* United States Senate, 96th Cong. 245, 417 (1979), *available at* http://babel.hathitrust.org/cgi/pt?id=umn.31951d00817104i [hereinafter Taiwan Hearings].

12. Richard Nixon, Joint Statement Following Discussions with Leaders of the People's Republic of China, Feb. 27, 1972, *available at* http://www.presidency.ucsb.edu/ws/?pid=3754.

13. *See, e.g.,* Robert Sutter, *The Taiwan Relations Act and the United States' China Policy, in* A Unique Relationship: The United States and the Republic of China under the Taiwan Relations Act 49–78, 63–64 (Ramon H. Myers ed., 1989).

14. *Id.* at 62.

15. *Id.* at 50.

16. Hungdah Chiu, *The Taiwan Relations Act and Sino-American Relations*, Occasional Papers/Reprints Series in Contemporary Asian Studies, No. 5, U. Md. Sch. L. at 5–6 (1990), *available at* http://digitalcommons.law.umaryland.edu/cgi/viewcontent.cgi?article=1099&context=mscas.

17. *Id.* at 7–8.

18. *Id.* at 9.

19. Prior to the adoption of the pinyin system of romanization in 1979, Deng Xiaoping's name was rendered as Teng Hsiao-ping, as seen in the text of the Second Communiqué.

20. Chiu, *supra* note 16, at 10.

21. Taiwan Hearings, *supra* note 11.

22. Jimmy Carter, United States Relations with the People on Taiwan Memorandum from the President, Dec. 30, 1978, *available at* http://www.presidency.ucsb.edu/ws/index.php?pid=30347.

23. *See* Chiu, *supra* note 16.

24. Wolff, Lester, *Crafting the Taiwan Relations Act*, ROLL CALL, Apr. 1, 2014, *available at* http://www.rollcall.com/news/crafting_the_taiwan_relations_act_commentary-231851-1.html.

25. Chiu, *supra* note 16, at 2–3.

26. *Id.* at 3.

27. *Id.* at 14.

28. Sutter, *supra* note 13, at 57.

29. Taiwan Hearings, *supra* note 11, at 11.

30. *Id.* at 1.

31. *Id.* at 2.

32. *Id.* at 11.

33. *Id.* at 125.

34. *Id.* at 618.

35. *Id.* at 439.

36. *Id.* at 509.

37. *Id.* at 16.

38. *Id.* at 24.

39. *Id.* at 127.

40. *Id.* at 292.

41. *Id.* at 292–93.

42. *Id.* at 293.

43. *Id.* at 295.

44. *Id.* at 307.

45. *Id.*

46. *Id.* at 90.

47. *Id.* at 410.

48. *Id.* at 11.

49. *Id.* at 127.

50. *Id.* at 145.

51. *Id.* at 149.

52. Chiu, *supra* note 16, at 21.

53. Sutter, *supra* note 13, at 76.

54. Joint Communiqué of the United States of America and the People's Republic of China, Aug. 17, 1982, *available at* http://www.taiwandocuments.org/communique03.htm.

55. Senate Committee on the Judiciary, Subcommittee on Separation of Powers, Taiwan Communiqué and Separation of Powers, 97th Cong. 7 (Sept. 17, 1982), *available at* http://babel.hathitrust.org/cgi/pt?id=pur1.32754077533457;view=1up;seq=1.

56. Senate Committee on Foreign Relations, U.S. Policy Toward China and Taiwan, 97th Cong. 5 (Aug. 17, 1982), *available at* http://babel.hathitrust.org/cgi/pt?id=pur1.32754074681622;view=1up;seq=1.

57. *Id.* at 13.

58. For a study on the practice of treaty termination under international law, *see* Myres S. McDougal & W. Michael Reisman, *Who Can Terminate Mutual Defense Treaties?*, 1 NAT'L L.J. 36 (May 21, 1979) and 1 NAT'L L.J. 37 (May 28, 1979).

59. Goldwater v. Carter, 481 F. Supp. 949, 965 (D.D.C. 1979).

60. Goldwater v. Carter, 617 F. 2d 697, 709 (D.C. Cir. 1979).

61. Jacob K. Javits, *Congress and Foreign Relations: The Taiwan Relations Act*, 60 FOREIGN AFF. 55 (1981).

62. CONGRESSIONAL RESEARCH SERVICE, TREATIES AND OTHER INTERNATIONAL AGREEMENTS: THE ROLE OF THE UNITED STATES SENATE, A STUDY PREPARED FOR THE COMMITTEE ON FOREIGN RELATIONS UNITED STATES SENATE 198 (2001) [hereinafter SENATE REPORT ON TREATIES].

63. *Id.* at 201–11.

64. *See* Goldwater v. Carter, 444 U.S. 996 (U.S. 1979).

65. SENATE REPORT ON TREATIES, *supra* note 62, at 23.

66. SUSAN V. LAWRENCE & THOMAS LUM, CONGRESSIONAL RESEARCH SERVICE, U.S.-CHINA RELATIONS: POLICY ISSUES 4 (2011), *available at* http://assets.opencrs.com/rpts/R41108_20110112.pdf.

67. SENATE REPORT ON TREATIES, *supra* note 62, at 60 ("Thus, whether or not a joint statement is titled a 'joint statement' or 'joint communiqué' or 'declaration' has no effect on whatever legal standing it may hold independent of its title.").

68. *Id.* at 3–4, 50–53.

69. *Id.* at 50.

70. United States of America-People's Republic of China Joint Communiqué of Feb. 27, 1972, *available at* http://www.taiwandocuments.org/communique01.htm.

71. *Id.*

72. SENATE REPORT ON TREATIES, *supra* note 62, at 52.

73. *Id.*

74. Joint Communiqué of the United States of America and the People's Republic of China, Jan. 1, 1979, *available at* http://www.taiwandocuments.org/communique02.htm.

75. Joint Communiqué of the United States of America and the People's Republic of China, Aug. 17, 1982, *available at* http://www.taiwandocuments.org/communique03.htm.

76. SENATE REPORT ON TREATIES, *supra* note 62, at 52.

77. *Id.*

78. *Id.* at 59.

79. *Id.*

80. *See* ERWIN CHEMERINSKY, CONSTITUTIONAL LAW: PRINCIPLES AND POLICIES 3D ED. 368 (2006).

81. *Id.* at 368–71.

82. Lung-Chu Chen, *Constitutional Law and International Law in the United States of America*, 42 AM. J. COMP. L. Supp. 453, 476 (1994).

83. *Id.* (The three U.S.-Sino joint communiqués are not congressional-executive agreements because they never obtained ratification by both houses of Congress.)

84. *Id.* at 477.

85. *Id.* at 485.

86. *See* RICHARD F. GRIMMETT, CONGRESSIONAL RESEARCH SERVICE, FOREIGN POLICY ROLES OF THE PRESIDENT AND CONGRESS (1999), *available at* http://fpc.state.gov/6172.htm.

87. Zivotofsky v. Kerry, 76 U. S. ___, at 18 (2015).

88. Joint Communiqué of the United States of America and the People's Republic of China, Aug. 17, 1982, *available at* http://www.taiwandocuments.org/communique03.htm.

89. SHIRLEY A. KAN, CHINA/TAIWAN: EVOLUTION OF THE "ONE CHINA POLICY"—KEY STATEMENTS FROM WASHINGTON, BEIJING, AND TAIPEI, CONGRESSIONAL RESEARCH SERVICE, at 44 (2014), *available at* http://www.fas.org/sgp/crs/row/RL30341.pdf.

90. SENATE REPORT ON TREATIES, *supra* note 62, at 4. ("Non-binding agreements may take many forms, including unilateral commitments and declarations of intent, joint communiqués and joint statements (including final acts of conferences), and informal agreements." *Id.* at 59.)

III Trends in Development and Conditioning Factors

6   U.S.-Taiwan Relations

THE U.S.-TAIWAN RELATIONSHIP has endured through tremendous changes over the course of the last century. During the period of Japanese occupation, American interests in Taiwan were limited. However, at the end of World War II, when the Nationalist Chinese forces took control of the island on behalf of the Allied Powers, Taiwan became a major concern. U.S. soldiers and diplomats quickly established a presence on Taiwan, working closely with the Republic of China (ROC) regime to secure the territory and ensure a stable transfer from the retreating Japanese. Chiang Kai-shek's decision to move his government to the island following the Kuomintang (KMT) defeat in the Chinese civil war, combined with the onset of the Korean War, ensured that Taiwan would remain a focal point of U.S. policy in the Pacific. After President Carter's decision in 1978 to normalize relations with the People's Republic of China (PRC), the United States adopted informal relations with the people of Taiwan under the Taiwan Relations Act (TRA) and established the American Institute in Taiwan (AIT) to fulfill some of the functions performed by the former U.S. embassy. Throughout the 1980s and 1990s, the United States supported Taiwan through its dramatic democratic transformation. Taiwan remains one of the United States' major strategic and trading partners in the Asia Pacific. Today, the two countries share a deep affinity built on the shared values of democracy, freedom, and human rights.

I. U.S.-Taiwan Relations before the Taiwan Relations Act

A. U.S.-TAIWAN RELATIONS IN THE 1940S AND 1950S

The United States' involvement in Taiwan emerged from the disorder of post–World War II Asia. In 1942, the ROC government—still in power on the Chinese mainland—made a unilateral declaration that it would annex Taiwan and the Pescadores, which it regarded as lost territories unjustly taken by the Japanese under the Treaty of Shimonoseki in 1895. As late as 1943, President Franklin Delano Roosevelt contemplated this outcome and agreed to its inclusion in the Cairo Declaration, which stipulated that the territories taken by Japan should be restored to the ROC. However, immediately following the war, Taiwan remained a Japanese colony under the terms of the Treaty of Shimonoseki. The United States took possession of the island in its capacity as chief occupying power in the Pacific and delegated responsibility for its administration to the ROC. Recognizing the island's strategic importance, U.S. leaders saw it paramount that Taiwan be denied to any hostile powers. Between 1941 and 1942, officials in the War, Navy, and State Departments were engaged in a "battle of memoranda" over the future of Taiwan. Officials were divided over the island's legal status and the role the United States should play in resolving the question. Some wished to limit U.S. involvement as much as possible, hoping to avoid an entanglement in the intensifying civil war between the KMT and the Chinese Communist Party (CCP). Others saw Taiwan as a strategic asset and an important foothold in the Pacific.

The outbreak of the Korean War settled the matter. During the height of the Chinese civil war, President Truman and Secretary of State Dean Acheson maintained that "the United States considered Taiwan a part of China and that there would be no support for the ROC government or intervention."[1] Their apparent rationale was that the territorial dispute began on the Chinese mainland and thus was an internal affair to be resolved by the Chinese themselves. This policy of nonintervention quickly gave way to strategic realities when hostilities erupted on the Korean Peninsula in June 1950. Truman dispatched the Seventh Fleet to neutralize the Taiwan Strait until such time that peace and stability could be restored in the Pacific.

After taking office in 1953, President Dwight Eisenhower moved to "unleash" Chiang Kai-shek and ordered the United States Seventh Fleet to cease neutralizing the Taiwan Strait. In early February, Eisenhower appointed Karl Rankin as ambassador to the ROC. Eisenhower's approach to Taiwan contrasted with Truman's policy of maintaining a "diplomatic distance from the Nationalist government."[2] Instead, the administration utilized tensions in the Taiwan Strait—fueled in part by the KMT's desire to retake the Chinese mainland—to place further pressure on the PRC, which was simultaneously engaged in hostilities in Korea. International tensions surrounding Taiwan continued to grow during the Cold War. Until the Sino-Soviet split, the Soviet Union was generally supportive of the PRC's strategic interests. Soviet Party leader Nikita Khrushchev supported the PRC's position on Taiwan and warned President Eisenhower that a U.S attack on China would be seen as an attack on the Soviet Union. U.S. officials were cautious to avoid emboldening Chiang Kai-shek in fear of triggering a wider conflict. Quemoy and Matsu were initially omitted from U.S. defense commitments toward Taiwan because war planners feared a battle for the islands could ignite a large-scale war, even a nuclear conflict.

The First Taiwan Strait Crisis occurred in September 1954 when the Chinese Communists launched artillery attacks on the strategically important islands of Quemoy and Matsu, which lie close to China's Fujian coast. The ROC had fortified the islands with more than 70,000 troops prior to the attack. The crisis spurred the United States and the ROC to sign a mutual defense treaty in December 1954, whereby the United States committed to defending Taiwan (Formosa) and the Pescadores (Penghu) and "such other territories as may be determined by mutual agreement." On January 29, 1955, prior to ratifying the treaty, Congress enacted the Formosa Resolution, further authorizing President Eisenhower to "employ the armed forces of the United States" to protect Taiwan and "related positions and territories" in case of attack by the PRC. By 1955, President Eisenhower and Secretary of State John Foster Dulles were searching for ways to resolve tensions in the Taiwan Strait. The United States began "pursuing a general, bilateral agreement with the PRC that would commit each side not to use force" to resolve political issues, including issues surrounding the Taiwan question.[3] These efforts were ultimately unsuccessful, but the United States did secure a semirenunciation from Chiang and the ROC in the process. The ROC agreed to "stress political means as it pursued the goal of mainland recovery."[4]

Fighting between the PRC and the ROC continued throughout the 1950s. A second offshore crisis occurred in 1958 when the PRC launched fresh attacks on Quemoy and Matsu in an effort to retake them. This prompted the United States to extend its defensive commitment to the two islands. The United States placed howitzer guns on Quemoy which were capable of shelling the Chinese mainland and provided the ROC military with Sidewinder air-to-air missiles for the first time. PRC leaders were reportedly shocked at the United States' resolve and gave up their attempts to retake the islands.[5] Following the Second Taiwan Strait Crisis, China adopted a policy of shelling Quemoy on odd days of the month. The ROC returned the favor on even days. The ceremonial exchange of fire on every other day of the month symbolized the continued existence of the civil war between the Communist and Nationalist regimes. At the same time, the continuing ROC occupation of

Quemoy and Matsu supported its claim to occupy the whole of China. The Chinese artillery bombardment of Quemoy and Matsu in 1958 became a hotly debated topic in the 1960 American presidential election between John F. Kennedy and Richard Nixon. During the presidential debates, Kennedy was asked if the line of defense in the Far East should include Quemoy and Matsu. He responded that the United States' commitment should not extend beyond Taiwan. Nixon countered, criticizing Kennedy for his unwillingness to defend Quemoy and Matsu and arguing that no territory should be surrendered to the Chinese Communists.

B. U.S.-TAIWAN RELATIONS IN THE 1960S AND 1970S

During the 1960s, the Kennedy and Johnson administrations put focus on the Taiwan question within the context of the United Nations. Both administrations regarded China and Taiwan as effectively two separate states and sought a way to accommodate both the ROC and the PRC in the United Nations. Chiang Kai-shek strenuously opposed any such proposals, famously insisting on *hanzei buliangli*—there was no room for patriots and traitors to live together. The issue remained unresolved until the passage of General Assembly Resolution 2758 in 1971. As described in Chapter 1, during the late 1960s, members of the Nixon administration and PRC leaders began laying the groundwork for negotiations over normalizing relations. In the wake of the Sino-Soviet split, President Nixon sought to isolate the USSR through closer relations with the PRC. The administration modified its long-held position that Taiwan's legal status remained undetermined. Instead, it advocated for a peaceful settlement of the Taiwan question by the Chinese themselves. In 1971, Henry Kissinger, the presidential assistant for National Security Affairs, made a secret trip to China as the administration took steps to end its policy of isolation against the PRC.

On July 15, 1971, the Chinese and American governments issued simultaneous announcements that Nixon would visit China. On February 27, 1972, Nixon's week-long visit to China culminated in the signing of the Shanghai Communiqué. For the first time the United States proclaimed:

All Chinese on either side of the Taiwan Strait maintain there is but one China and that Taiwan is a part of China. The United States Government does not challenge that position. It affirms its interest in a peaceful settlement of the Taiwan question by the Chinese themselves.[6]

Meanwhile in the United Nations, the PRC was assembling a bloc of friendly nations to support its bid to replace the ROC as China's representative in the United

Nations. Before the vote, the United States had led an unsuccessful effort to preserve the ROC's seat in the General Assembly and to allow both the ROC and the PRC to be UN members. On October 25, 1971, the General Assembly adopted Resolution 2758, acting to:

> . . . restore all its rights to the People's Republic of China and to recognize the representatives of its Government as the only lawful representatives of China to the United Nations and to expel forthwith the representatives of Chiang Kai-shek from the place which they unlawfully occupy at the United Nations and in all the organizations related to it.[7]

Relations between the United States and Taiwan deteriorated throughout the remainder of the decade. When Jimmy Carter became president in 1977, he was determined to finish the task Nixon had started. This meant establishing diplomatic relations with Beijing and terminating official ties with Taipei. Carter was also committed to withdrawing U.S. military personnel from Taiwan. The White House kept the ROC government in the dark during the final stages of negotiations with the PRC, fearing that the ROC, and its friends in Congress, would disrupt the normalization process. In December 1978, Carter announced that the United States would end diplomatic relations with the ROC and normalize its relationship with the PRC.

II. Application of the TRA Since 1979

As described in Chapter 5, while U.S. officials generally agreed on the need to establish diplomatic relations with the PRC, Carter's approach to the issue angered many in Congress. Congress had called hearings on the issue of normalization as early as 1977, and many lawmakers felt that Congress should have played a larger role in negotiations with the PRC. Furthermore, lawmakers feared the "package of legislation [submitted by] the White House to govern future unofficial relations with Taiwan . . . did not go far enough in protecting either Taiwan or U.S. interests."[8] On January 29, 1979, twenty-eight days after the U.S. terminated diplomatic relations with Taiwan, Senator Frank Church introduced Senate Bill S.245, titled the Taiwan Enabling Act. On the same day, Representative Clement Zablocki introduced H.R. 1614, a companion bill to S.245, in the House of Representatives. The Act provided a basic legal framework for the United States to maintain commercial, cultural, and other ties with the people of Taiwan on an unofficial basis. The bill, renamed the Taiwan Relations Act (TRA), received overwhelming bipartisan support and passed by a vote of 339 to 50 in the House on March 28, 1979, and 85 to 4 in the Senate on March 29, 1979. On April 10, 1979, President Carter signed the Taiwan Relations Act into law.

The effectiveness of the TRA rests largely on the commitment of successive presidential administrations to carry out its provisions. The TRA, along with the three communiqués, establishes the basis for U.S.-Taiwan relations, and every U.S. president since 1979 has affirmed the importance of the TRA in some fashion. However, the vigor with which each administration has carried out its duties under the TRA has varied. This is especially true on the issue of defensive arms sales, which came under fire as early as the Reagan administration. The following sections explore the application of the major provisions of the TRA under each U.S. presidential administration since 1979.

A. JIMMY CARTER (1979 TO 1981)

When President Carter signed the TRA into law, he issued a signing statement certifying that the Act was "consistent with the understandings we reached in normalizing relations with the Government of the People's Republic of China." Carter's statement underscored that the TRA gave the president discretion in implementing the Act's provisions. Carter promised to "exercise that discretion in a manner consistent with our interest, in the well-being of the people on Taiwan, and with the understandings" with the People's Republic of China.[9]

Carter's record at implementing the full scope of the TRA's provisions was mixed. Some critics charged that the president—who had threatened to veto more robust versions of the law—sought to placate the PRC and even took actions that were detrimental to Taiwan. Examples included the administration's decision to shutter several of Taiwan's consulate offices in the United States, even though TRA Section 10(b) expressed Congress' wish that Taiwan would be permitted to maintain "the same number of offices and complement of personnel" as before 1979. On the other hand, the Carter administration moved forward with the establishment of the American Institute in Taiwan (AIT) and approved more than USD 800 million in arms sales to Taiwan from 1979 to 1980 despite the PRC's protests that the sales violated the terms of both the first and second communiqués. The sales included forty-eight F-5(E) fighter planes; air-to-ground, anti-tank, and surface-to-air missiles; and missile systems.

The AIT was officially registered as a nonprofit organization on January 16, 1979. The first chairman of the AIT was David Dean, who served in the role from 1979 to 1986. The AIT's first director, Charles T. Cross, served from the Institute's inception in 1979 until the end of the Carter administration in 1981. Dean, who died in 2013, spoke frequently about his experiences working in Taiwan. His memoir,

Unofficial Diplomacy: The American Institute in Taiwan, recalls the early days of the Institute and its role in stabilizing U.S.-Taiwan relations following derecognition. Both Dean and Cross would go on to serve as important conduits between the U.S. government and members of the ROC government, including President Chiang Ching-kuo.

According to Dean, the first employees of the AIT, many of whom had volunteered for the post, worked for several months without pay while the Institute awaited funding from the U.S. government. Resources were scarce during the AIT's first years, while the staff faced the momentous task of organizing the business that had previously been conducted directly between the ROC government and various U.S. agencies. Discussions regarding everything from agriculture to military sales would from that point on take place under the auspices of the AIT. It took some time for the staff to work through its initial large backlog. However, as Dean later recalled, the AIT was in some ways more efficient than official government agencies because its unofficial nature allowed it to avoid bureaucratic red tape. The AIT was also able to leverage the American Chamber of Commerce in Taipei to facilitate contacts with Taiwan's business community. By 1980, trade between the United States and Taiwan had increased significantly thanks to renewed confidence in the stability of U.S.-Taiwan relations.

In June 1980, roughly one year after the TRA's passage, the Government Accountability Office (GAO) (then called the General Accounting Office) and the Senate Committee on Foreign Relations issued reports on the implementation of the TRA. Both reports found that the TRA had achieved its primary objective of establishing informal relations between the United States and the people of Taiwan. The AIT had, in the words of the Senate report, "worked better than anyone expected."[10] Trade with Taiwan had increased more than 20 percent since 1979. The United States had restarted arms sales to Taiwan, announcing a USD 280 million dollar package in 1980. Taiwanese officials had adjusted to the new reality of informal relations, and the PRC had also largely acquiesced to the status quo. Overall, the TRA was a resounding success in the eyes of U.S. policymakers.

However, both reports also criticized the executive branch for showing too much deference to the PRC out of fear of disrupting the development of U.S.-PRC relations. The GAO report found that the executive branch had not consulted adequately with members of Congress over key decisions, including approving defensive arms sales and terminating the 1946 U.S.-Taiwan Air Transport Agreement in favor of a replacement adopted by the AIT and Taiwan's Coordination Council for North American Affairs (CCNAA). In particular, the State Department was seen as being oversensitive to offending PRC.

While the AIT was generally praised, both reports found that the AIT and its counterpart, the CCNAA, were under-resourced. The AIT worked out of a former military facility in Taipei with half the staff of a typical embassy. The facility lacked adequate security and sanitation features. Furthermore, AIT staff relied on the U.S. Consulate in Hong Kong for the issuance of nonimmigrant visas, and accounting was conducted by hand because the State Department had denied the AIT access to a government data center in the region. AIT staff members were forbidden from attending meetings at government offices in Taiwan, while many U.S. officials could not receive State Department approval to travel to Taiwan to conduct business. Meanwhile, the CCNAA was permitted a smaller presence in the United States than the former ROC embassy. The Senate report argued that the restriction ran afoul of Section 10(b) of the TRA, which requested that Taiwan be permitted the same number of offices and personnel as before derecognition.

The Senate report also noted that Taiwan appeared to be at a political crossroads as some stakeholders within the KMT increasingly called for democratic reform. However, this momentum could only be maintained by furthering Taiwan's economic growth and security. The report stated:

For the United States the challenge is to maintain this balance, and, most important, to take no actions which would create a crisis in Taiwan about its security. For without this sense of confidence, Taiwan's economic future could be adversely affected and its willingness to move toward political reform and liberalization undermined.

Finally, it is quite likely that unless the Taiwan part of the equation works, U.S. policy toward the PRC has, over time, little chance of success. The failure in one could well lead to a failure in the other. A stable and prosperous Taiwan is therefore important to the stability of East Asia and to the national interests of the United States.[11]

B. RONALD REAGAN (1981 TO 1989)

President Reagan's views on the PRC and Taiwan evolved rapidly during his first term. As governor of California, Reagan represented the United States at the ROC's National Day celebrations in 1971 on behalf of President Nixon. As a candidate for president, Reagan railed against Communism in China and suggested that he would "upgrade" relations with Taiwan if elected, a promise that some interpreted to mean re-establishing diplomatic relations with the ROC. As a candidate, Reagan openly criticized Carter's approach to normalizing relations with the PRC and was a vocal supporter of the TRA. However, at the urging of his aides, Reagan began to moderate his tone toward the PRC. In 1980, he sent vice presidential running mate George H. W. Bush to Beijing in hopes of easing concerns of PRC officials. The trip largely failed to convince the PRC of Reagan's benevolent intentions. Upon taking office, Reagan selected Alexander Haig as his Secretary of State. Haig, a veteran of the Nixon administration, viewed the PRC as a potential strategic ally in the Cold War against the Soviet Union.

The first diplomatic crisis of the Reagan administration occurred even before the president's inauguration. Anna Chennault, a well-known Republic operative and wife of the late Lieutenant General Claire Lee Chennault, extended an invitation to the inauguration to a delegation of Taiwanese officials, including KMT Secretary-General Tsiang Yien-si. Upon learning of this, PRC Ambassador Chai Zemin threatened to boycott the event. The inauguration organizing committee responded by disinviting Tsiang, who was already in Washington, D.C., by this time. Tsiang feigned having the flu (Tsiang is often said to have come down with a "diplomatic illness") and checked himself into Jefferson Memorial Hospital two days before the inauguration. Tsiang's absence ensured that Chai would be the only representative of China at the ceremony.

The U.S.-Taiwan relationship was shaken once again in 1982 with the issuance of the Third U.S.-PRC Joint Communiqué. During negotiations with the Carter administration, PRC officials were vocal about their dissatisfaction with the U.S. decision to continue arms sales to Taiwan. Although the PRC ultimately acquiesced to the reality of the situation, they reserved the right to revisit the issue, which they did with vigor soon after Reagan took office. In particular, the PRC took issue with the increased volume of sales to Taiwan since 1978 as well as the planned sale of Northrop FX fighter jets. As a result of increasing pressure from the PRC, in 1982, three years after the TRA's enactment, the United States issued a third joint communiqué with the PRC. The countries agreed that the United States would "continue to maintain cultural, commercial, and other unofficial relations with the people of Taiwan."[12] The United States again acknowledged (without affirming) the Chinese position that "there is but one China and Taiwan is a part of China," but refined its position by proclaiming that it had "no intention of infringing on Chinese sovereignty and territorial integrity, or interfering in China's internal affairs, or pursuing a policy of "two Chinas" or "one China, one Taiwan." With respect to arms sales to Taiwan, the United States expressed that it did not seek to carry out a long-term policy of arms sales to Taiwan. However, President Reagan wrote in a secret memorandum:

> The U.S. willingness to reduce its arms sales to Taiwan is conditioned absolutely upon the continued commitment of China to the peaceful solution of the Taiwan-PRC differences. It should be clearly understood that the linkage

between these two matters is a permanent imperative of U.S. foreign policy. In addition, it is essential that the quantity and quality of the arms provided Taiwan be conditioned entirely on the threat posed by the PRC. Both in quantitative and qualitative terms, Taiwan's defense capability relative to that of the PRC will be maintained.[13]

In 1998, James Lilley, former AIT director and ambassador to the PRC, offered some insight into Reagan's interpretation of the 1982 communiqué. According to Lilley, Reagan assumed that the Taiwan issue would be resolved peacefully because "if the PRC became belligerent or built up a power projection capability in the Strait which threatened Taiwan, President Reagan [would] consider that . . . a violation of the 1982 communiqué and that the U.S. would be free to increase it arms sales to Taiwan."[14] President Reagan's memorandum and Ambassador Lilley's later recollections reveal that the president was not willing to preemptively abandon arms sales without a peaceful resolution of the Taiwan question.

In an attempt to assuage Taiwanese concerns over the third communiqué, Reagan issued an unsigned memorandum to ROC President Chiang Ching-kuo through Vice Foreign Minister Frederick Chien offering "Six Assurances." The Assurances, whose content was inspired by recommendations made by AIT Chairman David Dean, were made public soon after. They were:

> In negotiating the third Joint Communiqué with the PRC, the United States:
>   1) Has not agreed to set a date for ending arms sales to Taiwan;
>   2) Has not agreed to hold prior consultations with the PRC on arms sales to Taiwan;
>   3) Will not play any mediation role between Taipei and Beijing;
>   4) Has not agreed to revise the Taiwan Relations Act;
>   5) Has not altered its position regarding sovereignty over Taiwan;
>   6) Will not exert pressure on Taiwan to negotiate with the PRC.[15]

The Reagan administration attempted to reassure officials in Taiwan, as well as U.S. lawmakers, that the above-mentioned arms sale reduction was conditioned upon China's commitment to a peaceful resolution of the dispute over Taiwan. The day after the communiqué was issued, Assistant Secretary of State John Holdridge testified before Congress that the reduction in arms sales was consistent with the TRA insofar as Taiwan's defense needs were considered in the context of continued improvements in cross-strait relations. In 1984, Reagan visited China, signaling a warming of the U.S.-PRC relationship. While there, he reaffirmed the substance of the Six Assurances, lending Taiwan a measure of support.

As a practical matter, the policy of reducing arms sales was informally bench-marked at about USD 750 million based on sales in 1982, with approximately USD 20 million in reductions per year.[16] At the same time, the Reagan administration permitted increased technology transfers and other arrangements, such as the construction of Perry-class frigates in Taiwan under license. U.S. arms sales to Taiwan totaled over USD 1.5 billion during the eight years of the Reagan administration. These included the 1983 sale of sixty-six F-104G jets. President Reagan also authorized the sale of twelve C-130 cargo planes and Grumman S-2 submarine tracker planes and the licensing of co-production for a Taiwanese version of the U.S. Perry-class frigate. These became the Cheng Kung class frigate, of which eight were ultimately produced from 1993 to 2002. In 1982, plans to sell Taiwan an advanced fighter jet, the Northrop FX (later renamed the F-20 and ultimately canceled), were scrapped in favor of extending an existing F-5E co-production arrangement, which permitted the construction of fighter jets locally in Taiwan.

In 1981, Representative Stephen J. Solarz of New York, who was instrumental in pressuring the ROC regime to undertake political reforms during his tenure in Congress, introduced an amendment to the International Security and Development Cooperation Act to establish a separate quota of immigrant visas for Taiwan. Under the Immigration and Nationality Act, the State Department could approve no more than 20,000 visa applications for immigrants from China annually. Since the establishment of diplomatic relations with the PRC in 1979, the available pool of visas was shared between immigrants from China and Taiwan. Applicants from Taiwan, who in the past had a relatively good chance of gaining approval, were suddenly forced to compete with approximately 1 billion potential applicants from the Chinese mainland. With support from Senator Edward Kennedy, the amendment passed both the House and the Senate, before being signed into law on December 29, 1981. Hundreds of thousands of Taiwanese have immigrated to the United States since.

The AIT's leaders played a crucial role in maintaining communications between the White House and Chiang Ching-kuo during the Reagan administration. David N. Laux took over the chairmanship of the AIT in 1986, serving in the role until 1990. Under Reagan, the AIT's directors were James R. Lilley (1981 to 1984) and Harry E. T. Thayer (1984 to 1986). Lilley would later serve as ambassador to the PRC under George H. W. Bush. David Dean, the AIT's chairman until 1986, stepped into the director's role in 1987, serving until 1990. In 1982, just before the issuance of the Third Communiqué, Lilley personally delivered Reagan's Six Assurances to ROC Vice Foreign Minister Fredrick Chien, who then communicated them to Chiang Ching-kuo. Shortly after, Lilley informed the ROC on behalf of President Reagan that the United States would adhere to the Third Communiqué only if the PRC maintained a peaceful approach to cross-strait relations.

C. GEORGE H. W. BUSH (1989 TO 1993)

George H. W. Bush had served in the Beijing liaison office from 1974 to 1975. A year and a half into his term, the Tiananmen Square Incident forced Bush to take a tough stance toward the PRC. Reports of human and civil rights violations in China increased sharply during the first year of the George H. W. Bush administration. In April 1989, after the death of former PRC General Secretary Hu Yaobang, demonstrators called for "the establishment of a dialogue with government and party leaders on democratic reforms, including freedom of expression, freedom of assembly, and the elimination of corruption by government officials."[17] Protestors converged on Tiananmen Square in Beijing. On June 3, security forces led by the People's Liberation Army cracked down, using weapons and tanks to disperse the crowd. Thousands of demonstrators were wounded or killed. The Tiananmen Square massacre fundamentally altered the course of the U.S.-PRC relationship. Amid an international outcry over the events, the Bush administration suspended all military exports to the PRC. Although arms sales to the PRC had been minimal since normalization, there were plans to increase sales. These included the Peace Pearl F-8 fighter upgrade program, which was then canceled. Congress took steps to prohibit the export of U.S.-built satellites unless the PRC undertook political and human rights reforms.

The collapse of the USSR had opened the Russian arms market to the world, permitting the PRC to acquire dozens of advanced Sukhoi SU-27 fighters in 1991 and 1992. Taiwan had nothing comparable. In September 1992, Bush informed Congress that the United States would sell Taiwan one hundred fifty F-16 fighter jets worth USD 5.8 billion. In remarks to employees at General Dynamics in Fort Worth, Texas, Bush explained that "the sale of F-16s to Taiwan will help maintain peace and stability in an area of concern to us, the Asia-Pacific region, in conformity with [the Taiwan Relations Act]."[18] The decision to approve the sale was significant because the United States had never before sold current-generation F-16 fighters to Taiwan. The move angered the PRC, which promptly ended its participation in the ongoing Middle East arms control talks. In all, the George H. W. Bush administration approved roughly USD 8.2 billion in sales to Taiwan, including the sale of standard missiles, 110 M60A3 battle tanks, and radar upgrades for the F-5, F-104, and C-130 planes.

Thomas Brooks served as AIT director under the Bush administration from 1990 to 1993. Natale (Nat) H. Bellocchi was named chairman of the AIT in 1990. Bellocchi served as an important intermediary during negotiations over the sale of F-16 jets in 1992. The U.S.-Taiwan relationship deepened under the George H. W. Bush administration in the early 1990s. In 1992, Bush sent U.S. Trade Representative Carla Hills to Taiwan, the first cabinet level official to visit Taiwan since the termination of diplomatic relations in 1979.

D. BILL CLINTON (1993 TO 2001)

The Clinton administration was forced to recalibrate its policy toward Taiwan when faced with fundamental changes in Asia. Among these changes was the welcomed progress in Taiwan's democratization, including the country's first direct presidential election in 1996, roughly a decade after the end of martial law on the island. At the same time, the PRC continued on its path toward greater militarization. The Third Taiwan Strait Crisis occurred from 1995 to 1996 when China conducted military exercises, including the test-firing of missiles near Taiwan, in protest of President Lee Teng-hui's private visit to the United States and to influence the upcoming historic democratic election in Taiwan.

Once in office, President Clinton undertook a comprehensive review of the United States' Taiwan policy, which led to the publication of the 1994 Taiwan Policy Review. The Review affirmed the U.S. commitment to maintaining unofficial relations with Taiwan through the AIT and reiterated that the TRA and the three communiqués would continue to form the basis for U.S.-Taiwan relations. Additionally, the Review acknowledged the "changing circumstances" that had taken place in both the PRC and Taiwan, economically and politically, and called for a refinement in U.S. policy to "advance . . . mutual interests in light of a changed environment."[19] The Clinton administration's proposed policy changes included:

1) Permitting Taiwan's top leadership to transit U.S. territory for their travel convenience [on a case-by-case basis];

2) Initiating, under AIT auspices, a sub-Cabinet economic dialogue and Trade Investment Framework Agreement (TIFA) talks with Taiwan;

3) Actively supporting Taiwan's membership in international organizations accepting non-states as members;

4) Permitting high level U.S. Government officials, from economic and technical agencies to visit Taiwan, as well as more senior economic and technical officers from the Department of State;

5) Permitting U.S. government officials to travel to Taiwan to meet with [Taiwan's] officials at whatever level;

6) Permitting all AIT employees, including the Director and Deputy Director, access to [Taiwan's] Foreign Affairs Ministry;

7) Permitting U.S. Cabinet-level officials from economic and technical departments to meet with Taiwan representatives and visitors in official settings [in the United States]; and

8) Permitting State Department Officials at the Under Secretary level and below, who handle economic and technical issues to meet Taiwan's representatives in unofficial settings.[20]

The 1994 Review also emphasized that certain aspects of the U.S.-Taiwan relationship would remain unchanged. These included U.S. arms sales. At the same time, the United States appeared to be withdrawing its support for other measures thought to be in Taiwan's interest. For example, the Review provided that the United States would not support Taiwan's membership in organizations such as the United Nations where statehood was a requirement for entry, but would support greater international participation by Taiwan in organizations that accepted nonmember states. Some commentators recognized that this declaration could undermine Taiwan's status under international law and may even have contradicted the Six Assurances made by President Reagan in 1982. Nevertheless, the 1994 Review was viewed as having generally expanded opportunities for meetings between Taiwanese and U.S. representatives.

In 1995, Taiwan President Lee Teng-hui planned a private visit to the United States to attend a graduate school reunion at his alma mater, Cornell University. The White House was initially opposed to this visit. But Lee's visit became a *cause célèbre* among members of Congress. In 1994, Congress passed the Immigration and Nationality Technical Corrections Act of 1994, which granted approval for the president of Taiwan or any high-level official of Taiwan to "apply to visit the United States for the purposes of discussions with United States Federal or State government officials concerning 1) trade or business with Taiwan that will reduce the United States–Taiwan trade deficit; 2) prevention of nuclear proliferation; 3) threats to the national security of the United States; 4) the protection of the global environment; 5) the protection of endangered species; or 6) regional humanitarian disasters." Requests under the Act would be granted as long as the applicant was not excludable under U.S. immigration laws.

On March 6, 1995, the House of Representatives proposed a resolution urging President Clinton to "promptly indicate that the United States will welcome a private visit by President Lee Teng-hui to his alma mater, Cornell University, and will welcome a transit stop by President Lee in Anchorage, Alaska, to attend the USA-ROC Economic Council Conference."[21] The final vote tallies for the measures were 396–0 in the House of Representatives and 97–1 in the Senate. The State Department relented and granted Lee a visa to attend the reunion, provided that he made the trip in a personal, and not a public, capacity. In explaining his decision to allow Lee's visit, President Clinton remarked that "in our country, we have the constitutional right to travel. It is very difficult in America to justify not allowing a citizen of the world . . . to come to his college reunion and to travel around our country and to say whatever's on his mind."[22]

The PRC strongly protested the decision to approve Lee's visit. The PRC first retaliated against the United States by canceling official visits and high-level talks. Chinese leaders feared that Lee's visit would set a precedent allowing other Taiwanese presidents to make future trips to the United States or to other major countries. The situation further escalated in March 1996 when the PRC launched missiles near Taiwan, leading to the deployment of two U.S. aircraft carrier battle groups headed by the U.S.S. *Independence* and *Nimitz* to positions near Taiwan (though not in the Taiwan Strait). In his 2005 book *Untying the Knot*, former AIT Chairman and Managing Director Richard C. Bush wrote that President Lee's actions may have been calculated to bring attention to Taiwan's exclusion from the international community.[23] Lee's actions effectively gave voice to Taiwanese frustrations over the PRC's policy of suffocation.

During the crisis of 1995 to 1996, some members of Congress had, as Michael O'Hanlon wrote, "lost patience with the existing U.S. policy of strategic ambiguity—by which Washington suggested to both Taipei and Beijing that it might help Taiwan defend itself, but did not commit itself to doing so."[24] By the end of the crisis, the U.S.-Sino relationship had deteriorated to the point that State Department officials called for a state-level U.S.-PRC visit as a way to ease tensions. The United States and the PRC soon agreed to reciprocal visits between President Jiang Zemin and President Clinton. President Jiang visited the United States October 27 to November 3, 1997, marking the first visit to the United States by the Chinese head of state in more than a decade. During a news conference with Jiang, President Clinton stated in regard to Taiwan:

A key to Asia's stability is a peaceful and prosperous relationship between the People's Republic of China and Taiwan. I reiterated America's longstanding commitment to a "one China" policy. It has allowed democracy to flourish in Taiwan and provides a framework in which all three relationships can prosper—between the United States and the PRC, the United States and Taiwan, and Taiwan and the People's Republic of China.

I told President Jiang that we hope the People's Republic of China and Taiwan would resume a constructive cross-strait dialog and expand cross-strait exchanges. Ultimately, the relationship between the PRC and Taiwan is for the Chinese themselves to determine—peacefully.[25]

During his subsequent visit to China in June 1998, President Clinton proclaimed his "Three Noes" policy in remarks at the Shanghai Library:

I had a chance to reiterate our Taiwan policy, which is that we don't support independence for Taiwan, or two Chinas, or one Taiwan–one China. And we don't believe that Taiwan should be a member of any organization for which statehood is a requirement.[26]

As one commentator remarked, President Clinton's statements in Shanghai "put . . . Taiwan at a severe disadvantage in [its] 50-year struggle with the communist government of mainland China."[27] In particular, U.S. opposition to Taiwan's participation in international organizations made the United States "an accomplice in China's campaign to squeeze Taiwan into submission by isolating the island internationally."[28] President Clinton's statement was in apparent contradiction to existing U.S. policy, as the TRA made clear that the termination of U.S.-ROC diplomatic relations could not be construed as supporting Taiwan's exclusion or expulsion from continued membership in international organizations. In February 2000, Clinton moderated his Three Noes in a speech to the Business Council, when he stated: "We'll continue to reject the use of force as a means to resolve the Taiwan question. We'll also continue to make absolutely clear that the issues between Beijing and Taiwan must be resolved peacefully and with the assent of the people of Taiwan."[29]

In March 1999, Congress passed a concurrent resolution commemorating the twentieth anniversary of the TRA and expressing concerns over China's recent military modernization and weapons procurement program. The resolution sought to "reaffirm the United States' commitment to the TRA and the specific guarantees for the provision of legitimate defense articles to Taiwan." In testimony before the Senate Committee on Foreign Relations, Harvey Feldman, former U.S. Ambassador and a long-time expert in U.S.-Taiwan relations, stated that the "TRA and its formulations remained the law of this land," and urged the United States to "return to the former policy of . . . [taking] no position on what the final status of Taiwan should be, because [it was] a matter of negotiation between the two sides."[30] Feldman's statements were likely directed at President Clinton's Three Noes policy. Feldman further suggested that the United States should "continue to press for a renunciation of the use of force against Taiwan," even if it was "a neuralgic point for the PRC."[31] Citing the TRA, Feldman stressed the importance of determining Taiwan's future by peaceful means, as the United States' decision to establish diplomatic relations with the PRC rested upon that expectation. Last, Feldman recommended that the United States "cease its passivity and support Taiwan's membership in international organization as a matter of law and as a matter of realism."[32] Feldman contended that such legal obligation came from the "implicit injunction of the TRA to support Taiwan's membership in the international financial institutions, the World Trade Organization, and other international organizations."[33] Accordingly, Feldman believed that "Beijing's continuing campaign to squeeze Taiwan utterly out of international life, including the work of purely humanitarian organizations as well as technical bodies in fields such as telecommunications, aviation, marine transport, and the regulation of intellectual property, cannot be defended and should not be accepted."[34] He insisted that a U.S. policy which "took account only of . . . interests vis-à-vis the PRC, and failed to take account of the . . . substantial interests in Taiwan's democracy and its future, cannot be considered realistic."[35]

Within two months, Congress considered the Taiwan Security Enhancement Act (TSEA).[36] The TSEA, if passed, would have directed the Department of Defense and Department of State to assess Taiwan's defensive needs and to provide technical and material support in areas including training, communications, missile defense, and air defense. Specific measures included requiring the executive branch to report on Taiwan's defensive needs, holding positions for Taiwan military officers at the National Defense University and other training centers, increasing technical staff at the AIT upon the request of the Defense Security Cooperation Agency, and promoting combined training and personnel exchange programs, annual reports, and direct secured communications between armed forces of the United States and Taiwan. Referring to the policy of strategic ambiguity adopted by the Clinton administration, the bill found it was in the national interest of the United States to "eliminate ambiguity and convey with clarity continued U.S. support for Taiwan, its people, and their ability to maintain their democracy free from coercion and their society free from the use of force against them."[37] Supporters of the bill feared that the lack of clarity on the U.S. position on Taiwan could, as articulated in the bill, lead to "unnecessary misunderstandings or confrontations between the U.S. and the PRC, with grave consequences for the security of the Western Pacific region." Though the TSEA achieved a vote of 341–70 in the House of Representatives, the Senate did not take a final vote on the bill, in the face of opposition from the White House.

In 2000, Representative Doug Bereuter cited Section 6 of the TRA in proposing the American Institute in Taiwan Facilities Enhancement Act to authorize funding for the construction of a new AIT office complex in Taiwan.[38] The Act's findings included that the AIT played a successful role in "sustaining and enhancing the U.S. relations with Taiwan," and that given the AIT's importance to that relationship, Congress had a "special responsibility to ensure [its] requirements for safe and appropriate office quarters were met." Congress also found it necessary to upgrade the AIT's facility to ensure adequate security and welfare for its American and local employees. President Clinton signed the Enhancement Act into law on May 26, 2000.

Throughout the Clinton administration, members of Congress showed tremendous support for Taiwan's participation in international organizations in spite of the president's Three Noes policy. Lawmakers specifically advocated for Taiwan's membership in the World Trade Organization (WTO). The issue of Taiwan's accession to the WTO generated significant debate in the 106th Congress, where some law-makers expressed concern that China might try to force WTO members to block Taiwan's accession or recognize Taiwan as a part of China. Lawmakers on Capitol Hill urged the Clinton administration to clarify its position on the matter and sought to avoid the outcome through legislation. In May 2000, lawmakers introduced H.R. 4444, seeking to "authorize extension of nondiscriminatory treatment (normal trade relations treatment) to the PRC and to establish a framework for relations between the U.S. and the PRC" upon its accession to the WTO."[39] Section 601 of the bill provided:

> It is the sense of the Congress that—
> 1) immediately upon approval by the General Council of the WTO of the terms and conditions of the accession of the People's Republic of China to the WTO, the United States representative to the WTO should request that the General Council of the WTO consider Taiwan's accession to the WTO as the next order of business of the Council during the same session; and
> 2) the United States should be prepared to aggressively counter any effort by any WTO member, upon the approval of the General Council of the WTO of the terms and conditions of the accession of the People's Republic of China to the WTO, to block the accession of Taiwan to the WTO.

The bill's language gave a hefty endorsement to Taiwan's own WTO accession, indicating that Congress would not only adhere to Section 4(d) of the TRA, opposing the exclusion of Taiwan from international organizations, but go further by advocating Taiwan's participation and membership in them. This bill was signed into law on October 10, 2000 as the U.S.-China Relations Act of 2000.

There were no signature large arms sales to Taiwan during the Clinton administration, but the administration did authorize approximately USD 8.7 billion in arms sales to Taiwan over eight years. In 1996, President Clinton approved the sale of roughly thirteen hundred Stinger surface-to-air missiles, as well as seventy-four Avenger vehicle-mounted guided missile launchers and ninety-six HMMWV vehicles. In 1997, the president approved the sale of twenty-one AH-1W Super Cobra helicopters and thirteen OH-58D Kiowa Warrior Armed Scout Helicopters. Other notable sales during the Clinton administration included nine CH-47SD Chinook helicopters, twelve C-130H transport planes, and four E-2T early warning aircraft. In 2000, about USD 500 million was approved for radar and targeting upgrades for Taiwan's F-16s.

During the Clinton administration, the AIT was the focus of a short-lived scandal involving Chairman James C. Wood, Jr., a close associate of the president who served in the role for one year from 1996 to 1997. Wood was accused of soliciting financial contributions from wealthy Taiwanese donors on behalf of the U.S. Democratic Party. Following Wood's resignation, Richard C. Bush, a well-known expert in Asia affairs took on the chairmanship and served in the role until 2002. The AIT directors during the Clinton administration were B. Lynn Pascoe (1993 to 1996), Darryl Norman Johnson (1996 to 1999), and Raymond Burghardt (1999 to 2001). Burghardt would later serve again as AIT chairman. Bush was often called upon to represent the United States in Taiwan at sensitive moments. He briefed Taiwan's leaders during Jiang Zemin's 1997 state visit to the United States and President Clinton's subsequent visit to the PRC in 1998. Following President Lee's characterization of the PRC-Taiwan relationship as a "state-to-state" relationship, Bush traveled to Taipei with a special envoy to urge Lee to moderate his stance. In 2005, Bush documented many of the lessons learned during a long career in Taiwan affairs in his book *Untying the Knot*.

E. GEORGE W. BUSH (2001 TO 2009)

At the beginning of George W. Bush's first term, his administration was perceived as the "most Taiwan-friendly administration since the termination of diplomatic relations [between the United States and Taiwan in 1979]."[40] In an interview with ABC network's "Good Morning America" in April 2001, President Bush stated, "[I]f Taiwan were attacked by the PRC, the United States has an obligation to use whatever it took to help Taiwan defend herself."[41] Later that day, Bush appeared on "CNN Inside Politics" and said that his administration was willing to "uphold the spirit of the TRA" and that Taiwan's legal status must be resolved peacefully.[42] Vice President Dick Cheney weighed in four days later, saying, "[W]hen we get into an area where one side is displaying increasingly aggressive posture, if you will, toward the other, then it's appropriate to clarify here that in fact we're serious about this. It is an important step for the United States, and we don't want to see a misjudgment on the part of the Chinese."[43] These comments appeared to signal a shift from Clinton's policy of strategic ambiguity and led to speculation that, as Shirley Kan observed, the "U.S. had changed its policy toward Taiwan's security or was preparing to change its position on Taiwan's independence."[44] A visit by Taiwan's defense minister, the first since the ending of official relations with Taiwan in 1979, signaled further strengthening of the administration's commitment to the Taiwan issue.

During this period, tensions between Taiwan and China grew. In 2003, President Chen Shui-bian campaigned for a referendum on topics including "whether to build a nuclear plant, to cut the number of legislators by half, to mobilize more resources to gain representation on the World Health Organization" and "whether [Taiwan] should demand that Beijing remove hundreds of missiles aimed at it and renounce the use of force." President Chen's efforts triggered a warning by PRC officials, who stated that further provocation could lead to a PRC military response, since the "very act of holding a referendum on such issues implied that Taiwan was an independent state."[45]

The United States moderated its position toward Taiwan over the course of the Bush administration. In December 2013, during a visit by PRC Premier Wen Jiabao to the United States, President Bush hinted at yet another shift in U.S. policy toward Taiwan. President Bush said that the United States will "oppose any unilateral decision by either China or Taiwan to change the status quo . . . and the comments and actions made by the leader of Taiwan indicate that he may be willing to make decisions unilaterally, to change the status quo. . . ."[46] One analyst described President Bush's comments as the "toughest American language used against a Taiwanese leader in decades."[47] According to former U.S. Ambassador Harvey Feldman, the Bush administration was "in direct contradiction with Section 4(d) of the TRA" when it made restricting statements concerning the status of Taiwan's statehood.[48] At an October 19, 2003, press conference, Bush stood next to President Hu when the latter said, "President Bush reiterated his government's position of adhering to the one China policy, the three China-U.S. joint communiqués, and his opposition to Taiwan independence."[49] On October 25, 2004, Secretary of State Colin Powell declared on Phoenix TV in Beijing that "[t]here is only one China. Taiwan is not independent. It does not enjoy sovereignty as a nation, and that remains our policy, our firm policy."[50]

The Bush administration approved approximately USD 15.6 billion in arms sales to Taiwan in the span of seven years, from 2001 to 2008, announcing only one sale to Taiwan in both 2003 and 2005, and no sales in 2006. In 2001, the Bush administration announced that the annual U.S.-Taiwan arms sales talks would be ended, replaced instead with ad hoc requests and reviews. The move was intended to depoliticize the process, but appeared to have the effect of causing lengthy deferrals in responding to requests from Taiwanese officials. When Taiwan submitted letters of request for sixty-six new F-16C/D fighters in mid-2006 and early and late 2007, the Bush administration refused to accept them. Reasons included Taiwan's ongoing development of land-attack cruise missiles and President Chen's mid-2007 proposal to hold a referendum on applying for membership in the United Nations. The final year of the Bush administration saw an estimated USD 6.5 billion in approvals for arms sales to Taiwan.[51] The 2008 package authorized "upgrades and repairs of [Taiwan's] existing systems and gave Taiwan new weapons to use against

Chinese ground forces in the unlikely event that the People's Liberation Army decided to invade by way of Taiwan's beaches."[52] However, the Bush administration did not fulfill Taiwan's request for upgraded F-16C/D fighter aircrafts, causing some commenters to question the president's commitment to Taiwan's security. Notably, 2008 was the year of the Beijing Olympics and the U.S. presidential election.

Submarine warfare represents an area where U.S. hesitation has had the greatest impact on Taiwan's defensive capabilities. Taiwan's submarine fleet, which numbers four vessels, is dwarfed by that of the PRC. Since 1995, Taiwan's Ministry of Defense has requested submarines from the United States. In April 2001, the Bush administration provided an in-principle approval of the sale of submarines with the intention of Taiwan acquiring foreign-manufactured vessels. The acquisition was estimated to cost upward of USD 10 billion for eight ships. In April 2003, the tentative agreement was upset in a dispute over the start-up costs to the program and whether some of the ships could be manufactured in Taiwan. The Bush administration was urging Taiwan to focus on anti-submarine surveillance and detection to deal with the PRC submarine threat, rather than purchase new ships of its own. In 2006 a two-stage compromise was proposed whereby Taiwan would pay the United States to procure a submarine design, and as a second step, potentially procuring and building its own submarines. In January 2008, the U.S. Navy accepted Taiwan's letters of request for a submarine design phase. But the Bush administration did not follow through by submitting notice of the program to Congress.

In mid-2008, some members of Congress complained that the Bush administration had adopted a policy of freezing arms sales to Taiwan. The administration had failed to notify Congress of requested arms sales totaling over USD 12 billion, including submarines, PAC-3 Patriot missile defense systems, Apache and Black Hawk helicopters, upgrades of E2-T early warning aircraft, aircraft parts, and Harpoon and Javelin missiles. In October 2008, President Bush responded to congressional pressure and approved USD 6.5 billion in pending sales. The Bush administration did support arms sales in the areas of computer enhancements, detection systems, and missile defense. Large approvals included USD 725 million in sales of Joint Tactical Information Distribution Systems, fifty-four AAV7A1 amphibious assault vehicles for USD 250 million, four decommissioned Kidd-class destroyers for USD 875 million, Multi-function Information Distribution Systems for USD 775 million, two UHF Long-Range Early Warning Radars for USD 1.7 billion, twelve P-3C patrol/ASW planes for USD 1.9 billion, a Patriot missile defense configuration-2 systems upgrade for USD 939 million, 330 advanced Patriot PAC-3 missiles for USD 3.1 billion, and thirty Apache attack helicopters (along with 1,000 Hellfire and 173 Stinger missiles) for USD 2.5 billion. Separately, the Bush administration authorized almost

USD 1 billion in various missile sales. In total, Bush authorized about USD 15.6 billion in sales to Taiwan, or almost USD 2 billion a year.[53]

Under the George W. Bush administration, Therese Shaheen served as AIT chairman from 2002 to 2004. William A. Brown served as acting chairman from 2004 to 2006 upon Shaheen's resignation, followed by Raymond F. Burghardt, the AIT's former director, who remains the AIT chairman as of 2015. The AIT's directors during this period were Douglas H. Paal (2002 to 2006) and Stephen M. Young (2006 to 2009).

F. BARACK OBAMA (2009 TO THE PRESENT)

The Obama administration's stance toward Taiwan has shifted considerably over the course of eight years. Early in his first term, President Obama appeared to acquiesce to the PRC's characterization of the Taiwan question as being a matter of its core interests. However, improving relations across the Taiwan Strait, combined with the United States' strategic "pivot" toward the Asia Pacific, have provided an opportunity to enhance the U.S.-Taiwan relationship. Taiwan was accepted into the U.S. Visa Waiver Program in 2012, and in 2013 President Obama signed a bill supporting Taiwan's participation in the International Civil Aviation Organization (ICAO). High-level visits between officials increased, and trade talks advanced along a number of fronts. In April 2015, Secretary of State John Kerry stated that Taiwan was a crucial element in the U.S. strategy in the Asia Pacific and affirmed the administration's support for the Taiwan Relations Act.

The Obama administration did not begin auspiciously for Taiwan, whose status in Washington had suffered over the course of the Chen-Bush years. In November 2009, President Obama issued a joint statement with PRC President Hu Jintao during his state visit to China which alarmed many of Taiwan's supporters. The statement said:

> President Obama on various occasions has reiterated that the U.S. side adheres to the one-China policy, abides by the three Sino-U.S. joint communiqués, and respects China's sovereignty and the territorial integrity when it comes to the Taiwan question and other matters.[54]

The joint statement's failure to include the TRA as a part of the framework that shaped Washington's One China Policy was a first since the Carter administration. Though President Obama referenced the TRA in conjunction with the three communiqués in a subsequent press conference, its elimination in the joint press statement between the United States and China likely "added doubt in Beijing's mind about the U.S. commitment to a peaceful resolution of [Taiwan's] future."[55] In an attempt to ease fears, Raymond F. Burghardt, chairman of the AIT, assured Taiwanese officials and opposition leaders that there "would be no change in the U.S. policy and stance on Taiwan-related issues . . . and that the U.S. would abide by the TRA in helping Taiwan to safeguard its security with continuing arms sales."[56]

In other areas, goodwill between the United States and Taiwan was unaffected. In 2009, Taiwan qualified for a new U.S. visa waiver program that would allow Taiwanese travelers visa-free entries to Guam and the Commonwealth of the Northern Mariana Islands. In 2012, Taiwan was accepted for the visa waiver program for entry to the United States. Within the realms of trade and the economy, Taiwan and the United States resumed talks pursuant to the Trade and Investment Framework Agreement (TIFA), through which Taiwan hoped to secure a bilateral investment agreement with the United States. In May 2010, Congress introduced a resolution encouraging the Obama administration to make a Taiwan free trade agreement a priority and to order the U.S. Trade Representative to expedite negotiations.[57] However, later that summer, the United States decided to postpone TIFA negotiations following a dispute over Taiwan's ban on U.S. beef imports. The talks did not resume again until 2013 and are still ongoing.

In 2009, Taiwan was granted observer status at the 2009 World Health Assembly (WHA) (under the name "Chinese Taipei"), due in large part to a campaign by the United States that resulted in a compromise with the PRC over Taiwan's participation. Taiwan's attendance at the 2009 WHA meeting fell far short of full membership in the World Health Organization (WHO), an organization in which Taiwan had long sought membership. However, it was the first time Taiwan had been present at an annual meeting of a UN-affiliated organization since the ROC's ouster from the General Assembly in 1971. Although Taiwan's involvement did not amount to full membership in WHO, its invitation was seen as a major breakthrough following years of efforts by Taiwan officials to gain membership in the WHO. The Obama administration has also supported Taiwan's efforts to participate in the International Civil Aviation Organization (ICAO) and has offered support for "Taiwan's meaningful participation in multilateral organizations where its membership is not possible."[58]

The Obama administration has averaged about USD 2 billion in arms sales to Taiwan annually.[59] In January 2010, the administration made its first notification to Congress of an arms sale to Taiwan. The deal, valued at roughly USD 6.4 billion, included PAC-3 Patriot missile defense (a follow-up installment from the Bush administration), sixty Black Hawk utility helicopters, high-tech computer system support, various missiles, and Osprey-class mine hunters. Like the Bush administration, President Obama continued to silently pass over notification of the submarine design program and still did not accept the request for new F-16C/D fighters. In September 2011, the Obama administration approved upgrades to Taiwan's F-16A/B fighters for USD 5.3 billion, renewed the U.S.-Taiwan pilot training program, and approved the sale of USD 52 million of spare parts for aircraft.

The AIT has had the same chairman, Raymond Burghardt, since 2006. Burghardt, who served as AIT director from 1999 to 2001 has served in high-ranking positions at the AIT under three presidents. The AIT's directors under the Obama administration have been William A. Stanton (2009 to 2012) and Christopher J. Marut (2012 to 2015). In May 2015, Kin Moy, Deputy Assistant Secretary of State for East Asia, was named as Marut's successor. The AIT has experienced continued transformation during the Obama administration. In 2009 William Stanton began his tenure as director, vowing to strengthen bilateral relations between the U.S. and Taiwan. Stanton had been known as a supporter of more meaningful participation for Taiwan in UN specialized agencies. The AIT also began construction of a new facility in the Neihu District of Taipei. In 2009, the U.S. State Department approved funding for a USD 170 million AIT office complex, double the USD 75 million budget approved by Congress in 2000. The approval signaled the United States' long-term intentions to remain in Taiwan and to commit itself to maintaining commercial, cultural, and other ties.

III. Interim Appraisal of Past Successes and Failures

Policy making is not a one-shot affair. It is an ongoing process of authoritative decision carried out in phases: information gathering, promotion, prescription, invocation, application, appraisal, and termination. A verdict rendered yesterday may be overturned today in response to drastically changed conditions or power configurations. Participants, be they groups or individuals, engage in the promotion of new policies at every level of society in both formal and informal arenas. Decisions made in the public sphere are subject to constant appraisal from all quarters as decision makers seek to satisfy the demands of constituents and achieve an optimal distribution of values for the community as a whole. Institutions that once seemed enlightened and stable are reshaped with each new generation in light of evolving perspectives. This description of the global constitutive process of authoritative decision characterizes the New Haven School of international law.

The effects of this process of decision making are plainly visible in the sequence of development of U.S. policy toward Taiwan over the twentieth century. Policymakers shifted course rapidly in response to the changing context of conditions in the Asia Pacific. Immediately following World War II, President Truman was content to "let the dust settle," but the outbreak of the Korean War changed the Allies' strategic calculations dramatically. Three decades later, during the height of the Cold War, President Nixon seized the opportunity to play the China card against the Soviet Union, adopting the Shanghai Communiqué and laying the foundation for diplomatic relations between the United States and the PRC. In 1979, President Carter finished the work that Nixon started, assenting, in the Second Communiqué, to China's demands to derecognize the ROC government on Taiwan. Congress, whose members embodied the broad perspectives of the U.S. people, responded to Carter's surprise announcement by adopting the TRA to support and preserve the United States' relationship with the people of Taiwan and to ensure peace and stability in the Asia Pacific region. In 1982, President Reagan adopted the Third Communiqué, which called for a reduction in the sale of arms to Taiwan over the long term. He clarified in a secret memorandum that the reduction was premised on China's commitment to the continuation of peaceful cross-strait relations.

The formulation of U.S. policy toward Taiwan did not stop with the adoption of the Third Communiqué in 1982. It has continued to evolve within the framework established by the TRA and the three communiqués. After the June 4, 1989 massacre on Tiananmen Square, President George H. W. Bush increased arms sales to Taiwan and adopted an arms embargo against the PRC which remains in place to this day. Under President Clinton, the United States embarked on a policy of constructive engagement with the PRC, supporting China's accession to the World Trade Organization (along with Taiwan), and encouraging China to integrate itself into the world community. During the Third Taiwan Strait Crisis of 1995 to 1996, the United States relocated navy resources near Taiwan to counteract aggressive Chinese military exercises. After September 11, 2001, the United States and China deepened their cooperation while China increasingly flexed its economic might. Presidents George W. Bush and Barack Obama have encouraged China and Taiwan to hew to the status quo, warning against unilateral moves toward independence or unification. In 2014, President Ma Ying-jeou's policies of cross-strait economic integration at all costs spurred an anti-KMT movement that culminated in the Sunflower Movement and the KMT's crushing electoral defeats. All the while, China's growing military strength and provocative actions in the East and South China Seas have led the Obama administration to undertake a strategic rebalancing to the Asia Pacific.

An interim appraisal of past successes and failures finds that U.S. policy toward Taiwan has succeeded in achieving its stated objectives in many respects. However, changing conditions must be taken into account. There are clear opportunities—some which are long-standing, some emerging—to reform existing policies to meet the challenges facing the United States, Taiwan, and the Asia Pacific community as a result of China's rise as a regional power. This concluding section will consider some of these areas in anticipation of recommendations for concrete measures which are offered in Chapter 11.

A. UNOFFICIAL RELATIONS

Although it lacks the stamp of formal diplomatic relations, in breadth and content the United States' relationship with Taiwan is as significant as any other. Through the policies enacted in the TRA, the United States has forged close and productive ties with the people of Taiwan and encouraged Taiwan's profound economic, political, social, and cultural development over more than three decades. Above all, the American Institute in Taiwan (AIT) has been the principal organ for the growth of the informal, but substantive, U.S.-Taiwan relationship. As former AIT Chairman and Managing Director Richard Bush remarked, it is the AIT that is "arguably the most successful" outcome of the legislation because it created concrete mechanisms through which the U.S. and Taiwan can conduct meaningful relations.[60] Pursuant to its authority under the TRA, the AIT, and the Taipei Economic and Cultural Representative Office (TECRO) have entered into nearly two hundred agreements since January 1, 1979, addressing a wide range of topics such as agriculture, aviation, the environment, scientific and technical cooperation, trade, energy, and intellectual property.

The AIT makes it convenient for American citizens who are physically in Taiwan to receive services, such as applying for consular reports of births abroad, performing notarial acts, and issuing and renewing U.S. passports. Additionally, the AIT allows Taiwanese citizens to apply for nonimmigrant visas, for those making temporary visits to the United States, and offers consular processing for those applying for U.S. immigrant visas. The AIT helps to promote trade between Taiwan and the United States by providing marketing assistance to U.S. companies and associations seeking to export U.S. agriculture products to Taiwan through its Agriculture Trade Office and assists Taiwanese importers in finding reliable U.S. agricultural suppliers. The AIT also provides assistance to U.S. companies seeking to export goods to Taiwan by arranging meetings with potential business partners or authorities in Taiwan, providing information on the domestic market, and maintaining a directory of U.S. companies that supply goods to Taiwan.[61] The AIT promotes cultural exchanges through its American Cultural Center, which hosts arts and cultural events and maintains a resource library of U.S. history and culture.[62]

From the beginning, the AIT has served as an advocate for the protection of human rights in Taiwan. Following the Kaohsiung Incident in 1979, AIT Chairman David Dean encouraged Chiang Ching-kuo to authorize civilian trials for members of the *tangwai* movement. Chiang assured Dean that only the eight organizers of the Kaohsiung protests would receive military trials, while all others would be tried in civilian courts, and prosecutors would not seek the death penalty. Throughout his tenure, AIT Director Charles Cross focused the Institute's efforts on reporting on human rights in Taiwan, with an emphasis on political oppression and persecution of dissidents. Under Cross, the AIT cultivated ties with activists and arranged for meetings between the families of jailed protesters and prominent Americans, among them Senator John Glenn. Over time, the AIT's efforts helped influence the development of Taiwan's democratic movement and hastened the end of authoritarian rule on the island.

The role of the AIT's counterpart organization in Taiwan is not to be overlooked. Following derecognition and the establishment of the AIT, the ROC established the CCNAA to serve as its representative organization in the United States. (The CCNAA was renamed the Taipei Economic and Cultural Representative Office following President Clinton's Taiwan policy review in 1994.) The first director of the CCNAA in the United States was Konsin Shah, a close associate of the Chiang family. With the termination of official relations, ROC officials were forced to cope with a diminished status in the United States. High-level visits between the United States and Taiwan ceased, and meetings between U.S. agencies and representatives of the ROC government were relegated to hotel meeting rooms and other temporary spaces. Shah and other representatives from the CCNAA were reportedly treated with suspicion by some members of the Carter administration, who believed the ROC government was attempting to undermine the burgeoning U.S.-PRC relationship.

The CCNAA's influence in Washington grew tremendously under its third director, Frederick Chien. Chien, a Ph.D. graduate of Yale University, worked vigorously to cultivate relationships with U.S. policymakers and was a powerful lobbyist for Taiwan's interests on Capitol Hill. According to David Dean, Chien "was off to a running start and didn't seem to slow down the entire time he was in Washington." Chien was given access to many high-level officials in the Reagan administration in sharp contrast to his CCNAA predecessors. When Chien stepped down from the CCNAA directorship in 1988, dozens of members of Congress took to the floor to give farewell speeches in his honor.

Visits by Taiwanese officials to the United States have been a source of friction ever since the Third Taiwan Strait Crisis of 1995 to 1996, which began when the United States issued a travel visa to President Lee to allow him to give a speech at Cornell University. In practice, U.S. policy has been inconsistent since the termination of diplomatic relations with the ROC in 1979. The State Department has wide authority to regulate the issuance of visas to foreign visitors, and the granting of visas to Taiwanese officials has largely followed the policies of successive presidential administrations. Under the Clinton administration, President Lee was forced to spend a night on his plane when it landed for a refueling stop in Honolulu in 1994 because the State Department refused to grant an entry visa to him. The following year, under pressure from Congress, the State Department granted Lee a visa for his visit to Cornell. In the early years of the George W. Bush administration, President Chen Shui-bian was permitted to meet with members of Congress and to attend consultations with the State Department. During a transit stop in New York in October 2003, Chen received a human rights award from the International League of Human Rights in a ceremony at the Grand Ballroom of the Waldorf Astoria Hotel, attended by more than twelve hundred guests and covered by both national and international media, and on his return from a visit to Panama, he met with sixteen members of Congress and representative of the AIT. Deputy Secretary of State Richard Armitage spoke with Chen by phone. Chen made additional extended transit stops in Honolulu and Seattle in 2004. In January 2005, Chen stopped on Guam while returning to Taiwan from Palau and the Solomon Islands. In September, the State Department allowed Chen to stop in Miami for one day on his way to Latin America and in San Francisco during his return voyage. While Chen was in Miami, the Congressional Human Rights Caucus presented him with an award via teleconference. However, in 2006, Chen was once again subject to strict travel restrictions following his termination of Taiwan's National Unification Council. Chen was no longer permitted to make extended transits, and future stops would be relegated to Honolulu and Anchorage, Alaska. Chen refused the new flight path, choosing to transit through other countries on future international trips. In May 2006, Representatives Thomas Tancredo and Dana Rohrabacher sent a letter to Secretary of State Condoleezza Rice suggesting the travel restrictions were inconsistent with the Taiwan Relations Act.[63] Following his election in 2008, Ma has enjoyed several extended transit stops in the United States, permitting enough time to attend public events and meet with members of Congress, including a visit to Harvard University, his alma mater, in fall 2015.

U.S. policy toward Taiwan has been highly impactful in many respects since the inception of the TRA in 1979. The AIT in particular has been instrumental to the success of informal U.S.-Taiwan relations. But more can be done to enhance official and nonofficial contacts to increase mutual understanding and interactions at all levels of government and society in both countries. Travel restrictions on Taiwan's presidents should be formally lifted to afford an appropriate level of predictability and prestige to their visits to the United States. For all intents and purposes the AIT is serving the function of a U.S. embassy in Taiwan. However the AIT's effectiveness is hampered by limitations placed on its activities. Restrictions on meetings between U.S. and Taiwanese officials should be lifted wherever possible. Diplomatic and consular privileges should be extended to appropriate AIT and CCNAA staff members to permit them to carry out their work unimpeded. Eventually, the United States may wish to upgrade the CCNAA to the level of a liaison office, as was done for the PRC during the lead-up to the normalization of U.S.-China relations in the 1970s.

B. PRESERVING TAIWAN'S DISTINCTIVE STATUS

The United States has never advocated for unification between China and Taiwan. At the very most, U.S. presidents have agreed not to contradict the PRC's One China Principle, which holds that there is one China which includes Taiwan. This diplomatic compromise is embodied in the language of the joint communiqués in which the United States acknowledges—but does not recognize—the Chinese position. After the derecognition of the ROC government in 1979, many lawmakers were concerned that the PRC would eventually overpower Taiwan. The prospect of losing a long-time strategic and economic ally to a communist rival was unthinkable. The passage of the TRA attempted to forestall this possibility by giving Taiwan the means to resist China and to engage confidently in cross-strait relations without the overriding threat of violence.

What many policymakers did not predict in 1979 was that Taiwan would soon undergo a transformative process of democratization that would reshape every aspect of Taiwanese society. As noted above, the United States supported this transition through the efforts of the AIT and through diplomatic pressure applied to the Chiang Ching-kuo regime to secure fair treatment of defendants following the Kaohsiung Incident and for political reforms near the end of Chiang's life. The result was the gradual creation of a state that expressed the self-determination of the people of Taiwan, not only the interests of the KMT exiled regime. But for all its optimism, the TRA was not written with these conditions in mind. And it is difficult to imagine Congress, then or now, countenancing the derecognition of a democratic government such as the one that exists on Taiwan today. It is crucial, therefore, that U.S. policy be updated to reflect Taiwan's evolution as a democratic state. The framework adopted under the three communiqués and the TRA, which has been modified only slightly in the years since, is, to borrow a phrase from Senator Church, "woefully inadequate" to secure Taiwan's future as a democracy without additional measures to recognize and normalize Taiwan's status.

The TRA's method for preserving Taiwan's *de facto* independence was the continuation of defensive arms sales. Lawmakers believed that ROC leaders would be more capable of standing up to the PRC if they were confident in the government's ability to defend itself by force if needed. Section 2(b)(5) of the TRA states that "it is the policy of the United States to provide Taiwan with arms of a defensive character." Section 3(a) of the TRA states that the United States "will make available to

Taiwan . . . defense articles and defense services" in quantity that is necessary to give Taiwan sufficient self-defense capabilities. This is a needs-based determination that will be made by the president and Congress in accordance with their judgments and through the recommendations of the U.S. military authorities. Furthermore, the TRA recognized that the peace and security of the Asia Pacific was a matter of national interest for the United States and that the United States would not tolerate attempts to isolate Taiwan through embargoes, blockades, or other measures. The implied threat of U.S. intervention is the reason that the TRA is often referred to as the functional equivalent of the Mutual Defense Treaty that was allowed to expire under the Carter administration in 1979.

In 1982, the TRA's arms sales provisions were nearly vitiated by the Third Communiqué which was adopted by President Reagan. The communiqué suggested that the United States would not increase the quantity or quality of arms sold to Taiwan and would eventually end weapons sales to Taiwan, seemingly in contradiction to the TRA's policy of providing defensive arms. The administration argued that the Third Communiqué was necessary to retain the PRC's goodwill, while Reagan's secret memorandum made clear that the reduction was premised on the continuation of peaceful cross-strait relations, a point that was emphasized by John Holdridge in congressional testimony. Reagan held to his pledge; however, his successor, President George H. W. Bush, authorized the sale of 150 F-16 jets in 1992, a few years after the Tiananmen Square massacre of 1989. President Clinton authorized roughly USD 8.9 billion in sales during his administration. Then, the George W. Bush administration, which began by showing strong support for Taiwan's defense, was accused of adopting a virtual freeze on arms sales after ending annual U.S.-Taiwan arms talks in favor of ad hoc reviews. Since 2008, the majority of sales have included upgrades to previously acquired equipment or training services related to existing equipment, and the Obama administration has appeared to deemphasize arms sales in its efforts to manage cross-strait relations. Taiwan's requests for submarines and advanced fighter jets have gone unfulfilled.

Despite improvements in cross-strait relations during the Ma administration, the PRC's rapid militarization and its continued focus on unification with Taiwan presents an ongoing danger. The ROC military, in close cooperation with U.S. military planners, should maintain sufficient defensive capabilities to thwart any attempt by the PLA to seize control of Taiwan. The United States meanwhile should protect its own interests in the region by projecting adequate offensive power to counter the PLA's denial-of-access strategy. Both objectives fall within the broader context of regional stability and defense, which includes the maintenance of open waterways in compliance with international law and the prevention of unauthorized seizures of territory in the East and South China Seas. The United States may wish to bring Taiwan under the umbrella of a broader Asia Pacific defensive coalition comprising Japan, South Korea, and other regional strategic allies.

C. TAIWAN'S DEMOCRATIC DEVELOPMENT

Since its inception, the TRA has served as a catalyst for political development in Taiwan. The law contains no declaration of support for, nor outlines methods for promoting, democratic governance in Taiwan. Nevertheless, by ensuring Taiwan's security, the United States gave the ROC regime space—backed by the imperative to retain international support—to undertake broad political reforms. Without it, the insecure KMT government may have doubled down on its repressive tactics to stave off political intervention from communist China, as it had done often during the period of martial law. Instead, ROC leaders had an opportunity to engage in a democratic transformation under the leadership of President Lee Teng-hui, who ended the Temporary Provisions Effective During the Period of Communist Rebellion in 1991. The development of an open economy and the protection of foreign investments, as supported by TRA sections 4, 5, and 6, allowed private enterprises to flourish within a dynamic modern economy. By the late 1990s, Taiwan was already recognized as one of the four "Asian Tigers," alongside Hong Kong, Singapore, and South Korea, thanks to what has come to be known as its economic miracle.

President Ma's policy of economic dependence and integration with China has threatened to undo this progress. The KMT's China-centric policies have made Taiwan more dependent on China than at any time in its history. The Economic Cooperation Framework Agreement (ECFA), a cross-strait free-trade agreement adopted in 2010, has allowed Taiwanese businesses to export manufacturing to the Chinese mainland, leading to unemployment for many of Taiwan's lower-skilled workers. A 2011 study found that most of the benefits of the ECFA have accrued to wealthy business owners, who, perhaps not surprisingly, are overwhelmingly aligned with the KMT. The proposed Cross-Strait Service Trade Agreement (CSSTA) would have exacerbated the trend and likely devastated small and medium-size businesses in Taiwan while threatening the autonomy of local media. Proponents of these agreements argued that foreign investors would be attracted to Taiwan as an alternative to China, while gaining the benefits of free trade with the China mainland market. However these benefits have yet to materialize under the ECFA. Meanwhile, Taiwan has not been able to conclude free-trade agreements with many of its largest trading partners, including the United States. Rather than globalizing in the true sense, Taiwan's economy has become over focused and over dependent on China.

Meanwhile, KMT politicians have pushed for a peace-pact with the PRC that would cement this trend and preclude Taiwan from ever asserting its *de jure* independence.

Over the past decade, with the opening up of cross-strait trade, Taiwan's economy has rapidly shifted its orientation toward China. KMT-style economic integration has brought Taiwan dangerously close to losing its independent status. The framers of the TRA recognized that the United States was uniquely able to assist Taiwan in preserving its distinctive status by providing material support and maintaining unofficial relations with the people of Taiwan. In addition to historical, military, and political ties, the United States had significant business and financial interests in Taiwan that lawmakers sought to protect. This aspect of the U.S.-Taiwan relationship remains true and should not be neglected. The United States should deepen its economic ties with Taiwan by taking steps to adopt a U.S.-Taiwan free-trade and bilateral investment agreement and by promoting Taiwan's inclusion in the Trans-Pacific Partnership. Doing so will benefit Taiwan's economic well-being—at a time when China's own economy appears to be slowing—while strengthening its ability to resist the PRC's overtures for unification. This policy would most certainly contribute to the objectives of the TRA, as illuminated by the legislative history described above, and would be within the bounds of the three communiqués and the peaceful conduct of cross-strait affairs.

D. FOSTERING TAIWAN'S PARTICIPATION IN INTERNATIONAL ORGANIZATIONS

Section 4(d) of the TRA provided that nothing in the law was meant to support "the exclusion or expulsion of Taiwan from continued membership in any international financial institution or any other international organization." It was Congress' view that Taiwan should remain a member of organizations in which it held membership in 1979. A broader reading holds that Taiwan should not be excluded from seeking future membership in international organizations. Unfortunately, these words were not enough to save Taiwan a seat at the world table. Since the KMT regime's expulsion from the United Nations in 1971, Taiwan's participation in international forums fell dramatically. The ROC soon left the World Bank and the International Monetary Fund, and retained only ten international memberships by 1984.[64] Taiwan's numerous attempts to join the United Nations have been equally unsuccessful. This is in large part due to the actions of the PRC, which has actively sought Taiwan's ostracization from the international community. In particular, China has used its clout in the United Nations to keep the question of Taiwan's participation or membership off the General Assembly's agenda, despite repeated attempts by Taiwan and its allies to raise the issue. Were the United Nations to consider the matter of Taiwan's membership, China's permanent seat on the Security Council ultimately would allow it to veto Taiwan's membership—though some of Taiwan's proponents make a strong case that China would be disqualified from voting under Article 27(3) of the Charter, which requires Security Council members to abstain from voting on matters concerning disputes to which they are a party, as elaborated in Chapter VI and Article 52 of the Charter.

With limited success the United States has assisted Taiwan in its efforts to seek membership in some international organizations. In 1994, the Taiwan Policy Review conducted by the Clinton administration stipulated that the United States would "actively support Taiwan's membership in international organizations accepting non-states as members, and look for ways to have Taiwan's voice heard in organizations of states where Taiwan's membership was not possible." With U.S. assistance, Taiwan became a member of the World Trade Organization in 2002 and an observer at the World Health Assembly in 2009. More recently, President Obama and Congress have actively supported Taiwan's participation in the International Civil Aviation Organization (ICAO). The United States should continue to assist Taiwan in its campaign to achieve meaningful participation in international organizations, including UN specialized agencies. In accordance with the 1994 Taiwan Policy Review, the United States should support Taiwan's participation, as a full member, in international organizations where statehood is not a requirement and, at the very least, as a recognized observer where statehood is a prerequisite.

Under the TRA and the three joint communiqués, the United States has adhered to a One China Policy while encouraging Taiwan and China to resolve their differences peacefully. Throughout the administrations of George W. Bush and Barack Obama, the United States has opposed actions by either China or Taiwan that would unilaterally change the status quo of Taiwan's *de facto* independence. Seventy years since the end of World War II, Taiwan has evolved from a militarily occupied territory under martial law to a vibrant and peaceful democracy with an advanced economy. This transformation likely could not have taken place without the support of the United States under the TRA. However, increasingly Taiwan is at danger of finding itself dependent on China and isolated in the world community. U.S. policymakers should reaffirm their support for the objectives of the TRA and for the preservation of Taiwan's unique political and cultural identity. As a concrete measure, the United States should reappraise its One China Policy by evaluating whether changes could be made to better suit the reality in Taiwan. Furthermore, the United States ought to abandon its reliance on strategic ambiguity and clarify its stance on Taiwan's international legal status. As will be described in Chapters 11 and 12, the United States and members of the world community could, and should, go further by supporting an internationally supervised plebiscite to allow the people of Taiwan to decide their country's future path of development.

Notes

1. RICHARD C. BUSH, AT CROSS PURPOSES: U.S.-TAIWAN RELATIONS SINCE 1942, at 88 (2015).

2. *Id.* at 189.

3. *Id.* at 100.

4. *Id.* at 102.

5. *Id.*

6. United States of America-People's Republic of China Joint Communiqué of Feb. 27, 1972, *available at* http://www.taiwandocuments.org/communique01.htm.

7. UN General Assembly, Resolution 2758, A/RES/2758 (XXVI), Oct. 25, 1971.

8. KERRY DUMBAUGH, TAIWAN-U.S. RELATIONS: DEVELOPMENTS AND POLICY IMPLICATIONS, CONGRESSIONAL RESEARCH SERVICE, at 3 (2009), *available at* http://www.fas.org/sgp/crs/row/R40493.pdf.

9. U.S. Department of State, Foreign Relations of the United States, 1977–1980, Vol. XIII, China, Document 235, *available at* http://history.state.gov/historicaldocuments/frus1977-80v13/d235.

10. IMPLEMENTATION OF THE TAIWAN RELATIONS ACT: THE FIRST YEAR, A STAFF REPORT TO THE COMMITTEE ON FOREIGN RELATIONS, UNITED STATES SENATE at 7 (June 1980).

11. *Id.* at 4.

12. United States of America–People's Republic of China Joint Communiqué of Aug. 17, 1982, *available at* http:// www.taiwandocuments.org/ communique03.htm.

13. SHIRLEY A. KAN, CHINA/TAIWAN: EVOLUTION OF THE "ONE CHINA POLICY"—KEY STATEMENTS FROM WASHINGTON, BEIJING, AND TAIPEI, CONGRESSIONAL RESEARCH SERVICE, at 46 (2014), *available at* http://www.fas.org/sgp/crs/row/RL30341.pdf.

14. DUMBAUGH, *supra* note 8, at 9.

15. KAN, *supra* note 13, at 44.

16. NANCY BERNKOPF TUCKER, STRAIT TALK: UNITED STATES–TAIWAN RELATIONS AND THE CRISIS WITH CHINA 155–66 (2009).

17. H.R. Res. 178, 106th Cong. (1999).

18. KAN, *supra*, note 13, at 50.

19. 1994 Taiwan Policy Review (summary reprinted by the Formosan Association for Public Affairs), *available at* http://www.fapa.org/generalinfo/TPR1994.html.

20. *Id.*

21. H.R. Con. Res. 53, 104th Cong. (1995).

22. Jim Mann, *Clinton Struggling to Shape Foreign Policy and America's Place in World*, L.A. TIMES, Oct. 2, 1995, *available at* http://articles.latimes.com/1995-10-02/news/mn-52459_1_foreign-policy/2.

23. *See* RICHARD C. BUSH, UNTYING THE KNOT 210 (2006).

24. Michael E. O'Hanlon, *Can China Conquer Taiwan*, BROOKINGS INSTITUTION (2000), *available at* http://www.brookings.edu/views/articles/ohanlon/2000fall_IS.pdf.

25. KAN, *supra* note 13, at 62.

26. *Id.* at 64.

27. Stephen J. Yates, *Clinton Statement Undermines Taiwan*, HERITAGE FOUNDATION, July 19, 1998, *available at* http://www.heritage.org/research/asiaandthepacific/em538.cfm.

28. *Id.*

29. KAN, *supra* note 13, at 69.

30. Statement of Harvey J. Feldman, Former U.S. Ambassador, Senior Fellow, The Heritage Foundation, United States–Taiwan Relations: The Twentieth Anniversary of the Taiwan Relations Act: Hearing Before Senate Committee on Foreign Relations, 106th Cong., *transcript available at* http://www.gpo.gov/fdsys/pkg/CHRG-106shrg55823/pdf/CHRG-106shrg55823.pdf.

31. *Id.*

32. *Id.*

33. *Id.*

34. *Id.*

35. *Id.*

36. Taiwan Security Enhancement Act (TSEA), H.R. 1838, 106th Cong. (2000).

37. *Id.*

38. H.R. 3707, 106th Cong. (2000).

39. H.R. 4444, 106th Cong. §106 (2000).

40. Richard C. Bush III, *U.S.-Taiwan Relations: What's the Problem?*, BROOKINGS INSTITUTION, Dec. 3, 2007, *available at* http://www.brookings.edu/speeches/2007/1203_taiwan_bush.aspx.

41. KAN, *supra* note 13, at 71.

42. *Id.* at 64 n.169.

43. *Id.* at 71 n.172.

44. *Id.*

45. Ted Galen Carpenter, *Prospects for the Taiwan Security Enhancement* at 2, CATO INSTITUTE, Mar. 15, 2001, *available at* http://www.cato.org/pub_display.php?pub_id=4347.

46. KAN, *supra* note 13, at 76.

47. *Chen Stands Up to Bush*, CNN, Dec. 10, 2003, *available at* http://edition.cnn.com/2003/WORLD/asiapcf/east/12/10/taiwan.us.china/index.html.

48. *See* Jim Hwang, *Editorial: From the Stage to the Page*, TAIWAN TODAY, July 1, 1999, *available at* http://taiwantoday.tw/ct.asp?xitem=1438&ctnode=1343&mp=9.

49. KAN, *supra* note 13, at 76.

50. *Id.* at 79.

51. John J. Tkacik, Jr., *Taiwan Arms Sales: Less Than Meets the Eye*, HERITAGE FOUNDATION, Oct. 8, 2008, *available at* http://www.heritage.org/Research/AsiaandthePacific/wm2098.cfm.

52. *Id.*

53. SHIRLEY A. KAN, TAIWAN: MAJOR U.S. ARMS SALES SINCE 1990, CONGRESSIONAL RESEARCH SERVICE, at 58–59 (2014), *available at* https://www.fas.org/sgp/crs/weapons/RL30957.pdf.

54. Joint Press Statement by President Obama and President Hu of China, Nov. 17, 2009, http://www.whitehouse.gov/the-press-office/joint-press-statement-president-obama-and-president-hu-china.

55. Peter Brookes, *O's China Kowtow: Punting on Security, Trade*, N.Y. POST, Nov. 19, 2009, *available at* http://www.nypost.com/p/news/opinion/opedcolumnists/china_kowtow_JpkM6Xk8ocogXfEFsDvEUO.

56. *Taiwan Expected to Honor Beef Trade Pact*, CHINA POST, Nov. 24, 2009, *available at* http://www.chinapost.com.tw/taiwan/2009/11/24/233930/Taiwan%2Dexpected.htm.

57. William Lowther, *Taiwan-US FTA Resolution Introduced in Congress*, TAIPEI TIMES, May 10, 2010, *available at* http://www.taipeitimes.com/News/front/archives/2010/05/10/2003472624.

58. *See* U.S. Department of State, Taiwan's Participation in the International Civil Aviation Organization (ICAO), Sept. 24, 2013, http://www.state.gov/r/pa/prs/ps/2013/09/214658.htm.

59. *See* Sam LaGrone, *Taiwan Wants to Buy U.S. Frigates Despite Chinese Objections*, USNI NEWS, Dec. 9, 2014, *available at* http://news.usni.org/2014/12/09/taiwan-wants-buy-u-s-frigates-despite-chinese-objections; Ankit Panda, *US Finalizes Sale of Perry-class Frigates to Taiwan*, THE DIPLOMAT, Dec. 20, 2014, *available at* http://thediplomat.com/2014/12/us-finalizes-sale-of-perry-class-frigates-to-taiwan/.

60. Richard C. Bush III, *Thoughts on the Taiwan Relations Act*, BROOKINGS INSTITUTION (2009), *available at* http://www.brookings.edu/opinions/2009/04_taiwan_bush.aspx?p=1.

61. American Institute in Taiwan, About Us, Commerce Section, http://www.ait.org.tw/en/commercial-section.html.

62. American Institute in Taiwan, Education & Culture, Research Information Services, http://www.ait.org.tw/en/information-resources.html (last visited July 18, 2011).

63. *See* Nadia Tsao, *U.S. Officials Protest Chen's Treatment*, TAIPEI TIMES, May 7, 2006, *available at* http://www.taipeitimes.com/News/taiwan/archives/2006/05/07/2003306592.

64. *Id.*

7 U.S.-China Relations

THE UNITED STATES' strategic interests in the Asia Pacific evolved enormously in the decades following World War II. This shift is illustrated most dramatically in the case of Taiwan. By the end of the war, U.S. officials, including President Harry Truman, were content to walk away from Taiwan, allowing events between the People's Republic of China (PRC) and the Republic of China (ROC) to take their course. With the onset of the Korean War, Taiwan became strategically priceless, both as a regional ally and as a forward base in any potential military conflict with the PRC. U.S. support for the ROC was unequivocal throughout the 1950s and 1960s. Meanwhile, the United States had few diplomatic interactions with China. This dynamic was sharply reversed in the 1970s. The Nixon administration saw an opportunity to align with the PRC to further Soviet isolation. In 1979, the United States established formal diplomatic relations with the PRC. Since that time, the U.S.-PRC relationship has grown remarkably. Today, the United States' and China's economic and security interests are firmly intertwined. Yet areas of conflicting interests and mutual suspicions remain.

I. U.S.-China Relations from 1945 to 1971

A. THE CHINESE CIVIL WAR

When the Allied Forces declared victory in the Pacific, Chiang Kai-shek's Chinese Nationalist Party still exercised control over most of the Chinese mainland. On August 17, 1945, U.S. General Douglas MacArthur of the Allied Command issued General Order No. 1 which instructed Chiang to engage in a military occupation of Taiwan on behalf of the Allied Powers pending the conclusion of a peace treaty with Japan. The Chinese Nationalists undertook an immediate military occupation of the island that manifestly exceeded the scope of the trusteeship. The exercise was met with little objection from the United States or others in the international community. In early 1947, the Nationalist government unilaterally declared Taiwan to be one of the thirty-five provinces of the Republic of China, an act in violation of the Allied accords and international law. In January 1949, as the civil war worsened, Chiang resigned his presidency. Soon after, the Communists seized power after overrunning the Nationalist capital of Nanjing and, on October 1, 1949, Mao declared the founding of the PRC on the Chinese mainland, with its capital in Beijing. Defeated, Chiang Kai-shek and more than one million of his supporters sought refuge on Taiwan. There, Chiang proclaimed the re-establishment of the ROC in Taipei. The Chinese Nationalists were effectively a regime in exile.

At first, the United States adopted a policy of ambivalence toward the development, choosing "to let events take their course." However, the eruption of the Korean War in 1950 changed the U.S. calculus in the region and prompted the United States to rethink the cost of impartiality toward Taiwan. With support from the PRC, North Korean forces invaded South Korea on June 25, 1950. Fearing that a similar scenario was imminent in Taiwan, the United States found it necessary to intervene. Two days after the North Korean aggression, President Truman declared the "neutralization of Formosa" and dispatched the U.S. Seventh Fleet to the Taiwan Strait to maintain peace. Truman stated that "the determination of the future status of Formosa must await" the occurrence of one of the following events: the restoration of security in the Pacific; a peace settlement with Japan; or consideration by the United Nations.[1]

In 1951, Japan and the Allied Powers began formal negotiations to end the war in the Pacific. Although a large part of the negotiations concerned the disposition of Japan's overseas territories, neither the ROC nor the PRC received an invitation to attend the negotiations. On September 8, 1951, forty-nine nations signed the Treaty of Peace with Japan—commonly known as the San Francisco Peace Treaty. On the matter of Taiwan, the Treaty called for Japan to renounce "all right, title and claim to Formosa [Taiwan] and the Pescadores [Penghu]." As emphasized in previous chapters, the provisions failed to state to whom Formosa would be delivered; therefore, Taiwan's title and its legal status under international law remained unresolved. The San Francisco Peace Treaty entered into force on April 28, 1952. The same day, the ROC and Japan agreed to a separate bilateral peace treaty called the Treaty of Taipei, in which Japan again renounced "all right, title, and claim to Taiwan and Penghu." Like the San Francisco Peace Treaty, the Treaty of Taipei did not specify which state, if any, would benefit from the renunciation.

Even after the founding of the People's Republic of China, both the Nationalist ROC and the Communist PRC governments each claimed to be the only legitimate government of the entirety of China. But it was the ROC that maintained diplomatic recognition by most states and consequently a seat in the United Nations. As early as the summer of 1950, U.S. and Allied leaders contemplated whether to admit the newly victorious PRC to the United Nations. The question was complicated by the fact that the Republic of China was a permanent member of the Security Council, as prescribed in Article 23(1) of the UN Charter. In the absence of a formal pronouncement to the contrary, Chiang Kai-shek's government remained the sole lawful representative of China (that is to say, the whole of China) in the United Nations. The major powers decided that decisions concerning the PRC representation in the UN would have to wait until after the end of the Korean War.

B. THE TWO CHINAS AND THE UNITED NATIONS

Throughout the 1950s, the United States used its influence in the United Nations to advance a "moratorium formula" concerning the question of China's representation in the United Nations. Under this approach, the General Assembly would neither include in its agenda a proposal to unseat the ROC regime in favor of the PRC nor debate the merits of any such proposal. The Truman administration focused on preserving the status quo in the United Nations in which the Republic of China, a charter member of the United Nations, retained its original seat in the General Assembly and on the Security Council, while the People's Republic of China went unrepresented in either body. During the Eisenhower administration, however, it became apparent that the PRC's participation was inevitable. The White House began looking for ways to accommodate both the PRC and the ROC as UN members. This was consistent with the belief expressed by some senior-level officials that Taiwan constituted a unique state, and that the ROC was the government of Taiwan, but not the government of China. Nevertheless, no action was taken during Eisenhower's time in office, and the situation in the United Nations remained unchanged. The influx of new members to the United Nations in the 1960s, including many recently de-colonized states which were aligned with the PRC, made the question irresistible. By the time President Kennedy entered office, the issue of Chinese representation in the United Nations could no longer remain in abeyance. One of the biggest challenges facing U.S. officials was Chiang Kai-shek's refusal to relent his claim to the Chinese mainland. Chiang made clear that he would not tolerate coexistence with the PRC at the United Nations. Both the Kennedy and Johnson administrations attempted to accommodate the PRC and the ROC, arguing that both retained a right to membership as successors to the Chinese government that signed the UN Charter. Such a formulation would permit the ascension of both governments to the United Nations. To the contrary, Chiang's staunch position was that the ROC represented the "whole of China," rejecting both the "two Chinas" and the "one China, one Taiwan" proposals. During this period, the United States shifted from the moratorium formula to the "important question" strategy, which held that any proposal to deprive the ROC of representation was an important question under Article 18 of the UN Charter, thereby requiring a two-thirds majority vote. The strategy more or less stalled the issue until such time that the PRC could muster a parliamentary majority in its favor.

After 1969, the "frequency and intensity of . . . diplomatic exchanges [between the United States and the PRC] increased markedly."[2] The relationship between the two countries advanced rapidly beginning in 1971, when President Nixon sought to exploit growing tensions between the PRC and the Soviet Union. The Sino-Soviet split presented Nixon with an opportunity to normalize relations with the PRC and to leverage the PRC to constrain the Soviet Union (a decision referred to as Nixon's playing of "the China card"). Under Nixon, the United States came to the UN General Assembly with a changed attitude toward the ROC. U.S. diplomats would no longer use their influence to block moves unfriendly to the Chiang regime.

In 1971, the PRC's allies in the United Nations ramped up their efforts to expel the ROC and seat the PRC. On July 15, more than a dozen member states requested that the issue be included in the General Assembly's provisional agenda for the upcoming session. Over the course of the summer, the General Assembly entertained three proposals. The first, made by Albania and other states supporting Communist China, advocated the one-China formula, which called for seating the PRC and expelling the ROC from the United Nations. The second, submitted by the United States and allies, advocated the "two China proposal," which would permit the PRC's admission to the United Nations while allowing the ROC to keep its current seat. The third proposal, suggested by the Saudi Arabia delegation, supported a "one-China, one-Taiwan" formula, by which China would be seated as the representative of China and a permanent member on the Security Council, while Taiwan remained in the United Nations as Taiwan. The Saudi Arabian representative also proposed that Taiwan conduct a plebiscite under the auspices of the United Nations, believing that such action was necessary in order to respect the will of the people of Taiwan.

On September 25, a draft resolution, A/L.630, was presented in the General Assembly to "restore to the People's Republic of China all its rights and expel forthwith the representatives of Chiang Kai-shek." Four days later, on September 29, 1971, a coalition of twenty-two member states led by the United States introduced A/L.632, which would have deemed any proposal to expel the ROC as an "important question" under Article 18 of the UN Charter—requiring a separate, two-thirds majority vote. The vote failed, 59 to 55, with 15 abstentions. The United States then proposed a motion for a separate vote on the proposal "to expel forthwith the representatives of Chiang Kai-shek from the place which they unlawfully occupy at the United Nations" in the draft of A/L.630. If accepted, the U.S. proposal would have welcomed the PRC in the United Nations as the official representative of China, while retaining a seat for the ROC. The proposal also failed, 61 to 51, with 16 abstentions.

On October 25, 1971, the General Assembly accepted the Albanian proposal and adopted UN Resolution 2758, which recognized the PRC as the only lawful representative of China at the United Nations and one of the five permanent members of the Security Council. Simultaneously, the resolution expelled Chiang Kai-shek's ROC representatives and characterized their presence at the United Nations as an unlawful occupation. The resolution stated:

> THE GENERAL ASSEMBLY . . . *Recognizing* that the representatives of the Government of the People's Republic of China are the only lawful representatives of China to the United Nations and that the People's Republic of China is one of the five permanent members of the Security Council,
> *Decides* to restore all its rights to the People's Republic of China and to recognize the representatives of its Government as the only legitimate representatives of China to the United Nations, and to expel forthwith the representatives of Chiang Kai-shek from the place which they unlawfully occupy at the United Nations and in all the organizations related to it.[3]

It is worth noting that the resolution dealt solely with the issue of China's representation in the United Nations and did not take a position on sovereignty over Taiwan.

After the passage of Resolution 2758, the ROC delegation protested that its expulsion was a violation of Article 18 of the UN Charter, which expressly requires a two-thirds vote on questions of expulsion. The seating of the PRC in place of the ROC marked the beginning of Taiwan's diplomatic isolation and the rise of the PRC on the international stage.

II. Building the U.S.-China Relationship

A. PRESIDENT NIXON'S VISIT TO CHINA (1972)

Beginning in early 1971, President Nixon's national security advisor Henry Kissinger made a series of secret visits to China. Nixon and Kissinger had concluded that diplomatic relations with the PRC would provide the United States with leverage in its Cold War struggle against the USSR, which shared a long border with China and with whom it was increasingly at odds. U.S. officials also hoped that improved relations with Beijing would help hasten the ending of the Vietnam War. Through intermediaries in Pakistan, Kissinger communicated with Chinese Premier Zhou Enlai and arranged for a face-to-face meeting. On July 9, 1971, Kissinger met with Zhou in Beijing. President Nixon revealed Kissinger's mission in an address broadcast by the NBC TV network on July 15. A statement that was broadcast simultaneously in China said:

> Knowing of President Nixon's expressed desire to visit the People's Republic of China, Premier Chou En-lai, on behalf of the Government of the People's Republic of China, has extended an invitation to President Nixon to visit China at an appropriate date before May 1972. President Nixon has accepted the invitation with pleasure.[4]

Kissinger made a second trip to China, in October 1971, around the time of the adoption of Resolution 2758 in the United Nations. With the groundwork laid, President Nixon embarked on a new and crucial phase in U.S.-PRC relations with his own visit to China in February 1972. Nixon visited China from February 21 to 28, 1972, with a delegation that included First Lady Pat Nixon, Kissinger, Secretary of State William Rogers, and others. While Premier Zhou served as the U.S. party's escort for much of the visit, Nixon was granted a meeting with Chairman Mao Zedong, leader of the Chinese Communist Party, on the first day of his visit, which lasted approximately one hour.

The magnitude of Nixon's visit was heightened with the issuance of the joint Shanghai Communiqué on February 28. The communiqué has served as one of the pillars of the U.S.-PRC relationship ever since and expressed the countries' understandings and preferences on a number of topics related to Asia. As to Taiwan, the communiqué stated, in part:

> The leaders of the People's Republic of China and the United States of America found it beneficial to have this opportunity, after so many years without contact, to present candidly to one another their views on a variety of issues. They reviewed the international situation in which important changes and great upheavals are taking place and expounded their respective positions and attitudes . . . .
>
> The two sides reviewed the long-standing serious disputes between China and the United States. The Chinese side reaffirmed its position: the Taiwan question is the crucial question obstructing the normalization of relations between China and the United States; the Government of the People's Republic of China is the sole legal government of China; Taiwan is a province of China which has long been returned to the motherland; the liberation of Taiwan is China's internal affair in which no other country has the right to interfere; and all U.S. forces and military installations must be withdrawn from Taiwan. The Chinese Government firmly opposes any activities which aim at the creation of "one China, one Taiwan", "one China, two governments", "two Chinas", an "independent Taiwan" or advocate that "the status of Taiwan remains to be determined."
>
> The U.S. side declared: The United States acknowledges that all Chinese on either side of the Taiwan Strait maintain there is but one China and that Taiwan is a part of China. The United States Government does not challenge that position. It reaffirms its interest in a peaceful settlement of the Taiwan question by the Chinese themselves. With this prospect in mind, it affirms the ultimate objective of the withdrawal of all U.S. forces and military installations from Taiwan. In the meantime, it will progressively reduce its forces and military installations on Taiwan as the tension in the area diminishes. . . .[5]

B. ESTABLISHMENT OF LIAISON OFFICES (1973)

On May 1, 1973, the United States and the PRC established reciprocal liaison offices in Beijing and Washington, D.C. The U.S. Liaison Office (USLO) in Beijing sought to address all matters in the U.S.-PRC relationship "except the strictly formal diplomatic aspects of the relationship."[6] For several years, until February 28, 1979, these liaison offices were maintained simultaneously with the United States' embassy in Taiwan.

The first Chief Liaison Officer in Beijing was David K. E. Bruce, who served from March 1973 to September 1974. Bruce previously headed the U.S. delegation at the Paris talks that led to the end of the Vietnam War. John H. Holdridge, one of the two initial Deputy Chiefs of Mission (DCMs) under Bruce, wrote in his later account that the USLO in Beijing was to be "a more or less conventional Foreign Service mission, the staff of which was to be selected by the Department of State."[7] On the ULSO's status in China, Holdridge wrote:

> [T]he general outlines of the liaison office arrangement agreed upon by Premier Zhou Enlai and Dr. Kissinger in February were similar to those of a normal diplomatic mission. We discovered shortly after we opened the liaison office in Beijing that, with certain exceptions, we were indeed treated as a diplomatic mission. The exceptions were that we did not attend functions in the Great Hall of the People held in honor of visiting VIPs, nor was the chief of the U.S. Liaison Office invited to go along on the semiannual tour of various parts of China that the Foreign Ministry organized for chiefs of mission. Otherwise, we participated actively in the life of the diplomatic community, enjoyed diplomatic license tags on our cars, had ready access to the Foreign Ministry—sometimes more than we wanted—and maintained unrestricted contacts with fellow diplomats and members of the foreign press. We were also able to travel to parts of China open to foreigners on about the same basis as regularly accredited diplomats.[8]

In 1976, the Chief of the Chinese Liaison Office in Beijing was upgraded to the rank of ambassador. Three years later, on January 1, 1979, the United States recognized the PRC government as the only government of China. On March 1 of that year, the USLO in Beijing was converted into an official embassy. Shortly after, the process of normalization between the United States and the PRC was unexpectedly delayed by leadership changes in both countries. Nixon's resignation from office in the wake of the Watergate scandal brought Gerald R. Ford to office in 1974. In China, Mao Zedong and Premier Zhou Enlai were in declining health, and Zhou was increasingly delegating authority to his heir apparent Deng Xiaoping. In 1975, President Ford visited China for five days, but the future of U.S-Sino relations remained uncertain, and no official joint communiqué was produced. Upon his return from Asia, President Ford proclaimed the Pacific Doctrine, which called for normalization of relations with China and economic cooperation throughout Asia. Zhou died the next year in January 1976, followed by Mao Zedong in September.

C. THE SECOND COMMUNIQUÉ AND FORMAL RECOGNITION
OF THE PRC (1978)

Responsibility for completing the normalization process fell to President Jimmy Carter, who took office in 1977. In September 1978, Congress passed the Dole-Stone Amendment to the International Security Assistance Act of 1978 Concerning the Mutual Defense Treaty with the ROC. The amendment stated it was "the sense of the Congress that there should be prior consultation between the Congress and the Executive Branch on any proposed policy changes affecting the continuation in force of the Mutual Defense Treaty of 1954."[9] As described in Chapter 5, the Carter administration opted not to inform Congress of developments in discussions with the PRC until the last moment. In late 1978, PRC leaders signaled their willingness to soften their position on Taiwan, and Carter authorized Leonard Woodcock, Chief of the U.S. Liaison Office in China, to begin negotiations on normalization. The Chinese maintained their position that the resolution of the Taiwan question was an internal affair. However, in December, Vice Premier Deng Xiaoping stated that the Chinese government would "take note" of Carter's suggestion that the situation should be resolved peacefully.[10]

On December 15, 1978, the two countries issued their Second Communiqué, reaffirming the core principles expressed in the Shanghai Communiqué seven years earlier. The Second Communiqué restated the acknowledgment formula in the Shanghai Communiqué declaring that the U.S. government "acknowledged the Chinese position that there was but one China and Taiwan was part of China." (Importantly, neither communiqué stated that the United States recognized or shared China's viewpoint.) Further, the United States recognized the PRC as the "sole legitimate government of China." The statement effectively terminated any official ties that the United States held with the ROC. In 1979, President Jimmy Carter permitted the 1954 Mutual Defense Treaty between the United States and the ROC to lapse.

In late January 1979, shortly after the United States and the PRC established diplomatic relations, Deng Xiaoping began a goodwill visit to the United States. This was the first visit by a Chinese leader to the United States since the founding of the PRC in 1949. The visit was a diplomatic success, with photos and videos of Deng's activities broadcast around the globe. Deng had been purged from the Chinese Communist Party twice during his lifetime, but after Mao's death in 1976, he rapidly consolidated power and embarked on a reformist agenda. By the time of his visit to the United States, he had shifted many of China's Communist economic programs and had begun implementing limited private property and market reforms, including opening up the country to foreign investment. Deng's tour included visits to the headquarters of corporations including Boeing and Coca-Cola. Following Deng's visit, in July 1979, the United States and the PRC signed an agreement permitting Chinese products to receive temporary most favored nation tariff status.

D. THE TAIWAN RELATIONS ACT (1979) AND THE THIRD COMMUNIQUÉ (1982)

Notwithstanding statements made in the Second Joint Communiqué, disagreements between the United States and the PRC regarding Taiwan arose almost immediately. The negotiations over normalization left a number of crucial issues unresolved. Among them were the PRC's unwillingness to commit to not using force against Taiwan and the United States' continued arms sales to the island. In his signing statement, Carter stated that he would interpret the TRA "in a manner consistent with our interest in the well-being of the people on Taiwan and with the understandings we reached on the normalization of relations with the People's Republic of China." One of those understandings was a commitment to a one-year moratorium on arms sales to Taiwan, which the United States honored throughout 1979. Arms sales resumed in 1980. As described in Chapter 6, the Reagan administration's plan to sell Northrop FX fighter jets to Taiwan triggered vocal protests from the PRC. Chinese leaders warned that continued arms sales risked undermining U.S.-PRC relations.

In August 1982, three years after the enactment of the TRA, the United States and the PRC issued a third joint communiqué. The two sides agreed the United States would continue to maintain cultural, commercial, and other unofficial relations with the people of Taiwan. The United States again acknowledged but did not assent to the Chinese's position that "there is but one China and Taiwan is a part of China," but moderated its position by proclaiming that it had "no intention of infringing on Chinese sovereignty and territorial integrity, or interfering in China's internal affairs, or pursuing a policy of 'two Chinas' or 'one China, one Taiwan.'" With respect to the issue of arms sales to Taiwan, the United States expressed that, though it did not seek to carry out a long-term policy of arms sales to Taiwan, it would continue to do so pursuant to the TRA and consistent with the qualitative and quantitative terms agreed to between Taiwan and the United States in recent years.

As recounted in Chapter 6, at the time of the issuance of the third U.S.-Sino joint communiqué, President Reagan wrote in a secret memorandum:

> The U.S. willingness to reduce its arms sales to Taiwan is conditioned absolutely upon the continued commitment of China to the peaceful solution of the Taiwan-PRC differences. It should be clearly understood that the linkage between these two matters is a permanent imperative of U.S. foreign policy.

In addition, it is essential that the quantity and quality of the arms provided Taiwan be conditioned entirely on the threat posed by the PRC. Both in quantitative and qualitative terms, Taiwan's defense capability relative to that of the PRC will be maintained.[11]

Before the third joint communiqué was made public in August 1982, President Reagan offered his "Six Assurances" to Taiwan. The Six Assurances signaled that the United States would support but not actively orchestrate or coerce cross-strait dialogues. Additionally, the Assurances demonstrated the continued force of the TRA, as the United States would not alter the terms of the TRA; would not set a date for termination of arms sales; and would not consult the PRC in advance before making decisions about arms sales to Taiwan. Furthermore, the Assurances promised that the United States had not "altered its position regarding sovereignty over Taiwan," which meant that Taiwan's legal status would remain undetermined in the eyes of the United States, an approach consistent with prior U.S. policy.

E. CHINA JOINS MULTILATERAL ECONOMIC INSTITUTIONS (1980 TO 1991)

Since the 1980s, China has joined numerous intergovernmental organizations (IGOs) and nongovernmental organizations (NGOs). During the 1980s and into the early 1990s, China slowly began integrating itself into multilateral institutions. Under the leadership of Deng Xiaoping, the PRC carried out policies aimed at reforming and opening up the Chinese economy. In 1978, the Third Plenum of the Eleventh Chinese Communist Party (CCP) Congress adopted the Four Modernizations for developing the rural economy, encouraging some free-market activities, and attracting foreign investment. In 1982, the Twelfth CCP Congress adopted a new constitution that legitimized the use of foreign assistance in the country's economic development. The PRC went from being a member of 21 IGOs and 71 NGOs in 1977 to 49 IGOs and 1,013 NGOs in 1995, and 52 IGOs and 1,163 NGOs by 1997.[12] Today, China is a member of some 73 IGOs.[13] Beyond mere membership, the PRC has started to exercise significant influence and leadership.

Although the Republic of China was an original founding member of the International Monetary Fund (IMF) and the World Bank in 1945, the PRC did not participate in the institutions until 1980, when it assumed responsibility for China's seat in both organizations. In 1980, China resumed participation in the Interim Commission for the International Trade Organization, which had been set up under the General Agreement on Tariffs and Trade (GATT) in 1947 to foster the development of a permanent trade organization (which would become the World

Trade Organization some fifty years later). That year, China also joined the World Intellectual Property Organization. In 1983, it joined the Multi-Fibre Arrangement (MFA), a textiles trade pact that had been established in 1974 and that was largely favorable to developing countries. In 1986, China joined the Asian Development Bank (ADB). The same year it applied for permanent membership in GATT, having received observer status in 1983.

At first, the U.S. lawmakers did not support the PRC's entry into GATT or the ADB over concerns about the lack of transparency in the Chinese economy. In the case of the ADB, one of its founding members was the ROC, which joined the organization in 1966, after its exile from China. Therefore, unlike the United Nations and its associated organizations, the PRC was not able to easily claim that Taiwan was unrightfully occupying its seat. Although the PRC demanded that Taiwan be expelled from the ADB, a compromise was reached in 1985 that permitted Taiwan to stay in the ADB by changing its name to "Taipei, China." Taiwan boycotted the organization for two years as a result of this slight, only resuming participation in 1988.

In 1991, the PRC joined the Asia-Pacific Economic Cooperation (APEC). Taiwan joined at the same time as "Chinese Taipei." APEC serves as a forum for cooperation on economic and trade issues for twenty-one countries in the Pacific. The PRC and Taiwan are both active members of the organization, although APEC sometimes serves as a forum for diplomatic sparring between the two. APEC has also provided a stage for signature moments in the U.S.-PRC relationship. For example, in 2014, the United States and the PRC announced an agreement providing for ten-year multiple entry visas intended to promote greater tourism and business travel between the two countries.

F. THE TIANANMEN SQUARE MASSACRE OF JUNE 4, 1989

In 1989, George H. W. Bush entered office with intentions of broadening the United States' strategic relationship with the PRC. Then, on June 4, 1989, the PRC's People's Liberation Army (PLA) massacred scores of demonstrators in Beijing's Tiananmen Square during a rally in support of democratic reforms and an end to corruption. The aftermath of the Tiananmen crackdown prompted outrage and shock in the United States and around the world. In the wake of Tiananmen, the United States suspended military-to-military relations and arms sales to China. According to the firsthand observations of Robert L. Suettinger, an expert on U.S. policy in Asia, the Tiananmen Square incident marked a drastic turning point in the U.S.-China relationship that went from "amity and strategic cooperation to hostility, distrust, and misunderstanding." It was not until 1993 that both countries cautiously resumed military contacts, although with less enthusiasm than during the 1980s when the Soviet Union was a common enemy. The U.S. arms sale embargo put in place in the immediate wake of the massacre has never been lifted. The United States and the PRC began engaging in frequent high-level exchanges soon after establishing diplomatic relations in 1979. High-level exchanges were temporarily suspended following the incident and did not resume until February 1992 when President George H. W. Bush and Chinese Premier Li Peng met on the sidelines of a UN Security Council summit.

In 1993, President Clinton proposed conditioning the renewal of the PRC's most favored nation (MFN) status on its overall progress in human rights practices. However, the PRC's MFN status continued to be renewed annually, as it had been since 1980, and by 1994, the renewal was delinked from human rights conditions. Opponents of Clinton's proposal argued that maintaining the PRC's MFN status was beneficial to U.S. exporters, particularly in the agricultural sector, and that continued trade was the best form of engagement for promoting human rights. In 2000, the PRC was granted normal trade relations status, smoothing the way for its accession to the WTO.

G. THE THIRD TAIWAN STRAIT CRISIS (1995 TO 1996)

In May 1995, the U.S. State Department granted a visa to Taiwan President Lee Teng-hui permitting him to deliver an address at his alma mater, Cornell University. Granting the visa was a departure from the U.S. practice of restricting travel by top Taiwanese officials. The Clinton administration had planned to deny Lee's request, but gave in to pressure from Congress, which overwhelmingly passed a concurrent resolution supporting Lee's visit. The PRC reacted furiously to the State Department's about-face. Chinese officials believed that the Clinton administration had committed to denying Lee's visit. Furthermore, Lee's speech, entitled "Always in My Heart," focused on Taiwan's democratic transformation and was perceived by Beijing as overtly pro-independence. The PLA undertook military exercises in the East China Sea and the Taiwan Strait in July and August 1995. Later in the year, President Clinton admitted to Jiang Zemin on the sidelines of the November APEC conference that Lee Teng-hui's comments had caused trouble. In March 1996, the PLA unleashed a new wave of military exercises near Taiwan which coincided with the island's first direct presidential election since the beginning of Lee's tenure. The demonstrations, which included test firing missiles across the Strait, breached Taiwan's territorial waters and disrupted flights and shipping traffic in the vicinity of Chilung and Kaohsiung. Despite reassurances from Chinese Vice Premier Qian Qichen that the maneuvers were merely tests, the actions were widely viewed as an attempt to intimidate the Taiwanese people on the eve of their first direct presidential election. President Clinton responded by ordering two aircraft carrier battle groups to the region, the largest deployment of U.S. naval forces in the Pacific since the Vietnam War. However, the ships were never ordered into the Taiwan Strait. Lee gained 5 percent in the polls and won Taiwan's presidential election with clear 54 percent majority.

The Third Taiwan Strait Crisis was an inflection point in the triangular U.S.-Taiwan-China relationship. The U.S. navy's show of force spurred the PRC to accelerate its military build-up. At the same time, Beijing adjusted its strategy toward Taiwan to emphasize diplomatic, economic, and ideological persuasion over military force. On Taiwan, many were shocked by the rapid escalation in tensions and wished to avoid further provoking the PRC. U.S.-PRC relations cooled somewhat in the wake of the Third Taiwan Strait Crisis.

H. JIANG ZEMIN'S VISIT TO THE UNITED STATES (1997)

In October 1997, Chinese President Jiang Zemin made an official state visit to the United States at the invitation of President Bill Clinton. It was the first such visit in twelve years. At the end of their meeting on October 29, the presidents released a joint statement reiterating their countries' adherence to the three U.S.-PRC joint communiqués as the basis for relations. The statement summarized a myriad of specific discussions and agreements on areas for mutual cooperation and development, including greater military cooperation, negotiations over North Korea's nuclear weapons program, stopping the proliferation of weapons of mass destruction, and encouraging trade. On the matter of Taiwan, the joint statement reaffirmed the U.S. One China policy and the three joint communiqués:

> China stresses that the Taiwan question is the most important and sensitive central question in China-U.S. relations, and that the proper handling of this question in strict compliance with the principles set forth in the three China-U.S. joint communiqués holds the key to sound and stable growth of China-U.S. relations. The United States reiterates that it adheres to its "one China" policy and the principles set forth in the three U.S.-China joint communiqués.[14]

According to later reports, PRC officials had requested issuing the statement as a communiqué on par with the prior three that would include a version of the "Three Noes" that President Clinton had expressed privately to President Jiang in 1995. At that time, Clinton had reportedly assured Jiang that the United States would (1) "oppose" Taiwan independence; (2) would not support "two Chinas" or one China and one Taiwan; and (3) would not support Taiwan's admission to the United Nations.[15] However, U.S. diplomats refused the request. Several days later, a State Department spokesperson clarified:

We certainly made clear that we have a one-China policy; that we don't support a one-China, one-Taiwan policy. We don't support a two-China policy. We don't support Taiwan independence, and we don't support Taiwanese membership in organizations that require you to be a member state. We certainly made that very clear to the Chinese.[16]

The State Department's release was neither a bilateral statement nor a policy statement by the president; however, it did offer PRC officials a compromise without changing official U.S. policy.

The following year President Clinton paid his own visit to China for a second summit with Jiang. Clinton's visit spanned nine days from June 25 to July 3 and included stops in the cities of Xi'an, Beijing, Shanghai, Guilin, and Hong Kong. It was the first visit by a U.S. president since the Tiananmen Square incident. According to the Chinese press, the Chinese people were impressed with Clinton as a statesman. *The New York Times* described the mood as "elated."[17] Clinton lavished praise on Jiang, declaring him a "visionary leader" who had the "imagination" to transition China to a democracy. In praising Premier Zhu Rongji he said, "[t]here's a very good chance that China has the right leadership at the right time" to transition to a market economy.[18]

Clinton also used the trip as an occasion to openly advocate for progress on human rights. During a live, uncensored news conference and debate with Jiang, Clinton espoused U.S. views on human rights and criticized the 1989 crackdown on Tiananmen Square. Jiang responded by defending the PLA's actions and the importance of public order. "Had the Chinese government not taken the resolute measures we did then we could not have enjoyed the stability that we are enjoying today," Jiang said. Commenters noted that the exchange demonstrated both an increased candor on the part of the PRC's leadership and increased confidence.

On June 30, President Clinton publicly stated his "Three Noes" for the first time during a press conference in Shanghai. He said:

I had a chance to reiterate our Taiwan policy, which is that we don't support independence for Taiwan, or two Chinas, or one Taiwan–one China. And we don't believe that Taiwan should be a member in any organization for which statehood is a requirement. So I think we have a consistent policy. Our only policy has been that we think it has to be done peacefully. That is what our law says, and we have encouraged the cross-strait dialogue. And I think eventually it will bear fruit if everyone is patient and works hard.[19]

Stephen Yates of the Heritage Foundation was among the observers who questioned the statement's potential impact on Taiwan's security. Yates wrote that President Clinton's Three Noes statement in Shanghai "put . . . Taiwan at a severe disadvantage in [its] 50-year struggle with the communist government of mainland China."[20] He further remarked that the statement opposing Taiwan's participation in international organizations made the United States "an accomplice in China's campaign to squeeze Taiwan into submission by isolating the island internationally."[21] Indeed, Clinton's statement was in apparent contradiction with both the TRA and President Reagan's U.S.-Taiwan policy.[22]

The 1998 summit did not produce any joint statements of the sort made at the conclusion of the 1997 summit. The PRC did not, as U.S. officials were hoping, announce a firm date for the signing of the International Covenant on Civil and Political Rights (ICCPR), although PRC officials had announced the country's intention to sign the covenant earlier that year.[23] The PRC's ambassador to the United Nations eventually signed the covenant in October 1998; however, the PRC has yet to ratify the document.

I. THE BELGRADE EMBASSY BOMBING (1999)

On May 7, 1999, a squadron of U.S. B-2 Stealth Bombers taking part in Operation Allied Force in Yugoslavia dropped five guided missiles on the Chinese Embassy in Belgrade. The strike killed three Chinese reporters at the embassy and injured more than twenty other people. The embassy compound was extensively damaged. Following the incident, tens of thousands of protesters surrounded the U.S. embassy in Beijing, throwing rocks and other projectiles and trapping the staff inside for several days. The U.S. consulate in Chengdu, China was partially burned by protesters who stormed the compound. Protesters also attempted to burn the U.S. consulate in Guangzhou. Some observers questioned whether the PRC government tacitly endorsed the protests, having allowed them to take place for several days without intervening to restore order. Chinese state media did little to quell the public's outrage, failing at first to broadcast conciliatory statements from U.S. officials.

U.S. Ambassador James Sasser apologized for the "terrible mistake" in a statement made to the Chinese Foreign Ministry on May 8. Later in the day CIA Director George Tenet publicly accepted blame for the incident, stating that his agency had determined the wrong coordinates for the intended target, the Yugoslav Federal Directorate for Supply and Procurement. He offered his "deep regret" for the loss of life and injuries. That evening, President Clinton expressed his "regrets and condo-lences" for the "tragic mistake" in remarks to the press. On May 8 and 9, President Clinton and Secretary of State Madeline Albright sent letters to Jiang Zemin and Chinese Foreign Minister Tang Jiaxuan expressing their apologies. On May 9, President Clinton phoned President Jiang over the state-to-state hotline, but Jiang refused to accept the call. Military-to-military relations were suspended after the incident. On May 10, Tang presented Ambassador Sasser with four conditions for resolving the situation: make an open and official apology; carry out a complete and thorough investigation over the bombing; disclose promptly the results of the investigation; and punish severely those responsible for it. Later that day, President Clinton made his first public statement about the tragedy, offering an unqualified apology. On May 12, the U.S. embassy and consulates in China flew their flags at half-staff in honor of the bombing victims. On May 14, President Jiang accepted a call from President Clinton and agreed that there would be a special NATO inves-tigation of the bombing and that the results would be made public. These gestures restored the high-level relationship between the two countries to a functioning sta-tus. On June 12, Prime Minister Qian Qichen stated, "China does not want a con-frontation with the United States."[24]

In August 1999, following three days of negotiations, the U.S. government made a voluntary "humanitarian payment" of USD 4.5 million to the families of the three Chinese nationals killed during the bombing and the twenty-seven people who were injured. By the APEC Forum in September, U.S.-China relations had recovered sig-nificantly. Presidents Clinton and Jiang met face-to-face to restart discussions over China's WTO accession. On December 16, the U.S. and PRC governments agreed on a settlement under which the United States would pay USD 28 million in com-pensation for damage to the Chinese embassy in Belgrade, and China would pay USD 2.87 million for damage inflicted by rioters to U.S. diplomatic facilities. With the matter satisfactorily closed, the two countries agreed to resume military-to-military contact in January 2000.

J. CHINA JOINS THE WORLD TRADE ORGANIZATION (2001)

The immediate post–World War II global trade order was based on the General Agreement on Trade and Tariffs (GATT,) which preceded the formation of the WTO. The ROC was a founding signatory to the original GATT treaty in 1947, while still in power on the Chinese mainland. However, the Chinese civil war and eventual exile of the KMT regime prevented the ROC from meaningfully partici-pating, and the ROC voluntarily withdrew from GATT in 1950. For the next three decades, the PRC showed no interest in joining the global trade regime. Therefore, the Chinese people were effectively unrepresented in the development of global trade law for much of the twentieth century.

In 1986, after more than a decade of market reforms and increased trade with the outside world, the PRC sought to join GATT. It applied and obtained observer status that year, but progress toward full membership was interrupted by the 1989 Tiananmen Square incident. Prior to this, in 1965, Taiwan also sought to enter GATT and was granted observer status. But in 1971, its observer status was revoked following the ROC's dismissal from the United Nations. The lack of UN recognition stymied Taiwan's efforts to join GATT as a full member. Rather, its path would run through Section XXVI:5(c) of the treaty, the "customs territory" provision. The provision generally requires that a customs territory be admitted only upon the sponsorship of a parent that is a state contracting party to GATT. As a result, it was generally assumed that Taiwan would have to wait until after the PRC's accession to pursue its own membership. Accordingly, in 1990, Taiwan applied to GATT as a customs territory, and in 1992, it gained observer status with an informal agreement that it would be admitted to the organization after the PRC.

China's own accession to GATT and the WTO was delayed due to concerns that included its status as a developing country, its centrally controlled economy, and its large size, which some analysts warned could lead to worldwide market disruptions. These factors combined raised questions about the PRC's ability to adhere to the requirements of the treaty, which generally favors market-based and nonprotectionist national policies. Furthermore, the country's large size meant that it represented a potential threat to U.S. dominance in global trade.

Gaining permanent normal trade relations (PNTR) status was a crucial step for the PRC to achieve membership in the WTO. In April 1999, Chinese Premier Zhu Rongji traveled to Washington in an attempt to finalize an agreement. According to a report from the BBC, the PRC conceded more in three weeks than "in the prior three years."[25] Yet, it was still not enough. Congress pushed for the PRC to make further concessions. On April 8, the United States and the PRC issued a joint statement reporting that they had failed to reach a deal. Although the two sides had struck agreements on a number of issues, touching on agricultural and industrial goods, the service sector, and WTO rules concerning trading rights, technology transfer, state enterprises, and subsidies, more still remained to be worked out in areas including banking and securities, the importation of certain U.S. agricultural products, dumping provisions, product safeguards, and textiles. Negotiations resumed later that year. Finally, on November 15, 1999, the United States and the PRC signed a watershed agreement encompassing China's accession to the WTO. However, permanent normal trade relations status had yet to be granted.

The United States granted China normalized trade status under the U.S.-China Relations Act, which was passed by the House of Representatives in May 2000 and signed into law by President Clinton on October 10, 2000. The law's purpose was to "authorize extension of nondiscriminatory treatment (normal trade relations treatment) to the PRC and to establish a framework for relations between the U.S. and the PRC upon its accession to the [World Trade Organization]."[26] Additionally, the bill's language heavily endorsed Taiwan's own accession to the WTO and indicated that Congress would adhere to Section 4(d) of the TRA, which prohibits the U.S. government from supporting the exclusion or expulsion of Taiwan from international organizations. On September 17, 2011, the PRC's accession to the WTO was approved, and the PRC formally acceded to the WTO on December 11, 2001, becoming the organization's one hundred and forty-third member. Taiwan's admission was approved the following day, allowing it to become the one hundred and forty fifth member on January 1, 2002.

III. Recent Trends in U.S.-China Relations

The beginning of George W. Bush's first term brought renewed focus on U.S. commitments to Taiwan. The administration was initially considered, in the words of Richard Bush, the "most Taiwan-friendly administration since the termination of diplomatic relations [between the United States and Taiwan in 1979]." Taiwanese leaders, however, soon found themselves sidelined as global events brought new opportunities for cooperation between the United States and China. U.S.-China relations improved significantly over the course of the George W. Bush administration, as the two countries found greater alignment in the global fight against terrorism and a shared interest in maintaining peace on the Korean Peninsula. China's economic stature grew after the global financial crisis and elevated the PRC's stature among global powers. Chinese leaders are now seeking to define the concept of "new great power relations" as a foundation for future interactions with the United States. There are more than one hundred mechanisms through which the United States and China may convene to discuss a broad range of topics, among them the global economy, trade, nuclear nonproliferation, climate change, and human rights. In 2004, President George W. Bush and Chinese President Hu Jintao initiated the Senior Dialogue, a high-level meeting for the discussion of issues of mutual interest. The talks were upgraded to the Strategic and Economic Dialogue under President Obama in 2009. The Dialogues represent the highest-level platform for both nations to address bilateral, regional, and global issues.

A. THE EP-3 RECONNAISSANCE PLANE INCIDENT (2001)

On the morning of April 1, 2001, two Chinese F-8 jets intercepted a U.S. EP-3 reconnaissance plane on a patrol mission over the South China Sea about fifty miles from China's coast. One of the jets made a number of intentionally close passes to the U.S. EP-3. On the third pass, the F-8 collided with the EP-3. Both Chinese pilots on the jet were killed in the collision. The EP-3, still maneuverable despite having lost a propeller, made an emergency landing at Lingshui air base on Hainan Island, China. PLA soldiers immediately detained the twenty-four-man flight crew.

The PRC had previously protested that U.S. reconnaissance flights, which took place four to five times per week, amounted to spying over China's territorial waters. However, the United States maintained that the flights took place over international waters and were permissible under international law. To bolster its position, the Chinese air force increased the frequency and aggressiveness of its intercept flights, which the United States in turn complained were unjustified and dangerous. Amid this brinkmanship, the April 1, 2001 accident was one that was perhaps waiting to happen. The PRC further complained that the EP-3 had breached Chinese territory when it landed on Hainan. It demanded an apology from the United States—which U.S. officials refused—sparking a diplomatic standoff. On April 2, the U.S. Pacific Command requested that the Chinese "respect the integrity of the aircraft and well-being and safety of the crew in accordance with international practices, expedite any necessary repairs to the aircraft, and facilitate the immediate return of the aircraft and crew."[27] On April 2, President Bush demanded the "prompt and safe return of the crew and aircraft without further damage or tampering" and that a diplomatic staff be permitted to visit the crew. U.S. Ambassador Joseph Prueher reportedly waited approximately twelve hours before being granted a meeting with China's Assistant Minister of Foreign Affairs, Zhou Whenzong. On April 3, staff from the U.S. embassy and Consulate General in Guangzhou, accompanied by Brigadier General Neal Sealock, were permitted to meet with the crew. However, the PLA made no moves to release them.

President Bush and other U.S. officials, including Secretary of State Colin Powell expressed "regret" and "sorrow" over the incident, but pointedly refused to apologize. Behind the scenes, U.S. and Chinese diplomats worked to resolve the incident. The steps included an initial brief statement of regret from the United States, followed by a more comprehensive statement. After four days, the two sides agreed the United States would state that it was "very sorry" for the death of the Chinese pilots and for breaching Chinese airspace. However it would not explicitly apologize, thus avoiding implying culpability for the incident. The result was a letter signed and delivered by Ambassador Prueher on April 11. The U.S. flight crew was released the following day.

The U.S. Department of Defense then commenced its own negotiations over the return of the EP-3 aircraft and other matters, including compensating the PRC and taking measures to avoid future incidents. On April 29, a U.S. inspection team was permitted to inspect the aircraft; however, the PLA would not allow the plane to be repaired on site. Instead, the U.S. Pacific Command, working with engineers from Lockheed Martin, would dismantle the plane and deliver it from Hainan on a cargo aircraft. The mission was completed on July 3. Finally, in September, U.S. and Chinese officials met on Guam under the Military Maritime Consultative Agreement to agree on procedures for preventing similar events in the future.

B. U.S.-CHINA RELATIONS AFTER SEPTEMBER II, 2001

The events of September 11, 2001 and the global fight against terrorism worked to both stabilize and transform the U.S.-China relationship. The George W. Bush administration reshaped its approach to the PRC and Taiwan believing that "smooth U.S.-PRC relations might be an important tool in cooperating against terrorism" and advancing other U.S. objectives, including maintaining stability on the Korean peninsula.[28] Meanwhile, U.S.-Taiwan relations "eroded significantly" due to "problems of trust . . . between Taiwan's President and U.S. officials."[29] The administration began to "balance its criticisms of China's military [proliferation against] Taiwan with periodic warnings to the Taiwan government that U.S. support was [no longer] unconditional."[30]

PRC officials also viewed this period as an opportunity to improve relations with the United States. Immediately following the attacks, Chinese President Jiang Zemin condemned the attacks and offered condolences in a message to President Bush. On the same day, the PRC joined members of the UN Security Council in support of Resolution 1373, reaffirming the call to combat terrorism. On September 20, 2001, China promised to offer the United States its unconditional support in combating terrorism. China permitted President Bush to use the APEC meeting in China as a forum to rally support for antiterrorist action. President Bush recognized the PRC as a key player in the fight against global terrorism and reminded President Jiang that "the war on terrorism must never be an excuse to prosecute minorities."[31] (Unfortunately, President Jiang did not heed Bush's reminder, as evidenced by China's harsh treatment of Uyghurs, Tibetans, and other minority groups who have been labeled as separatists by the PRC.) Since 2001, PRC officials began closer cooperation with U.S. antiterrorism, intelligence, and other specialists.[32] In his State of the Union speech in January 2002, Bush stated that "America is working with Russia and China and India, in ways we have never before, to achieve peace and prosperity."[33]

C. CHINA AND NORTH KOREA (2002 TO THE PRESENT)

In 2002, during a visit by James Kelly, Assistant Secretary of State for East Asian and Pacific Affairs, North Korean officials raised suspicions that the country maintained a clandestine program to enrich uranium in violation of the 1994 Agreed Framework. The North Korean government did not deny the allegations, and the Bush administration suspended fuel oil deliveries to North Korea. In response, North Korea nullified the Framework and restarted its nuclear weapons program and, in January 2003, withdrew from the Nuclear Non-proliferation Treaty (NPT). In February, the country began harvesting plutonium from its reactor at the Yongbyon nuclear complex. In August 2003, China invited the United States, Russia, South Korea, and Japan to join negotiations over North Korea's nuclear program. The "Six Party Talks," hosted in Beijing, have come to represent a major area of cooperation for Washington and Beijing. In September, 2005, North Korea agreed to a draft agreement to end its nuclear weapons program in return for certain security, economic, and energy guarantees.

In October, 2006, North Korea violated the draft agreement by conducting underground testing of a small nuclear device. The United Nations unanimously passed—with China's support—Resolution 1781, which condemned North Korea for the test and imposed sanctions. Within weeks, North Korea agreed to restart the Six Party Talks. In February 2007, the parties agreed to USD 400 million in fuel and other aid to North Korea in exchange for the dismantling of its nuclear weapons program. By September 2008, North Korea had once again restarted processing plutonium, claiming that the Bush administration had reneged on a promise to remove it from the U.S. list of state sponsors of terrorism. In October the United States did remove North Korea from the list, which led to a resumption in the talks, but the talks collapsed again in December after the parties failed to reach an agreement on the inspection of North Korean nuclear facilities. In April 2009, North Korea launched a rocket which international observers viewed as a step in developing a nuclear-capable intercontinental ballistic missile (ICBM). The UN Security Council condemned the launch. In May, North Korea announced that it had performed a second, more powerful nuclear test. In June 2009, the United Nations passed Resolution 1874, which the Security Council followed by unanimously approving additional sanctions against Pyongyang. The sanctions were strengthened in February 2013 after a third nuclear test. The latest round of sanctions was unique, as China participated in writing the resolution for the first time. In May 2013, PRC President Xi Jinping advised a North Korean envoy that the country should return to the Six Party Talks, something North Korea has failed to do as of 2015.

Since its founding in 1949, the PRC has maintained close ties with neighboring North Korea. However, Pyongyang's unpredictability has increasingly made the North Korea relationship a political liability. Meanwhile, the China–North Korea border has become a source of troubles including refugees and smuggling, which would certainly increase should the North Korean government collapse suddenly, while likely requiring U.S. intervention to stabilize the Korean Peninsula. Whereas China has challenged U.S.-led efforts to punish states such as Iran, Syria, and Russia through sanctions and other means in response to violations of international norms, China has shown a willingness to try to rein in Pyongyang's belligerent behavior in concert with other nations. In terms of outcomes and effects, the situation leaves much to be desired—the Kim Jong-un regime remains free to talk ceaselessly without taking substantive actions to curb the development of weapons of mass destruction. However, the establishment of Six Party Talks and subsequent UN resolutions targeting North Korea's nuclear program offer a relative bright spot in the United States' and China's common efforts to maintain regional peace and security.

D. THE GLOBAL FINANCIAL CRISIS (2008 TO 2009)

The global economic crisis and recession that began in 2008 dominated the attention of both U.S. and Chinese governments. China's economy is now the second largest in the world. Some observers saw the 2008 financial crisis as a turning point in the U.S.-China relationship, marking the beginning of China's rise and the United States' decline as the world's dominant economy. As one commentator remarked, the perceived deterioration in the United States' status prompted Chinese authors to launch a "flood of declinist commentary about the United States."[34] The most common version of this commentary predicted that "Asia was adjusting to an emerging China-centered order and that the U.S. influence was in decline."[35] Many assessments in mainstream Asian and Western media focused on China's economic strengths and the United States' weaknesses. In China, editorialists painted a picture of a United States bogged down in costly wars in Iraq and Afghanistan and unable to manage its own economic troubles. Meanwhile, Chinese leaders appeared reluctant to make costly commitments. Seven years on, it appears that the most dire predictions have gone unfulfilled. The United States remains the world's preeminent economic power. While China's economy continues to grow, it faces many challenges, including a slowing manufacturing sector, concerns over a rise in defaults among corporate borrowers, demographic weaknesses, and the devastating effects of industrial pollution on the country's water and air.

E. THE UNITED STATES' AND CHINA'S "CORE INTERESTS" (2009 TO THE PRESENT)

In the 2000s, Chinese officials and media began to speak of the country's "core interests." The term refers to issues that the PRC regards as purely domestic in nature and about which it will tolerate no foreign intervention. Many commentators characterize China's core interests as those issues for which it is willing to wage war. According to Michael D. Swaine, Senior Associate in the Asia Program at the Carnegie Endowment for International Peace, the PRC's use of the phrase may at times signify "a marker, or a type of warning, regarding the need for the United States and other countries to respect (indeed, accept with little if any negotiation) China's position on certain issues."[36]

The components of China's core interests were defined by Chinese State Councilor Dai Bingguo at the 2009 U.S.-China Strategic and Economic Dialogue. These were: preserving China's state system and national security, national sovereignty and territorial integrity, and continued stable development of China's economy and society.[37] The elements were reiterated in a white paper called "China's Peaceful Development," issued by the PRC in 2011. Sovereignty and territorial integrity are the most frequently cited of the elements. Many commentators have noted that the concept, while conforming to the parameters laid out by Dai, is also flexible, tending to expand to suit the geopolitical issues of the day. PRC officials have made reference to core interests to defend Chinese claims to Taiwan, Tibet, and Xinjiang, and they have been increasingly assertive in invoking the concept in discussions of international issues, among them U.S. arms sales to Taiwan, foreign meetings with the Tibetan Dalai Lama, and disputed territories in the East and South China Seas.

In November 2009, President Obama made his first state visit to China. During his visit, the United States and the PRC issued a joint statement emphasizing the significance of Taiwan as a factor in U.S.-PRC relations, among other topics. The statement declared that "the two sides agreed that respecting each other's core interests is extremely important to ensure steady progress in U.S.-China relations."[38] The reference to "core interests" was surprising to many observers, as over the past decade China has increasingly employed the term as a watchword for topics that are beyond compromise. Among these is the sanctity of the PRC's sovereignty over China and the inviolability of its territorial claims. AIT Chairman Raymond Burghardt later clarified that the phrase, as used in the 2009 U.S.-China joint statement, was intended only to refer to Tibet and Xinjiang.[39] However, PRC officials have also repeatedly used the phrase in reference to Taiwan. The phrase "core interests" was dropped in the next U.S.-China joint statement issued on January 9. According to Burghardt, the omission was intentional and was made at the request of U.S. negotiators.[40]

Over the course of eight presidential administrations, from Richard Nixon in the 1970s to Barack Obama in the 2010s, the U.S.-China relationship has grown rapidly, from a total détente to conditions of frequent and intense engagement. China's view of itself has also changed. Once isolated and scarcely developed, China is now undergoing a process of economic and social development on a scale never before seen in human history. Throughout this period, Chinese leaders have been resolute in projections of their country's interests, especially in regard to territorial claims. As some observers have suggested, the PRC is growing increasingly confident—sometimes to the point of arrogance—and is pressing these claims both in word and deed, projecting its power—ideological, military, diplomatic, and economic—across the region and the globe. With these recent trends in mind, Chapter 9 will consider whether the United States and China are on the verge of a developing rivalry or whether, through dialogue and mutual cooperation, the two countries will be able to accommodate their interests while promoting the shared goal of peace and security within an evolving global order.

Notes

1. 23 DEP'T STATE BULL. 5 (1950); Lung-chu Chen & W. Michael Reisman, *Who Owns Taiwan: A Search for International Title*, 81 YALE L.J. 599–671, 615–16 (1972).

2. Chen & Reisman, *supra* note 1, at 618.

3. UN General Assembly, Resolution 2758, A/RES/2758 (XXVI), Oct. 25, 1971.

4. Remarks by President Nixon to the Nation, July 15, 1971, U.S. Dept. of State, Office of the Historian, Foreign Relations of the United States, 1969–1976, Volume I, Foundations of Foreign Policy, 1969–1972, Document 92; *available at* https://history.state.gov/historicaldocuments/frus1969-76v01/d92.

5. Joint Communiqué of the United States of America and the People's Republic of China, Jan. 1, 1979, *available at* http://www.taiwandocuments.org/communique02.htm.

6. *See* U.S. Dept. of State, A Guide to the United States' History of Recognition, Diplomatic, and Consular Relations, By Country, Since 1776, https://history.state.gov/countries/china.

7. JOHN H. HOLDRIDGE, CROSSING THE DIVIDE: AN INSIDER'S ACCOUNT OF NORMALIZATION OF U.S.-CHINA RELATIONS 113 (1997).

8. *Id.* at 114.

9. Public Law 95-384, §26, Sept. 26, 1978.

10. Hungdah Chiu, *The Taiwan Relations Act and Sino-American Relations*, Occasional Papers/Reprints Series in Contemporary Asian Studies, No. 5, U. MD. SCH. L. at 10 (1990), *available at* http://digitalcommons.law.umaryland.edu/cgi/viewcontent.cgi?article=1099&context=mscas.

11. SHIRLEY A. KAN, CHINA/TAIWAN: EVOLUTION OF THE "ONE CHINA POLICY"—KEY STATEMENTS FROM WASHINGTON, BEIJING, AND TAIPEI, CONGRESSIONAL RESEARCH SERVICE, at 40–41 (2014), *available at* http://www.fas.org/sgp/crs/row/RL30341.pdf.

12. *See* DAVID M. LAMPTON, SAME BED, DIFFERENT DREAMS: MANAGING U.S.-CHINA RELATIONS 1989–2000, at 162–63 (2001).

13. CIA World Factbook, Field Listing: International Organization Participation, https://www.cia.gov/library/publications/the-world-factbook/fields/2107.html.

14. U.S. Dept. of State, Joint U.S.-China Statement, Oct. 29, 1997, *available at* http://1997-2001.state.gov/www/regions/eap/971029_usc_jtstmt.html.

15. KAN, *supra* note 11, at 62.

16. *Id.* at 63.

17. *See* Erik Eckholm, *Visit by Clinton Leaves Chinese Feeling Elated*, N.Y. TIMES, July 4, 1998, *available at* http://partners.nytimes.com/library/world/asia/070498china-assess.html.

18. John M. Border, *Clinton Optimistic on China's Future as He Heads Home*, N.Y. TIMES, July 4, 1998, *available at* http://partners.nytimes.com/library/world/asia/070498china-clinton.html.

19. KAN, *supra* note 11, at 64.

20. Stephen J. Yates, *Clinton Statement Undermines Taiwan*, HERITAGE FOUNDATION, July 19, 1998, *available at* http://www.heritage.org/research/asiaandthepacific/em538.cfm.

21. *Id.*

22. *Id.*

23. *See* Erik Eckholm, *Clinton Urged to Meet Top China Dissident*, N.Y. TIMES, June 20, 1998, *available at* http://partners.nytimes.com/library/world/asia/062098china-dissidents.html.

24. *See* China and Taiwan—From Flash Point to Redefining One-China, TAIWAN INFO, May 1, 2001, *available at* http://taiwaninfo.nat.gov.tw/ct.asp?xItem=609&CtNode=124&htx_TRCategory=&mp=4.

25. *Final Negotiations' on China's WTO Bid*, BBC NEWS, Mar. 30, 1999, *available at* http://news.bbc.co.uk/2/hi/business/306191.stm.

26. Pub. L. 106-286 (2000).

27. *China Blames Jet Crash on U.S.*, BBC NEWS, Apr. 1, 2001, *available at* http://news.bbc.co.uk/2/hi/asia-pacific/1254397.stm.

28. KERRY DUMBAUGH, TAIWAN-U.S. RELATIONS: DEVELOPMENTS AND POLICY IMPLICATIONS, CONGRESSIONAL RESEARCH SERVICE, at 15 (2009), *available at* http://www.fas.org/sgp/crs/row/R40493.pdf.

29. *Id.*

30. *Id.*

31. The President's News Conference with President Jiang Zemin of China in Shanghai, China, Oct. 19, 2001, *available at* http://www.presidency.ucsb.edu/ws/?pid=64116.

32. ROBERT G. SUTTER, CHINESE FOREIGN RELATIONS: POWER AND POLICY SINCE THE COLD WAR 126 (2010).

33. George W. Bush, State of the Union Address, Jan. 29, 2002, *available at* http://georgewbush-whitehouse.archives.gov/news/releases/2002/01/20020129-11.html.

34. *See* Joseph Nye, *American and Chinese Power after the Financial Crisis*, WASH. Q. (2010), *available at* http://www.tandfonline.com/doi/abs/10.1080/0163660X.2010.516634.

35. *See* SUTTER, *supra* note 32, at 163.

36. Michael D. Swaine, *China's Assertive Behavior Part One; On "Core Interests"* at 6, CHINA LEADERSHIP MONITOR (2010).

37. *See* CAITLIN CAMPBELL ET AL., CHINA'S "CORE INTERESTS" AND THE EAST CHINA SEA, U.S.-CHINA ECONOMIC AND SECURITY REVIEW COMMISSION STAFF RESEARCH BACKGROUNDER (May 10, 2013), *available at* http://www.uscc.gov/sites/default/files/Research/China%27s%20Core%20Interests%20and%20the%20East%20China%20Sea.pdf.

38. *Id.*

39. KAN, *supra* note 11, at 84.

40. Raymond Burghardt, AIT Chairman Raymond Burghardt Press Roundtable Taipei, The American Institute in Taiwan, Official Texts, Jan. 25, 2011, http://www.ait.org.tw/en/officialtext-ot1102.html.

8 Taiwan-China Relations

IT BEARS REPEATING that China has never exerted meaningful control over Taiwan. And there is little evidence to support the People's Republic of China's (PRC) historical claim of sovereignty over Taiwan. This was true during the country's premodern era, when the emperors dismissed the island as far away and backward, and it has been the case since the establishment of the PRC in October 1949. As noted in Chapter 1, Taiwan was designated as a province by the Qing government in 1887, but Beijing scarcely managed the island before ceding it to Japan in perpetuity a mere eight years later. Even Mao Zedong once famously voiced his support for an independent Taiwan in response to a question from American journalist Edgar Snow in 1936, which was reported in the first edition of Snow's book *Red Star over China*:

> It is the immediate task of China to regain all our lost territories, not merely to defend our sovereignty below the Great Wall. This means that Manchuria must be regained. We do not, however, include Korea, formerly a Chinese colony, but when we have re-established the independence of the lost territories of China, and if the Koreans wish to break away from the chains of Japanese imperialism, we will extend them our enthusiastic help in their struggle for independence. The same thing applies for Formosa.[1]

From a historical perspective, the intensity of China's claims over Taiwan are a fairly recent phenomenon. Indeed, one could reasonably conclude that these claims are rooted in a blatant desire for territorial gain, rather than a nostalgia for an imagined national past. For more than a century, Taiwan has evolved along a distinct path from China into a separate, independent state, as elaborated in Chapter 2. From 1895 to the entry into force of the San Francisco Peace Treaty in 1952, Taiwan was a Japanese territory. Where China was underdeveloped, dysfunctional, and closed off, Taiwan was industrialized, modern, and relatively open. This was a period of enforced separation between the two countries, and there was little contact between them. While Taiwan enjoyed massive growth in its economy and infrastructure under Japanese management, the Chinese mainland saw turmoil and stagnation through the fall of the Qing dynasty and the events of two world wars. From 1945 to 1987 Taiwan was under a military occupation by the Kuomintang (KMT) regime, enforced by thirty-eight years of martial law. Even after the arrival of the Republic of China (ROC) occupation, Taiwan continued to develop along unique cultural, political, and economic paths. From 1988 to the present, Taiwan has undertaken a dramatic democratic transformation from which has emerged a vibrant, self-determined national identity. The Chinese dream of unification is based on fantasy. The PRC's claim of sovereignty over Taiwan make less sense today than ever. It ignores more than a century of profound historical developments on both sides of the Taiwan Strait. No amount of repetition will make China's claims any more valid.

The recent collaboration of the CCP-led PRC and the KMT-led ROC—once arch enemies—as partners in a mutually beneficial relationship is an important historical development. Trade, communications, and transportation links have multiplied since the 1980s. China is Taiwan's largest economic partner and Taiwan's number-one source of tourists. Taiwanese music, films, and television programs are widely popular in China and Hong Kong. There is a superficial impression that the PRC has somehow succeeded in bringing Taiwan within its sphere of influence without resorting to force (although it has never renounced the threat of force). Indeed, peaceful cross-strait relations ought to be encouraged. Yet it should be done with care. The PRC has deliberately enacted a strategy toward Taiwan with tactics designed to condition the Taiwanese people to accept closer ties with China, exclude Taiwan from international organizations, and discourage other states from establishing diplomatic relations with the Taiwan government. Chinese officials and media outlets continuously assert that Taiwan is a part of China, while the PRC uses its economic might to threaten deprivations against nations that extend diplomatic recognition to Taiwan. As a result, while most nations do not formally assent to China's claim over Taiwan, they remain silent on the matter. The United States, for its part, initially supported Ma ying-jeou's efforts to develop the cross-strait relationship, but has stopped short of promoting steps toward unification, especially after the PRC's display of expansionist intent and behavior in the South China Sea and elsewhere.

The trend toward stability and prosperity in the region is to be valued. But the Taiwanese people should not have to bear an unreasonable cost to maintain it. As demonstrated by the recent Sunflower Movement and the resounding KMT electoral defeats, the Taiwanese people are not willing to sacrifice their country's ultimate sovereign authority. It is essential that Taiwan's elites remain cognizant of the promises and the perils of closer cross-strait ties, proceeding cautiously, transparently, and with the consent of the people. Taiwan's leaders must work to secure conditions favorable to Taiwan's continuation as a free, democratic, and sovereign country.

I. Taiwan-China Relations before 1949

A. TAIWAN AND CHINA BEFORE 1895

As explained in Chapter 1, ties between China and Taiwan were historically intermittent and tenuous. The island was regarded as an inferior tributary by Chinese emperors, and there was little contact between the two sides before the arrival of Western powers in the region in the sixteenth and seventeenth centuries. Late Ming and early Qing descriptions of Taiwan emphasized the island's separation from the Chinese mainland. It was variously described as "faraway overseas," "hanging alone beyond the seas," "an isolated island surrounded by the ocean," or "far off on the edge of the oceans."[2] These words hardly evince a sense of dearness on the part of the imperial court.

Immigration from the Chinese mainland to Taiwan did not occur significantly prior to the 1620s. Dutch colonizers encouraged large-scale Han immigration to provide manpower for developing the island. When the Dutch East India Company arrived on the island in 1624, there was no reported evidence of administration by the imperial Chinese government. The Dutch period saw an influx of Japanese, Spanish, English, and Chinese soldiers and traders vying to set up commercial outposts and exploit the island's resources. The island's population during this period consisted of Han Chinese, Japanese, Dutch missionaries and officials, Portuguese mercenaries working for the Dutch East India Company, and African slaves.[3]

Dutch rule came to an end when Koxinga (Cheng Cheng-kung), foreshadowing the ROC exile centuries later, brought the remnants of the defeated Ming dynasty to Taiwan. Koxinga's forces expelled the Dutch and used the island as a base for harassing the newly established Qing dynasty. After Koxinga's death in 1662, his son, Cheng Ching, became the island's ruler. Two decades later, the Dutch partnered with the Qing to reoccupy the island in 1683. An expedition sent by Qing Emperor

Kangxi crushed the Ming loyalist forces, after which Taiwan was left mostly to its own devices. For nearly two centuries, the Qing government did virtually nothing to govern or develop the territory. In Peking, many Qing officials wished to abandon Taiwan, with some arguing that the Chinese population there should be repatriated to the mainland. It was Admiral Shi Lang who convinced the emperor to incorporate the island into the empire, despite advisors' objections that the island was no better than "a ball of mud." Thereafter, the Qing implemented a set of quarantine policies. The government limited cross-strait transportation and communication and restricted Han immigration to Taiwan. During this period, the island merited little attention from the Qing court, except in times of crisis.

Following the Mudan Incident of 1871, in which Taiwanese villagers massacred members of a Japanese fishing crew, the Qing government was forced to pay closer attention. In response to a Japanese inquiry into the event, Qing officials claimed that the indigenous people belonged to a barbarian land outside Peking's jurisdiction. The ministers claimed that the Qing government could not be held responsible for the actions of the "raw barbarians" since "they are beyond the reach of our government and culture. . . ."[4] In the spring of 1874, the Japanese government launched a military expedition to Taiwan to exact punitive measures. In the negotiations that followed, the Qing government agreed to pay damages for the loss of the ship and crew in exchange for recognition of its claim over the island. Thereafter, the Qing intensified its efforts to extend Chinese administration of Taiwan, which included measures to incorporate the aboriginal territory into the prefectural administrative system. China aimed at "opening up the mountains and pacifying the aborigines" in order to bring Taiwan's underdeveloped central mountain belts under Han Chinese settlement.[5]

The Qing designated Taiwan as a province of China in 1887, with Liu Ming-ch'uan as its first provincial governor. From 1884 to 1891, Liu undertook a series of reforms aimed at modernizing the island. This period of modernization would last only eight years before China ceded Taiwan to Japan in perpetuity under the Treaty of Shimonoseki after the Chinese defeat in the Sino-Japanese War of 1894 to 1895.

B. TAIWAN UNDER JAPANESE COLONIAL RULE (1895 TO 1945)

Taiwan was Japan's first colony, and the Office of the Governor General undertook strict measures to control Taiwan's interactions with China. Relations between Taiwan and the mainland were drastically reduced and restricted. From 1919 onward, the Japanese policy of *doka* (assimilation) sought to repress the Chinese culture as a means of transforming the Taiwanese people into fully assimilated colonial subjects. Meanwhile, the Japanese implemented policies to suppress local resistance to

Japanese rule. Although several minor incidents of armed resistance incidents took place during the early years of Japanese colonial rule, the Japanese colonial government ensured that Taiwan saw vast economic and industrial gains. The Taiwanese soon saw their standard of living rise to be among the highest in Asia. The colonial government made massive investments in infrastructure leading to improvements in the island's railway, road, irrigation, and communications networks as well as central governmental buildings, many of which remain in use to this day.

The Japanese made primary education mandatory for the Taiwanese population as a measure to both increase productivity and stem anti-Japanese sentiment among the people. Schools were initially segregated, with separate facilities for Japanese nationals, Taiwanese, and indigenous peoples. Desegregation efforts were later undertaken in the latter days of Japanese rule in the early 1940s, as social groups became increasingly comingled. Throughout the colonial period, the Office of the Governor General adopted policies and campaigns designed to eliminate Chinese cultural practices. The rapid development in agricultural and industrial output and overall living standards under Japanese rule was a far cry from the social and economic turmoil in China. Civil war erupted between the Nationalists and Communists after the collapse of the Qing dynasty. The Japanese saw an opportunity to further indulge their expansionist ambitions and launched an invasion of Manchuria in 1931. Japan would remain the dominant force in the region until the end of World War II.

C. THE CHINESE CIVIL WAR AND THE BIRTH OF THE PRC (1927 TO 1949)

On January 1, 1912, the Chinese Nationalist Party declared the founding of the Republic of China (ROC) after the successful Xinhai Revolution brought an end to the Qing dynasty. The Nationalist leader Sun Yat-sen established the first incarnation of the Kuomintang (KMT) Party in August of that year. In 1914, following months of infighting, the KMT was dismantled and many of its members exiled. The party re-established itself in October 1919 in Shanghai and soon gained political dominance with assistance from the Soviet Union. Following Sun Yat-sen's death in 1925, control of the KMT fell to Generalissimo Chiang Kai-shek. Within three years, Chiang had subdued rival factions in the north and south of the country and succeeded at uniting China under a single government based in Nanking (Nanjing).

The Chinese Communist Party (CCP) was founded on July 1, 1921. By the mid-1920s, tensions were brewing between the KMT and the Communists led by Mao Zedong. Although Chiang Kai-shek had received some military training and support from the Soviet Union (Chiang began his military education at Japan's Tokyo

Shunbu Gakko academy from 1907 to 1911), he resisted pressures from the Chinese Communists and sought to consolidate his own authority within the KMT and the ROC government. To Chiang, the Communists presented an obstacle to the country's unification. In April 1927, KMT forces loyal to Chiang undertook a purge and massacred hundreds of Communists in Shanghai. In retaliation, Communist forces, aided by rural peasants, launched an insurgency that would last for ten years.

In 1937, the KMT and the CCP agreed to a temporary truce, forming the Second United Front to jointly defend China from the Japanese in Manchuria. The fragile alliance was shattered in 1941 when KMT troops killed thousands of Communists in Anhui and Jiangsu Provinces in an ambush known as the New Fourth Army Incident. The incident ended what little cooperation existed between the KMT and the CCP. Fighting between the two parties continued for the duration of World War II, and a full-scale civil war broke out following the Japanese surrender in 1945. The CCP, under the command of Mao Zedong, had grown considerably larger during the fight against Japan with support from the country's rural populations. Meanwhile Soviet forces were collaborating with the CCP during the Soviet withdrawal from Manchuria, giving the Communists a foothold in the country's northeast. American troops assisted the KMT to prevent liberated territory from falling under Communist control. Battles raged across China from 1946 until 1949. On October 1, 1949, Mao's army overran the KMT at the Nationalist capital of Nanjing, and the Communists proclaimed the founding of the PRC, with its capital in Beijing. By December 1949, Chiang and his supporters had fled China, taking refuge on Taiwan, whose military occupation had been entrusted to the ROC by the Allied Forces at the end of the war with Japan, although no transfer of title was involved.

II. Taiwan-China Relations from 1945 to 1987

A. MILITARY OCCUPATION OF TAIWAN BY THE KMT

In 1945, four years before the Chinese Nationalists' defeat, General Douglas MacArthur tasked Chiang Kai-shek with administering Taiwan on behalf of the Allied Powers. In early 1947, the Nationalist government unilaterally declared Taiwan to be one of the thirty-five provinces of the Republic of China, an act in violation of the Allied accords and international law. In 1951, Japan signed the San Francisco Peace Treaty, renouncing its rights over Taiwan without specifying to whom the island would be assigned. Neither the ROC nor the PRC governments was invited to be present at the treaty's signing. The treaty became effective in 1952—between 1945 and 1952, Taiwan remained a Japanese territory under the ROC's military administration.

At first, the Taiwanese welcomed their Chinese brothers and sisters, who they believed would liberate them from the Japanese. However, the KMT administration, led by Chiang Kai-shek's close associate General Chen Yi, and accompanied by an influx of exiled Chinese mainlanders, quickly clashed with Taiwanese locals. As Steven Phillips describes, Chen's administration of the island was marred by "inflation, grain shortages, corruption, lack of military discipline, unemployment, industrial collapse, and cultural conflict."[6] The KMT took it upon itself to implement a campaign of Sinicization on the island to re-educate the Taiwanese who had been influenced by the Japanese. The KMT mandated the use of Mandarin in public places including schools and government offices. As described in Chapter 1, Chen's policy of "Necessary State Socialism" wrecked the economy. By 1947, tensions came to a head. On February 28, KMT troops cracked down on a public demonstration, leading to a series of events that culminated in the slaughter of upwards of 20,000 Taiwanese. The massacre is commemorated today as the 228 Incident on Taiwan's annual Peace Memorial Day.[7]

The 228 Incident cemented the KMT's repressive one-party rule on Taiwan by wiping out an entire generation of Taiwanese leaders from all walks of life. The era of "White Terror" had begun. The KMT declared martial law on May 19, 1949. Over the next several decades, tens of thousands of Taiwanese would be imprisoned or killed on charges of treason or Communist sympathizing, including many local leaders and educated professionals. The brutality with which the KMT subdued the local population assured that Chiang and his son, Chiang Ching-kuo, would rule without opposition for many years to come. As David Yang writes, "Taiwanese society in the authoritarian era was characterized by the domination of the mainlander elite over the majority native Taiwanese."[8]

In January 1949, as the Chinese civil war worsened, Chiang Kai-shek resigned his presidency of the ROC. Soon after, the Communists seized Nanjing. Defeated, Chiang and more than one million of his supporters sought refuge on Taiwan. There, Chiang proclaimed the re-establishment of the ROC in Taipei. On May 19, 1949, Chiang declared a permanent state of martial law on the island. On March 1, 1950, Chiang Kai-shek named himself president of the ROC and appointed representatives of the KMT to various positions in the new government. For the next four decades, the KMT regime, through the ROC government on Taiwan, carried on the fight against the Chinese Communists intermittently, taking advantage of the situation as a justification for imposing martial law to deprive the Taiwanese people of their human rights. Indeed, the Taiwanese became the victims of the so-called civil war between the CCP and the KMT, which was generally regarded as having ended in 1949. Under martial law, the state criminalized political speech, association, and assembly perceived as subversive or critical of government policy.

The Taiwan Garrison Command was tasked with suppressing activities perceived to challenge the KMT's power. As of 1949, the ROC regime's controlled territory had been reduced to an island of about 8 million people, consisting of Taiwanese and Chinese mainlanders fleeing CCP rule. However, it continued to claim sovereignty over all of China and its then-population of roughly 500 million. As representation in the government was apportioned by China's total population, Taiwan's citizens were allotted just 3 percent of the legislative seats in Taiwan, while KMT members were entitled to the remainder, as so-called representatives of their constituents on the Chinese mainland—based on the myth that the exiled KMT regime on Taiwan continued to represent the whole of mainland China.

Had the ROC won the Chinese civil war, and returned its forces to China, it is possible that Taiwan would be a normalized state today. However, history took a very different turn. Defeated in the civil war, the ROC regime took exile on Taiwan, beginning an illegal military occupation and declaring a martial law that would last for almost forty years. The Allied Powers, hesitant to involve themselves in another Pacific conflict, acquiesced to the situation. The question of Taiwan's disposition after the war was clouded by the ROC's unexpected exile to Taiwan and the imminent threat of a PRC invasion from across the strait.

B. KMT-CCP HOSTILITIES (1949 TO 1987)

Following the KMT's exile, remnants of the ROC's army continued for a short while to wage isolated battles against the Communists on the Chinese mainland. The People's Liberation Army was successful in seizing several offshore islands, including Hainan Island, from the ROC. However, they were unable to overtake Quemoy and Matsu. The potential for the continuation of major fighting ended with the onset of the Korean War in June 1950. The Korean War was a blessing for Chiang as he quickly became a part of the United States' containment strategy against Communism in Asia. President Truman, acknowledging the strategic value of Taiwan, ordered the neutralization of the Taiwan Strait. The presence of the U.S. Seventh Fleet prevented what many observers assumed would be a rapid end for the ROC's exiled regime on the island.

Territorial disputes between the PRC and the ROC persisted throughout the 1950s. In 1953, President Eisenhower removed the Seventh Fleet from the Taiwan Strait. Hostilities renewed in September 1954 during the First Taiwan Strait Crisis, when the PRC engaged in heavy artillery bombardment of Quemoy. Subsequently, the United States and the ROC signed a Mutual Defense Treaty in December 1954, which entered into force in 1955 and placed Taiwan and Penghu (the Pescadores) (but not Quemoy and other ROC-held offshore islands) under U.S. protection. In

January 1955, the PRC seized the Yijiangshan Islands north of the Dachen Islands. In response, the U.S. Congress passed the Formosa Resolution on January 29, 1955, authorizing President Eisenhower to defend Taiwan and the Pescadores "as he deems necessary."[9] The PRC's military advances forced Chiang Kai-shek to abandon the Dachen Islands offshore from Zhejiang Province in February 1955. Active hostilities ended in April 1955, when the PRC signaled its willingness to enter negotiations at the Bandung Conference in Indonesia.

The Second Taiwan Strait Crisis erupted three years later, in 1958, when PRC and ROC forces shelled each other's positions at Amoy (Xiamen), Quemoy, and Matsu Islands. The Chinese artillery bombardment of Quemoy and Matsu spurred the United States into providing fighter jets and anti-aircraft missiles to the ROC. Cross-strait hostilities became a hot topic in U.S. foreign policy discussions. During the 1960 U.S. presidential debates, then Vice President Richard Nixon famously criticized John F. Kennedy for stating that he would not defend Quemoy and Matsu in a hypothetical attack by the PRC.[10]

While military tensions flared in Asia, a diplomatic battle between the PRC and the ROC was ensuing in the United Nations. As explained in Chapter 6, the United States and Allied leaders contemplated the PRC's admission into the United Nations as early as 1950. As a signatory to the UN Charter, Chiang Kai-shek's government remained the sole lawful representative of China in the United Nations. Diplomats opted to wait until the end of the Korean War to address the issue. By the time of the Eisenhower administration, it became apparent that the PRC's participation in the United Nations was inevitable. The White House began exploring scenarios for seating both the PRC and the ROC as UN members, but no action was taken. Throughout the Kennedy and Johnson administrations, Chiang Kai-shek revolted against the notion of the PRC's membership. He made it abundantly clear that he would not tolerate coexistence with the PRC in the United Nations.

The ROC's occupation of China's seat in the United Nations persisted until 1971, when relations between the United States and the PRC began to improve rapidly. The Sino-Soviet split presented Nixon with an opportunity to normalize relations with the PRC as part of his containment strategy against the USSR. This shift undermined Chiang's bargaining power. Under Nixon, U.S. diplomats would no longer block moves to elevate the PRC's participation in the United Nations. Finally, in 1971, the General Assembly voted in favor of Resolution 2758, which expelled Chiang Kai-shek's regime and seated the PRC in the United Nations.

At one fell swoop, Resolution 2758 recognized the PRC as the only lawful representative of China in the United Nations and one of the five permanent members of the Security Council. The ROC was summarily expelled from the world body. Chiang Kai-shek and the KMT quickly found themselves isolated in the international community as more countries established relations with the PRC. In Taiwan, the ROC-controlled media accused the United Nations of moral bankruptcy and lauded the ROC delegation for walking out before the final Assembly vote was taken. In private, Chiang reportedly made inquiries to his confidants as to whether the ROC could re-enter the United Nations under the compromise offered prior to the adoption of Resolution 2758. However, by that point, there was no turning back. To this day, many people in Taiwan look upon Chiang's "original sin" in the United Nations as the moment of truth when Taiwan and its people lost their position in the international community. Chiang, in his emotional commitment in the struggle against Mao and the Chinese Communists, stubbornly refused the advice given to him by friendly nations to accept a two-China or one-China, one-Taiwan solution to the question of UN representation. By the time the General Assembly passed Resolution 2758, Chiang's opportunity had been squandered. As a result, Taiwan's quest for normalized statehood suffered a tremendous blow that resonates to this day. Taiwan has since become an international orphan to be kicked around by the PRC, its allies, and others.

The trend toward Taiwan's international isolation was hastened with President Carter's decision to derecognize the ROC in 1979. During this period, the PRC and the ROC each vied to one up the other through "checkbook diplomacy," offering economic incentives to potential diplomatic partners in exchange for political recognition. To this day, Taiwan maintains formal relations with some twenty-one countries and the Holy See. The vast majority of its past allies have shifted their recognition to the PRC. The PRC enforces these decisions by refusing to deal with states that maintain formal diplomatic relations with the ROC.

Relations between the PRC and the ROC brightened somewhat following Chiang Kai-shek's death in 1975. In January 1979, Deng Xiaoping promoted the concept of "one country, two systems," promising that "so long as Taiwan returns to the embrace of the motherland, we will respect the realities and the existing system there."[11] PRC leaders also attempted to persuade Taiwan's leaders to rebuild the "Three Links"— postal, transportation, and trade contacts—across the Taiwan Strait. Chiang Ching-kuo responded to the overtures by announcing the "Three-Noes Policy," promising "no contact, no compromise, and no negotiation" with the PRC. Yet, the younger Chiang was reported to have had regular contact with China's Deng Xiaoping via Singapore Prime Minister Lee Kuan Yew, who carried letters between the two leaders during his frequent trips to Taiwan and the PRC.[12] Chiang Ching-kuo softened his stance in 1986 in order to negotiate for the release of a hijacked China Airlines cargo plane that had been diverted to Guangzhou.

Toward the end of his life, the younger Chiang sought modest political changes aimed at giving native Taiwanese more influence in the government. An attempt on his life by a Taiwanese activist in New York in April 1970, sometimes called the 424 Incident, was said to have awakened Chiang to the deep discontent of the Taiwanese people and the ultimate need for reforms. By the late 1980s, under pressure from the United States and Taiwanese abroad and at home, Chiang Ching-kuo had little choice but to finally abandon authoritarian rule. However, powerful forces within the ROC, including exiled mainlanders within the KMT and the military, did not wish to see their influence diminished in the process. With demands mounting on both sides, Chiang gradually opened the door to democracy in Taiwan. In 1984, Chiang selected Lee Teng-hui, a Taiwanese and former mayor of Taipei and governor of Taiwan Province, to serve as his vice president. Two years later, in 1986, Chiang acquiesced to the formation of the Democratic Progressive Party (DPP) to act as the main opposition to the KMT. Martial law was lifted in 1987. That same year, the government began to permit traveling to China, mostly for aging KMT soldiers who longed to see their families across the strait.

III. The Era of Taiwanese Presidents (1988 to 2008)

A. LEE TENG-HUI (1988 TO 2000)

Lee Teng-hui became Taiwan's president after Chiang Ching-kuo's death in January 1988. The ascendency of a Taiwanese to the country's top post invited opposition by some conservative mainlanders in the KMT. In order to continue implementing political reforms, Lee would also need to win the KMT chairmanship. He secured his victory on July 8, 1988, and quickly moved to add more Taiwanese to the party's Central Standing Committee. With his power then consolidated, Lee pushed forward with his agenda, which included the enormously important task of divesting the KMT of its day-to-day operation of the ROC government and instituting a genuine democracy in Taiwan.

During his twelve years in power, Lee shepherded enormous changes in Taiwanese politics and brought the country closer to the dream of a full multiparty democracy.[13] Alongside these dramatic changes was the culmination of a social movement toward Taiwanization in all areas of life on the island. What had started as an effort to include more native-born people in the KMT grew into an emphasis of a distinct Taiwanese social and cultural identity. Taiwan's government was no longer that of an exiled regime, and with the period of repression ended, Taiwan's people were free to express new perspectives and demands rooted in the local experience unburdened of the KMT's historical preoccupations.

By 1990, relations between China and Taiwan had progressed significantly. The two sides agreed to establish a forum for nonofficial discussions of topics of mutual interest. On February 19, 1991, the ROC's Mainland Affairs Council created the semi-official Straits Exchange Foundation (SEF) as the country's representative in dealings with the PRC, acknowledging "the complex and unique nature of relations across the Taiwan Strait."[14] In December, the PRC reciprocated with the establishment of the Association for Relations Across the Taiwan Straits (ARATS). In November 1992, representatives of the SEF and the ARATS met in Hong Kong for a practical meeting on topics including certificate registration and registered mail exchanges. It was this meeting that gave rise to the myth of the so-called "1992 Consensus." There is no official record from the meeting. But PRC attendees stated that the two sides agreed that there was "one China," which includes Taiwan, but that the two sides disagreed as to which government, the ROC or the PRC, was its legitimate government.[15] KMT officials agreed on this version of events, and in 2000, the KMT's Su Chi fabricated the term "1992 Consensus," asserting that the agreement was implied during the summit to build "mutual trust between the KMT and the CCP [Chinese Communist Party]."[16] Years later, the 1992 Consensus would become a key symbol of the Ma Ying-jeou administration in order to appease, and establish closer ties with, the PRC. In reality, the term has become a code word for the PRC's One China Principle, which holds that Taiwan is a part of China.

President Lee refused to acknowledge that a consensus had been struck at the meeting. Indeed, a press release issued by the SEF after the meeting stated: "On November 3, a responsible person of the Communist Chinese ARATS said that it is willing to 'respect and accept' SEF's proposal that each side 'verbally states' its respective principles on 'one China.'"[17] ARATS responded by stating: "At this working-level consultation in Hong Kong, SEF representatives suggested that each side use respective verbal announcements to state the one China principle. On November 3rd, SEF sent a letter, formally notifying that 'each side will make respective statements through verbal announcements.' ARATS fully respects and accepts SEF's suggestion."[18] Neither release alludes to a "consensus" other than the fact that both sides would make "verbal announcements" regarding the One China principle. The November 1992 meeting was followed in April 1993 by the Wang-Koo Summit in Singapore between ARATS Chairman Wang Daohan and SEF Chairman Koo Chen-fu. The meeting resulted in a set of agreements on matters including postal services. Wang and Koo met again in October 1998 in Shanghai. A third meeting scheduled for 1999, which was to be held in Taiwan, was canceled by the PRC following comments by President Lee suggesting that Taiwan and China were two separate states.

Lee increasingly asserted Taiwan's separate political identity throughout his presidency. In 1991, Lee formally terminated the Temporary Provisions Effective During the Period of Mobilization for Suppression of the Communist Rebellion, which the National Assembly adopted in 1948 as a pretext for depriving and curtailing rights under the ROC constitution. He abolished other constitutional provisions adopted to secure the Chiangs' position after the KMT's exile to Taiwan. In 1994, the National Assembly voted to allow the people of Taiwan to elect the president in a popular vote beginning in 1996. Positions including mayors of the cities of Taipei and Kaohsiung were opened for popular election for the first time beginning in 1994. In the diplomatic field, Lee's administration moved away from the mindset of the Chinese civil war by recognizing that "the PRC controls the Chinese mainland while the ROC's jurisdiction includes only Taiwan and . . . Penghu, Kinmen [Quemoy], and Matsu."[19] In August 1993, Lee undertook what would become an annual campaign to seek Taiwan's participation in the United Nations, initially under the banner of the Republic of China on Taiwan. These efforts were co-sponsored by member states friendly to Taiwan. However, the PRC used its influence to prevent the matter from ever appearing on the General Assembly's agenda.

In 1995, the Third Taiwan Strait Crisis erupted when Lee, a graduate of Cornell University, accepted an invitation to speak at the school on the topic of Taiwan's democratization. The PRC vehemently opposed the invitation and protested to the U.S. State Department to deny Lee a visa. The U.S. Congress then passed a concurrent resolution urging the State Department to grant the visa. The PRC responded by conducting missile tests near Taiwan followed by live-fire and amphibious assault exercises. With Taiwan's first democratic presidential election scheduled for March 23 of the following year, the PRC announced that a second set of missile tests would be held two weeks before the election, followed by additional live-fire exercises. Amphibious assault exercises were to be held from March 18 to 25. As tensions rose, the United States dispatched two carrier battle groups to patrol near the Taiwan Strait. The PRC's moves were unquestionably timed to intimidate Taiwanese voters on the eve of their first direct presidential election and to warn its leaders not to stray from the One China Principle. But the PRC's threats were counterproductive. Lee won 54 percent of the popular vote in the 1996 elections.

In 1999, toward the end of his administration, Lee responded to a question in an interview with the Voice of Germany, regarding how the PRC views Taiwan as a renegade province. In the interview he emphasized the cross-strait realities in the following terms:

[T]he two sides of the Taiwan Strait are under separate administrations of different governments, [that] the Chinese communist authorities have been threatening us with force is actually the main reason why cross-strait ties cannot be improved thoroughly.... Since the PRC's establishment, the Chinese communists have never ruled Taiwan, Penghu, Kinmen, and Matsu, which have been under the jurisdiction of the Republic of China.... Since our constitutional reform in 1991, we have designated cross-strait ties as nation-to-nation, or at least as special state-to-state ties, rather than internal ties within "one China" between a legitimate government and a rebellion group, or between central and local governments. . . .[20]

The PRC reacted furiously to Lee's characterizations of the cross-strait relationship as one of sovereign equals, warning him against his "extremely dangerous step" suggesting a move toward Taiwanese independence.[21]

B. CHEN SHUI-BIAN (2000 TO 2008)

Democratic Progressive Party (DPP) candidate Chen Shui-bian succeeded Lee Teng-hui after winning the 2000 presidential election. Born to an impoverished family in southern Taiwan in 1951, Chen excelled as a student at the National Taiwan University, College of Law, and later rose to prominence for his courageous defense of activists who were arrested, detained, and tried following the Kaohsiung Incident of 1979. He served on the Taipei City Council in the early 1980s and then as a DPP member of the Legislative Yuan. He was the first popularly elected mayor of Taipei City in twenty-seven years, as well as the first DPP candidate to win such a position. Although he lost the Taipei mayoral bid for a second term to Ma Ying-jeou in 1998, he began campaigning for the presidency soon after. Chen's election to the presidency marked the first peaceful transfer of power from the KMT to the DPP since Taiwan's transition to democracy in the 1990s.

The Chen administration inherited a largely KMT bureaucracy along with a KMT dominated legislature, which significantly checked the new president's power. At the same time, PRC leaders showed little interest in developing high-level contacts with Chen's government. Nevertheless, he managed to take several important unilateral steps to buttress cross-strait ties even while taking a strong stance in favor of Taiwan independence. In 2002, Chen gave a speech stating that the PRC and Taiwan were "each one country on each side of the [Taiwan] strait."[22] And in 2004, he proposed that Taiwan should reform the ROC constitution, an act the PRC considered provocative, as it could strengthen the legal basis for Taiwan's statehood claim.[23] In 2007, after fourteen previous attempts to participate in the United Nations as the Republic of China on Taiwan, Chen's administration for the first time submitted an application for membership—as distinguished from mere participation—to join the United Nations under the name Taiwan. The UN Secretary-General, citing Resolution 2758, refused the application, bypassing the Security Council in violation of the Council's rules of procedure for dealing with an application for UN membership.

Throughout the Chen administration, gradual steps were taken to re-establish direct contact with China. Beginning in 2001, registered residents of Quemoy and Matsu islands were permitted to visit the PRC directly. In 2003, Taiwanese carriers were given permission to charter indirect flights for travelers between Taiwan and the PRC. This led to limited direct flights beginning in 2005. The administration also lifted the fifty-year direct trade and investment ban between Taiwan and the PRC. Despite these changes, PRC leaders chose to avoid direct dealings with the Chen administration on many matters. Around 2004, the PRC began courting the opposition KMT. KMT Chairman Lien Chan visited the PRC in 2005. Chen extended an invitation to then PRC president Hu Jintao to visit Taiwan, but the invitation was ignored.

IV. The Era of Ma Ying-jeou (2008 to the Present)

Relations between Taiwan and the PRC have warmed considerably under President Ma Ying-jeou. Ma, who was the mayor of Taipei, had served as an English-language interpreter to Chiang Ching-kuo. The KMT's interests ironically had evolved since Chiang's era, and the KMT's fortunes are increasingly aligned with that of their former arch-enemies, the Chinese Communists across the Taiwan Strait. Members of the KMT, including Ma, have even advocated for a permanent peace pact between Taiwan and China. Born in Hong Kong, Ma's perspective regarding his own relationship with China differs significantly from his predecessors. His willingness to put aside the question of sovereignty to focus on economic matters initially made him an asset, and PRC leaders hoped to secure policies that would further integrate the two countries' economies. However, the Taiwanese public's vocal opposition to new trade agreements and the KMT's stunning defeat in 2014 nine-in-one island-wide elections undermined Ma's credibility with Beijing. Above all else, the Ma administration's downfall demonstrates that Taiwan's democratically elected leaders must first and foremost answer to the Taiwanese people.

A. MA'S "THREE NOES"

Though President Ma promised in his 2008 inaugural speech to adhere to a policy of "no independence, no unification, and no use of force," his actions have hinted at ulterior motives. *Time* reported that since 2008 "relations between Taiwan and China had arguably seen the most rapid advancement in the six-decade standoff between the two governments."[24] In less than three months of his presidency, Ma's government approved direct charter flights between China and Taiwan, opened Taiwan to Chinese tourists, and eased restrictions on investment and stock trading by Chinese investors. Under Ma, the SEF and the ARATS were brought out of dormancy to take up negotiations that would culminate in the Economic Cooperation Framework Agreement (ECFA) of 2010. As reported by the *Washington Post*, Ma took credit in developing cross-strait relations by "addressing the easiest and most pressing issues first, such as economic ties, rather than tackling more-difficult political questions."[25] But many Taiwanese voiced concern that the president was eroding the country's self-governing status in the process. Ma argued that characterizing Taiwan and the PRC as "two areas," rather than "state to state" or "one country on each side," allowed "both sides of the Taiwan Strait to sidestep sovereignty questions in pursuing closer ties."[26] His characterization of an "area to area relationship" drew vocal opposition from DPP representatives and others who feared Ma was hinting at a basis for unification.

Ma has held to the outdated KMT line that the ROC is still the government of all of China, as embodied in the ROC constitution of 1947—totally ignoring the reality that the PRC has controlled and ruled the Chinese mainland since October 1949. In an interview with a Japanese magazine in 2008, he reaffirmed the party's version of the One China principle by stating that the ROC "definitely is an independent sovereign state, and [that] Mainland China is also part of the territory of the ROC."[27] However, KMT leaders no longer pretend that the ROC will retake the Chinese mainland. During his campaign for the presidency in 2008, Ma proclaimed his own version of a "Three Noes" policy, promising not to pursue unification, independence, or the use of force in building relations with the PRC.

Ma's pro-China leanings were evident in September 2009 when, contrary to the wishes of the Taiwanese people, he declined to pursue Taiwan's annual bid for UN membership or participation. Earlier that year, the PRC allowed Taiwan to gain observer status in the World Health Assembly (WHA), the annual meeting of all members of the World Health Organization (WHO), under the name "the Department of Health, Chinese Taipei." Ma's opponents, including DPP presidential candidate Tsai Ing-wen, questioned whether this and other arrangements had forsaken Taiwan's "sovereignty, security, democracy and economic leverage."[28] In 2013, the PRC proposed Taiwan's participation in the International Civil Aviation Organization (ICAO) in 2013 as a guest, rather than an observer. Critics suggested that Ma's strategy of kowtowing accommodation had created the presumption that Taiwan's future participation in international organizations would be subject to the PRC's approval. Ma rebutted the charges by playing up the economic benefits of token participation in even a few international forums, at the expense of Taiwan's sovereign authority and dignity.

B. CROSS-STRAIT ECONOMIC INTEGRATION AND DEPENDENCY

Throughout his administration, Ma has been accused of adopting policies designed to foster Taiwan's economic dependence on the PRC. The ROC and the PRC have signed more than twenty agreements during Ma's administration on topics ranging from investment protection to meteorology. These include the Economic Cooperation Framework Agreement (ECFA), which the Ma administration began promoting shortly after he took office in 2008. The ECFA was intended to relax trade restrictions on both sides of the strait by lowering tariffs and facilitating the sale of hundreds of goods. The ECFA was signed on June 29, 2010, and went into effect on September 12, 2010. Ma claimed that Taiwan's adoption of the ECFA would smooth the way for free trade agreements with the United States and the Association of Southeast Asian Nations (ASEAN). He also argued that the agreement would make Taiwan more attractive to foreign investors. Ma also claimed that fostering closer economic ties with the PRC through the ECFA would demonstrate Taiwan's progress in liberalizing trade, facilitating Taiwan's conclusion of bilateral free-trade agreements with other countries and its eventual entry into the Trans-Pacific Partnership (TPP).[29] To date, many of the promises made by the ECFA's proponents have yet to materialize.

Some observers have compared the ECFA with the PRC–Hong Kong Closer Economic Partnership Agreement (CEPA), a trade agreement signed by the PRC and the Hong Kong Special Administrative Region in 2003. Both agreements contain provisions relating to trading in goods and services, financial cooperation, and other areas. But the agreements also differ in important ways. The CEPA is essentially an internal trade agreement between a central and regional government. Article 2 of the CEPA affirms this dynamic by providing that implementation and amendment of the CEPA shall abide by the "one country, two systems" principle. The ECFA's signatories in contrast are the Chairman of the SEF for Taiwan and the President of the ARATS for the PRC. The SEF is claimed to be a private organization, but is in fact funded and controlled by Taiwan's Executive Yuan. It has limited authority to handle cross-straits matters with the PRC. The ARATS is a counterparty to the SEF founded by the PRC to facilitate cross-strait relations. A second important difference between the documents is the CEPA's waiver of certain provisions of China's WTO Accession Legal Document for trade between mainland China and Hong Kong. No similar provision is found in the ECFA. The ECFA and the CEPA also differ on the issue of termination. Neither the CEPA nor its nine supplemental agreements contain termination clauses. ECFA's Article 16(1), meanwhile, contains a clause for termination. It is not unusual that an intragovernmental agreement such as the CEPA would lack a termination clause. On the other hand, the ECFA does provide for termination, as would be expected of an agreement between two sovereign powers under international law.

Support for the ECFA was high at the time of its adoption. One survey found roughly 60 percent of the Taiwanese public were in favor.[30] (It is worth noting that a separate poll found nearly 90 percent of the public lacked extensive knowledge of the agreement's purposes or functions.[31]) Perhaps not surprisingly, while the ECFA has succeeded in fostering increased economic activity between Taiwan and China, the benefits of increased trade have not accrued equally to all segments of society. A 2011 report commissioned by the Research, Development, and Evaluation Commission of Taiwan's Executive Yuan found that "[p]eople who possess large amounts of capital appeared to reap benefits from the [ECFA], while those on the lower end of the economic scale absorbed the costs."[32] According to critics, the real beneficiaries of Ma's policies have been wealthy KMT constituents with business ties in China as opposed to everyday Taiwanese. After more than half a century in power, the KMT's members have acquired commercial holdings in industries including sugar cane production, petrochemicals, media, and financial services. The KMT itself retains extensive corporate holdings despite a self-proclaimed divestment process that supposedly began in the 1990s. A lack of transparency of the KMT's dealings is a constant source of debate in Taiwanese politics, and the party has leveraged its business connections for political advantage. In 2012, some Taiwanese companies gave employees working in China time off to vote in the island's presidential election, with the expectation of supporting the KMT ticket.

In August 2012, shortly after Ma won his second term, the SEF and the ARATS signed the Cross-Strait Bilateral Investment Protection and Promotion Agreement that established a mechanism for resolving trade and investment disputes. In June 2013, the two sides signed the Cross-Strait Service Trade Agreement (CSSTA), opening "further cross-strait exchanges" of the PRC and Taiwan's service sectors.

The CSSTA would allow exchanges in banking, healthcare, transportation, travel, communications, and construction, and permit cross-strait investment by citizens from both countries. Like the ECFA, the agreement was negotiated by the SEF and the ARATS. Critics immediately raised alarms over the lack of transparency during negotiations for the CSSTA and criticized the Ma administration for throwing open the doors to the PRC without securing protections for Taiwan's ongoing sovereignty. In the Legislative Yuan, opposition lawmakers demanded a close review of the agreement. In June 2013, the KMT and the DPP agreed to a process for a clause-by-clause review. In March 2014, the KMT attempted to force the CSSTA through the legislature by disregarding the agreed procedures, sparking immediate strong protests. On the evening of March 18, hundreds of protestors stormed the Legislative Yuan building in Taipei and occupied the legislature floor. A massive rally on March 30 saw hundreds of thousands of people take to the streets of Taipei in support of the occupiers' demands. By May 2014, Ma's approval rating had dropped again, to below 18 percent, and commentators accused his government of being out of touch with the Taiwanese people.[33] Polls found that half of those who identified themselves as KMT voters believed Ma had "flunked" as president.[34] In November 2014, voters dealt the KMT a crushing defeat in the crucial, nine-in-one island-wide elections, positioning the opposition DPP for a strong showing in upcoming presidential and legislative elections in January 2016.

V. Conclusion: Security and Dignity for Taiwan

The Taiwan-China relationship has followed the general trend toward peaceful coexistence that has emerged in the post–Cold War global order. Before the end of World War II, China and Taiwan had weak and infrequent ties. Although the Qing dynasty attempted to assert governance over Taiwan as a province in 1887, it ceded Taiwan to Japan in perpetuity in 1895 under the Treaty of Shimonoseki. The two sides had minimal contact during the era of Japanese colonization that lasted until 1945. After the inception of Chiang Kai-shek's military occupation in 1945 and the KMT exile to Taiwan in 1949, the PRC government in China and the exiled ROC regime in Taiwan were locked in a stalemate that lasted until the era of Taiwanese presidents that began in 1988. In recent decades, both sides have emphasized the use of the diplomatic and economic instruments in lieu of the military in sharp contrast to the situation in the mid-twentieth century. However, profound ideological differences remain, despite the PRC and the KMT's collaboration to undermine Taiwan's independence against the evident wishes of the Taiwanese people. The trend toward peace and stability in the Taiwan Strait and the Asia Pacific region is welcomed. But it cannot be purchased in the long term by sacrificing other cherished values, among them freedom, democracy, and human rights. Human security and human dignity are of equal essentiality in the drive toward the achievement of minimum world order (minimization of unauthorized coercion and violence) and optimum world order (widest shaping and sharing of values).

In 1969, U.S. Attorney General John Mitchell speaking to activists protesting the Nixon administration's civil rights policies, was reported to have remarked: "You'd be better informed if instead of listening to what we say, you watch what we do."[35] Mitchell's cynical-sounding admonishment may be taken as a universal rule in politics. In Taiwan, President Ma's self-proclaimed achievements must be subject to scrutiny by examining his deeds as well as his words. During his campaigns for election and reelection, Ma advertised his Taiwanese upbringing and made a pledge of "three noes"—no unification, no independence, and no use of force in dealing with China. He swore he would die a Taiwanese. But once in office, he betrayed his campaign promises and slogans, taking actions that strengthened the PRC's hand and downplaying Taiwan's *de facto* independence. In 2008, when ARATS Chairman Chen Yunlin visited Taipei for a meeting of the SEF and the ARATS, ROC flags were removed from prominent locations around the capital. Prior to Chen's arrival, Ma remarked that Chen would be free to call him "Mr. Ma," in lieu of his presidential title. The obscuring of ROC symbols was an obvious attempt to placate PRC officials, but it also denied the reality of Taiwan's hard-won political status. The tendency to kowtow before China defined the ROC's cross-strait policy throughout Ma's administration. (Some of Ma's more fervent supporters believed he was on track for a Nobel Peace Prize for his efforts to ease cross-strait tensions, possibly as a joint recipient with Chinese President Xi Jinping. These hopes seem to have been dashed—and weren't helped by the Ma-Xi meeting in Singapore in November 2015, which generated more controversy than anything in Taiwan and elsewhere, owing in part to the invocation of the so-called 1992 Consensus as a basis for continued cross-strait interactions.) In 2010 and 2013, Ma redoubled efforts to marry the Chinese and Taiwanese economies by promoting the ECFA and the CSSTA. By this point he had earned the moniker "9 percent president" in reference to his lowest single-digit approval ratings. In 2014, the KMT's last-ditch attempt to pass the CSSTA in the Legislative Yuan triggered widespread protests. In the end, the Ma administration had little to show for its cross-strait strategy save for the Sunflower Movement and unprecedented disapproval among the Taiwanese electorate.

In evaluating the outcomes of the KMT's pro-China policies, the predispositions of the Taiwanese people cannot be forgotten. After many decades of *de facto* independence and the emergence of a vibrant democratic society and national culture, the Taiwanese people will never be content to see their country become the next Hong Kong under a flawed "one country, two systems" formula. President Ma, in emphasizing economic matters and cross-strait appeasement over preserving Taiwan's distinctive status, failed to satisfy the Taiwanese people's aspirations for sovereignty and self-determination. Policymakers inside and outside of Taiwan should keep recent events in mind in making estimations about the future. In the global context, an emerging U.S.-China rivalry is bound to shape Taiwan's possible future developments and conditions of peace and security in the Asia Pacific region. Prospects for the U.S.-China relationship will be considered more deeply in Chapter 9.

Notes

1. EDGAR SNOW, RED STAR OVER CHINA 88–89 (1937).

2. EMMA JINHUA TENG, TAIWAN'S IMAGINED GEOGRAPHY: CHINESE COLONIAL TRAVEL WRITING AND PICTURES 1683–1895, at 38 (2004).

3. MELISSA J. BROWN, IS TAIWAN CHINESE? THE IMPACT OF CULTURE, POWER, AND MIGRATION ON CHANGING IDENTITIES 37 (2004).

4. Nagao Ariga, *Diplomacy, in* JAPAN BY THE JAPANESE 163 (Alfred Stead ed., 1904).

5. Robert Gardella, *From Treaty Ports to Provincial Status, 1860–1894, in* TAIWAN: A NEW HISTORY 164 (Murray A. Rubinstein ed., 2015).

6. Steven Phillips, *Between Assimilation and Independence: Taiwanese Political Aspirations Under Nationalist Chinese Rule, 1945–1948, in* TAIWAN: A NEW HISTORY 293 (Murray A. Rubinstein ed., 2015).

7. *See* TSUNG-YI LIN, AN INTRODUCTION TO 2-28 TRAGEDY IN TAIWAN: FOR WORLD CITIZENS (1998).

8. David D. Yang, *Classing Ethnicity: Class, Ethnicity, and the Mass Politics of Taiwan's Democratic Transition*, 59 WORLD POL. 503–38, 509 (July 2007) .

9. Public Law 84-4 (H.J. Res. 159), Jan. 29, 1955.

10. Commission on Presidential Debates, Oct. 13, 1960 Debate Transcript, http://www.debates.org/index.php?page=october-13-1960-debate-transcript.

11. *See* Ministry of Foreign Affairs of the People's Republic of China, A Policy of "One Country, Two Systems" on Taiwan, http://www.fmprc.gov.cn/mfa_eng/ziliao_665539/3602_665543/ 3604_665547/t18027.shtml.

12. *See e.g.,* DAVID DEAN, UNOFFICIAL DIPLOMACY: THE AMERICAN INSTITUTE IN TAIWAN (2014).

13. *See* ANDREW J. NATHAN & ANDREW SCOBELL, CHINA'S SEARCH FOR SECURITY 226–33 (2012).

14. Straits Exchange Foundation, History of the SEF, http://www.sef.org.tw/ct.asp?xItem=4 8843&CtNode=3987&mp=300.

15. SHIRLEY A. KAN, CHINA/TAIWAN: EVOLUTION OF THE "ONE CHINA POLICY"—KEY STATEMENTS FROM WASHINGTON, BEIJING, AND TAIPEI, CONGRESSIONAL RESEARCH SERVICE, at 46 (2014), *available at* http://www.fas.org/sgp/crs/row/RL30341.pdf.

16. *See* Chris Wang, *KMT Beyond "1992 Consensus": DPP*, TAIPEI TIMES, July 26, 2013, *available at* http://www.taipeitimes.com/News/taiwan/archives/2013/07/26/2003568197.

17. KAN, *supra* note 15, at 50.

18. *Id.* at 51.

19. *See* Eric Ting-Lun Huang, *Taiwan's Status in a Changing World: United Nations Representation and Membership for Taiwan*, 9 ANN. SURV. INT'L L. 55, 85 (2003).

20. KAN, *supra* note 15, at 66.

21. Seth Faison, *Taiwan President Implies His Island Is Sovereign State*, N.Y. TIMES, July 13, 1999, *available at* http://www.nytimes.com/1999/07/13/world/taiwan-president-implies-his-island-is-sovereign-state.html.

22. KAN, *supra* note 15, at 73.

23. *Chen Vows Constitutional Reform*, BBC NEWS, Mar. 30, 2004, http://news.bbc.co.uk/2/hi/asia-pacific/3581407.stm.

24. *Talking to Taiwan's New President*, TIME MAGAZINE, Aug. 11, 2008, *available at* http://www.time.com/time/world/article/0,8599,1831748,00.html.

25. William Wan, *Taiwan's President, Ma Ying-jeou, Plans to Expand Relations with China*, WASH. POST, Oct. 24, 2013, *available at* http://www.washingtonpost.com/world/taiwans-president-ma-ying-jeou-plans-to-expand-relations-with-china/2013/10/24/0e38bb7e-3cbd-11e3-b6a9-da62c264f40e_story.html.

26. *Ma Clarifies "Two Areas," Reaffirms Non-denial*, CHINA POST, Oct. 25, 2008, *available at* http://www.chinapost.com.tw/taiwan/china-taiwan-relations/2008/10/25/180363/Ma-clarifies.htm.

27. Ko Shu-Ling, *Ma Refers to China as ROC Territory in Magazine Interview*, TAIPEI TIMES, Oct. 8, 2008, *available at* http://www.taipeitimes.com/News/taiwan/archives/2008/10/08/2003425320.

28. William Lowther, *Tsai Warns of Strategic Collapse*, TAIPEI TIMES, May 8, 2009, *available at* http://www.taipeitimes.com/News/front/archives/2009/05/08/2003443067. *See also* Jacques deLisle, *Taiwan in the World Health Assembly: A Victory, with Limits*, BROOKINGS INSTITUTION (May 2009), *available at* http://www.brookings.edu/research/opinions/2009/05/taiwan-delisle.

29. Russell Flannery, *Taiwan President Ma Ying-jeou Says Services Pact Would Open Up New Business*, FORBES, June 25, 2014, *available at* http://www.forbes.com/sites/russellflannery/2014/06/25/taiwan-president-ma-ying-jeou-says-services-pact-would-open-up-new-business/.

30. *60% of People Support ECFA*, CHINA POST, June 2, 2009, *available at* http://www.chinapost.com.tw/taiwan/china-taiwan-relations/2009/06/02/210496/60%25-of.htm.

31. *Most People Clueless about ECFA: Poll*, TAIPEI TIMES, Dec. 18, 2009, *available at* http://www.taipeitimes.com/News/taiwan/archives/2009/12/18/2003461241.

32. Su Yung-yao, *ECFA Benefiting Wealthy: Report*, TAIPEI TIMES, Mar. 27, 2011, *available at* http://www.taipeitimes.com/News/front/archives/2011/03/27/2003499218.

33. Stacy Hsu & Rich Chang, *Separate Polls Put Ma's Approval Rate Under 18 Percent*, TAIPEI TIMES, May 14, 2014, *available at* http://www.taipeitimes.com/News/front/archives/2014/05/14/2003590295.

34. Crystal Hsu, *Trade Pact Siege: Majority Opposes Trade Agreement: Poll*, TAIPEI TIMES, Mar. 27, 2014, *available at* http://www.taipeitimes.com/News/taiwan/archives/2014/03/27/2003586647.

35. *Watch What We Do*, WASH. POST, July 7, 1969.

IV Projections of Probable Future Developments

9   A Developing U.S.-China Rivalry?

TAIWAN'S SECURITY HINGES on the continuation of constructive diplomacy between the United States and China. But, as any casual observer would know, the United States and China are deeply divided in their perspectives. Historically, relations between the two countries have been characterized by equal measures of stability and volatility, of goodwill and enmity. Within the relatively new international frameworks established since the collapse of the Soviet Union, the prospects of the U.S.-China relationship remain highly uncertain. Some commentators see great potential for good in China's rise on the global stage. Others speculate on the beginnings of a new Cold War, like the one that divided East and West for much of the twentieth century. With memories of that era still fresh, one cannot help but speculate whether the United States and China are destined for a similar fate. Chinese leaders, for their part, insist they are pursuing a peaceful rise and peaceful development. But the country's accelerating military expansion and aggressive tactics in the East and South China Seas and elsewhere suggest other intentions.

China's rapid expansion in economic and political stature since the 1970s has destabilized familiar patterns and aroused anxiety within old power centers. Throughout history, interactions between powerful nations have always been marked by apprehension and rivalry, and at times violence. The rise of a new global power invariably will lead to tensions in a world that is increasingly crowded and where resources are ever-more scarce. Taiwan's status is only one of the matters complicating the situation in the Asia Pacific—disputes over China's territorial expansion, claims over maritime resources, human rights, trade, and economic development threaten to undermine regional and global stability. Yet the United States and China have shared interests that are profound and which cannot be overlooked in the final analysis. As outlined in Chapter 3, peaceful development depends in large measure on the ability of participants to broaden and integrate their perspectives and, when necessary, to elevate the interests of the world community above parochial aims. Under the right circumstances, the twenty-first century could be one of peace, cooperation, and prosperity for all—conditions heretofore unseen on the global stage.

I. Evolving Chinese Perspectives

The traditional Chinese worldview placed China at the center of the universe. Its Mandarin name, *Zhongguo*, literally means "the middle kingdom." Historical China was first among nations and regarded itself as the pinnacle of civilization. Neighboring countries including Japan, Korea, and Vietnam were viewed as vassal states and were required to make tributes to the Chinese emperor. This Sino-centric view prevailed in Asia until the arrival of Western powers and the eventual decline of the Qing dynasty in the late nineteenth and early twentieth centuries. The period between 1839 and 1949 was China's "century of humiliation" during which it suffered political, military, and cultural indignities at the hands of foreign powers. The low points included the First Opium War, the Taiping Rebellion, the Second Opium War, the Sino-French War, the First Sino-Japanese War, and the British invasion of Tibet. In the twentieth century, China was subjected to the Twenty-One Demands by Japan during World War I and the Second Sino-Japanese War during World War II. China's past humiliation, and the dream of national resurgence, serves as a cornerstone of the People's Republic of China's (PRC) governing narrative and a basis for Chinese skepticism of the international system. As Professor Aaron Friedberg remarked, China is not simply a new rising power. Rather, it is "returning to the position of regional preeminence it once held."[1]

A. FROM PEACEFUL COEXISTENCE TO CORE INTERESTS

Chinese foreign policy in the mid-twentieth century was characterized by the Five Principles of Peaceful Coexistence as first enumerated in the Panchsheel Treaty between China and India in 1954 concerning disputed territory in the Tibet region. The Five Principles were: mutual respect for sovereignty and territorial integrity, mutual nonaggression, noninterference in internal affairs, equality and mutual benefit, and peaceful coexistence. Although the Principles originated from negotiations between China and India, they soon became a common banner for developing nations around the world which were emerging from the era of colonization. The Principles featured prominently at the Bandung Conference (also known as the Asian-African Conference) and were ultimately incorporated into a ten-point declaration aimed at charting a new path for global development that was not dependent on the support of the Soviet Union or the industrialized West. China played a major role at the conference and used the opportunity to build its relationships with other developing countries. The outcomes of the Bandung Conference laid the foundation for the establishment of the Conference of Heads of State or Government of Non-Aligned Countries (the Non-Aligned Movement) in 1961. The Non-Aligned Movement also made use of the Five Principles as a cornerstone for peaceful relations among states. To this day, the PRC formally maintains a policy of nonalignment in foreign affairs.

In the early years of the PRC, Chinese leaders sought to influence the evolution of global Communism, providing ideological and material support to revolutionary causes around the globe. However, by the 1970s, following the disaster of the Cultural Revolution, Chinese leaders charted a more moderate course in foreign affairs. Tensions with the Soviet Union led the PRC to establish diplomatic relations with the United States in the 1970s, while Chinese elites increasingly sought opportunities to develop the country's economic and social resources with the help of outside aid. Throughout the 1970s, the number of governments with which Beijing maintained state-to-state relations increased dramatically. The country's international profile grew steadily under the presidency of Li Xiannian, who represented China in frequent visits abroad, and Communist Party Chairman Deng Xiaoping, who promoted a policy of opening up in stark contrast to Mao's economic isolationism. The positive trend continued until the Tiananmen Square massacre of June 4, 1989, where the People's Liberation Army violently ended a pro-democracy demonstration in Beijing, slaughtering an untold number of people. By some estimates, thousands were killed. The PRC government has never given a full official account of the incident and continues to suppress internal discourse concerning the events. The brutality of the Tiananmen Square massacre shocked the world, and called into question the veracity of Chinese leaders' commitments to reforms. World leaders reassessed their support for the PRC regime. Many Western governments severed or severely curtailed diplomatic relations with China. As explored in Chapter 7, relations with the United States suffered a major setback as a result of the crackdown, images of which were broadcast globally. To this day the United States maintains an arms embargo against the Chinese government.

Chinese foreign policy during the 1990s was focused on rebuilding the damage done from the events at Tiananmen Square. In 1989, Deng Xiaoping advised the Chinese people to "maintain a low profile, hide brightness, do not seek leadership, but do some things." During this period China undertook a series of economic reforms, opening itself to foreign investment and trade which would become the foundation for its rapid economic growth in the late 1990s and 2000s. In 1986, China became an observer to the General Agreement on Tariffs and Trade (GATT) and by 2001 had obtained membership in the World Trade Organization (WTO). With a booming middle class and increasingly internationalized society, Chinese leaders no longer adhered to the Communist tenets popularized under Mao Zedong. Rather, successive Chinese leaders have modified party doctrine to incorporate new elements. Today's Chinese Communist Party (CCP) luminaries, led by Xi Jinping, speak of "socialism with Chinese characteristics" and promise to build a "moderately prosperous society in all respects."

Nationalism has played an important role in the development of the modern Chinese state. The CCP's legitimacy rests in large part on its ability to maintain economic growth through top-down management of most sectors of the country' s economy. In doing so, PRC's leaders project a future of regional dominance and political unification in contrast to the humiliations of the past two centuries. This project has found concrete expression in the annexation of Tibet in 1951 and the reacquisition of Hong Kong and Macau in 1997 and 1999, respectively. The mission of unification has also formed the basis for territorial aspirations that are not well-founded in historical facts, such as claims to broad swaths of the South China Sea and Taiwan. While everyday people in China may only deserve moderate prosperity—according to their leaders—they can take heart in the great destiny they are helping to build for the Chinese nation, however far-fetched.

The themes of Chinese national pride and economic development are closely intertwined. Not surprisingly, Chinese foreign policy has become increasingly aggressive as the country amasses resources and influence. In the 2000s, Chinese officials and media began to speak of the country's "core interests." The term refers to issues that the PRC regards as purely domestic in nature. As highlighted in previous chapters, many commentators characterize China's core interests as those issues for which it is willing to wage war. According to Michael D. Swaine, Senior Associate in the Asia Program at the Carnegie Endowment for International Peace, the PRC's use of the phrase may at times signify "a marker, or a type of warning, regarding the need for the United States and other countries to respect (indeed, accept with little if any negotiation) China's position on certain issues."[2]

The components of China's core interests were defined by Chinese State Councilor Dai Bingguo at the 2009 U.S.-China Strategic and Economic Dialogue. These were: preserving China's state system and national security, national sovereignty and territorial integrity, and continued stable development of China's economy and society.[3] The elements were reiterated in a 2011 white paper called "China's Peaceful Development."[4] Although sovereignty and China's territorial integrity are the most frequently invoked of these elements, Chinese officials have made reference to core interests to signal displeasure in a variety of contexts. As noted before, PRC officials have made reference to core interests to defend Chinese claims to Taiwan, Tibet, and Xinjiang, and they have been increasingly assertive in invoking the concept in discussions of international issues, among them U.S. arms sales to Taiwan, foreign meetings with the Tibetan Dalai Lama, and disputed territories in the East and South China Seas. Indeed, the concept seems quite elastic in its usage.

Since the 1970s, the United States has for the large part supported and accommodated China's development. In recent years, U.S. diplomats have shown a marked willingness to accept Chinese assertions of China's core interests rather than court controversy or threaten disruptions in bilateral affairs. This tendency is visible in the U.S. One China Policy, which does not challenge the PRC's claims of sovereignty over Taiwan. Even after the passage of the Taiwan Relations Act (TRA), U.S. policymakers have shown great deference in the execution of the TRA's provisions. For example, President Reagan issued the Third Joint U.S.-PRC Communiqué in 1982, which pledged that the United States would gradually reduce arms sales to Taiwan, following protests from the Chinese government. More recently, in November 2009, the United States and China issued a joint statement during President Obama's visit to China, in which the countries "agreed that respecting each other's core interests is extremely important to ensure steady progress in U.S.-China relations."[5] This was the first time the term *core interests* was used in a high-level joint statement. The inclusion of the phrase alarmed those who felt the White House was going too far in accommodating Chinese demands.

At the insistence of U.S. negotiators, the term was omitted from the joint statement issued during President Hu Jintao's visit to the United States in January 2011. Instead, the document stated simply that "the two sides reaffirmed respect for each other's sovereignty and territorial integrity," a formulation that had been used previously in the joint communiqués.[6] The 2011 statement also proclaimed that the two sides were "committed to work together to build a cooperative partnership based on mutual respect and mutual benefit" to promote their common interests and meet the challenges and opportunities of the new century. In these statements, Chinese commentators saw an upgrading of U.S.-China relations. According to the Xinhua news agency, the term "mutual respect" called for a recognition of each country's "core interests and path of development."[7] In 2012, Chinese Vice President Xi again called on the United States to respect China's core interests in a policy speech delivered during his five-day visit to the United States. U.S. officials have hesitated to endorse or parrot the terminology.

Chinese President Xi Jinping and other PRC officials have also urged the adoption of a "new type of great power relations" as a model for interactions with the United States. President Xi has highlighted the phrase frequently during high-level meetings with U.S. officials. Xi emphasized the concept at the U.S.-China Strategic and Economic Dialogue in July 2014 and the Sunnylands summit with President Obama in November that year. During the Sunnylands summit, Xi explained that the concept comprised three elements: the avoidance of conflict or confrontation through dialogue and objective recognition of strategic interests; mutual respect of core interests and major concerns; and mutually beneficial cooperation. Many Western commentators have observed that Chinese leaders hope to persuade the United States to adopt the concept as a model for the development of bilateral relations in order to neutralize U.S. incentives to disrupt China's continuing development and regional influence.

U.S. officials have so far declined to endorse the new great power model. Adopting the concept would include accepting implicitly the assertion of China's core interests, which would not sit well with many U.S. allies in Asia, such as Japan, Korea, the Philippines, and Taiwan. Furthermore, the language employed by Chinese leaders implies an equal status between the two countries. Gaining this recognition would buoy PRC leaders seeking to legitimize themselves to domestic audiences. But for the United States and other countries, elevating China to the level of a new great power would favor the PRC's designs as regional hegemon and signal a weakening of U.S. influence in the region in contradiction to the Obama administration's push for a strategic rebalancing toward the Asia Pacific region. While the United States has shown considerable accommodation, it is unlikely that U.S. policymakers will grant Chinese leaders this affirmation in the near future.

II. U.S.-China Economic Rivalry

China's economy has experienced tremendous growth since the country's opening up in the 1970s, and continued economic growth is central to the Chinese Communist Party's long-term viability. China's economic success can be attributed to a number of factors, which include strong state-driven investments in key industries, investment in education, the rapid growth of the country's private sector and middle class, and the continuity of Beijing's economic planning over several decades. Millions of people have been lifted out of poverty, while increased trade and investment have benefited countries throughout Asia. Access to technology and modern infrastructure has improved the quality of life for countless people and will continue to do so for the foreseeable future.

A. CHINA'S ECONOMIC EXPANSION

With the advent of a global knowledge economy, human beings—along with their knowledge, skills, talents, and abilities—have become critical to a country's ability to compete economically. In this regard, China's 1.34 billion people are a magnificent asset. Education, more than any other component, is the key to developing this human capital. China's educational system has undergone significant changes since the middle of the twentieth century. In the 1970s, Deng Xiaoping advocated for raising the education level of China's population and developing the country's intellectual resources, especially in the areas of science and technology. China's nine-year compulsory education system, which was established in 1986, has helped to raise the country's literacy rate from 77 percent in 1990 to 94 percent in 2015. Under the PRC's Medium- and Long-term Plan for Education Reform and Development, government spending on education increased to roughly 3.7 percent of total gross domestic product (GDP) in 2010, compared with less than 3 percent in the mid-1980s. As a result, millions of young people have been prepared for the workforce and are helping to develop the country's economy in new and unexpected ways while competing effectively against their peers globally. Significant emphasis has been placed on training China's leadership within both the Community Party and the military. China sends more students to the United States for higher education than any other nation, with more than 157,000 Chinese students studying in American universities during the 2010–11 academic year. In comparison, the United States sent about 14,000 students to China during the same period.

The relationship between the world's two largest economic powers is a symbiotic one. Economically, the United States and China have become deeply intertwined. Modest trade and investment links begun in the 1970s grew steadily over the 1980s and 1990s and then exploded in the new millennium following China's accession to the World Trade Organization. The growth of the bilateral U.S.-China economic relationship has had a significant impact on the global economy. China is the second largest U.S. trading partner, with trade between the two countries totaling an estimated USD 590.7 billion in 2014. China sends by far the most imports to the United States. Chinese exports to the United States totaled roughly USD 466.7 billion in 2014 (Canada and Mexico totaled USD 346.1 billion and USD 294.2 billion, respectively). China is also the United States' largest agricultural export market. By 2010 U.S. firms had invested a cumulative USD 60.5 billion in the Chinese market, an increase of more than 21 percent from 2009 and more than double the cumulative total of U.S. foreign direct investment in China in 2007. Meanwhile, cumulative Chinese investment in the United States totaled just USD 3.2 billion in 2010, a threefold increase over the year before. China is now one of the largest holders of U.S. Treasuries, giving the PRC some leverage over economic policy in the United States. In August 2015, the Chinese government began selling a significant share of its U.S. Treasury holdings to fund its efforts to stabilize the value of the yuan. Some observers warned that the United States was vulnerable to China's efforts to manipulate the value of its currency relative to the U.S. dollar. Others countered that China depends too heavily on continued U.S. investment and trade to risk triggering an economic slowdown in the United States.

Intense focus on science and technology has made China into the second largest spender on research and development, accounting for 14.2 percent of total global spending. By contrast, the United States accounted for more than 30 percent of global spending in 2012. According to *R&D Magazine*, China's annual output of scientific papers has grown to more than 120,000 annually, second only to the United States.[8] However, Chinese enterprises have also been accused of expropriating technology from competitors in order to gain an advantage in the market. In his book, *The Hundred-Year Marathon*, defense expert Michael Pillsbury notes that Chinese corporations, aided by government-funded spies and hackers, routinely steal technology and intellectual property from Western targets. Meanwhile, foreign firms are pressured to transfer technology to Chinese partners in exchange for the right to do business in the country. Expropriation is one of the main drivers of China's economic growth, according to Pillsbury and other scholars.

China's leaders have acted with increased confidence since the global financial crisis of 2008. The PRC managed to navigate the perils of both the 1998 Asian financial crisis and the 2008 crisis, maintaining strong growth while others stagnated. China's prosperity was on full display during the 2008 Olympic Games in Beijing and the 2010 Shanghai Expo. While the Chinese economy appeared to slow over the course of 2014 and 2015, it continues to expand at a faster rate than that of the United States. In 2011, the International Monetary Fund (IMF) predicted that the Chinese economy would surpass that of the United States by 2016, as measured by GDP-purchasing power parity. This milestone was reached two years earlier than expected, when the Chinese economy edged ahead of the United States in the IMF's October 2014 figures. Other predictions hold that China will surpass the United States in most other measures of economic performance within the next decade.

The country's dramatic economic growth over the past three decades has given birth to an ever-changing and modernizing urban landscape. The movement of millions of people into cities has undermined rural communities and led to unprecedented social and environmental problems throughout the country. Forced evictions are common, and local officials have often been accused of conspiring with property developers to seize land and dwellings with little or no compensation for displaced residents. Migrant workers living in cities are marginalized by the *hukou* system that denies education and other social services to individuals who are not registered as local citizens. China's infamous "one-child policy" (now a two-child policy) has led to severe demographic imbalances, while its workforce is aging faster than other similarly developed countries. By 2040, an estimated 28 percent of China's population will be aged sixty or older, compared to 25 percent for the United States. The trend is likely to strain pensions, healthcare, and other social programs. China has benefited so far from a huge labor force made up of working-age people. But the demographic window that has enabled this growth may be closing.

B. EXPANDING REGIONAL INFLUENCE

China's rapid growth has increased the country's dependence on foreign resources such as oil and natural gas, construction materials, capital, and technology. China became a net oil importer by 1993. Chinese state-owned enterprises, with support from the central government, have sought to secure exploration and supply agreements with energy-rich nations in Africa, Central Asia, and Latin America. China has also looked increasingly to Russia as an important source of natural resources, particularly hydrocarbons. The Chinese government woos supplier states by providing developmental aid and other forms of assistance such as loans and resource extraction partnerships. China is now a major donor and investor in Africa and is increasingly a major force in Latin America.

Many critics have accused the Chinese government of adopting exploitative financial arrangements and seeking unfair advantages for Chinese companies. Its practices have raised particular concern in countries such as Angola where corruption and mismanagement threaten the well-being of the Angolan people. Moreover, China's investment activities do not appear to be bounded by concerns for the protection of social, cultural, economic, or political rights by its partner regimes. China's actions in the developing world sometimes frustrate Western efforts to promote democracy in countries such as Myanmar, Cambodia, Sudan, and elsewhere. Moreover, China's growing economic presence in Africa has been a mixed blessing for the continent's local economies and China's image abroad. The caricature of the "ugly Chinese" draws on the perception of China as a resource-hungry nation that cozies up to corrupt officials with little concern for local populations. Chinese companies have been accused of causing environmental damage, importing cheap workers, and abusing local labor and engaging in unfair practices. In December 2014, workers at a Chinese-owned sugar mill in Madagascar rioted, demanding better pay and treatment of workers. The company evacuated all of its Chinese nationals after the factory was looted and burned. In June 2013, police in Ghana arrested more than 160 Chinese who were accused of illegal mining. Earlier in the year, locals in Tanzania protested the construction of a 530-kilometer gas pipeline undertaken by the China National Petroleum Corporation at a cost of USD 1.2 billion. More than a dozen people were killed during demonstrations. Similar events took place in Sudan and Zambia in 2010 and 2012. In January 2012, armed rebels abducted twenty-nine workers from a Chinese Sinohydro site to use as leverage in negotiations and to draw attention to the plight of refugees in the region.

Chinese business activities have also at times challenged U.S. security objectives. The U.S. Treasury Department imposed economic sanctions against Xinjiang-based Bank of Kunlun, an affiliate of the China National Petroleum Corporation, for providing financial services to Iranian banks in contravention of international sanctions. China has become one of Iran's largest trading partners, with bilateral trade projected to increase to USD 100 billion by 2016. China has provided Iran with technological support in the energy sector and infrastructure development and has helped build infrastructure projects in Iran.

China's regional development efforts have also encompassed bilateral accords with Russia. The number of agreements has grown since the onset of the crisis in Ukraine in 2014. In May 2014, China and Russia announced a thirty-year, USD 400 billion gas pipeline and supply deal, which the partners called The Power of Siberia. In January 2015, China announced that it would build a 4,350-mile high-speed rail link from Beijing to Moscow at a cost of about USD 242 billion. The project is expected to cut the duration of a trip between the two cities from five days to about thirty hours. Other deals included a USD 25 billion lending arrangement, a USD 2 billion agricultural investment fund, and a USD 5.4 billion investment in a high-speed rail line between Moscow and Kazan, Russia, which will be completed by 2020. Commenting on the China-Russia relationship in 2015, Chinese Foreign Minister Wang Yi called the bilateral relationship "mature and stable."[9]

In 1996, China established the Shanghai Cooperation Organization (SCO) (originally called the Shanghai Five) as a forum for coordinating national security initiatives in Central Asia among China, Russia, Kazakhstan, Kyrgyzstan, and Tajikistan. Uzbekistan was admitted as a member in 2001. In 2015, the SCO approved membership applications for India and Pakistan, which are expected to join the organization in 2016. All told, the SCO's current and future members account for roughly half of the world's population. China's involvement in SCO gives it added leverage with geostrategically important nations in Central Asia. Some military analysts have described SCO as a potential challenger to NATO in the West.

The PRC government has been vigorous in developing its regional economic influence. Chinese leaders have sought closer ties with Association of Southeast Asian Nations (ASEAN) members—Indonesia, Malaysia, the Philippines, Singapore, Thailand, Brunei, Myanmar, Cambodia, Laos, and Vietnam. A free trade agreement between China and the ASEAN member states went into effect in January 2010. The China-ASEAN free trade zone is the largest in the world in terms of population and third in terms of trade volumes behind the European Economic Area and the North American Free Trade Area. China has overtaken the United States as ASEAN's third largest trading partner, behind the European Union and Japan.

Under President Xi, China has undertaken the New Silk Road Economic Belt and Maritime Silk Road initiative (also called the One Belt, One Road initiative). The initiative, which was first detailed in 2015, will bring large-scale development of railroads, highways, ports, and other infrastructure in areas commonly associated with the historical Silk Road that carried Chinese goods to the West for centuries. The Chinese government intends to fund billions of dollars in projects connecting cities in Central and Western China, Kazakhstan, Russia, and Europe. Maritime infrastructure will be built from Shanghai, through the South China Sea and Indian Ocean, through the Suez Canal, the Mediterranean Sea, and the Adriatic Sea. New shipping facilities will enhance connections from Indonesia, India, North Africa, the Middle East, and Europe. Some commentators have compared the initiative to the U.S.-led Marshall Plan in the years following World War II. The Chinese government has announced a USD 40 billion New Silk Road development fund to support the projects.

The New Silk Road initiative coincides with the establishment of the China-led Asian Infrastructure and Investment Bank (AIIB) announced in October 2014. More than fifty nations including the United Kingdom and several European countries have pledged to join the AIIB despite U.S. concerns over the quality of governance of the proposed Bank. Taiwan submitted an application to join the AIIB, but was rejected. A Chinese government spokesperson said that Taiwan could resubmit its application in the future under an "acceptable" name. In March 2015, the United States announced it would cooperate with the AIIB via institutions including the Asia Development Bank and the World Bank.

China has also spearheaded the creation of a development bank to support the BRICS countries of Brazil, Russia, India, China, and South Africa. The idea, which was first proposed by India in 2012, led to the opening of the BRICS Bank headquarters in Shanghai in 2014. The bank's assets include a USD 100 billion Contingent Reserve Arrangement (CRA) to act as a source of emergency financial assistance, as well as a USD 50 billion fund known as the New Development Bank. Membership in the BRICS Bank is open to all UN members, although the combined ownership of the BRICS countries cannot fall below 55 percent, while non-BRICS countries are prohibited from owning more than 7 percent of the Bank.

China's efforts to develop its economic leadership appear to be gaining traction. In March 2015, the International Monetary Fund (IMF) declared that the Chinese yuan was no longer considered undervalued—a position that broke with the U.S. Treasury Department's long-standing assessment. In December 2015, the IMF voted in favor of the yuan's inclusion in the IMF's currency basket. In recent years China has established yuan clearing arrangements with about a dozen countries and currency swap arrangements with nearly thirty foreign central banks. The yuan's inclusion in the IMF currency basket will greatly expand China's influence in the global economy. The world's confidence in the PRC's ability to competently manage its economy was shaken in the summer of 2015 when signs of an economic slowdown triggered a sharp decline in the value of the Chinese stock market. The central government took extraordinary steps to stabilize markets and the Chinese currency, reportedly liquidating in excess of USD 100 billion in U.S. Treasuries to fund its efforts. Rather than address the underlying weakness in the country's economic structure, Chinese officials ordered the country's large investors to commit funds to prop up the value of stocks, while punishing financial professionals and journalists for "destabilizing" markets and "rumormongering." Around the same time a massive industrial explosion in the port city of Tianjin killed scores and spewed pollution into the surrounding areas, bringing new focus to the country's corrupt and ineffective regulatory system.

C. THE BEIJING CONSENSUS

The Washington Consensus is a term often used to describe the global free-market agenda promoted by the United States and other Western nations after the Cold War. Its proponents encourage the adoption of liberal policies aimed at the development of national economies and globalized free trade. To the contrary, the Beijing Consensus (or China Economic Model) embraces authoritarian-style economic policies characterized by state intervention and the suppression of individual rights. In China, government authorities wield immense power over state-run corporations and deploy national resources to shape the economy in accordance with long-term economic planning.

While many of China's people are enjoying the benefits of modern life, the country's rapid growth has had a massive impact on society, driving millions of people from rural areas into crowded urban centers plagued with air and water pollution. Development has not been accompanied by an increase in political rights.

The Chinese government has adopted a raft of security laws aimed at suppressing political opposition and negative media that could challenge the Communist Party's rule. Unlawful detention, excessive violence, torture, and harassment are common. Estimates of the number of political prisoners range as high as thirty thousand. In 2013, numerous reform activists were detained for their association with the New Citizens' Movement (NCM), which promotes the rule of law, transparency, and human rights in China. Xu Zhiyong, a Beijing lawyer and the movement's primary leader, was detained for "gathering a crowd to disturb public order," a charge that carries a prison term of up to five years. The Chinese government tightly regulates public discussion, speech, or reporting of sensitive or controversial political matters, which includes the Tiananmen Square incident of 1989, Taiwan, Tibet, Falun Gong, and criticism of CCP leadership. Meanwhile, corruption among government officials is endemic. President Xi's efforts to root out corruption in the CCP ranks has been a topic of constant focus in the Western press, with some commentators noting that the anticorruption campaign has provided Xi with an opportunity to liquidate political opponents at the same time.

As China's influence grows, it may seek to promote the PRC's values as an alternative to Western liberalism. Stefan Halper, author of *The Beijing Consensus: How China's Authoritarian Model Will Dominate the Twenty-First Century*, argues that the apparent success of the Chinese model is leading other developing countries to emulate it.[10] China encourages this trend through direct financial aid and investment to governments in Central and Latin America, Africa, and elsewhere. It asks for little in the way of reforms. In the West, economic development was widely viewed as a driver for the growth of free markets and human rights after the fall of the Soviet Union. China's growing presence in the developing world may very well have the opposite effect and may even reinforce the power of some despotic regimes.

While many of the world's people are realizing the transformative force of information technology, China's citizens are still subject to extreme censorship on the Internet and on their personal communication devices. By the end of 2010, the total number of Internet users in China had grown to approximately 457 million—about 23 percent of the world's total online population. Electronic forums for the discussion of politics and current events have proliferated. The advent of mobile communication technology has made it more difficult for officials to regulate the flow of information. Yet, as visitors to China quickly discover, many websites and services that are popular outside of China are virtually unavailable through local Internet service providers thanks to the "Great Firewall." Additionally, the government employs an unknown number of media censors as well as paid commentators who post pro-government commentary on popular websites in order to help shape public opinion. In February 2011, overseas activists called on the Chinese people to take part in a Jasmine Revolution inspired by the Arab Spring taking place in the Middle East and North Africa. The Chinese government blocked the Chinese characters for the word *jasmine* in text messages and online posts. Censors reportedly also blocked videos of President Hu Jintao singing "Mo Li Hua," a Qing-era song dedicated to the flower.

III. U.S.-China Strategic Rivalry

A. CHINA'S MILITARY MODERNIZATION

For the past two decades, China's military has rapidly modernized and expanded its capabilities. China has focused on strengthening its overall military capabilities in the air, on the sea, in space, and even in cyberspace. Despite a reduction in cross-strait tensions since 2008, the PRC is estimated to maintain more than sixteen hundred ballistic missiles aimed at Taiwan. Moreover, defense experts believe that much of China's military modernization and training is aimed at deterring or denying any attempt by the U.S. military to come to Taiwan's defense. In March 2012, the Chinese government announced a double-digit increase in its national military expenditures. The country's military budget for 2012 represented an 11.2 percent increase from USD 95.6 billion to USD 106.4 billion.

The United States still dwarfs China in terms of conventional military strength. U.S. military spending accounts for nearly 40 percent of the combined global total for all countries. The United States has troops stationed in approximately one hundred fifty countries, with military bases in more than seventy countries and dozens of military alliances. The U.S. Navy boasts eleven aircraft carrier groups. China is just developing its first. As part of the recently announced policy of rebalancing toward the Asia Pacific, the United States has begun rotating its military presence through different locations in Asia. President Obama, speaking to the Australian Parliament in 2011, said the United States is determined to maintain and strengthen its military presence in Asia.[11] In September 2015, the PRC staged an enormous military parade in Beijing to commemorate the country's victory over the Japanese in World War II. Soldiers commanding tanks and missile batteries marched through Tiananmen Square while helicopters and fighter jets soared overhead. The highly televised event gave Chinese officials an opportunity to boast about their country's growing military strength—interviewees repeatedly stressed that China's focus was on defense only—while sending a clear message to the United States and other powers about China's readiness to use force to protect its "core interests."

According to a 2011 Pentagon report, Chinese military planners are aiming to develop a "Blue Water Navy" complete with nuclear-powered ballistic missile submarines and sophisticated radar systems for targeting enemy assets. Rear Admiral

Zhang Huachen, deputy commander of the East Sea fleet, said in an interview with Xinhua news agency that part of China's new naval strategy is to transition from defending the coast to projecting force across the sea. He clarified that "the navy wants to better protect the country's transportation routes and the safety of our major sea lanes" to protect the country's growing economic resources.[12] PRC leaders insist that the country's navy will be defensive in nature; however, the nature of self-defense may be broadly interpreted. In 2011, China launched its first sea trial of an aircraft carrier, a refurbished Soviet-era carrier purchased from Ukraine in 1998.

Conventional military strength is only part of the picture. The Chinese military has concentrated on developing its arsenal of unconventional weaponry, ranging from antisatellite missiles to computer hacking that can be deployed asymmetrically against a more powerful opponent. Michael Pillsbury observes in his book *The Hundred-Year Marathon* that China is perfecting unconventional strategies inspired by military conquests from China's Warring States Period.[13] Chinese computer hackers are reportedly well-versed in penetrating U.S. servers, including those belonging to corporations and the military. The PRC is believed to cultivate numerous professional hacking groups which engage in cyber-espionage against U.S. targets. These groups have been linked to hundreds of intrusions since the early 2000s. In 2006, Chinese hackers are said to have downloaded up to 20 terabytes of data from a Pentagon computer network. In 2013, a classified study revealed that cyber intruders had accessed designs for two dozen weapons systems. In 2015, hackers reportedly associated with the Chinese government, gained access to millions of records of individuals who had applied for U.S. security clearances. Experts warned that the information could be used in recruiting spies or committing blackmail against individuals with inside knowledge of the U.S. government.

The United States' ability to project power globally is heavily dependent on satellite-based communications. In 2007, the Chinese military destroyed one of its own satellites in orbit using ground-based missiles. The demonstration alarmed military observers who believed the technology could be used to target U.S. satellite networks during a conflict. According to Pillsbury, the Chinese military has continued to develop such technology and is eying a number of methods for striking U.S. communications capabilities. Other exotic weapons under developing include weapons based on electromagnetic and microwave energy and lasers. These weapons could be used to destroy or disable electronic devices and high-tech systems with devastating effectiveness. Next-generation weapons in China's arsenal include highly accurate ballistic missiles, rocket-propelled sea mines, and drones that are designed to evade U.S. defenses. Military experts do not believe that China will have the ability to defeat the U.S. military in a head-to-head military context in the near future. However, it is developing the tools to prevent the United States from deploying forces in the Asia Pacific region. This would have serious consequences for U.S. allies, especially Taiwan, which relies on the likelihood of U.S. military support to ensure its security.

B. REGIONAL SECURITY ISSUES

China is the fourth largest country in the world in terms of geography, encompassing an area of about 9.6 million kilometers. It shares land borders with fourteen states: Vietnam, Laos, Myanmar (Burma), India, Bhutan, Nepal, Pakistan, Afghanistan, Kazakhstan, Kyrgyzstan, Tajikistan, Russia, Mongolia, and North Korea. China has close maritime proximity with South Korea, Japan, Taiwan, and the Philippines. Since 1949, China has fought armed conflicts with four neighboring states: India, the Soviet Union, Vietnam, and South Korea. Among China's fourteen contiguous land neighbors, four have nuclear weapons: Russia, India, Pakistan, and North Korea.

Given China's size and the rapidity of its military development, smaller countries welcome the United States' presence in the region as a means of countering the threat posed by their larger neighbor. Allies such as Japan, South Korea, Vietnam, and the Philippines are greatly concerned about China's growing military capabilities and its ability to project force in the region, which may be used to challenge their claims to territory and resources. This is especially so in the East and South China Seas, where China has aggressively pursued claims over territory by reclaiming land and designating an Air Defense Identification Zone (ADIZ). Heightened tensions have compelled many governments in the region to seek closer ties with the United States.

There are many shared interests among Asia Pacific countries, but territorial disputes, several of which have been unresolved since the end of World War II, have led to frequent tensions. China and five other nations—Taiwan, Vietnam, Malaysia, the Philippines, and Brunei—claim parts of the South China Sea. The islands of the South China Sea hold great significance, as the region is rich in natural resources, and the waterways are critical to international shipping. This is especially the case with oil, liquefied natural gas, and other fossil fuels, with some 80 percent of China's energy imports traveling through the South China Sea via the Strait of Malacca—in 2003, Chinese President Hu Jintao coined the phrase "the Malacca Dilemma" to describe this aspect of China's strategic vulnerability.

China claims about 90 percent of the South China Sea, marking the claim on maps with a U-shaped, "nine-dashed line," which outlines virtually the entire sea extending almost to Indonesia. PRC leaders base their claim on perceived historical precedents. However, the claims represented by the nine-dashed line almost certainly violate the UN Convention on the Law of the Sea (LOS Convention), which the PRC ratified in 1996. The LOS Convention recognizes claims to territorial waters and exclusive economic zones that are described by a country's coastlines and the islands over which it definitively exercises control. Rather than appeal to dispute resolution mechanisms prescribed in the LOS Convention, China insists on resolving the claims on a bilateral basis. In 2002, China concluded an agreement with the ASEAN member nations aimed at avoiding conflicts in the South China Sea. Under the agreement, the countries agreed to "resolve their territorial and jurisdictional disputes by peaceful means, without resorting to the threat or use of force, through friendly consultations and negotiations." However, the parties have yet to negotiate a binding code of conduct.

Noting the dangerous situation, Secretary of State Hillary Clinton issued a declaration in July 2010 linking U.S. national interests to the maintenance of freedom of navigation, open access to Asia's maritime commons, and respect for international law in the South China Sea.[14] The Chinese Foreign Minister dismissed Secretary Clinton's statements as "in effect an attack on China," and warned the United States against making the South China Sea "an international issue or multilateral issue."[15] Both sides have backed their stances with action. The United States has continued conducting military and surveillance activities in the South China Sea, while Chinese vessels have continued to harass foreign ships and aircraft. Since 2014, China has also been engaging in aggressive land reclamation projects on shoals throughout the South China Sea. The projects include the construction of aircraft landing ships and other facilities.

China has also asserted disputed claims in the East China Sea, where China's exclusive economic zone overlaps with that of Japan. Within this area lie the contested, but uninhabited Diaoyutai (Senkaku Islands). Taiwan also maintains a residual claim to the islands, as some argue that the islands were included in the terms of the Treaty of Shimonoseki, under which China ceded Taiwan and surrounding isles to Japan in perpetuity in 1895. The situation is further complicated by Japan's mutual defense treaty with the United States. In 2013, China asserted an ADIZ over the East China Sea which covered the disputed areas and parts of Japan's own ADIZ. The United States responded by dispatching B-52 bombers to fly over the zone, which failed to elicit a response from the Chinese military. In September 2015, Japan's parliament adopted legislation that would permit its military to fight overseas in response to attacks on Japan or its allies in cases that severely threaten the country or its people. The law, which was heavily promoted by Prime Minister Shinzo Abe, was the biggest change to the country's pacifist constitution since World War II. Observers in Taiwan and elsewhere noted that the development sent a clear message to China that Japan is increasingly willing to deploy its military to protect its interests if necessary.

C. U.S. "PIVOT" TO THE ASIA PACIFIC

Since World War II, the United States has acted as a superpower in the Asia Pacific, with formal alliances and a significant military presence throughout the region. Beginning in 2009, the Obama administration made efforts to engage more closely with regional multilateral institutions. In 2011, the Obama administration declared that the United States would "pivot" or "rebalance" attention to the region after years of heavy engagement in the Middle East. As America's self-proclaimed first Pacific president, Hawaii-born Barack Obama has vowed that "the United States is a Pacific power, and we are here to stay."[16] In a speech in Honolulu in 2011, Secretary of State Clinton articulated a vision of "America's Pacific Century," proclaiming that "it is becoming increasingly clear that the world's strategic and economic center of gravity will be the Asia Pacific, from the Indian subcontinent to the western shores of the Americas."[17] Concrete steps included strengthening security alliances with Australia, Japan, the Philippines, South Korea, and Thailand; expanding relations with emerging powers such as India, Indonesia, Singapore, and Vietnam; sending new military deployments to Australia and Singapore; joining the East Asia Summit; and redoubling negotiations for the Trans-Pacific Partnership (TPP), a landmark free trade agreement among the United States and eleven Pacific countries, including Australia, Canada, Singapore, Brunei, New Zealand, Chile, Mexico, Japan, Malaysia, Peru, and Vietnam. The prospective TPP member countries are estimated to account for roughly 40 percent of the world's total economic output. The TPP is often compared to the proposed Regional Comprehensive Economic Partnership which, if concluded, would cover the ASEAN countries and Australia, India, Japan, South Korea, New Zealand, and China.

In 2011, the Pentagon announced plans to deploy twenty-five hundred Marines to Darwin, Australia, a decision that incensed Chinese officials. PRC foreign ministry spokesman Liu Weimin commented that "it may not be quite appropriate to intensify and expand military alliances and may not be in the interest of countries within this region."[18] An editorial in the *Global Times*, a government-controlled Chinese newspaper, warned that if "Australia uses its military bases to help the U.S. harm Chinese interests, then Australia itself will be caught in the crossfire."[19] Nevertheless, Australia and China concluded a major free trade agreement in June 2015 after roughly a decade of negotiations. Subsequently, the United States announced broader plans to bolster its permanent military presence in the Asia Pacific. In 2012, Defense Secretary Leon E. Panetta announced that naval forces would be shifted toward the Pacific. The U.S. Navy is divided equally between the Pacific and the Atlantic Oceans. By 2020, roughly 60 percent of U.S. naval forces will be deployed in the Pacific. This would amount to a fleet of about sixty-seven ships. The People's Liberation Army plans to maintain upwards of four hundred ships by 2030.

Secretary of State Clinton, writing in *Foreign Policy* in 2011, declared that the United States seeks to "build a web of partnerships and institutions across the Pacific that is as durable and as consistent with American interests and values as the web we have built across the Atlantic."[20] The adoption of the term *community* emphasized that the Asia Pacific was not solely China's backyard. Rather, the term encompasses the shared interests of many countries in the region. Clinton chastised China for its human rights record, making reference to numerous human rights violations and environmental ills, and stated that U.S. leadership would benefit the Chinese people and encourage a humanitarian focus for regional policies. Among the violations cited by Clinton were reports of lawyers and other political activists who were detained. In those cases, "the United States speaks up both publicly and privately," Clinton wrote.[21] Meanwhile, the TPP would bring together both developed and developing economies into a single trading community, providing "unprecedented opportunities for investment, trade, and access to cutting-edge technology."[22]

Chinese officials have reacted coolly to U.S. plans for greater involvement in the Asia Pacific. In the broader context, the U.S. rebalancing coincides with the advent of numerous disagreements between the two sides. The Obama administration has stepped up rhetoric targeting Chinese favoritism toward Syria and North Korea and the country's record on human rights, currency manipulation, and cyber attacks. During Chinese Vice President Xi Jinping February 2012 visit to the United States, President Obama assailed China's human rights record, saying that the United States has "tried to emphasize that because of China's extraordinary development over the last two decades, that with expanding power and prosperity also comes increased responsibilities."[23] When it comes to the global economy, Obama declared that "we want to work with China to make sure everyone is working by the same rules of the road when it comes to the world economic system."[24] The Obama administration was equally critical of China's position on Syria, stating that the United States "strongly disagreed with China and Russia's veto of a [UN] resolution against the unconscionable violence being perpetrated by" the regime of Syrian President Bashar al-Assad.[25] In March 2012, in a ninety-minute meeting before a nuclear security summit meeting in South Korea, President Obama pressed Chinese leader Hu Jintao to use the country's influence over North Korea to prevent a planned satellite launch. Commentators wrote that the discussion appeared to catch Hu off guard.[26]

The United States and China have also clashed over the conflict in Ukraine. U.S. officials have blamed Russia for enabling separatists in Eastern Ukraine to carry on a sustained civil war. Western powers including the United States and the European Union have imposed economic sanctions against entities in Russia's financial, energy, and defense sectors for their role in the turmoil. Meanwhile, China has expanded its diplomatic cooperation with Russia and has forged ahead with long-term investments in Russian energy resources and infrastructure. China also abstained from a UN Security Council resolution condemning a referendum undertaken in Crimea in March 2014 in support of joining the Russian Federation. As described in Chapter 12, the Crimean referendum suffered from serious procedural flaws, including that Russian troops were present on the peninsula during the vote. The resolution received overwhelming support from the other Security Council members, despite being vetoed by Russia itself. In early September 2015, U.S. media reported that the U.S. Treasury Department was seeking to introduce economic sanctions against Chinese firms suspected of profiting from U.S. intellectual property stolen through cyber hacking. The reports coincided with President Xi Jinping's planned state visit to Washington, D.C., in late September. Xi took the opportunity to stop in Seattle, Washington, to attend a technology summit hosted by Microsoft, signaling China's influence over the U.S. technology sector. The events highlighted the growing importance of the economic instrument as a tool of foreign policy.

IV. The Future of U.S.-China Relations

Like all authoritarian regimes, the Chinese Communist Party (CCP) is secretive about its internal deliberations. While dissension certainly exists within the CCP, its leaders are careful to project an image of consensus. Debates over policy, when they occur, are tightly regulated and scripted by state-controlled media. Discourse from outside the party is simply forbidden. For these reasons, it is difficult to discern the long-term intentions of China's political elites. Experts outside the country are increasingly divided on this subject. Some view China as a promising, but imperfect, developing nation that will, like most affluent societies, undertake liberalizing reforms eventually, albeit cautiously. In the opposite camp are those who see China as primarily self-interested, even deceitful, and a danger to the prevailing world order led by the United States and Europe. Commentators of all stripes look for signs of China's intentions in every official pronouncement or action while promoting strategies that range from peaceful cooperation to preemptive containment. The following sections consider some of the key themes and concepts in popular theories about China's rise and future as a global power.

A. INTERNATIONAL COOPERATION

Participating in multilateral institutions is thought to encourage countries to adhere to international norms. Experts such as Daniel W. Drezner have warned that unless rising powers such as China and India are incorporated into the prevailing international institutional frameworks, the future of these international regimes will be threatened. Some experts have postulated that rising powers will not seek to overturn the existing system's current rules and norms, but rather seek to gain more authority within the existing order. To this point, John G. Ikenberry has described today's international institutions as "easy to join, hard to overturn."

China has become increasingly active in international and multilateral institutions since joining the United Nations in 1971. Between 1984 and 1996, China's membership in international organizations almost doubled from 29 to more than 50, and its membership in international nongovernmental organizations tripled from 355 to 1,079. China's involvement with international economic institutions provides access to resources and strategies to support the country's rise, and its participation ensures that it will have a say in decisions affecting global norms. Whereas the PRC previously avoided or participated only passively in multilateral organizations, the country is increasingly taking a more prominent role in them.

China has successfully sought entry into existing regional groups such as the Asia-Pacific Economic Cooperation (APEC), ASEAN Regional Forum, the Forum for East Asia and Latin America Cooperation, the Inter-American Development Bank, and the Organization of American States. China has also created several multilateral institutions in which the United States is not a member, including the East Asia Summit, the Shanghai Cooperation Organization in Central Asia, the China-Arab Cooperation Forum, and the Forum on China-Africa Cooperation. China has spearheaded the creation of a number of parallel international economic institutions such as the BRICS Bank and the Asian Infrastructure Investment Bank (AIIB). China has sought to strengthen bilateral relations through high-level visits and multilateral engagement. In 2002, the PRC signed the Declaration on the Conduct of Parties in the South China Sea with the ASEAN member states; however, as noted above, a binding code of conduct has yet to be adopted.

Since establishing formal diplomatic ties in 1972, the United States and China have engaged in frequent high-level visits and dialogues on a broad and expanding range of issues. In the post–Cold War world order, a dual pattern has emerged characterized by constructive engagement on the one hand and suspicion and hedging on the other. Professor Thomas J. Christensen has said that the central theme of U.S. policy toward China is one that "combines active engagement to maximize areas of common interest and cooperation, along with a recognition that we need to maintain strong U.S. regional capabilities in case China does not eventually move down a path consistent with our interests."[27] To that end, the bilateral relationship now includes almost one hundred dialogue mechanisms to discuss issues related to the global economy, trade, nuclear nonproliferation, climate change, human rights, and others. These mechanisms include the highest-level dialogue, the Strategic and Economic Dialogue (S&ED), the Joint Commission on Commerce and Trade, and military forums such as the Defense Consultative Talks, the Defense Policy Coordination Talks, and the Military Maritime Consultative Agreement. Meetings between the U.S. Secretary of State and China's state councilor in charge of foreign affairs are seen by both governments as useful to achieve better understanding of each other's policies and to identify common interests over which to take joint action. A 1999 study by the Center for Naval Analyses noted that the United States and China took diametrically opposed approaches to developing their bilateral military relations. The United States has pursued a strategy of developing lower-level contacts between the two sides to work toward mutual understanding and strategic agreements. The PRC seeks a top-down relationship where broad agreements on strategic principles can be developed in specificity over time.

The United States has encouraged China's involvement in organizations such as the G20 and the WTO, which offers rules-based mechanisms for resolving trade disputes. The United States has engaged with China on global problems, including climate change through meetings under the UN Framework Convention on Climate Change. The United States has also urged China to follow norms on foreign aid, export credit finance, and overseas investment established by the Paris-based Organisation for Economic Co-operation and Development(OECD), and to accept principles related to freedom of navigation contained in the LOS Convention.[28] The United States and China are both permanent members of the UN Security Council. Working together, the two countries have cooperated on passing sanctions targeting North Korea's nuclear programs. However, China has also used its veto in the Security Council to block several U.S.-supported resolutions.

Showcasing the fruits of the bilateral relationship, the two countries reached a bilateral climate accord in November 2014. The deal came a half decade after the failed attempt to reach a multilateral accord at the 2009 Copenhagen Climate Change summit. Under the deal, the United States plans to reduce its carbon emissions by up to 28 percent below their 2005 level by 2025. China promised to reach a peak in emissions by 2030. The bilateral deal could have a major impact on combating climate change, as the United States and China are the largest producers of man-made greenhouse gases. Their joint effort contributed to the successful adoption of a multilateral climate accord in Paris in December 2015.

B. SOFT AND SMART POWER

In the 1990s, political scientist Joseph Nye, Jr. popularized the concept of soft power to describe "the ability to get what you want through attraction rather than through coercion."[29] The currency of soft power includes a state's values, culture, policies, and institutions. According to Nye, a country's military resources and economic strength can be sources of appeal and attraction to other countries, thereby increasing a country's influence in the world. The term *smart power* is complementary and refers to the combination of hard power and soft power strategies. According to Nye's framework, the most effective strategies in foreign policy require a combination of hard and soft power resources. This kind of power can be cultivated through economic assistance and cultural exchanges aimed at influencing public opinion and perceptions of credibility. The Center for Strategic and International Studies (CSIS) has defined smart power as "neither hard nor soft—it is the skillful combination of both … It is an approach that underscores the necessity of a strong military, but also invests heavily in alliances, partnerships, and institutions at all levels."[30] In 2009, the CSIS offered several policy recommendations for developing the U.S.-China relationship based on the strategy of smart power with a focus on three objectives: implementing a policy of engagement, taking action on energy and climate issues, and increasing dialogue on financial and economic matters. A 2008 survey by the Chicago Council attempted to measure these dimensions of soft power in a questionnaire posed to respondents in China, Japan, South Korea, Vietnam, Indonesia, and the United States. The survey found that the United States ranked highest in measurements of soft power in Asia, while China trailed behind. Factors included low ratings of China's human rights record and weak rule of law.[31]

China, too, is evolving to make use of its smart power potential. According to a Chinese academic quoted by Professor David Lampton, this evolving process of Chinese power can be viewed in the following terms: "[T]he first generation [Mao Zedong] paid more attention to military power; the second generation [Deng Xiaoping] placed more emphasis on comprehensive national strength. The third generation [Jiang Zemin], in the late 1990s, began to pay more attention to soft power."[32] In the 1990s, China expanded its diplomacy beyond executive branches to include ideological and economic appeals to whole governments and even whole societies. This strategy was undertaken in part to influence national debates over China's most favored nation status and to smooth the way for its entry into the WTO. Since being endorsed by President Hu Jintao in 2007, soft power has been widely embraced by China's leadership. Clearly aware of the benefits in wielding soft power, China has sought to utilize a variety of tools to increase its influence in the developing world to achieve its desired outcomes. Beijing's triumph in being named the host city for both the 2008 Summer Olympic Games and 2022 Winter Olympic Games is indicative of its success in this area.

China's tools of soft power encompass foreign investment, humanitarian aid, exchange programs, diplomacy, and participation in multilateral institutions. Between 2004 and 2013 China funded the opening of more than three hundred Confucius Institutes in more than ninety countries to educate visitors about Chinese history and culture. However, some critics have accused the Institutes of promoting a flawed view of history which glosses over events such as the Tiananmen Square massacre of 1989 and presents a skewed perspective on Taiwan and other political matters. According to Nye and other commentators, the PRC government has a track record of undermining its own soft power by engaging in behavior that damages its reputation, whether through aggression in the South China Sea or oppressing human rights internally. Moreover, China does not have a private sector equivalent to the U.S. entertainment industry or nongovernmental organizations that are free to promote Chinese values around the world. Whereas the U.S. government reaps the benefits of the soft power generated by private citizens, the Chinese government is attempting, and often failing, to centrally manage a positive image.

C. CHINA AS A RESPONSIBLE STAKEHOLDER

In 2005, then Deputy Secretary of State Robert B. Zoellick introduced the phrase "responsible stakeholder" to describe China's possible future role on the global stage. In a highly regarded speech before the National Committee on U.S.-China relations, Zoellick provided a detailed assessment of China's rise and addressed U.S. concerns regarding China's integration into the international economy and global institutions.[33] Zoellick suggested that the United States' response to Zheng Bijian's policy of a "peaceful rise" should be to "foster constructive action by transforming our thirty-year policy of integration." According to Zoellick, "[w]e need to encourage China to become a responsible stakeholder. As a responsible stakeholder, China would be more than just a member—it would work with us to sustain the international system that has enabled its success."[34] The responsible stakeholder concept further entails that "[a]ll nations conduct diplomacy to promote their national interests. Responsible stakeholders go further, they recognize that the international system sustains their peaceful prosperity, so they work to sustain that system."[35] Put another way, the role of a responsible stakeholder is to work to strengthen and nurture the international system, and not simply to reap benefits from it. In his speech, Zoellick suggested a host of changes China could undertake in its domestic and foreign policies—from North Korea to Iran to trade—to enhance its status as a responsible global player. Zoellick addressed the fairness of competition within the Chinese market, piracy, intellectual property, and currency manipulation; in foreign policy, he cautioned against the use of a mercantilist energy strategy, called for participation in halting the proliferation of weapons of mass destruction and fighting terrorism; and criticized China's support for regimes that violated human rights or supported terrorist groups. Zoellick stressed that U.S.-China cooperation would make it easier to handle the wide range of global challenges ahead: terrorism, the proliferation of weapons of mass destruction, poverty, and threats to public health. Cooperation as stakeholders, according to Zoellick, means that the parties recognize "a shared interest in sustaining political, economic, and security systems that provide common benefits."[36]

In contrast, others have criticized China for falling short of the obligations of a responsible stakeholder. Dan Blumenthal, a resident fellow at the American Enterprise Institute, offered this perspective:

[I]t is difficult to count China as a responsible stakeholder. While it has taken low-cost actions to help solve some of the challenges to the system, it has done so, for the most part, to alleviate U.S. pressure. It still refuses, however, to take high-cost or risky actions to sustain the international system. When it comes to tradeoffs between narrow interests such as oil, or thwarting threats to the system, it has chosen the former. Moreover, in some instances, China's approach has taken on the cast of a spoiler, perhaps even a balancer, to America's vision of international order.[37]

D. CHINA'S LONG-TERM INTENTIONS

Western policymakers hoped that China's rise on the global stage would be accompanied by an evolution toward freer markets and democracy. Greater prosperity and internationalization would encourage the Chinese people to adopt new perspectives as members of a global community. Economic advancement would spur demands for wider participation in power processes and an end to corruption and political oppression. By and large, these changes have failed to materialize. As detailed above, China today is characterized by widespread repression under an authoritarian single-party political system. The PRC government suppresses the free flow of ideas and punishes those who dare advocate for human rights. State-owned enterprises dominate the Chinese economy, and central authorities routinely intervene in markets to promote the Communist Party's self-interested policies. Since the events at Tiananmen Square on June 4, 1989, China has moved backward, not forward, in many respects. Nowadays, President Xi often speaks of the glory of the "Chinese Dream," which, unlike the American Dream it mirrors, embraces national revitalization over individual happiness. A growing body of scholarship in the United States and elsewhere is trying to come to grips with this disparity. Professor David

M. Shambaugh writes in his book *China Goes Global: The Partial Power* that China may never surpass the United States in some aspects of economic, military, or ideological power. To Shambaugh, the behavior of the PRC's leaders belies "deep insecurities" and an "obsession with control" that is at odds with the country's image as a stable and rising power. Joseph Nye writes in his book *Is the American Century Over?* that Chinese leaders, whose power hinges on a mix of economic growth and nationalism, will be challenged in the coming decades by economic and demographic trends beyond their control.[38] Meanwhile, the United States continues to occupy a dominant power position owing to its advanced military force and global strategic alliances. Furthermore, the U.S. government benefits from the abundant soft power generated by nongovernmental organizations, the U.S. entertainment industry, and other private actors who expound the virtues of the American system—something the PRC struggles to emulate through propaganda alone. According to Nye, under current conditions, China's ascendency over the United States is anything but certain. Professor Thomas Christensen argues in *The China Challenge* that the PRC is insecure and that Western leaders must find ways to integrate China into the international system without threatening the Communist Party's authority. In this sense, China is not thought of as a growing menace, but rather as a typical—albeit large— developing nation with many of the same challenges of smaller, less affluent countries. Other scholars such as Michael Pillsbury take a more pessimistic view. While agreeing that China is not nearly as powerful as often perceived, Pillsbury holds that Chinese leaders are actively misleading the international public about their long-term designs. Using himself as an example, he writes that many China experts in the West have been slow to question the veracity of Chinese leaders' promises of a peaceful rise. According to Pillsbury, the CCP has no intention of constraining itself in the long term or being weighed down by the existing international system, which it perceives as a foreign construct.

President Xi and other Chinese leaders insist that China does not seek hegemony or military conquest, and Chinese leaders often proclaim that the PRC is committed to maintaining peace and stability in the Asia Pacific, including in the South China Sea. They contend that the country's security policies are purely defensive in nature. Foreign Minister Li Zhaoxing, spokesman for the Fifth Session of the Eleventh National People's Congress, in announcing China's 2012 military budget, sought to assuage concerns over the new spending program by saying that "China is committed to the path of peaceful development and follows a national defense policy that is defensive in nature."[39] Yet according to some military observers, China's increasingly assertive policies can only threaten regional stability. University of Chicago Professor John Mearsheimer has argued that China is pursuing "its own Monroe Doctrine for Asia's seas." Mearsheimer warns that China is "likely to try to push the United States out of Asia, much the way the United States pushed the European great powers out of the Western Hemisphere."[40]

Combining observations of China's diplomatic behavior with readings of Chinese-language military and political tracts, Pillsbury concludes that China's foreign policy hawks (*ying pai*) are now in control of the country's strategic development.[41] Top Chinese officials are characterized by their overriding adversarial perspective. They perceive the United States as a hegemon and a major rival. They call for the use of the military instrument to counteract U.S. influence in the region. Pillsbury supports his thesis by pointing to Chinese military leaders' continuous invocation of stratagems from the country's Warring States period. The viewpoint is characterized by the continuous pursuit of rivalry, emphasizing nonmilitary tactics implemented in times of peace; the championing of deception as a legitimate mode of state behavior, including diplomatically; and the belief that adversaries have adopted a similar perspective and tactics. Over time, leaders hope to accumulate advantages that, when taken in the aggregate, will secure China's supremacy over its adversaries. The approach favors the adoption of asymmetric warfare. Pillsbury argues that framing the thinking of Chinese leaders in this manner helps to explain the country's behavior over the past several decades, including its reinvigorated authoritarianism; retention of state control over corporations; increased aggression in the South China Sea; continued threat of military force against Taiwan; efforts to create economic dependencies in Africa, Latin America, Russia, and elsewhere; and its flouting of global norms in trade and economic policy. Pillsbury suggests that Deng Xiaoping's outwardly humble maxims are a pretense veiling a long-term strategy of amassing strategic assets to be used against the United States and other powers. Chinese officials do not intend to adopt a Western-style free market or liberal democratic system over time. Rather they seek to maximize China's influence and to shape the global system in its own image.

Analysts at the China Academy of Military Sciences have long sought to measure the country's "Comprehensive National Power," taking into account military capabilities as well as economic and cultural factors. Pillsbury maintains that China's preoccupation with its own power may allow it to gradually improve its position vis-à-vis the United States and other Western powers. In the years following the terrorist attacks of September 11, 2001, the U.S. military became preoccupied with wars in Iraq and Afghanistan, while U.S. diplomacy suffered from a depletion of goodwill. Chinese leaders saw an opportunity to take advantage of a perceived weakness. John Tkacik, a former State Department China specialist, assessed that Chinese officials believed that China had gained "tremendous economic and financial leverage, especially over the United States" and that "they will use it when they can."[42]

Professor Christensen offers a different view in his book *The China Challenge*. Christensen notes that many Chinese leaders still regard their country as a developing nation which is not yet prepared to shoulder the responsibilities of a super power on the world stage. However, over time, as China's capabilities grow, and its leaders become more confident, it is likely that China will become an increasingly important partner for the United States and others in promoting world order. What is required, Christensen argues, is for China to see how global initiatives align with its interests as a rising power, whether in the economic, military, diplomatic or ideological realms. "[T]he goal of the United States, its allies, and all like-minded states should not be to contain China but to shape Beijing's choices so as to channel China's nationalist ambitions into cooperation rather than coercion," Christensen writes.[43]

Christensen's book, released in 2015, follows in a vein of thinking highlighted by Professors Andrew J. Nathan and Andrew Scobell in *China's Search for Security*, in 2012, where they advocate a holistic agenda for managing U.S.-China affairs:

China's rise will be a threat to the U.S. and the world only if the U.S. allows it to become one. Therefore, the right China strategy begins at home. The U.S. must resume robust growth, continue to support a globally preeminent higher-education sector, continue to discover new technologies, protect intellectual property from espionage and theft, deepen trade relations with other economies, sustain military innovation and renewal, nurture relationships with allies and other cooperating powers, and by example, earn the respect of people around the world for American values. As long as the U.S. holds tight to its values and solves its problems at home, it will be able to manage the rise of China.[44]

Are the United States and China on a collision course destined for conflict and great power rivalry? Or will the two sides pursue a strategy of peaceful cooperation? The answer to this question will have immense consequences for the people of both countries and the world community as a whole. Should China play the part of a disruptive power, it could challenge the United States' influence in the region. Worse, it could destabilize the prevailing global order and undermine peace and security. In all likelihood, the relationship will continue to be a mixed one. Both countries operate from the context of vastly different historical and contemporary perspectives. For the time being, their interests are not easily reconciled. However, as observed throughout the preceding chapters, there are many common interests and shared expectations around which the United States and China can, and should, build positive relations. As Nye has observed, the American Century is not soon ending. The United States will continue to exert influence in the Asia Pacific for the foreseeable future. In doing so, it must encourage Chinese leaders to act responsibly, to adhere to the rule of law, and to work toward the maintenance of minimum world order. As for Taiwan, the island's future as an independent state depends in large part on the continuation of constructive relations between its larger allies. Chapter 10 will consider several possible developmental paths for Taiwan, taking into account regional and global power configurations. Whereas previous chapters have considered the development of bilateral relations, the next chapter will highlight the context of the triangular U.S-Taiwan-China relationship. Within this context, special focus will be given to the demands, expectations, and identifications of the Taiwanese people.

Notes

1. Aaron L. Friedberg, *Hegemony with Chinese Characteristics*, THE NATIONAL INTEREST 18–27, 20 (July/Aug. 2011).

2. Michael D. Swaine, *China's Assertive Behavior Part One; On "Core Interests"* at 6, CHINA LEADERSHIP MONITOR (2010).

3. *See* CAITLIN CAMPBELL ET AL., CHINA'S "CORE INTERESTS" AND THE EAST CHINA SEA, U.S.-CHINA ECONOMIC AND SECURITY REVIEW COMMISSION STAFF RESEARCH BACKGROUNDER (May 10, 2013), *available at* http://www.uscc.gov/sites/default/files/Research/China%27s%20Core%20Interests%20and%20the%20East%20China%20Sea.pdf.

4. White Paper: China's Peaceful Development, Sept. 6, 2011, *available at* http://www.cfr.org/china/white-paper-chinas-peaceful-development/p25850.

5. Press Release: U.S.-China Joint Statement, The White House, Nov. 17, 2009, *available at* https://www.whitehouse.gov/the-press-office/us-china-joint-statement.

6. Press Release: U.S.-China Joint Statement, The White House, Jan. 19, 2011, *available at* https://www.whitehouse.gov/the-press-office/2011/01/19/us-china-joint-statement.

7. *Hu's Visit Sketches Blueprint for China-U.S. Ties*, XINHUA, Jan. 23, 2011, *available at* http://news.xinhuanet.com/english2010/china/2011-01/23/c_13703037.htm.

8. Martin Grueber & Tim Studt, *2012 Global R&D Funding Forecast: China's R&D Momentum*, R&D MAGAZINE, Dec. 16, 2011, *available at* http://www.rdmag.com/articles/2011/12/2012-global-r-d-funding-forecast-chinas-r-d-momentum.

9. Ministry of Foreign Affairs of the People's Republic of China, Foreign Minister Wang Yi Meets the Press, Mar. 8, 2015, *available at* http://www.fmprc.gov.cn/mfa_eng/zxxx_662805/t1243662.shtml.

10. *See* STEFAN HALPER, THE BEIJING CONSENSUS: HOW CHINA'S AUTHORITARIAN MODEL WILL DOMINATE THE TWENTY-FIRST CENTURY (2010).

11. Press Release: Remarks by President Obama to the Australian Parliament, The White House, Nov. 17, 2011, *available at* https://www.whitehouse.gov/the-press-office/2011/11/17/remarks-president-obama-australian-parliament.

12. Edward Wong, *Chinese Military Seeks to Extend Its Naval Power*, N.Y. TIMES, Apr. 23, 2010, *available at* http://www.nytimes.com/2010/04/24/world/asia/24navy.html.

13. MICHAEL PILLSBURY, THE HUNDRED-YEAR MARATHON: CHINA'S SECRET STRATEGY TO REPLACE AMERICA AS THE GLOBAL SUPERPOWER (2015).

14. Hillary Rodham Clinton, U.S. Dept. of State, Remarks at Press Availability, July 23, 2010, *available at* http://www.state.gov/secretary/20092013clinton/rm/2010/07/145095.htm.

15. *Chinese FM Refutes Fallacies on the South China Sea Issues*, CHINA DAILY, July 25, 2010, *available at* http://www.chinadaily.com.cn/china/2010-07/25/content_11046054.htm.

16. Remarks by President Obama to the Australian Parliament, *supra* note 11.

17. U.S. Dept. of State, Remarks by Hillary Rodham Clinton, Secretary of State: America's Pacific Century, Nov. 10, 2011, *available at* http://www.state.gov/secretary/20092013clinton/rm/2011/11/176999.htm.

18. *Obama Visit: Australia Agrees U.S. Marine Deployment Plan*, BBC NEWS, Nov. 16, 2011, *available at* http://www.bbc.com/news/world-asia-15739995.

19. *Australia Could Be Caught in Sino-U.S. Crossfire*, GLOBAL TIMES, Nov. 11, 2011, *available at* http://www.globaltimes.cn/content/684097.shtml.

20. Hillary Clinton, *America's Pacific Century*, FOREIGN POLICY (Oct. 11, 2011), *available at* http://foreignpolicy.com/2011/10/11/americas-pacific-century/.

21. *Id.*

22. *Id.*

23. Press Release: Remarks by President Obama and Vice President Xi of the People's Republic of China before Bilateral Meeting, The White House, Feb. 14, 2012, *available at* https://www.whitehouse.gov/the-press-office/2012/02/14/remarks-president-obama-and-vice-president-xi-peoples-republic-china-bil.

24. *Id.*

25. William Lowther, *Obama Takes "Tougher" Tone with Xi*, TAIPEI TIMES, Feb. 16, 2012, *available at* http://www.taipeitimes.com/News/front/archives/2012/02/16/2003525588.

26. *See* Mark Landler, *Obama Urges China to Restrain North Korea as He Praises South's Successes*, N.Y. TIMES, Mar. 26, 2012, *available at* http://www.nytimes.com/2012/03/27/world/asia/president-obama-in-south-korea.html.

27. Thomas J. Christensen, *China's Role in the World: Is China a Responsible Stakeholder?*, Remarks before the U.S.-China Economic and Security Review Commission (Aug. 3, 2006), *available at* http://2001-2009.state.gov/p/eap/rls/rm/69899.htm.

28. *See* SUSAN V. LAWRENCE, U.S.-CHINA RELATIONS: AN OVERVIEW OF POLICY ISSUES, CONGRESSIONAL RESEARCH SERVICE, at 11 (2013), *available at* http://www.fas.org/sgp/crs/row/R41108.pdf.

29. JOSEPH S. NYE, JR., SOFT POWER: THE MEANS TO SUCCESS IN WORLD POLITICS at x (2004).

30. CENTER FOR STRATEGIC & INTERNATIONAL STUDIES, CSIS COMMISSION ON SMART POWER at 7 (2007), *available at* http://csis.org/files/media/csis/pubs/071106_csissmartpower-report.pdf.

31. *See* Chicago Council on Global Affairs, Soft Power in Asia: Results of a 2008 Multinational Survey of Public Opinion (2008), *available at* http://www.brookings.edu/~/media/Events/2008/6/17%20east%20asia/0617_east_asia_report.pdf.

32. DAVID M. LAMPTON, THE THREE FACES OF CHINESE POWER: MIGHT, MONEY, AND MINDS at 11 (2008).

33. Robert B. Zoellick, *Whither China, From Membership to Responsibility?*, Remarks to National Committee on U.S.-China Relations, *available at* http://2001-2009.state.gov/s/d/former/zoellick/rem/53682.htm.

34. *Id.* at 98.

35. *Id.* at 96.

36. *Id.* at 98.

37. Dan Blumenthal, *Is China at Present (or Will China Become) a Responsible Stakeholder in the International Community?*, Reframing China Policy: The Carnegie Debates, June 11, 2007, *available at* http://www.carnegieendowment.org/files/Blumenthal_Responsible%20Stakeholder%20 Final%20Paper.pdf.

38. *See* Joseph S. Nye, Jr., Is the American Century Over? at 46–70 (2015).

39. *See China's Defense Budget to Grow 11.2 pct in 2012: Spokesman*, Xinhua, Mar. 4, 2012, *available at* http://news.xinhuanet.com/english/china/2012-03/04/c_131445012.htm.

40. *See* John Mearsheimer, *Why China's Rise Will Not Be Peaceful*, Sept. 17, 2004, *available at* http://mearsheimer.uchicago.edu/pdfs/A0034b.pdf.

41. *See* Pillsbury, *supra* note 13.

42. *See* Elison Elliott, *Economic Warfare: China Threatens U.S. Debt as WMD*, Foreign Policy Association, Feb. 22, 2010, *available at* http://foreignpolicyblogs.com/2010/02/22/ economic-warfare-china-threatens-debt-as-wmd/.

43. Thomas J. Christensen, The China Challenge: Shaping the Choices of a Rising Power at xxi–xxii (2015).

44. Andrew J. Nathan & Andrew Scobell, China's Search for Security 359 (2012).

10 Possible Future Developments for Taiwan

THE PRECEDING CHAPTERS described the major features of the bilateral relationships between the United States and Taiwan, the United States and China, and Taiwan and China. This chapter will address the Taiwan question in the context of the dynamic and triangular U.S.-Taiwan-China relationship. What does the future hold for the people of Taiwan? And what is the significance of the possibility of a developing U.S.-China rivalry? A survey of past trends and conditioning factors, considered in light of both internal and external factors, finds a range of possible outcomes. Some of these outcomes would bring Taiwan closer to China. Others accentuate the island's prospects for independence and neutrality. Some scholars and advocates have argued persuasively that Taiwan may become Asia's answer to Switzerland. That is to say, a permanently neutral state. Others find that Taiwan is likely to seek independence while remaining close to China. This would entail a policy of Finlandization. To the contrary, Taiwan could seek to become a normalized state like any other in the region, maximizing its flexibility in foreign affairs, engaging with its neighbors on equal footing, confirming its status as a sovereign state, and obtaining membership in the United Nations. On the other hand, although less likely, Taiwan may never seek independence. It may someday opt to become a part of China, either as a new province or a member of a confederated system. There is even support for the notion that Taiwan could become an overseas territory of the United States. Each path carries the likelihood for negative and positive outcomes that must be considered and weighed in selecting among courses of action. Outcomes can be appraised in terms of both minimum and optimum world order and the ultimate goal of securing human dignity and human security for all. The best outcomes are those that promote peace and security and the widest possible shaping and sharing of all values for all people.

I. The Context of Conditions

Taiwan's future depends on a multitude of factors. Outcomes and effects will be shaped by innumerous interactions among participants engaged in a complex network of overlapping and interpenetrating domestic and international legal and power processes. The most influential participants are, of course, the governments of the United States, Taiwan, and China themselves. Other participants include intergovernmental and nongovernmental organizations, private associations, and individuals, who will influence the development of the U.S.-Taiwan-China relationship. The interests of the three countries are deeply entangled and yet easily distinguishable. The military, economic, diplomatic, and ideological strategies available to them are contingent on historical trends and conditions unique to each. Policymakers are restrained by the realities of foreign affairs while on the domestic front political elites are equally constrained by the demands and expectations of their constituents, who embody sometimes contradictory interests and perspectives. Cataloguing and interpreting these factors and extrapolating probable future developments demands the scholar's intellectual skills and no small portion of imagination. In accordance with the New Haven School's policy-oriented approach, future outcomes will be appraised in light of the goal of securing human security and human dignity for all.

A. EXTERNAL CONDITIONS

After World War II, the United States loomed large over the Asia Pacific, with Taiwan serving as a forward base of operations throughout the Korean and Vietnam Wars. For the People's Republic of China (PRC), reducing the U.S. military presence on Taiwan and ending the U.S.–Republic of China Mutual Defense Treaty were top priorities in negotiations with the United States over diplomatic normalization. In December 1978, President Carter accepted those conditions when he made the decision to derecognize the Republic of China (ROC). Congress, however, remained committed to protecting the people of Taiwan. In 1979, the Taiwan Relations Act cemented that commitment, marrying U.S. national security with conditions in the Asia Pacific and providing the means for Taiwan's self-defense. Cross-strait relations have been a focal point for U.S. foreign policy ever since—and will be so for a very long time. Meanwhile, the PRC persists in calling Taiwan a "renegade" province, advancing unfounded claims over the island, and stifling Taiwan's conduct as a state. The PRC, which has never controlled Taiwan for a single day during its existence of sixty-six years since 1949, has refused again and again to renounce the use of force in its campaign for annexation of Taiwan—in perpetual violation of the UN Charter and unworthy of a permanent member of the Security Council. Despite this, Taiwan has evolved as a state. With the eras of Chiang Kai-shek and Chiang Ching-kuo's authoritarianism behind them, the people of Taiwan are living freely and democratically.

As described at length in Chapters 2 and 8, Chiang Kai-shek managed to cling to the ROC's seats in the UN General Assembly and Security Council for two decades following the ROC's defeat in the Chinese civil war. Then, in October 1971, the General Assembly adopted Resolution 2758, which seated the PRC and moved to "expel forthwith the representatives of Chiang Kai-shek from the place which they unlawfully occupy at the United Nations and in all the organizations related to it." In the 1990s, President Lee embarked on a public and outspoken five-year campaign for Taiwan's participation in the United Nations.[1] In 2007, President Chen reinvigorated efforts initiated in the Lee administration and formally submitted an application for membership to join the United Nations under the name Taiwan. The application stated that Taiwan had evolved as a "free and peace-loving state." UN Secretary-General Ban Ki-moon denied the application by invoking General Assembly Resolution 2758, in violation of the provisional rules of procedure of the Security Council. The campaign for UN membership effectively ended under President Ma. Under Ma, however, Taiwan did gain observer status at the 2009 World Health Assembly and signed several bilateral agreements with Asia Pacific nations. Taiwan is an active participant in about thirty intergovernmental organizations (IGOs), including the Asian Development Bank; the World Trade Organization (as the "Separate Customs Territory of Taiwan, Penghu, Kinmen and Matsu"); and the Asia-Pacific Economic Cooperation forum (as "Chinese Taipei"—a degrading name the country is forced to use for its national Olympic Committee and in the World Health Assembly). Additionally, Taiwan has observer status or other membership in about twenty other IGOs and subsidiary bodies.

In recent years cross-strait relations have followed the general trend toward peace and stability in Asia. The situation today is markedly different from the state of cold war that persisted between the PRC and the ROC in the days of the two Chiangs. The current period of seemingly stable relations was preceded by a decade of high anxiety. Anti-independence maneuvering by the PRC heated up dramatically during the presidency of Lee Teng-hui, forcing the United States to deploy its navy to the region in the wake of the Third Taiwan Strait Crisis. Two weeks before Taiwan's election day in 1996, the People's Liberation Army began a series of ballistic missile tests off the coast of Taiwan. The move was largely interpreted as an intimidation tactic directed at Taiwanese voters. In 2005, during President Chen Shui-bian's second administration, the PRC adopted an antisecession law that threatened force against any alleged Chinese territory that moved toward independence, including notably Taiwan. The threat was reinforced by the deployment of more than sixteen hundred missiles aimed at the island as a deterrent to any declaration of independence. The PRC has never renounced the use of force against Taiwan. Yet, twenty years since the Third Taiwan Strait Crisis, politicians on both sides of the Taiwan Strait acknowledge that the threat of war may be lower than ever. Some Kuomintang (KMT) leaders are even calling for a peace pact between the two countries. However, for many the term itself evokes memories of China's 1951 peace pact with Tibet, which gave China sovereignty over the Tibetan territory and culminated in a massacre of the Tibetan people.

In its long-term quest to subjugate Taiwan, the PRC carries out a strategy focused on (1) conditioning Taiwan to accept closer ties with China through ideological and economic policies backed by an implicit threat of force for noncompliance, (2) discouraging other states from establishing diplomatic relations with the Taiwan government, and (3) excluding Taiwan from international organizations. Chinese officials and media outlets continuously assert that Taiwan is a part of China. The PRC uses its economic might to threaten deprivations against nations that extend diplomatic recognition to Taiwan. As a result, while most nations do not formally assent to China's claim over Taiwan, they remain silent on the matter. As elaborated in previous chapters, most of Taiwan's diplomatic relationships are informal in nature. The number of countries that maintain diplomatic relations with Taiwan has fallen from more than one hundred during the mid-twentieth century to today's total of twenty-one (plus the Holy See).

B. TAIWAN'S INTERNAL POLITICS

Taiwan's political scene is divided between those favoring closer ties with China, known as the Pan-Blue camp, and those favoring greater independence for Taiwan, known as the Pan-Green camp. The KMT is the leading Pan-Blue party. Today's KMT descends from the Nationalist movement that began in China in the early twentieth century. The KMT charter identifies Sun Yat-sen as the party's founder and adheres to the historical "Three Principles of the People and the Five-Power Constitution." For many years, the KMT's platform included a pledge to retake the Chinese mainland and restore the ROC as the government of all of China. Nowadays, however, most KMT politicians would settle for peaceful unification with a *democratized* PRC. Indeed, President Ma and Hung Hsiu-chu, the KMT's first 2016 presidential nominee, have advocated for a "peace pact" with China, which opponents fear would constrain Taiwan's policy choices and lay the groundwork for an eventual annexation of Taiwan. The KMT also observes the so-called 1992 Consensus, which holds that there is "one China" but that the PRC and the ROC disagree on its definition. (During the Ma administration, the 1992 Consensus has served as a code word for China's One China Principle. Lee Teng-hui, who was president during the 1992 summit, commented that the term was a "creative fabrication" and did not represent the substances of the discussions.)

On the other side of the spectrum is the Democratic Progressive Party (DPP), the island's historical opposition party, which leads the Pan-Green Coalition. The DPP rejects the existence of the 1992 Consensus. The party's charter, adopted in 1986, includes an "independence clause" calling for the creation of an independent Republic of Taiwan. Although the DPP is closely associated with the movement for independence, in practice, some DPP politicians today adhere to some version of the status quo, and a handful have advocated for "freezing" the charter's independence clause. Furthermore, the DPP's 1999 Resolution regarding Taiwan's future declared that Taiwan has already become a sovereign, independent state and that this independent status cannot be changed without a plebiscite by the Taiwanese people. What the parties have in common on the issue of cross-strait relations is that neither would tolerate unification with China under the current conditions of the Chinese Communist Party's (CCP) authoritarian one-party rule.

Taiwan's foreign policy is closely tied to the island's economic well-being. The island's economy is heavily dependent on foreign trade, especially with China, but also with Japan, the United States, and other countries. Interactions between Taiwan and China intensified in the early 1990s and developed further with the re-establishment of trade, travel, and communications. Much of this work began under the Chen administration, which permitted registered residents of Quemoy and Matsu to travel to the PRC directly beginning in 2001 and permitted indirect flights between Taiwan and the PRC beginning in 2003. The Chen administration also lifted the fifty-year direct trade and investment ban between Taiwan and the PRC.

Ma took credit in developing cross-strait relations by focusing on easy wins with the PRC, in effect putting less controversial economic issues ahead of more difficult and fundamental political questions. His policy of economic engagement has been credited with de-escalating cross-strait tensions. Indeed, the early years of the Ma administration showed that the Taiwanese public was willing to tolerate greater engagement with China in exchange for economic growth—to a point. The adoption of the Economic Cooperation Framework Agreement (ECFA), one of more than twenty PRC-ROC agreements signed during Ma's presidency, was a significant milestone. However, the public's tolerance for cross-strait integration and dependency is limited, as vividly illustrated by the Sunflower Movement and the results of the 2014 nine-in-one island-wide elections. The Taiwanese people understand that in a world where international relations revolve largely on economic matters, Taiwan's flexibility in foreign affairs is proportional to the strength and number of its economic relationships. Greater economic integration with China will eventually constrict Taiwan's foreign policy options because economic dependency will lead to an expectation of political concessions on the part of Taiwan in exchange for continued access to Chinese markets and other inducements. Ma's excessive policies alienated many Taiwanese. His approval rating fell to as low as 9 percent for a considerable period of time, earning him the nickname "the 9 percent president." There is now a visible divide between the KMT and the Taiwanese people. The next president will have an opportunity to rectify this gap and chart a new course of development.

C. THE PREDISPOSITIONS OF THE PEOPLE OF TAIWAN

Due regard should be given to the predispositional factors which include the Taiwanese people's demands, expectations, and identifications. In the case of Taiwan, the people's outlook has changed remarkably through the periods of authoritarian rule and democratic transformation and the successive DPP and KMT administrations. The people's demands are not limited to independence but also include freedom, democracy, and human rights within their existing political context. The overwhelming majority of people in Taiwan today consider themselves to be Taiwanese, not Chinese. They have experienced and cherish democracy. They cannot live without freedom and all the related human rights. These demands exist very much apart from the demand for independence for the whole nation. Taiwan's younger generations never lived under the KMT's authoritarian rule of martial law (commonly known as the reign of "White Terror")—and, of course, never under the Chinese Communist Party's authoritarian rule of the PRC, which has never governed or controlled Taiwan. Today's twenty-somethings have only known Taiwan as a free and democratic country. For them, China's propositions ring especially hollow.

Scholars and commentators who facilely assert that Taiwan is a part of China and who predict that the two sides are on the path to unification are overlooking the biggest factor: the wishes of the Taiwanese people. Recent events including the Sunflower Movement and the KMT's crushing defeat in the 2014 island-wide elections patently demonstrate that the Taiwanese public is against increased integration with dependency on China. As detailed in Chapter 2, the proportion of the island's population who identify as Taiwanese—not Chinese—has grown significantly over time. The number of people who identify as Taiwanese has increased from 40 percent in 1997, to 55 percent in 2004, to more than 60 percent in 2015. The number identifying as Chinese-only dropped from 16 percent in 1998 to 3.5 percent in 2015. According to a survey by the Taiwan Brain Trust conducted in November 2015, 82 percent of young people between the ages of twenty and twenty-nine believe Taiwan should be independent, while 98 percent identify themselves as Taiwanese, not Chinese. One need only look to the case of Hong Kong to see that Beijing is not capable of meeting the demands of a people accustomed to living freely and democratically—and Hong Kong has much closer historical, geographical, and political ties to China than Taiwan ever has. There is no reason to believe that China, in its current state, could effectively govern Taiwan, let alone fulfill the demands and expectations of the Taiwanese people more effectively than a sovereign democratic state could. It is more likely that the Taiwanese people would see unprecedented political oppression and untold deprivations of their fundamental human rights under Chinese rule. It is astounding that so many Western scholars and commentators advocate this step backward. This is why the principle of self-determination is so critical in this debate. Taiwan is not a piece of property to be traded. It is home to 23 million people who have chosen to live freely and democratically and who are entitled to continue doing so under international law. Naturally, the Taiwanese people want peaceful cross-strait relations. No one wants to live under the constant threat of violence or a state of perpetual warfare. However the Taiwanese people should not have to sacrifice their fundamental human rights to achieve this. China's continued threat of force, which is in violation of the UN Charter, is the problem. The world community, and especially the United States, should not countenance this unauthorized use of coercion in international affairs.

As detailed in earlier chapters, Chiang Ching-kuo's death was followed by a movement for democratization and Taiwanization under the leadership of President Lee Teng-hui. Lee's reforms ended many of the outmoded policies that characterized the military occupation and opened government positions to local Taiwanese. Under President Lee, the people of Taiwan forged a new national identity and local culture. Lee promoted the idea of a "New Taiwanese" identity that would embrace Taiwan's status as an island nation of immigrants with a shared destiny.

In 2009, the Legislative Yuan ratified the International Covenant on Civil and Political Rights and the International Covenant on Economic, Social and Cultural Rights. The government has made subsequent efforts to amend Taiwan's laws to conform with the covenants. Freedom House's *Freedom in the World* report named

Taiwan as one of the world's freest countries owing to the high degree of civil and political freedoms adopted in 1988. Since the ending of official censorship in the late 1980s, the Taiwanese people have enjoyed unrestricted access to information through every form of media. Contrast this with China, where government censors regularly restrict access to information about current events, and Internet users are largely prevented from using popular websites such as Facebook and Google. Individuals in Taiwan are free to speak their minds publicly on any topic. In China, dissenting voices are silenced through threats of imprisonment. The topic of cross-strait relations is hotly debated in every sector of Taiwanese society; political parties exist to promote every variant of opinion on the issue. Meanwhile, in China, the public is indoctrinated with the Communist Party's dogmatism, which leaves no room for compromise.

In March 2014, the KMT's policy of economic engagement was put to the test when students, civil society groups, and other concerned citizens coalesced under the banner of the Sunflower Protest Movement and undertook an unprecedented occupation of the Legislative Yuan. The movement started in response to lawmakers' attempts to pass the Cross-Straight Service Trade Agreement (CSSTA) between China and Taiwan without due process of review in the legislature. The CSSTA, a follow-up agreement to the ECFA, would allow exchanges in banking, healthcare, transportation, travel, communications, and construction, and permit cross-strait investment by citizens from both countries. Opponents believed that the CSSTA would endanger Taiwan's economy by leaving the country susceptible to pressure from Beijing. Opposition lawmakers in the Legislative Yuan demanded closer scrutiny of the agreement, and in June 2013, the KMT and the DPP agreed to a process for a clause-by-clause review. In September, the parties decided on public hearings to consult academics, businesses, and other nongovernmental organizations regarding the potential impact of the CSSTA.[2] Then, in March 2014, the KMT attempted to force the CSSTA through the legislature, sparking immediate protests. On the evening of March 18, about three hundred students, academics, and civic leaders barricaded themselves inside the Legislative Yuan, beginning a three-week long standoff. A massive rally on March 30 saw hundreds of thousands of people take to the streets of Taipei in support of the occupiers' demands. Solidarity protests were held in major cities around the world. The occupation was brought to a close when KMT legislative speaker Wang Jin-pyng visited the occupiers and agreed to postpone the CSSTA's ratification until after the Legislative Yuan adopted legislation concerning the monitoring of cross-strait agreements.

The size and impact of the Sunflower Movement was significant. It demonstrated that for a large portion of Taiwan's population tolerance of the status quo was on the wane and that a great many citizens were growing skeptical of the government's handling of cross-strait affairs. Subsequent events suggest that the movement's views are becoming mainstream. In November 2014, the KMT was dealt a stunning defeat in the nine-in-one island-wide elections. The KMT lost control of eight populous municipalities and counties, including the city of Taipei. The dismal KMT showing forced the resignation of Premier Jiang Yi-huah, followed by Ma, who resigned his post as chairman of the KMT shortly after the election. In early 2016, voters will elect a new president, and many observers expect the DPP to perform strongly. By late 2015, Tsai Ing-wen, the DPP's chairwoman and 2012 presidential candidate, had emerged as the clear front runner. In June, the KMT nominated Hung Hsiu-chu, vice president of the Legislative Yuan, as its candidate for the 2016 presidential elections. Like Ma, Hung has advocated for a peace pact with the PRC. Many commentators speculated that the 2016 election would be the equivalent of a referendum on the two parties' approach to cross-strait relations. Hung's pro-unification stance proved to be so unpopular with the public that the KMT moved to replace her on the presidential ticket with KMT Chairman and New Taipei Mayor Eric Chu in October 2015, approximately three months before the election day. The 2016 presidential election could set a new course for cross-strait relations regardless of which party prevails at the voting booth.

II. Future Projections

The sections that follow present several developmental constructs for how Taiwan's future could unfold, taking into account the facts and prevailing trends of today. These scenarios, each of which has its own proponents, range from the least ideal—annexation by China—to the most ideal—normalized statehood for Taiwan. Interested readers may consult the list of Suggested Readings in Chinese, which appears at the end of the book, for contemporary sources elaborating each of the alternatives described below.

The purpose of making projections is not to play the role of fortune teller or to persuade others that certain events are inevitable. Rather, it is to imagine how today's trends and predispositional factors, if conserved and amplified through policy, would bring about future outcomes. It is also to consider how conditions may be configured differently through policy to bring about desirable changes. This type of thinking about the future is not entirely a creative exercise. Projections of likely developments should be bounded by the current context of internal and external conditions. As elaborated in the previous chapter, there is the potential for a growing rivalry between the United States and China that cannot be overlooked. However, Taiwan's history of perseverance gives reason for optimism. Nothing is inevitable.

This chapter concludes by arguing that Taiwan should continue to develop along the path of normalization, in keeping with its evolution as a state, which was described in Chapter 4. What is clear is that any decision regarding Taiwan's future must represent the genuine desires of the Taiwanese people. The long-term goal of fostering a world community of human dignity and human security must not be forgotten. In the final analysis, what is good for the people of Taiwan should be, and is in fact, good for the people of Asia and the world community.

A. TAIWAN AS A PART OF CHINA

During the Cold War era, Mao Zedong and Chiang Kai-shek were arch enemies. There was little communication between the PRC in China and the ROC in Taiwan, and the prospect of a peaceful reconciliation was nonexistent. Neither side was strong enough to present a convincing military threat to the other. However, the PRC's effective power was growing steadily. In the United States, policymakers were debating supporting a policy of Two Chinas or One China and One Taiwan as an eventual solution for the impasse. Meanwhile, Communist and KMT forces continued their ceremonial shelling across the Taiwan Strait as a reminder of the ongoing civil war between them. The passage of Resolution 2758, which seated the PRC in the United Nations and expelled Chiang Kai-shek's representatives, was a major turning point. It seemed that it was only a matter of time before the discredited KMT would face its reckoning. The deaths of Chiang Kai-shek in 1975 and Mao in 1976 (preceded by the death of Zhou Enlai earlier that year) opened the door to new leaders and new thinking on both sides of the strait. Ideas were floated for ending the deadlock, which ranged from a confederacy of Chinese states to a commonwealth system modeled on that of the British Commonwealth. At that time, Taiwan's military was still superior to that of the People's Liberation Army (PLA), and the U.S.-ROC Mutual Defense Treaty remained in effect. By the late 1970s, Deng Xiaoping had settled on the "one country, two systems" formula as China's preferred solution for annexing Taiwan. His hand was strengthened considerably in 1978, when the United States decided to switch diplomatic recognition from the ROC to the PRC, concluding negotiations which had begun under the Nixon administration. Some assumed it was only a matter of time before the ROC on Taiwan would surrender. Yet the situation remained intractable. The adoption of the Taiwan Relations Act (TRA) in the United States, and the continuation of unofficial relations with most other countries, ensured that the ROC regime would remain in power and that Taiwan as a country would continue to exist independently of China. The Tiananmen Square massacre of June 4, 1989, irreparably damaged the PRC's image on the global stage and ended hopes that the Communist Party would entertain even the slightest move toward genuine democracy in China. Taiwan, in contrast, was just beginning its "Silent Revolution" under the leadership of President Lee Teng-hui, who had taken office upon Chiang Ching-kuo's death in 1988. During this period, the ROC government opened up to native Taiwanese, and the island began its remarkable progress toward democratization and Taiwanization. As described in Chapter 8, relations between Taiwan and China thawed during the era of Taiwanese presidents, as the two sides embarked on diplomatic and economic engagements for the first time since the 1940s. Tensions flared once again during the presidencies of Lee Teng-hui and Chen Shui-bian, which saw the Third Taiwan Strait Crisis of 1995 to 1996 and the passage of China's Anti-Secession Law in 2005. By the time Ma Ying-jeou took office in 2008, Chinese leaders realized that it would be easier to literally buy Taiwan than to take it by force. Under Ma's administration, economic integration between the two sides continued apace. KMT leaders are now talking of a "peace pact" that would preclude Taiwan from ever declaring its independence.

Under what circumstances would Taiwan give in to ultimate unification with China? An obvious, albeit increasingly less probable, scenario involves a forceful takeover by the PRC. A 2013 report by Taiwan's Ministry of Defense asserted that by 2020 the PLA would be capable of mounting a cross-strait invasion.[3] A 2014 Pentagon report outlined potential military strategies the PLA could undertake in a hypothetical attack on Taiwan.[4] Possible scenarios include naval blockades, cyber warfare, missile strikes, or a full-scale invasion by the PLA. The short-term and long-term costs of such a move would be staggering in every conceivable dimension. An attack by the PRC would almost certainly force the international community to reckon with Taiwan's international legal status—as an unprovoked attack against another state would clearly violate the UN Charter. Looking to the example of Crimea, the PRC may wish to encourage instability in Taiwan, opening a pretext for a military invasion in defense of the ethnic Chinese living on the island. Under the guise of a humanitarian mission, the PRC could coax Taiwanese elite into accepting the PLA's permanent presence or holding a referendum in support of annexation. The differences between Taiwan and Crimea, however, are evident. The majority of Crimea's people are ethnic Russians who resisted Ukrainian rule and sought closer ties with the Russian Federation. Taiwan's people could scarcely be expected to vote in favor of a referendum on annexation by China. It is unlikely that the presence of the Chinese military would be tolerated under any circumstances.

Scholars such as John Mearsheimer highlight Beijing's ambitions to accomplish regional hegemony. Mearsheimer's "offensive realism" theory holds that Beijing's actions can only be understood in this context. According to this view, foreign affairs in the Asia Pacific is a zero-sum game. According to Mearsheimer, China, like the United States in the West, will seek to become the regional hegemon of the East.

Mearsheimer's offensive realism holds that states exist in an anarchical system and cannot reliably predict how other states will act. Therefore, political decision makers, when given an opportunity, are not likely to forego an opportunity to further their security interests. They will seek to gain power whenever possible. According to Mearsheimer, the United States' strategy is to deny other countries the opportunity to become a regional or global hegemon. In this regard, the United States' recent "pivot" to the Asia Pacific may be interpreted as an effort to check the PRC's rising power.

From the perspective of the PRC's leadership, annexing Taiwan without the use of force would be ideal. This preference underlies many of the PRC's current economic and diplomatic strategies toward the island. Increasing economic dependency coupled by diplomatic isolation makes Taiwan susceptible to pressures from Beijing. Isaac Stone Fish, writing in *Foreign Affairs*, described the strategy succinctly: "As China continues to expand in influence, the world increasingly sees the Middle Kingdom, rather than the United States, as the future. When large numbers of Taiwanese begin to do the same, that's checkmate."[5] Thankfully, for the present, this is not the case—the Taiwanese people do not believe China represents the wave of the future. But in the eyes of many, the signing of the 2010 Economic Cooperation Framework Agreement brought the PRC one step closer to its goal of eventual unification. Absent meaningful free trade agreements with the United States and other economically powerful nations, Taiwan may someday find that China is its only economic lifeline. Should this trend continue, Taiwan's economic dependence on China will become so great that its cooperation with China on noneconomic issues will become equally vital to its existence. Taiwan's inability to participate in international organizations will only add to its isolation, furthering the conditions needed for Beijing to achieve annexation through nonmilitary means.

Any scenario involving the PRC's annexation of Taiwan would likely lead to Taiwan becoming a special administrative region of the PRC. This is the so-called "one country, two systems," first introduced by Deng Xiaoping in 1979, and currently implemented in Hong Kong and Macau. In theory, Taiwan would merge with China administratively while maintaining some aspects of its democracy and free-market economy.

However, recent events in Hong Kong demonstrate that the two-systems framework is built on empty promises. When the United Kingdom returned Hong Kong to China in 1997, the PRC signaled that it would preserve the political freedoms enjoyed by Hong Kong's citizens. Hong Kong's Basic Law—the equivalent of its constitution—was adopted ahead of the handover with the expectation that Hong Kong's future chief executives would be chosen by universal suffrage. In 2007, the PRC announced that 2017 would be the first year in which open voting for the chief executive would take place. However, Beijing would retain broad control over the selection of candidates for the post. In 2013, Qiao Xiaoyang, chairman of the Law Committee under the National People's Congress Standing Committee, elaborated on the proposal's flaws: "Firstly, the nomination committee will decide [the candidate.] Then the voters in Hong Kong will decide. Lastly, the central government will decide whether to appoint [the candidate] or not."[6] Further, Qiao stated that candidates "who confront the central government" would fail to qualify as candidates. What PRC leaders apparently meant by universal suffrage was that the people's political freedoms would be subject to maximum oversight. Currently a 1,200-member pro-Beijing committee selects Hong Kong's chief executive. Under the voting proposal, the committee will retain responsibility for selecting the candidates from which the people of Hong Kong will select their leader. The risk of political manipulation is high. A June 2014 PRC white paper elaborated the notion of "one country, two systems." According to the white paper, the "one country" is the premise and basis of the "two systems," and the "two systems" is subordinate to and derived from "one country."[7] In other words, the two systems are not equal and are secondary to Beijing's demands.

In 2015, the PRC hosted a military parade to honor the seventieth anniversary of the end of World War II in the Pacific. Former ROC vice president Lien Chan made headlines when he attended the ceremonies in Beijing. Lien, a scion of a political family and former honorary chairman of the KMT, lost the election to Chen Shui-bian in 2000. Chinese officials lauded the political reconciliation underway between the CCP and the KMT, who fought together against the Japanese before the end of the Chinese civil war. Meanwhile in Taiwan, both the KMT and the DDP criticized Lien's actions, making clear that Lien was not acting as a representative of Taiwan. Former Vice President Annette Lu and others asked prosecutors that Lien be criminally charged for treason.

B. THE FINLANDIZATION OF TAIWAN

Some observers have remarked that Ma's KMT regime has embarked on a process of Finlandization in forging closer ties with China. In 2010, Bruce Gilley, writing in *Foreign Affairs*, observed that Taiwan, like Finland, is a "small but internally sovereign state that is geographically close to a superpower with which it shares cultural and historical ties . . . Its fierce sense of independence is balanced by a pragmatic sense of the need to accommodate that superpower's vital interests."[8] Gilley argued that U.S.-China relations would improve as Taiwan's dependence on U.S. arms sales decreased. Lower tensions would increase the likelihood that the United States could win China's cooperation on a wide range of global issues, including climate change, economic development, and nuclear nonproliferation. Furthermore, Gilley proposed that a Finlandized Taiwan would benefit the United States because it would encourage Beijing to emulate Taiwan and eventually democratize.[9]

In the context of the Cold War the term *Finlandization* refers to "a policy or behavior of a country that, while not formally part of the Soviet bloc, wished to maintain close relations with the USSR and . . . was willing to distance itself from traditional allies and friends."[10] In 1948, Finland entered into a friendship treaty with the USSR committing Finland to "repel any attempt by other Western nations to use Finnish territory as a base for an attack against the Soviet Union."[11] Finland's decision to establish a cordial relationship with the Soviet Union was interpreted by many as a response to the Soviet's military strength and geographic proximity to Finland. In striking its deal, Finland also impeded its ability to form close relationships with nearby NATO countries. Were Taiwan to follow Finland's example, it may be forced to distance long-time allies such as the United States and Japan. Nevertheless, the proposal has supporters who see its practical advantages. An alliance with the PRC would lead to a reduction in cross-strait tensions. Although it contradicts the One China Principle, the PRC's leaders could save face by keeping an independent Taiwan firmly within their zone of influence. Taiwan's economic integration with the PRC could continue unabated.

Several conditions would have to be met for Taiwan to follow the Finnish model, and in practice, outcomes would invariably be different, owing to Taiwan's unique political and historical conditions. While Finland was able to retain its *de jure* sovereignty through a friendship treaty with the Soviet Union, Taiwan would risk developing into the next Hong Kong, in light of the PRC's strenuous opposition to Taiwanese independence. A Findlandized Taiwan would be further isolated from its long-time allies. Furthermore, proponents would have to overcome strong aversion to the idea among the Taiwanese people.

Gilley's article drew criticism, including from the late former American Institute of Taiwan chairman Nat Bellocchi, who called Gilley's analysis "so far removed from reality that it would be dismissed out of hand for its lack of understanding and its outright naiveté."[12] In Bellocchi's view, Gilley's essay made three incorrect assumptions: the false perception that Finlandization enjoyed wide support in Finland at the time; the notion that Taiwan and China only became separate political entities beginning in 1949; and the assessment that Finlandization will somehow "democratize and pacify a rising China rather than embolden it."[13] Bellocchi stressed that it would be a "fundamental error to sacrifice the hard-won achievements of a vibrant and democratic Taiwan and let it drift into an uncertain, fuzzy principled neutrality."[14] He also emphasized that, given the strategic importance of Taiwan in the Asia Pacific, the United States should continue to ensure Taiwan's self-defense and build new economic ties through trade agreements. Bellocchi emphasized that stability in the Asia Pacific could only be achieved by "bringing Taiwan into the international family of nations," and not by subjecting Taiwan to overbearing influence from China.

Jyrki Kallio, a senior Research Fellow for the Finnish Institute of International Affairs, argued that that Gilley's article was flawed in its premises and its conclusions.[15] Unlike Taiwan, Finland was already recognized as an independent sovereign nation in 1948. It was one of the few countries that had not been occupied in World War II. For Taiwan, appeasing Beijing would mean sacrificing any chance at genuine independence. Furthermore, Taiwan is more or less protected by the United States. Finland had no significant military backing during the Cold War and had little choice but to align with the Soviet Union. The Soviet Union was not opposed to Finland maintaining its defensive capabilities since Finland agreed to defend its territory against a German attack. However, Kallio distinguished that "it would be folly for Taiwan to stop buying weapons from the USA, and China certainly does not want Taiwan to have strong defence capabilities."[16]

Kallio also criticized Gilley for being "overly optimistic" in the view that "Taiwanese officials would gain more free access to the Mainland where they could influence their communist counterparts on the benefits of liberalization."[17] Kallio disagreed with Gilley's characterization that Beijing viewed Taiwan as a situation to be managed, rather than a fundamental interest. In Kallio's words, "[t]he legitimacy of the [PRC] is inseparably tied with the unity of the nation, and thus the idea of reunification has to be kept alive."[18] Therefore, the Taiwan question could not be solved by following the Finnish example.

Finlandization would ultimately be detrimental for Taiwan. Closer ties would increase Taiwan's dependence on China, making it more susceptible to diplomatic strong-arming. Taiwan would be further isolated from the international community. Contrary to Gilley's projections, the situation could undermine human rights on Taiwan. Finland was host to numerous human rights violations during the Cold War. There is little reason to believe that the PRC would not seek to curtail opposition elements in its satellite states. Indeed, the tendency has been demonstrated already in Hong Kong, which saw widespread civil disobedience in 2014 following Beijing's attempts to micromanage local elections.

C. TAIWAN AS ASIA'S SWITZERLAND

Taiwan could seek security through neutrality. This proposal was made popular by Chen Hsiu-li, a pro-independence leader who advocates for Taiwan to declare itself a permanently neutral state. Chen and his supporters believe that Taiwan could become, in effect, the Switzerland of Asia. Their analogy recognizes similarities between the countries' geopolitical situations. Switzerland, which achieved independence in 1648, is landlocked by France, Germany, Austria, and Italy. Since the early 1800s, it has opted to remain neutral amid conflicts involving its powerful neighbors. In 1815, European participants in the Congress of Vienna, which included France and Austria, collectively agreed to respect Switzerland's neutrality in all future wars. In 1938, just prior to the outbreak of World War II, Switzerland secured guarantees from Germany and Italy to do the same. As a neutral state, Switzerland abstains from armed conflicts. However, it maintains a defensive military. In 2002, Switzerland joined the United Nations following a successful national referendum. Taiwan, like Switzerland, has obvious incentives to avoid armed conflict. Taiwan is an island located in the middle of important waterways in the Asia Pacific. It is strategically important to the United States, China, Japan, and other regional powers. It is vulnerable due to its small size and proximity to the PRC. However, its strategic location makes it an ideal buffer state. As a neutral country, Taiwan would serve as an oasis of economic and political stability in the region.

Under international law, neutralization is attained through four modalities: unilateral declaration, notification and recognition, custom, and treaty. A unilateral declaration of neutrality would have little validity without a guarantee of security. Like Switzerland, Taiwan would require firm commitments to ensure its territory would be respected. Furthermore, the relevant powers would need to be convinced that Taiwan's neutralization would benefit their interests. As argued by Yao Meng-chang, Taiwan would need to undertake constitutional reforms to outline its responsibilities and duties as a neutral state.[19] Taipei would also need to engage in negotiations with neighboring states and the United States to obtain recognition of its neutrality. For both the United States and the PRC, Taiwan's neutrality could serve to lessen tensions over cross-strait relations and lead to a further reduction in U.S. arms sales. The PRC would be free to shift its military resources to other areas in pursuit of its genuine core interests. For Japan, the Philippines, and other neighboring countries, Taiwan's neutralization would help ensure long-term access to regional waters.

The idea of permanent neutrality has vocal supporters in Taiwan. Former Vice President Annette Lu leads a coalition called the Peace and Neutrality for Taiwan Alliance, which advocates for a referendum on declaring Taiwan's neutrality. Proponents argue that an authoritative declaration is needed to halt the momentum toward unification with China that has gained under the Ma administration. They point to examples like Singapore, which maintains a policy of neutrality backed by a strong military. Furthermore, Taiwan's neutrality would benefit Japan and other nations that rely on the surrounding waterways. Critics, however, argue that China is unlikely to accept Taiwan's declaration and that permanently excluding Taiwan from security alliances would make it vulnerable to pressure from the PRC.

D. TAIWAN AS A PART OF THE UNITED STATES

Taiwan's future is most often projected in terms of its relationship to China. But there is a perspective—more prevalent than often acknowledged—holding that Taiwan is a part of the United States. As the principal victor over Japan and an occupying power over Taiwan's territory following World War II, the United States, some argue, retains a residual claim to title over Taiwan. This argument was advanced in U.S. federal court in 2008 in *Lin v. United States.*[20]

The plaintiffs, who were residents of Taiwan and members of the Taiwan Nation Party, filed a civil lawsuit in the District Court for the District of Columbia seeking a judicial declaration of their personal legal rights under U.S. law. The plaintiffs had attempted several times to secure U.S. passports from the American Institute in Taiwan (AIT), but were denied and blocked from submitting future applications. In their complaint, the plaintiffs argued that they were, along with all residents of Taiwan, U.S. nationals and that the AIT's refusal to process their applications deprived them of constitutional rights.

The plaintiffs' principal argument was that the United States retained temporary *de jure* sovereignty over Taiwan at the end of World War II. Prior to the signing of the San Francisco Peace Treaty, the United States provided crucial assistance to the ROC regime that occupied Taiwan, which, until 1952, was still a Japanese territory. The plaintiffs argued that even after the treaty took effect, the United States retained sovereignty over Taiwan for two reasons. First, Article 2(b) of the treaty required Japan to renounce all right, title, and claim to Taiwan. Second, Article 23(a) named the United States as the principal occupying power. Since the treaty did not designate a recipient state to which right, title, and claim over Taiwan would devolve, the United States held sovereignty over the territory by default.

The AIT defended its actions with reference to the 1954 Mutual Defense Treaty between the United States and the ROC, which "recognized the ROC as the government of China and recognized Taiwan to be among its territories."[21] Moreover, in 1982, the United States and the PRC issued the Third Communiqué, in which the United States agreed that "respect for each other's sovereignty and territory integrity and non-interference in each other's internal affairs constitute the fundamental principles guiding U.S.-China relations" and expressed its intention to continue unofficial relations with the people of Taiwan. In 1996, President Clinton issued an executive order stating that relations with the people on Taiwan would continue unless otherwise terminated or modified in accordance with law. Based on the foregoing, the government asserted that the United States did not hold sovereignty over Taiwan.

The District Court held that the plaintiffs' case was barred by the political question doctrine and granted the government's motion to dismiss the complaint.

The court reasoned that the "determination of who is sovereign over specific territory is non-justiciable." The court added that the "judiciary is not equipped to interpret and apply, 50 years later, a wartime military order [issued by General MacArthur] entered at a time of great confusion and undoubted chaos."[22] The court chose to adhere to the separation of powers principle and maintained that "the foreign relations of the U.S. are conducted by the President of the U.S. and the Executive and Legislative Branches will decide whether and under what circumstances the United States will recognize a sovereign government over Taiwan."[23] The District Court's ruling was affirmed by the Court of Appeals for the D.C. Circuit. The U.S. Supreme Court subsequently denied plaintiff's petition for a writ of certiorari.[24]

Despite the court's holding, the plaintiffs' arguments in *Lin* resonate with a great many people in Taiwan. There are those who advocate that Taiwan should become a fifty-first state of the United States. Joining the United States would require a complex and contentious process through which the U.S. Congress would provide enabling legislation authorizing the people of Taiwan to draft a new constitution and form a state government. Then, the legislation would need to receive the signature of the president of the United States. It has been more than fifty years since Hawaii became a state. It seems perhaps far-fetched that Taiwan will become the next territory to do so. A less arduous, but equally improbable, outcome would be for the United States to establish Taiwan as an unincorporated territory. There are currently four such entities: Puerto Rico, Guam, Northern Mariana Islands, and the U.S. Virgin Islands. In this case, Taiwan would fall within U.S. legal jurisdiction and would enjoy the protection of the U.S. military while maintaining an autonomous government. However, becoming an unincorporated territory would still require congressional action and presidential approval.

As the plaintiffs in *Lin* demonstrated, there are some people in Taiwan who advocate that the United States holds sovereignty over Taiwan. By extension, the people of Taiwan are U.S. nationals. This notion remains deeply unpopular with the Taiwanese who retain a strong sense of national identity and yearn for a state of their own. It goes without saying that the PRC would be extremely hostile to any attempt by the United States to claim sovereignty over Taiwan.

E. MAINTAINING THE STATUS QUO

The *status quo* is a perennial theme in Taiwanese politics. Within Taiwan, the term connotes policies that preserve and make the most of the island's *de facto* independence without inviting reprisals from the PRC. However, there is no agreed-upon definition of what the status quo entails in practice. The term implies both an understanding of the underlying political realities—for example, that Taiwan acts as an independent state—as well as the limits placed on Taiwan's action—for example, that Taiwan will not declare its independence. Within the status quo, Taiwan's government avoids declaring or seeking formal independence and resists ultimate unification with China. Versions of the concept were suggested by President Chen's "Four Noes and One Shall Not" pledge (no declaration of Taiwan's independence, no changing of the ROC name to the Republic of Taiwan, no incorporation of the state-to-state doctrine in the ROC constitution, no referendum on unification or independence, and no abolishing of the National Unification Council—all subject to China's continuation of peaceful relations) and President Ma's "Three Noes" policy (no unification, no independence, and no use of force).

China, meanwhile, has its own interpretation of the status quo that runs counter to that of Taiwan. To China, the status quo is based on the One China Principle, which holds that there is only one China and that Taiwan is a part of China. China's interpretation of the status quo also incorporates the 1992 Consensus, under which China asserts that Taiwanese officials accepted the One China Principle as a basis for peaceful cross-strait relations. In the eyes of Chinese officials, a disavowal of the 1992 Consensus or a move toward *de jure* independence would constitute a change in the status quo. Under the 2005 Anti-Secession Law, the PRC could seek to use force to compel compliance with its conception of the status quo.

Further complicating the matter, U.S. officials appear to have their own interpretation of the status quo. The United States continues to hold to the acknowledgment formula of the three U.S.-China communiqués, which encourage the two sides to come to a peaceful resolution of the cross-strait dispute. President George W. Bush famously cautioned China and Taiwan against taking unilateral action to change the status quo. His remarks followed tensions after President Chen's efforts to define Taiwan's status as an independent, sovereign state. On the one hand, this position has allowed the United States to avoid antagonizing China; on the other hand, it precludes supporting Taiwan's efforts to actualize its independent status, while affording the PRC time to pursue its goal of unification.

Adhering to the status quo has permitted Taiwan to have beneficial relations with the United States, the PRC, and many other countries. Trade is strong. The threat of a military attack is lower than ever. For the time being Taiwan is enjoying the benefits of *de facto* independence. But the status quo does not immunize Taiwan from changing conditions. While the rest of the world globalizes, Taiwan is becoming economically dependent on China. It has been left out of major trade agreements such as the Trans-Pacific Partnership (TPP) and regional initiatives such as the China-led Asian Infrastructure Investment Bank (AIIB). As tensions among its neighbors rise, Taiwan's military is stagnating. Taiwan has no significant diplomatic partners (formally), and it cannot advocate for itself in most international forums. Like the proverbial frog in a pot of slowly boiling water, Taiwan will succumb to outside forces if it does not take decisive action. The most important choice facing the people of Taiwan today is whether to maintain the status quo or embark on a new path of peaceful development toward normalized statehood. For the United States, the choice whether to support Taiwan's efforts will be a critical one in the future of the U.S.-Taiwan-China relationship.

III. Taiwan as a Normalized State

Taiwan could move away from the status quo by embarking on a process of normalization. This would involve seeking greater representation in international organizations, including those for which statehood is a requirement for membership, up to and including the United Nations, and seeking greater diplomatic and governmental recognition from other states. Unlike a declaration of independence, normalization would not be a one-time affair. Rather, the term envisions a long-term, ongoing campaign to enhance Taiwan's international presence without ceasing. At the state-to-state level, normalization would entail entering new trade and investment agreements, granting reciprocal visa waivers, and hosting more frequent exchanges between foreign governmental agencies and their officials. At the international level, it entails participating fully in organizations for which statehood is not a requirement for membership and gaining access to organizations for which statehood is a prerequisite, whether as an observer or a full-fledged member. Ultimately the process would culminate with Taiwan's full membership in the United Nations, a goal long sought by the Taiwanese people since Chiang Kai-shek's representatives were expelled from the United Nations under General Assembly Resolution 2758. Normalization would involve decoupling Taiwan's diplomacy from that of the PRC (and even the United States), when necessary, and acting confidently as an equal stakeholder in the Asia Pacific region.

As elaborated in Chapter 4, contemporary international law recognizes four criteria for statehood, which are embodied in the 1933 Montevideo Convention. These are: control over a defined territory, a permanent population, maintenance of an effective government, and the ability to conduct foreign relations with other states.[25] This objective formula enjoys widespread acceptance in the international community. However, difficulties arise in applying it to the facts in certain cases. Who decides when a territorial community has fulfilled these four requirements? Does a territory become a state automatically, or should there be an authoritative process for conferring this status? What happens when a territory satisfies most, but not all, of the requirements? This is the problem of state recognition. There are competing theories as to how to resolve this problem in practice. The two most prominent are the *declaratory* and the *constitutive* theories of recognition. Under the constitutive theory, it is not sufficient to attain the four conditions of statehood. Rather, a new entity must receive formal recognition by existing states to become a full-fledged member of the community of nations.[26] The constitutive theory demands that a new state receive formal recognition from other states. The claim to statehood is strongest when a prospective state receives the recognition of most, if not all, other states. Recognition could come in the form of a diplomatic act, such as a declaration by a head of state or the reciprocal establishment of embassies and consular offices. The shortcoming of the constitutive theory is that it overpoliticizes what is essentially a legal analysis. By placing recognition within the purview of self-interested states, it ensures that the practice of recognition will be an outcome of effective power processes, rather than legal reasoning. In contrast, the declarative theory of state recognition does not call for any formal act on the part of other states. Under this view, a state may exist in fact even without formal recognition. As such, it is entitled to make the same claims under international law as other states. Decision makers, whether acting as representatives of other states, international judges, scholars, or in other roles, are free to consider and accept those claims. The declarative theory is the prevailing view. It is reflected in the Montevideo Convention as well as the Restatement of the Foreign Relations Law of the United States.[27]

In practice, statehood may be either *de facto* or *de jure*. In this sense, diplomatic recognition is not a precondition to interaction between states and nonstate actors. When a territory has *de facto* recognition, it is never fully excluded from international affairs—with or without diplomatic recognition life must go on. What then is the value of attaining recognition as a state? Recognition matters because states are still regarded as primary actors under international law. States have access to forums that other international entities do not. They can make claims that other entities cannot, either for themselves or on behalf of their nationals. They can exert control over resources within their boundaries and can exclude access to other actors. They are entitled to a presumption of national sovereignty and have the inherent right to defend themselves from attack under Article 51 of the UN Charter.

In Taiwan's case, there is near unanimity that the island's government fulfills the requirements of statehood. Therefore it is a *de facto* state. First, Taiwan has a defined territory that encompasses the island of Formosa, the Pescadores, Green Island, and Orchid Island. Importantly, an entity may "satisfy the territorial requirement for statehood even if its boundaries have not been finally settled, if one or more of its boundaries are disputed, or if some of its territory is claimed by another state."[28] Thus, any existing territorial disputes with the PRC do not preclude Taiwan from fulfilling the first requirement for statehood. Second, Taiwan has a permanent population of approximately 23 million people, greater than 75 percent of the member states of the United Nations. Third, Taiwan has a government capable of exercising effective authority over its territory. The threshold for this requirement is low. "[T]he state need not have any particular form of government . . . [so long as there is] some authority exercising governmental functions and able to represent the entity in international relations."[29] The ROC government on Taiwan has exercised control over Taiwan since 1945, first under a military occupation and then as a representative democracy. Fourth, Taiwan has the capacity to conduct formal relations with other states. Despite having been expelled from the United Nations in 1971, the ROC government on Taiwan continues to maintain diplomatic ties with nearly two dozen countries and unofficial relations with dozens more, including the United States.

Ordinarily a political entity with Taiwan's qualities would be embraced by the international community. Why is Taiwan in such an unfortunate position today? Because China claims it. And China's claims are not merely rhetorical—they are backed by the threat of force. The PRC has undertaken "Three Wars" against Taiwan: a public opinion war, a legal war, and a psychological war with the intention of undermining Taiwan's movement toward *de jure* recognition and discouraging other states from extending diplomatic relations. Take, for example, the Anti-Secession Law of 2005 and China's refusal to trade with countries that have formal diplomatic relations with Taiwan. Currently, only twenty-one countries and the Holy See continue to maintain formal diplomatic relations with the ROC government. Taiwan is not a member of the United Nations, and it has been excluded from international organizations for which statehood is a requirement for membership. How to resolve this problem? Given the confusion surrounding the practice of recognition, the United Nations could offer a mode of confirming a territory's statehood through collective action. A General Assembly resolution could define a framework under which a political entity would gain automatic or provisional UN membership upon satisfaction of certain requirements, such as those listed in the Montevideo Convention, or upon making a successful petition. This solution would benefit not only Taiwan but also nations such as Kosovo and Palestine. Kosovo, for example, has been denied UN membership, despite having diplomatic relations with 108 countries. What is needed is a mechanism for recognizing states that is not beholden to the power processes of individual states. Obviously, any procedure adopted by the United Nations could potentially be blocked by a member of the Security Council or through lobbying of General Assembly members. In Taiwan's case, China, a permanent member of the Security Council, would present a major obstacle. However, by shifting the debate into the UN forum, the burden is placed on the opposition to argue why a prospective member should not receive international recognition. The International Court of Justice could be called upon to render advisory opinions in difficult cases to ensure a fair application of standards adopted by the General Assembly.

While the prospects of a solution to the problem of recognition may be far off, Taiwan can nevertheless facilitate the process of normalization by working to distinguish itself from China in the eyes of the international community. This could involve changing its name to the Republic of Taiwan or adopting a new Taiwan constitution. Less drastically, it could involve an effort to rebrand Taiwan through a global educational campaign featuring the country's distinctive history and character. Taiwan should continue to use its economic resources to assist in developing other countries and providing aid in times of need. It should build strong ties with those countries with which it does maintain diplomatic relations, and it should establish instrumentalities for interacting with countries with which it does not. Developing along the path of a normalized state would give Taiwan the greatest chance of ensuring the security of its people in a comprehensive sense. The concept of human security is not limited to alleviating the threat of violence or coercion. It embraces positive values as well. To achieve its aims, Taiwan may require a guarantee from the United States or other powers, including the United Nations. Open aggression on the part of China, like Iraq's invasion of Kuwait in 1990, cannot be tolerated.

The world is not simply becoming smaller and more crowded. As the world's people grow increasingly interconnected and interdependent, our identifications become less separate and less parochial. Our common interests come into focus. From this emerges international law. The New Haven School of international law calls for a comprehensive education of the world's citizens to nurture a global consciousness and a broad understanding of the common good upon which a beneficial global order may be founded. In this regard, it offers an optimistic vision and a reference point from which to recommend and appraise policy, while remaining cognizant that there is a gap between that vision and our present reality. The outcomes of decisions are appraised in terms of the dual objectives of attaining minimum world order in the sense of minimizing unauthorized coercion and optimum world order in the sense of maximizing the shaping and sharing of all desired human values. The task of achieving normalized statehood and membership in the United Nations is a challenging and difficult one. The government and the people of Taiwan must be persevering. Taiwan must continue to make its case and to arouse the conscience of the world's people. Its precarious status cannot be left to drift from year to year.

Notes

1. Murray A. Rubinstein, *Political Taiwanization and Pragmatic Diplomacy: The Eras of Chiang Ching-kuo and Lee Teng-hui, 1971–1994, in* Taiwan: A New History 465 (Murray A. Rubinstein ed., 2015).

2. J. Michael Cole, *Taiwanese Occupy Legislature over China Pact*, The Diplomat, Mar. 20, 2014, *available at* http://thediplomat.com/2014/03/taiwanese-occupy-legislature-over-china-pact/.

3. *See, e.g., China Able to Attack Taiwan by 2020: Report*, Taipei Times, Oct. 9, 2013, *available at* http://www.taipeitimes.com/News/front/archives/2013/10/09/2003574061.

4. *See* Department of Defense, Military and Security Developments Involving the People's Republic of China (May 8, 2015), *available at* http://www.cfr.org/china/department-defense-military-security-developments-involving-peoples-republic-china/p28408.

5. Isaac Stone Fish, *An Offer They Can't Refuse*, Foreign Aff. (Feb. 2014), *available at* http://foreignpolicy.com/2014/02/12/an-offer-they-cant-refuse/.

6. Joshua But & Colleen Lee, *Opponents of Beijing Ineligible to Be CE: Top Chinese Official*, South China Morning Post, Mar. 25, 2013, *available at* http://www.scmp.com/article/1199015/opposition-camp-members-cant-run-chief-executive-says-npc-official.

7. *Full Text: The Practice of the "One Country, Two Systems" Policy in the HKSAR*, China Daily, June 10, 2014, *available at* http://www.chinadaily.com.cn/china/2014-06/10/content_17576281_11.htm.

8. Bruce Gilley, *Not So Dire Straits*, Foreign Aff. (Jan. 2010), *available at* https://www.foreignaffairs.com/articles/china/2010-01-01/not-so-dire-straits?cid=rss-foreign_affairs_report_a_year-not_so_dire_straits-000000.

9. *Id.*

10. Ruud van Dijk, 1 Encyclopedia of the Cold War 1st Ed. 319 (2008).

11. *Id.*

12. Nat Bellocchi, *Gilley's "Finlandization" Is Wrong*, Taipei Times, Jan. 18, 2010, *available at* http://www.taipeitimes.com/News/editorials/archives/2010/01/18/2003463745.

13. *Id.*

14. *Id.*

15. Jyrki Kallio, *Finlandization Is No Model for Taiwan to Follow*, Finnish Institute of International Affairs Blog, Feb. 5, 2010, http://www.fiia.fi/en/blog/259/finlandization_is_no_model_for_taiwan_to_follow/.

16. *Id.*

17. *Id.*

18. *Id.*

19. *See, e.g.,* Meng-chang Yao, *Permanent Neutral State: A New Vision for Taiwan?*, *available at* http://www.taiwanthinktank.org/ttt/attachment/article_618_attach2.pdf.

20. Lin v. United States, 539 F.Supp.2d 173 (D.D.C. 2008), *aff'd*, 561 F.3d 502 (D.C. Cir. 2009).

21. *Id.* at 11.

22. Lin v. United States, 539 F.Supp.2d 173 (D.D.C. 2008).

23. *Id.*

24. Lin v. United States, 130 S. Ct. 202 (2009).

25. Montevideo Convention on Rights and Duties of States Art. 1, Dec. 26, 1933, 49 Stat. 3097, 3100, 165 L.N.T.S. 17.

26. *See* Lung Chu-chen, An Introduction to Contemporary International Law: A Policy Oriented Perspective 3d Ed. 42 (2015).

27. Formal recognition is not a requirement for statehood under the Restatement (Third) of Foreign Relations. *See* Restatement (Third) of Foreign Relations Law § 201 (1987).

28. *Id.* §201 cmt. b.

29. *Id.* §201 cmt. d.

V Recommendations of Policy Alternatives

11 Recommendations of Policy Alternatives

OUR THINKING ABOUT international legal problems—even the most intractable ones—must be balanced with a regard for fundamental principles. The policy recommendations made throughout this book are inspired by the teachings and spirit of the New Haven School of international law. As such, they aim to serve not only the interests of the people of Taiwan but also those of the United States, China, the Asia Pacific region, and even the world community as a whole. With these goals in mind, this chapter introduces specific recommendations of policy alternatives in light of the foregoing discussions of present realities, past trends, conditioning factors affecting those trends, and possible future developments, with special emphasis on the common good—especially the goals of human dignity and human security.

The recommendations that follow are addressed primarily to decision makers and political elites in the United States and Taiwan, as they are most likely to encounter and consider this advice. However, the principles and objectives herein apply equally well to the Chinese political establishment. Policymakers in China, seizing their roles as members of a globally interconnected world community, would do well to adopt more accommodating policies toward Taiwan, whether in the interest of maintaining the peace and security of the Asia Pacific or, more parochially, to avoid costly and detrimental military or diplomatic conflicts that would harm the People's Republic of China (PRC) itself. Many of the recommendations in this chapter are well established and enjoy wide support, having been formulated and promoted by scholars, political activists, and other proponents. Others are novel and exhibit creative thinking about emerging conditions.

I. Enhance Taiwan-U.S. Trade through Bilateral Agreements and Taiwan's Participation and Membership in the Trans-Pacific Partnership

The Taiwan Strait is one of the world's busiest transportation routes, playing host to hundreds of commercial vessels and civilian aircraft each day. Taiwan's trade hubs include Kaohsiung, a major regional hub port, Chilung (Keelung), Hualian, and Taichung. Between 1952 and 2014, Taiwan's foreign trade expanded from USD 303 million to more than USD 575 billion. Total foreign direct investment in Taiwan reached approximately USD 220.8 billion in 2012, making Taiwan the twenty-first most popular location for foreign investment in the world. As an island nation, Taiwan relies on trade with other nations for its economic well-being. The island's economy must keep pace with its growing population to ensure a high quality of life. Exports in the form of goods and services provide much needed foreign exchange, while imports satisfy the various demands of domestic consumers and industries. Foreign investment provides capital and other resources needed for economic expansion. Without strong trade and investment relationships, the island's growth would likely stagnate—with dire effects. Greater economic strength also provides leverage in other areas, such as national defense and diplomacy.

At present, two interrelated trends are threatening Taiwan's long-term economic security. The first is an increasing dependency on China. Under President Chen, Taiwan adopted a series of reforms aimed at facilitating cross-strait interactions. Residents of Quemoy and Matsu were given permission to travel to China directly. Indirect and limited direct flights between Taiwan and the Chinese mainland were authorized in 2003 and 2005, respectively. Most significant was the lifting in 2001 of the trade and investment ban which had been in place for fifty years. President Ma took Chen's policies to the next level. Under President Ma, bilateral talks between the Straits Exchange Foundation (SEF) and the Association for Relations Across the Taiwan Straits (ARATS) resumed for the first time since the mid-1990s, leading to the adoption of more than twenty bilateral agreements on a range of subjects. Milestones included the lifting of restrictions on direct flights between China and Taiwan, relaxation of tourist limitations, and the signing of the cross-strait Economic Cooperation Framework Agreement (ECFA). Today, China looks to

Taiwan for electrical equipment, plastics, fuel, and other industrial products. China is now Taiwan's largest trading partner, accounting for 40 percent of Taiwanese exports. Approximately 1 million Taiwanese work in China, and thousands of Taiwanese students travel to China to study each year. China is Taiwan's number-one source of tourists. This growth is especially astounding considering that China was only in the top twenty of Taiwan's largest trading partners as recently as twenty years ago.

The second trend is Taiwan's weak participation in bilateral and multilateral trade agreements. In absolute terms, Taiwan's trade has increased tremendously over the past two decades, growing from roughly USD 180 billion in 1992 to more than USD 650 billion in 2012.[1] Much of this growth can be attributed to developments in the regional economy. Taiwan is an important source of computer chips and other high-tech components that are critical to manufacturing supply chains in the region. More than 85 percent of Taiwan's exports are consumed by just fifteen trading partners, eleven of which are located in the Pacific. Meanwhile, Taiwan's total share of global trade volumes has fallen by 30 percent since 2000.[2] Yet, with the exception of the ECFA, Taiwan does not participate in any major regional trade pacts, and it lacks bilateral treaties with some of its largest trading partners.

A. BILATERAL TRADE

Taiwan's largest trading partners are China (including Hong Kong), the United States, and Japan. In 2008, China surpassed the United States to become Taiwan's largest trading partner, accounting for more than USD 100 billion in total bilateral trade each year. Trade with the United States now accounts for less than 10 percent of Taiwan's total foreign trade. Since the early 2000s, Taiwan's trade with Association of Southeast Asian Nations (ASEAN) member economies has grown from approximately USD 500 million to more than USD 6 billion annually.

Bilateral investment and trade treaties are important tools in promoting economic growth. Bilateral investment treaties (also known as BITs) define standards for the protection of investments, technology, and other resources contributed by foreign parties in the local economy. It has signed bilateral investment treaties with twenty-four other nations; however, only fifteen of these are currently in force. Taiwan has signed free trade agreements with only eight other countries. (See Table 11.1.) In 2013, Taiwan signed free trade agreements with Singapore and New Zealand. By early 2014, as a result of the agreement, exports from New Zealand to Taiwan increased by more than 30 percent, making Taiwan New Zealand's eighth largest export market. Taiwan's exports to New Zealand increased by roughly 20 percent during the same period.[3]

TABLE 11.1.

TAIWAN FREE-TRADE AND BILATERAL INVESTMENT AGREEMENTS AS OF 2015

Taiwan Free Trade Agreements as of 2015	
Country	Year Adopted
Panama	2009
Guatemala	2009
Nicaragua	2009
El Salvador and Honduras	2009
PRC (ECFA)	2010
New Zealand	2013
Singapore	2013

Source: ROC Bureau of Foreign Trade

Taiwan Bilateral Investment Treaties in force as of 2015	
Country	Year Adopted
Singapore	1990
Panama	1992
Paraguay	1992
Philippines	1992
Malaysia	1993
Vietnam	1993
Nigeria	1994
Thailand	1996
Costa Rica	1999
Dominican Republic	1999
El Salvador	1999
Guatemala	1999
Macedonia	1999
India	2002
St. Vincent and the Grenadines	2009

Source: UNCTAD

Among the most significant of Taiwan's foreign-trade agreements is the Economic Cooperation Framework Agreement (ECFA) with China. The ECFA, which took effect in September 2010, was intended to relax trade restrictions on both sides of the strait. President Ma claimed that Taiwan's adoption of the ECFA would smooth the way for free trade agreements with the United States and ASEAN—however, these benefits have yet to materialize. Furthermore, while the ECFA has succeeded in fostering increased economic activity between Taiwan and China, the benefits of increased trade have not accrued equally to all segments of society. As previously highlighted, a 2011 report commissioned by the Research, Development, and Evaluation Commission of Taiwan's Executive Yuan found that "[p]eople who possess large amounts of capital appeared to reap benefits from the [ECFA], while those on the lower end of the economic scale absorbed the costs."[4]

In June 2013, the two sides signed the Cross-Strait Service Trade Agreement (CSSTA), opening "further cross-strait exchanges" of the PRC and Taiwan's service sectors.[5] As described in earlier chapters, the Legislative Yuan failed to ratify the CSSTA due to extreme public opposition. An attempt by Kuomintang (KMT) lawmakers to ratify the agreement without a proper legislative review led to the emergence of the 2014 Sunflower Movement. The movement's leaders decried their country's growing dependency on China and the fear of losing sovereignty in the rush for economic integration. Ma took credit in developing cross-strait relations by addressing economic ties rather than more fundamental and difficult policy questions.[6] But many Taiwanese were concerned that the president was eroding the country's sovereignty in the process.

The United States has dozens of bilateral investment treaties with nations around the world. It maintains free trade agreements with twenty countries and is in the process of negotiating the Trans-Pacific Partnership (TPP), a regional free trade pact for the Asia Pacific region. However, despite having a long-standing strategic relationship, the United States and Taiwan have signed neither a free trade agreement nor a bilateral trade agreement. This is not for a lack of interest on the part of Taiwanese leaders. U.S. policymakers have hesitated for reasons that include deference to the U.S.-China relationship and ongoing trade disputes with Taiwan on issues such as U.S. meat exports and intellectual property protections.[7] However, there is a growing chorus in the United States that is urging the adoption of trade and investment treaties with Taiwan. In 2011, U.S. Senator Joseph Lieberman argued for the adoption of a U.S.-Taiwan free trade agreement, remarking that "Taiwan's trade relations with China are now arguably more free than their trade relations with the United States."

Negotiations over a U.S.-Taiwan free trade agreement have progressed slowly. In 1994, the United States and Taiwan adopted a Trade and Investment Framework Agreement (TIFA) establishing a framework for the discussion of trade issues. However, TIFA talks were suspended between 2009 and 2012 as a result of Taiwan's food safety restrictions on U.S. beef imports. The talks resumed in 2013, with subsequent sessions focusing on Taiwan's protection of intellectual property rights and importation of U.S. agricultural products, among other topics. The agenda for the latest round of talks, held in October 2015 in Taipei, included a discussion of

Taiwan's desire to join the TPP agreement. The TIFA discussions are widely seen as a precursor to an eventual free trade agreement between the two countries.

Strengthening the U.S.-Taiwan relationship is a strategic imperative with important implications for relative power configurations in the Asia Pacific. The United States and Taiwan should continue negotiations for a TIFA and enter into talks for a bilateral free trade agreement. Taiwan should also enter into agreements with other large trading partners in the Asia Pacific region. Taiwanese business leaders should seek out opportunities in emerging markets to create demand for Taiwanese products and gain a foothold in new manufacturing centers that could utilize components produced in Taiwan. Importantly, Taiwanese policymakers must remain sensitive to the concerns of the public and avoid creating dependencies that could undermine the country's sovereignty.

Policymakers in Taiwan have a duty to protect and advance the interests of their domestic constituents. However, they must also continue to take reasonable steps to address U.S. concerns regarding domestic regulations and trade restrictions that could undermine the development of a healthy trading and investment relationship. The opportunity for bilateral agreements provides a strong incentive for Taiwan to adopt commonsense reforms in numerous economic sectors. At the same time, U.S. negotiators should take an accommodating view of Taiwan's efforts at reform. The United States is Taiwan's most important historical trading partner. It offers a much-needed foil to China. Policymakers in Taiwan must not lose the opportunity to build strong bilateral ties with the United States as a counterbalance to the growing Taiwan-China relationship. The United States, for its part, cannot miss the opportunity to lock in favorable agreements that will preserve its influence in Taiwan.

B. MULTILATERAL TRADE

Multilateral trade agreements allow groups of states to adopt uniform rules governing the exchange of goods and services within a free trade zone. Trade agreements can level the playing field by regularizing individual trade regimes, opening new markets for goods and services, and streamlining tariffs and other measures that create barriers to trade. Such agreements may also permit the formation of regional trading blocs through which member states can compete more effectively in the global economy. Examples of free trade agreements include agreements adopted by the World Trade Organization (WTO), the North American Free Trade Agreement (NAFTA), the ASEAN Free Trade Area (AFTA), and the Central European Free Trade Agreement (CEFTA), among others.

The most important and influential of all multilateral trade agreements is the WTO. The WTO, which was established in 1995, replaced the antiquated General

Agreement on Tariffs and Trade (GATT) of 1947. The WTO provides a framework for negotiating trade agreements between its more than 160 members. All told, the WTO's members account for approximately 95 percent of the world's trade. The WTO also provides a dispute resolution mechanism for resolving claims between member states arising under WTO agreements. The Republic of China (ROC) was previously a signatory to the GATT. In January 2002, Taiwan became the 144th member of the World Trade Organization under the name of the Separate Customs Territory of Taiwan, Penghu, Kinmen and Matsu. Taiwan's ascension came one month after China's own ascension to the WTO in December 2001. Since that time, Taiwan's economy has grown tremendously, with gross domestic product increasing by approximately 35 percent and foreign trade more than doubling.

While the WTO remains the world's preeminent trade agreement, regional trade agreements have grown in number and importance in recent decades. Regional agreements are often easier to negotiate than global treaties and can be tailored to the needs of member states, who, owing to their proximity to one another, often face similar economic challenges. The ASEAN, whose member states include Brunei Darussalam, Cambodia, Indonesia, Laos, Malaysia, Myanmar, the Philippines, Singapore, Thailand, and Vietnam, is the most important regional association in the Asia Pacific. ASEAN has adopted trade pacts with China and India. Indeed, the adoption of the China-ASEAN free trade agreement was one of the factors leading to the China-Taiwan ECFA. Policymakers in Taiwan feared that regional competitors would have a trade advantage with China because their products would not be subject to the same export tariffs as Taiwanese goods—underscoring again the dangers of Taiwan's exclusion from regional trade agreements.

Among the most significant multilateral trade agreement contemplated in recent years is the TPP. The TPP, which started as a free trade pact among New Zealand, Chile, Singapore, and Brunei in 2006, is now under negotiation between the United States and eleven Pacific countries, including Australia, Canada, Singapore, Brunei, New Zealand, Chile, Mexico, Japan, Malaysia, Peru, and Vietnam. The prospective TPP member countries are estimated to account for roughly 40 percent of the world's total economic output. The TPP seeks to promote uniform adoption of regulations among the member states and facilitate trade and investment in a variety of industries. The TPP is often compared to the proposed Regional Comprehensive Economic Partnership (RCEP), which, if concluded, would cover the ASEAN countries and Australia, India, Japan, South Korea, New Zealand, and China.

In 2012, President Ma set a goal for Taiwan to join the TPP by 2020. In 2013, Taiwan's Ministry of Economic Affairs considered the potential benefits of Taiwan's inclusion in the TPP. It reported:

> Statistics from the International Trade Centre . . . show that the 11 TPP Members accounted for 23.43% of Taiwan's trade in 2012, and if calculated on the basis of 12 Members (including Japan), the share in Taiwan's trade would have increased to 40.10%, demonstrating an impact that cannot be understated on Taiwan's foreign trade.[8]

In order to join the TPP, Taiwan, like any country seeking accession to the agreement, would have to engage in negotiations with the existing TPP members over the measures required to adhere to the TPP's standards. Taiwan's membership in the TPP would be subject to the approval of the other member nations. It has already received support from officials in the United States. Additionally, a 2014 report from the Brookings Institution's Center for East Asia Policy Studies concluded that Taiwan's participation in the TPP would benefit the Partnership's members by providing access to one of Asia's leading economies and would also leverage the benefits of the ECFA.

The United States should promote Taiwan's integration into the Pacific economy by supporting Taiwan's membership in the TPP. The United States can undertake bilateral negotiations with Taiwan over its inclusion in the TPP and exercise influence over other TPP member states to smooth Taiwan's entry into the treaty. In June 2015, the U.S. Congress granted President Obama with "fast-track authority" to conclude the TPP negotiations in their entirety before submitting a completed trade agreement for a simple majority vote. With the threat of a legislative veto gone, the likelihood of the TPP's adoption increased significantly, and the president's hand in the negotiations was strengthened considerably. The United States is in a position to promote Taiwan's inclusion in the TPP sooner rather than later. This should be no more difficult than winning support for Taiwan's accession to the WTO, in which the United States played a central role. Meanwhile, Taiwan should press for inclusion in other regional trade agreements including the ASEAN Free Trade Area and RCEP.

II. Enhance Official and Nonofficial Contacts to Increase Mutual Understanding at All Levels

The number of countries that maintain formal diplomatic relations with Taiwan has fallen from more than one hundred during the first half of the twentieth century to today's total of twenty-one (plus the Holy See). Since the 1970s, Taiwan has forged unofficial relations with many countries, adopting flexible arrangements that have permitted it to maintain a significant, albeit highly limited, international presence.

While most of the world's governments acknowledge some variation of the One China Policy, ruling out the possibility of full diplomatic relations, Taiwan continues to carry out unofficial relations with nearly sixty countries through *de facto* embassies and consulates. In the United States, Taiwan maintains the Taipei Economic and Cultural Representative Office (TECRO) (formerly known as the Coordination Council for North American Affairs). The TECRO is the counterpart to the U.S. American Institute in Taiwan (AIT). The AIT was modeled on the approach taken by the Japanese in 1972, when Tokyo terminated diplomatic relations with the ROC, but maintained informal relations through a nongovernmental instrumentality on the island.

The nongovernmental model has also been applied to the Taiwan-China relationship. In 1991, the ROC's Mainland Affairs Council established the nongovernmental Straits Exchange Foundation (SEF) as the country's representative in dealings with the PRC. The PRC established a counterpart organization called the Association for Relations Across the Taiwan Straits (ARATS). As discussed in earlier chapters, meetings between the SEF and the ARATS gave rise to the myth of the 1992 Consensus, which holds that representatives of the two sides agreed that there was "one China." Chinese leaders often assert that acceptance of the 1992 Consensus is a precondition for the continuation of peaceful cross-strait relations. However, many Taiwanese politicians, including former President Lee Teng-hui and members of the Democratic Progressive Party (DPP), reject the existence of the consensus.

As described in detail in Chapter 6, the AIT offers a range of services both to Taiwanese and U.S. citizens designed to preserve and promote extensive, close, and friendly commercial, cultural, and other relations between the people of the United States and the people of Taiwan. The AIT serves as the *de facto* U.S. embassy in Taiwan. The AIT, which was registered as a nonprofit organization in Washington, D.C. in January 1979, was empowered by the Taiwan Relations Act (TRA) to perform services for U.S. citizens that would be valid within the United States if performed by any other persons authorized under the laws of the United States to perform such acts. These include administering oaths and taking depositions, providing notary services, and acting as a provisional conservator for the estates of deceased U.S. citizens. The AIT renders consular services to individuals traveling to the United States and to U.S. companies seeking commercial or agricultural assistance in Taiwan. Today there are a total of four AIT offices, including a headquarters in Arlington, Virginia, a principal branch office in Taipei, and two smaller branch offices in Kaohsiung and Taichung in Taiwan. Pursuant to its authority under the TRA, the AIT and the TECRO have entered into nearly two hundred agreements since January 1, 1979, addressing a wide range of topics such as agriculture, aviation, the environment, scientific and technical cooperation, trade, energy, and intellectual property. From the beginning, the AIT served as an advocate for the protection of human rights in Taiwan. The AIT's efforts helped influence the development of Taiwan's democratic movement and hastened the end of authoritarian rule on the island.

Congressional funding for the AIT has increased from approximately USD 23 million per year to just over USD 37 million. In 2009, the AIT began construction of a new facility in the Neihu District in Taipei. Pursuant to the 2000 American Institute in Taiwan Facilities Enhancement Act, Congress authorized USD 75 million for the facilities. In 2009, the U.S. State Department approved funding for a USD 170 million AIT office complex, more than doubling the USD 75 million budget approved by Congress in 2000. The new facility is scheduled to open in late 2015.

Although the United States and Taiwan have informal relations, officials from the two countries continue to meet on a regular basis to discuss matters of mutual importance. The United States' 1994 Taiwan Policy Review declared that Taiwanese officials would not be able to attend meetings at the State Department, White House, or Old Executive Building in Washington, D.C. However, cabinet-level officials would be allowed to meet with Taiwanese representatives in other official settings. The Review expanded the scope of activities that U.S. representatives would be permitted to undertake in Taiwan. In April 2014, Taiwan hosted the first visit from a U.S. cabinet-level official in fourteen years when Environmental Protection Agency Administrator Gina McCarthy met with President Ma in recognition of the cooperation between the United States and Taiwan on environmental issues.[9]

Meetings with Taiwan's presidents are more strictly regulated than interactions between lower-level officials. The 1994 Review concluded that Taiwan's "top leaders" would not be permitted to visit the United States except for transit stops and would not be permitted to engage in public activities while on U.S. soil. For example, as explored in Chapter 6, the State Department placed restrictions on President Chen during transit stops in the United States. In 2006, Chen canceled a visit to the United States, when U.S. officials rejected his request for a layover within the lower forty-eight states. Instead, Chen was offered a fueling stop in Alaska, which he refused. The proposed Taiwan Policy Act of 2013 took exception with the executive branch's restrictive policy on high-level visits by Taiwanese officials. Section 103 of the bill called for overturning existing policies against high-level visits and would have authorized "senior leaders of Taiwan to enter the United States under conditions which demonstrate appropriate courtesy and respect for the dignity of such leaders."

Ordinary Taiwanese citizens are able to easily travel to the United States. The United States approved Taiwan for its Visa Waiver Program in 2012, permitting travelers from

Taiwan to enter the United States without a visa. Taiwanese presidential candidates are also able to freely travel to the United States. In June 2015, DPP candidate Tsai Ing-wen made a twelve-day visit to the United States, where she met with officials at both the White House and the State Department—a first for a Taiwanese political candidate.

Increasing the opportunities for contacts between representatives of the United States and Taiwan holds both symbolic and practical importance. The United States should remove restrictions on travel for high-level Taiwanese officials including the president. The president of Taiwan should be permitted to travel directly to the United States to conduct official business and attend public events and should not be limited to transit stops. Furthermore, the United States should increase the number of high-level officials who visit Taiwan and remove restrictions on meetings with Taiwanese representatives in U.S. government offices in Washington, D.C. Congress and the executive branch should also continue offering their strong support for the work of the AIT and ensure that the Institute is well resourced to carry out its functions on behalf of the United States government.

III. Support Taiwan's Membership or Meaningful Participation in International Organizations, Both Governmental and Nongovernmental

International governmental organizations provide a forum through which states and other participants can promote common purposes. Because of the increasing complexity and interdependence evident in international relations, the number of international organizations has grown tremendously. International organizations exhibit varying degrees of specialization and complexity. Their focus may include any value goal, and their work may be bilateral, regional, or global in scope. The most well-known international governmental organization is, of course, the United Nations. However, there are numerous other organizations of great importance. Examples include the World Trade Organization, World Health Organization, International Civil Aviation Organization, International Seabed Authority, International Energy Agency, International Atomic Energy Agency, Organisation for Economic Co-operation and Development, the World Bank, and many others. International organizations provide a forum through which states may secure benefits for their citizens and advocate preferred solutions to shared problems. When states are excluded from international forums they are denied an opportunity to represent the perspectives of their people. Their people are, in effect, denied a voice on the global stage.

The Republic of China was an early participant in many international organizations, and it continued its involvement in many of them after the ROC regime's exile to

Taiwan. As explored in earlier chapters, Chiang Kai-shek's ROC regime clung to its seat in the United Nations, where it claimed to represent the whole of China in the international community. The PRC's entrance on the global stage made Chiang's position difficult to defend. On October 25, 1971, the General Assembly adopted Resolution 2758, acting to "restore all its rights to the People's Republic of China and to recognize the representatives of its Government as the only lawful representatives of China to the United Nations and to expel forthwith the representatives of Chiang Kai-shek from the place which they unlawfully occupy at the United Nations and in all the organizations related to it."[10] Since the ROC's expulsion from the United Nations, Taiwan has seen its presence in a host of other international governmental organizations dwindle. In 1980, the ROC lost its seat in the World Bank and International Monetary Fund, two important pillars of the international economic system in which the ROC had participated since the 1940s. Taiwan currently participates in about thirty intergovernmental organizations (IGOs) including the Asian Development Bank, the World Trade Organization, and the Asia-Pacific Economic Cooperation forum (as "Chinese Taipei"). Additionally, Taiwan has observer status or membership in nineteen other IGOs or their subsidiary bodies, such as the World Health Assembly.

Taiwan has pressed for greater inclusion in international forums, whether in the form of re-entering organizations from which the ROC was expelled or joining organizations for the first time. President Chen strongly advocated for a national referendum on Taiwan's membership in the United Nations. In 2007, he submitted an application for Taiwan's membership, using the occasion as a platform to declare Taiwan as an independent, sovereign, and peace-loving state that possessed the ability and willingness to carry out the purposes, principles, and obligations of the UN Charter. In August 2009, to please the PRC, President Ma announced that his administration would forgo Taiwan's annual bid for UN membership or participation for the first time in seventeen years.

The PRC government has regularly exerted its growing political, military, and economic influence to exclude Taiwan from gaining increased international recognition. The PRC actively sought Taiwan's expulsion from intergovernmental organizations and the deletion of references to Taiwan in reports by the United Nations and other bodies. When Taiwan does achieve participation in an organization it must usually do so under a name such as "Taiwan, China," "Taipei, China," "Taiwan Province of China," or "Taiwan Province of the PRC." Taiwan's efforts to join the UN Framework Convention on Climate Change and the International Civil Aviation Organization (ICAO) have been stymied. In 2015, the PRC rejected Taiwan's application to join the newly formed Asian Infrastructure Investment Bank (AIIB).

The United States wields great influence over the international community and could facilitate Taiwan's participation in some organizations. The TRA provided that "nothing in the Act may be construed as a basis for supporting the exclusion or expulsion of Taiwan from continued membership in any international financial institution or any other international organization." The 1994 Taiwan Policy Review provided that the United States would not support Taiwan's membership in organizations where statehood was a requirement for entry, such as the United Nations, but would support greater international participation by Taiwan in organizations that accepted nonmember states. In May 2000, U.S. lawmakers introduced H.R. 4444, seeking to "authorize extension of nondiscriminatory treatment (normal trade relations treatment) to the PRC and to establish a framework for relations between the United States and the People's Republic of China." The bill endorsed Taiwan's own WTO accession, indicating that Congress would not only adhere to Section 4(d) of the TRA, opposing the exclusion of Taiwan from international organizations, but would go further by advocating Taiwan's participation and membership in them. This bill was signed into law on October 10, 2000, as the U.S.-China Relations Act of 2000.

Taiwan was granted observer status at the 2009 World Health Assembly (under the name "Chinese Taipei"), due in a large part to a campaign by the United States that resulted in a compromise with the PRC over Taiwan's participation. It was the first time Taiwan had been represented at a UN-affiliated organization since the ROC's ouster from the General Assembly in 1971. Although Taiwan's involvement did not amount to full membership, its invitation was seen as a major breakthrough following years of efforts by Taiwanese officials to gain membership in the World Health Organization. In 2013, President Obama and Congress expressed their support for Taiwan's participation in ICAO, from which it has been excluded since 1976.

The United States should continue to assist Taiwan in its campaign to achieve meaningful participation in international organizations, including UN specialized agencies. In accordance with the 1994 Taiwan Policy Review, the United States should support Taiwan's participation, as a full member, in international organizations where statehood is not a requirement and, at the very least, as a recognized observer where statehood is a prerequisite.

IV. Support and Encourage Taiwan's Ongoing Efforts to Enhance the Actualization of the Universal Values of Democracy, Freedom, and Other Human Rights

The evolution of Taiwan's democracy since the late 1980s represents one of the political highpoints of the late twentieth century. Today, Taiwan is a model of democracy in the Asia Pacific and proves that democratic principles can take hold and thrive in a country sharing some characteristics of the Chinese culture. People from all over the world are increasingly demanding the right to participate in public decisions. The tide of history is moving in favor of democracy. Supporting Taiwan's continued democratic development should be a paramount goal.

In 2013, the SEF and the ARATS signed the Cross-Strait Service Trade Agreement (CSSTA) with the objective of further opening trade in the service sectors. The CSSTA would allow exchanges in banking, healthcare, transportation, travel, communications, and construction, and permit cross-strait investment by citizens from both countries. Critics immediately raised alarms over the lack of transparency during negotiations for the CSSTA and criticized the Ma administration for throwing open the doors to the PRC without securing protections for Taiwan's ongoing sovereignty. These concerns are highlighted throughout the preceding chapters.

In the Legislative Yuan, opposition lawmakers demanded a close review of the agreement over the KMT's push for a hasty ratification. The two sides agreed to conduct a clause-by-clause review of the CSSTA and to hold public hearings on the agreement's potential effects on Taiwan's economy. Then, in March 2014, the KMT attempted to force the CSSTA through the legislature. In response, on the evening of March 18, hundreds of protestors stormed the Legislative Yuan building in Taipei and a group of about three hundred students, academics, and civic leaders occupied the legislature floor. The three-week long Sunflower Student Movement had begun. The protesters demanded that the president and KMT lawmakers reinstate the review process agreed to the year before in addition to the passage of legislation to monitor all cross-strait agreements. At a press conference on March 23, Ma reaffirmed his support for the CSSTA and urged its passage.[11] Hundreds of thousands of people joined a massive rally on March 30 in support of the occupiers' demands. Solidarity protests were held in major cities around the world, including New York, London, and Paris, garnering international media coverage and bringing the Sunflower Movement to the attention of the world community. The occupation of the Legislative Yuan ended peacefully on April 10 after KMT Legislative Speaker Wang Jin-pyng pledged to enact legislation to monitor cross-strait legislation before reviewing the CSSTA. Ma, claiming he had no knowledge of Wang's promise, again called for the quick ratification of the CSSTA.[12] By May 2014, Ma's approval rating had dropped to 17.9 percent, and commentators accused his government of being out of touch with the Taiwanese people.[13] Polls found that half of those who identified themselves as KMT voters believed Ma had "flunked" as president.[14] In November 2014, voters dealt the KMT a crushing defeat in the crucial, nine-in-one island-wide elections. The KMT lost control of eight populous municipalities and counties, including the city of Taipei. The dismal KMT showing forced Premier Jiang Yi-huah to resign, followed by Ma, who resigned his post as chairman of the KMT shortly after the election.

The size and impact of the Sunflower Movement was significant. It demonstrated that, for a large portion of Taiwan's population, tolerance of Ma's and the KMT's policies was on the wane and that a great many citizens were growing skeptical of the government's handling of cross-strait affairs. The occupation of the legislative floor by the Sunflower Student Movement was unprecedented in Taiwan's history. Dozens of civic and nongovernmental organizations participated in the protests against the CSSTA. The movement sparked a passionate interest among the island's younger generation in protecting their country's future. It soon became apparent that the Sunflower Movement signaled a broader shift in Taiwanese politics. In November 2014, the KMT was routed in Taiwan's nine-in-one island elections. In January 2016, voters will elect a new president, and many observers expect the DPP to perform strongly. As of late 2015, Tsai Ing-wen, the DPP's chairwoman and 2012 presidential candidate, was the clear frontrunner. In June, the KMT nominated Hung Hsiu-chu, vice president of the Legislative Yuan, as its candidate for the 2016 presidential elections. Like Ma, Hung has advocated for a peace pact with the PRC. Hung's pro-unification stance was highly unpopular with the public. She was replaced as the KMT presidential candidate in October 2015 after a contentious vote by the KMT, which nominated KMT Chairman and New Taipei Mayor Eric Chu to run in her place in an attempt to salvage the party's chances at retaining the presidency or at least a majority in the Legislative Yuan.

In the past the United States has openly shown its preference for KMT administrations in Taiwan because some U.S. policymakers have incorrectly associated the DPP with heightened cross-strait tensions. The United States repeatedly chastised the Chen administration for provoking China by making reference to the fact of Taiwan's independence. Increasingly, however, the Taiwanese people are looking to the DPP to counter the KMT's tendency toward promoting dependency on China. It is likely that the next president of Taiwan will be a member of the DPP. The United States must offer as much support to a DPP administration as to any other. Furthermore, the United States must support the Taiwanese people in the continued expression of their free political will and self-determination.

V. Fortify Taiwan's Defense Capabilities through Arms Sales and Related Measures

The threat of an armed conflict was for many years a principal theme shaping cross-strait relations. The two sides exchanged fire during the First and Second Taiwan Strait Crises in 1954 to 1955 and in 1958. Ceremonial shelling continued until the

1970s. In the mid-1990s, China fired missiles near Taiwan during the Third Taiwan Strait Crisis. In each of these cases, hostilities were tempered by the intervention of the United States. The overall threat of an armed conflict has decreased considerably over the past decade as the two sides have engaged each other diplomatically and economically. The military instrument is no longer the PRC's biggest source of leverage over its neighbors. The calculus in support of military action on both sides of the strait has shifted dramatically against the use of force. Military barracks and tunnels in Quemoy that once housed soldiers and weapons are now popular tourist attractions for Chinese tourists. Politicians in both countries acknowledge that once bitter tension has given way to mutually beneficial partnership.

But it must not be forgotten that China has never renounced the use of force against Taiwan. The PRC's 2005 antisecession law sought to legitimize the use of force against Taiwan. The People's Liberation Army is growing in strength and sophistication as China looks to project power in the region. The threat of an imminent military conflict over Taiwan has not disappeared. Meanwhile, long-standing territorial disputes between China, Japan, and Taiwan in the East China Sea and a cluster of disputes between China and Indonesia, Malaysia, the Philippines, Vietnam, and other countries in the South China Sea could spark an armed naval conflict. The United States has a strong interest in the outcome of these disputes. It is unlikely that the United States could avoid being dragged into any large conflict in the Asia Pacific involving its allies.

A. REGIONAL MILITARY IMBALANCE

There is no shortage of reports on the military balance between Taiwan and China. The issuance of military analyses relevant to Taiwan is virtually an industry onto itself. For example, a 2010 report from the Defense Intelligence Agency concluded that many of Taiwan's four hundred combat aircraft were not operationally capable.[15] The U.S. Department of Defense found in 2010 that, "in spite of the ongoing rapprochement [between the PRC and Taiwan], the PLA was continuing its military buildup and missile deployment aimed at Taiwan, leading to a further deterioration of the military balance across the Taiwan Strait."[16] A 2014 report found that Beijing has upgraded its cache of M-9 and M-11 ballistic missiles deployed near the Taiwan Strait and has acquired Type 071 amphibious boats that are capable of carrying marine battalions across the Strait and could be used in "Taiwan-related conflict scenarios."[17]

The gap between Taiwan and China's national defense budgets is widening. The PRC's military budget is now about twenty-one times that of Taiwan's.[18] The PRC's military spending is second only to the United States. Taiwan has strived to maintain an adequate defensive military capacity; however, the goal has proven increasingly difficult in the face of economic and political challenges. The country's defense budget fell from about 3.8 percent of gross domestic product (GDP) to 2 percent of GDP between 1994 and 2014. The nominal amount remained flat at around USD 10 billion. Both the KMT and the DPP have pledged to raise defense spending to 3 percent of GDP, a target that has so far gone unmet. Spending during the first six years of the Ma administration averaged about 2.2 percent of GDP. Nevertheless, Taiwan's defense spending amounts to about 16 percent of the national budget—a high level compared to many advanced economies, but far less than the 24 percent reported in 1994.[19]

B. ARMS SALES UNDER THE TAIWAN RELATIONS ACT (TRA)

As detailed in Chapters 2 and 6, the United States has contributed tremendously to the maintenance of Taiwan's defensive capabilities. Under the Taiwan Relations Act, every president since Jimmy Carter has authorized military sales to Taiwan. The sales have supported every branch of the Taiwanese military and have included the deployment of sophisticated computer-based communications systems and training for Taiwanese military personnel. Although the United States has not maintained a formal military presence on Taiwan since the late 1970s, the United States continues to influence military planning on the island. Since 1997, the U.S. Department of Defense has hosted closed-door talks with Taiwan national security officials at least annually in Monterey, California (the "Monterey Talks"). The summits include discussions on intermilitary coordination and how best to provide for Taiwan's defense. U.S. teams visit Taiwan periodically to evaluate specific aspects of the country's defensive capabilities. In 2002, the countries established a crisis hotline and have discussed joint undersea monitoring for Chinese submarines.

The quantity of arms sold to Taiwan was relatively minor throughout the 1980s, at around USD 500 million per year. President Reagan made clear that the United States' adherence to reduced arms sales under the Third Communiqué was premised on the continuation of peaceful cross-strait relations. On August 17, 1982, Reagan signed a secret memorandum that stated:

> The U.S. willingness to reduce its arms sales to Taiwan is conditioned absolutely upon the continued commitment of China to the peaceful solution of the Taiwan-PRC differences. It should be clearly understood that the linkage between these two matters is a permanent imperative of U.S. foreign policy. In addition, it is essential that the quantity and quality of the arms provided Taiwan be conditioned entirely on the threat posed by the PRC. Both in

quantitative and qualitative terms, Taiwan's defense capability relative to that of the PRC will be maintained.[20]

In 1992, three years after the Tiananmen Square Incident in China, President George H. W. Bush approved the sale of one hundred fifty F-16 jets to Taiwan. The Clinton administration authorized about USD 8.7 billion in arms sales to Taiwan over eight years. In 2001, the Bush administration announced that the annual U.S.-Taiwan arms sales talks would be ended, replaced instead with ad hoc ongoing requests and reviews. The move was intended to depoliticize the process, but appeared to have the effect of causing lengthy deferrals in responding to requests from Taiwanese officials. When Taiwan submitted requests for sixty-six new F-16C/D fighters in mid-2006 and early and late 2007, the Bush administration refused to accept them. In mid-2008, some members of Congress complained that the Bush administration had adopted a policy of freezing arms sales to Taiwan. The administration had failed to notify Congress of requested arms sales totaling over USD 12 billion. In October 2008, President Bush responded to congressional pressure and approved USD 6.5 billion in pending sales.

In April 2011, Congress passed a House concurrent resolution addressing its concerns regarding the state of Taiwan's security.[21] Citing the TRA, members of Congress considered the threats facing Taiwan. These included the PRC's antisecession law, which would permit the use of force against Taiwan, as dramatized by the more than sixteen hundred missiles aimed at the island. The resolution alluded to a report issued by the U.S. Department of Defense, which stated that, "in spite of the ongoing rapprochement [between the PRC and Taiwan], the PLA was continuing its military buildup and missile deployment aimed at Taiwan, leading to a further deterioration of the military balance across the Taiwan Strait."[22] Thus, in light of the foregoing factors, Congress recommended that the President "take immediate steps to redress the deteriorating balance of airpower . . . and move forward expeditiously with the sale to Taiwan of new F-16 C/D aircraft and upgrades of the existing F-16 A/B fleet."[23] On August 1, 2011, 181 members of Congress sent a joint letter to the White House to urge President Obama to sell advanced F-16C/D aircrafts to Taiwan. In the letter, lawmakers highlighted their concerns that "Taiwan was losing its qualitative advantage in defensive arms that had long served as a primary military deterrent."[24] Furthermore, the letter warned that Taiwan's situation could become "quite precarious" within the next decade if Taiwan "retired 70% of its jet fighter force . . . without new fighter aircraft and upgrades to its existing fleet of F-16s."[25] As of 2015, the White House has not approved the sale of F-16s to Taiwan.

The Obama administration has averaged about USD 2 billion in arms sales to Taiwan annually and has notified Congress of more than USD 12 billion in sales under the TRA as of mid-2015. In January 2010, the Obama administration made its first notification to Congress of an arms sale to Taiwan. The deal, valued at roughly USD 6.4 billion, included PAC-3 Patriot missile defense (a follow-up installment from the Bush administration), sixty Black Hawk utility helicopters, high-tech computer system support, various missiles, and Osprey-class mine hunters. Like the Bush administration, President Obama continued to silently pass over notification of the submarine design program and refused to accept a request for new F-16C/D fighters. In September 2011, the Obama administration approved upgrades to Taiwan's F-16A/B fighters for USD 5.3 billion, renewed the U.S.-Taiwan pilot training program, and approved the sale of USD 52 million of spare parts for aircraft. In late 2015, the Obama administration announced a USD 1.83 billion arms sale package which drew immediate protests from China.

Submarines are essential to patrolling the waters around Taiwan, and Taiwan's military officials have long sought U.S. support in building and modernizing their submarine fleet. Taiwan currently has just four submarines, two of which are used only for training purposes due to their age. Taiwan is now seeking to develop indigenous diesel-electric submarines to counter the PRC's growing underwater forces. In April 2001, the Bush administration provided an in-principle approval of Taiwan's acquisition of foreign-manufactured submarines. In April 2003, the tentative agreement was upset in a dispute over the start-up costs to the program and whether some of the ships could be manufactured in Taiwan. The Bush administration was urging Taiwan to focus on anti-submarine surveillance, rather than purchase new ships of its own. In 2006 a two-stage compromise was proposed whereby Taiwan would pay the U.S. to procure a submarine design, and as a second step, potentially procuring and building its own submarines. In January 2008, the U.S. Navy accepted Taiwan's letters of request for a submarine design phase. But the Bush administration did not follow through by submitting notice of the program to Congress. Taiwan's air force has also been pushing the United States to authorize the sale of advance fighter jets such as the F-35. The proposal gained additional urgency after China purchased a fleet of Sukhoi Su-35 jets from Russia. The Su-35's radar is reportedly capable of tracking Taiwan's outdated F-16 jets from a distance of 400 kilometers.

Arms sales to Taiwan are a perennial topic during meetings of high-level officials from the United States and the PRC. In January 2010, the White House approved a major arms sales package, which it stated was necessary to maintaining military balance in the Taiwan Strait. Chinese vice foreign minister, He Yafei, responded by issuing a message to the U.S. State Department via the Chinese embassy in Washington, D.C., expressing "indignation" over the sale, which he said would endanger China's national security and the U.S.-China relationship. Chinese President Xi Jinping reportedly urged President Obama to halt arms sales to Taiwan during a summit in Sunnylands, California, in June 2013.[26] Xi indicated that China would redeploy army units located along its coast if the United States stopped supplying Taiwan with defensive weapons.

The United States must continue to supply Taiwan with arms in support of its national defense in accordance with the TRA. This includes reinstating annual reviews of Taiwan's military needs which were suspended during the George W. Bush administration. Military sales made since the Carter administration have not been without controversy. In some cases, Taiwan has failed to allocate funds for the purchase of certain weapons, while the United States has declined to fulfill certain requests made by Taiwanese military officials. Some U.S. officials have also expressed concerns over the threat of corruption and espionage in Taiwan that could lead to the mishandling of military secrets or technology. However, delays by the United States in supplying much needed arms could send an incorrect signal to China regarding the U.S. commitment to defending Taiwan. Pending sales of fighter jets and submarines should be concluded, and the U.S. military should continue to engage in high-level exchanges with Taiwanese military leaders.

VI. Reaffirm the Taiwan Relations Act

The TRA remains popular with members of Congress and the U.S. people. In March 1999, Congress passed a concurrent resolution commemorating the twentieth anniversary of the TRA and expressing concerns over China's recent military modernization and weapons procurement program. The resolution sought to "reaffirm the United States' commitment to the TRA and the specific guarantees for the provision of legitimate defense articles to Taiwan."

In 2000, Congress considered the Taiwan Security Enhancement Act (TSEA).[27] The bill elaborated that it was in the national interest of the United States to "eliminate ambiguity and convey with clarity continued U.S. support for Taiwan, its people, and their ability to maintain their democracy free from coercion and their society free from the use of force against them." Supporters feared that the lack of clarity on the U.S. position on Taiwan could lead to "unnecessary misunderstandings or confrontations between the U.S. and the PRC, with grave consequences for the security of the Western Pacific region."[28] Additionally, the TSEA sought to enhance Taiwan's security through measures that included requiring the executive branch report on Taiwan's defensive needs; holding positions for Taiwan military officers at the National Defense University and other military schools; increasing technical staff at the American Institute in Taiwan upon the request of the Defense Security Cooperation Agency; and strengthening the defense of Taiwan through the use of combined training and personnel exchange programs, annual reports, and direct secured communications between armed forces of the United States and Taiwan.[29] Though the TSEA achieved a vote of 341–70 in the House of Representatives, the Senate did not take a final vote on the bill, in the face of opposition from the White House.

In 2000, Representative Doug Bereuter cited Section 6 of the TRA in proposing the American Institute in Taiwan Facilities Enhancement Act, which would authorize funding for the construction of a new AIT office complex in Taiwan.[30] The Act's findings included that the AIT played a successful role in "sustaining and enhancing the U.S. relations with Taiwan," and that given the AIT's importance to that relationship, Congress had a "special responsibility to ensure [its] requirements for safe and appropriate office quarters were met."[31] Congress also found it necessary to upgrade the AIT's facility to ensure adequate security and welfare for its American and local employees. President Clinton signed the Enhancement Act into law on May 26, 2000. A new AIT facility is due to open in late 2015.

In a concurrent resolution introduced in January 2009, Congress proclaimed that the president should adopt a more realistic "One China, One Taiwan Policy" that would recognize "Taiwan as a sovereign and independent country, separate from the Communist regime in Beijing."[32] The resolution even suggested resuming normal diplomatic relations with Taiwan and assisting Taiwan's full participation in the United Nations and any other international organization for which statehood was a requirement for membership. On March 24, 2009, a concurrent resolution introduced by Representative Shelley Berkley on the TRA's thirtieth anniversary passed with 124 co-sponsors and strong support from both sides of the aisle.[33]

The executive branch plays an important role in reinforcing the TRA's importance in the trilateral U.S.-Taiwan-China relationship. The TRA is the law of the land, and observers pay close attention to statements made by U.S. presidents to ensure that the TRA receives the recognition that it deserves. For example, in November 2009, President Obama issued a joint statement with PRC President Hu Jintao that alarmed many of Taiwan's supporters.[34] The statement said:

> President Obama on various occasions has reiterated that the U.S. side adheres to the one-China policy, abides by the three Sino-U.S. joint communiqués, and respects China's sovereignty and the territorial integrity when it comes to the Taiwan question and other matters.[35]

The joint statement's failure to include the TRA as a part of the framework that shaped Washington's One China Policy was a first since the Carter administration.[36] Though President Obama referenced the TRA in conjunction with the three communiqués in a subsequent press conference, its elimination in the joint press statement between the United States and China likely "added doubt in Beijing's mind about the U.S. commitment to a peaceful resolution of [Taiwan's] future."[37] In an attempt to ease fears, Raymond F. Burghardt, chairman of the AIT, assured Taiwanese officials and opposition leaders that there "would be no change in the U.S. policy and stance on Taiwan-related issues . . . and that the U.S. would abide by the TRA in helping Taiwan to safeguard its security with continuing arms sales."[38]

The continuation of peaceful cross-strait relations is of utmost importance to the people of Taiwan and China and the world community as a whole. U.S. policymakers should reaffirm and strengthen their commitment to the aims of the Taiwan Relations Act. Members of Congress may wish to do so by speaking individually or as representatives of congressional committees and caucuses, whether as witnesses, speakers, rallies, or guests on political talk shows. As a body, one or both houses of Congress can pass nonbinding resolutions, making declarations of findings and urging the continuation of U.S. policies. Congress may pass bills to strengthen provisions of the TRA or to carry out certain acts in reference to the TRA. For example, Congress may authorize the sale of defensive weapons or commit resources to supporting Taiwan's efforts to join international organizations.

VII. Reappraise the U.S. One China Policy

The U.S. One China Policy derives from the three U.S.-Sino joint communiqués and the TRA, although the policy goes beyond the scope of these documents. The policy can be traced to negotiations conducted by President Richard Nixon and his staff in the early 1970s, prior to the U.S. decision to recognize the PRC as the government of China. The first joint communiqué stated that the United States "acknowledged" the PRC's position "that all Chinese on either side of the Taiwan Strait maintain there was but one China and that Taiwan is a part of China." The Second and Third Communiqués continued the acknowledgment formula. During the Cold War period, when the three communiqués were adopted, the United States tolerated and condoned the ROC regime's reign of terror under perpetual martial law while Chiang Kai-shek clung to the fiction that the ROC was the rightful government of the whole of China. Beginning with the Shanghai Communiqué, the United States left the Taiwan question to be settled by the Chinese on both sides the Taiwan Strait. While convenient as a diplomatic elision, this approach overlooks that the vast majority of the island's people were then, and are today, not Chinese, but Taiwanese. Until the end of martial law in 1987, the Taiwanese people were not permitted to express their collective identity politically or culturally under the KMT's campaign of forced Sinicization. It was not until the adoption of the

Taiwan Relations Act in 1979 that U.S. policymakers acknowledged the separation between the ROC regime and the people of Taiwan, with whom the United States would maintain unofficial relations. The Taiwanese people emerged as a political force after the democratic transformation that began with President Lee Teng-hui's leadership in 1988 and continues to the present. The U.S. One China Policy has yet to catch up with this reality.

In 1998, President Clinton's Three Noes policy declared that the United States (1) opposed Taiwan independence, (2) would not support "two Chinas" or one China and one Taiwan, and (3) would not support Taiwan's admission to the United Nations. In some ways, the Three Noes policy was even more constraining to Taiwan's freedom of action than the acknowledgment formula because of its explicit limitations on Taiwan's statehood. In July 1999, President Bill Clinton described the U.S. One China Policy in the following words:

> We favor the "One-China" policy . . . we favor the cross strait dialogues . . . .
> The understanding [the United States has] had all along with both China and
> Taiwan is that the difference between them would be resolved peacefully . . .
> If that were not to be the case, under the Taiwan Relations Act [the United
> States] would be required to view it with the gravest concern.[39]

U.S. officials have also expressed the One China Policy in terms of maintaining the status quo. In 2001, President Bush—after committing to do whatever to help Taiwan defend itself—stated that "a declaration of independence was not the one China policy, and we would work with Taiwan to make sure that that doesn't happen."[40] In March 2002, Assistant Secretary of State James Kelly said at a conference that the Bush administration would continue to uphold the "Six Assurances," thus implying that there would be "no U.S. mediation and no pressure on Taiwan to go to the bargaining table."[41] In October 2003, then National Security Advisor Condoleezza Rice stated that "nobody should try unilaterally to change the status quo . . . there must be a peaceful resolution of the cross-strait issue."[42] Two months later, President Bush proclaimed, "the United States Government's policy is one China, based upon the three communiqués and the Taiwan Relations Act. We oppose any unilateral decision by either China or Taiwan to change the status quo. And the comments and actions made by the leader of Taiwan indicate that he may be willing to make decisions unilaterally to change the status quo, which we oppose."[43] In April 2004, a State Department official testified to the House International Relations Committee that "the United States does not support independence for Taiwan or unilateral moves that would change the status quo as we define it."[44] The expectation applies to the PRC as much as to Taiwan. In March 2005, Congress condemned the PRC's passage of its antisecession law, characterizing it as a "unilateral change to the status quo in the Taiwan Strait."[45]

In 2009, the Obama administration appeared to fall back on the acknowledgment formula, maintaining that the United States continued to "adhere to the one-China policy [and] abide by the three Sino-U.S. joint communiqués." As mentioned above, President Obama failed to reference the Taiwan Relations Act in his joint press statement with PRC President Hu Jintao in November 2009. The omission was quickly corrected in response to an outcry by concerned officials inside and outside of Taiwan.

As a concrete measure, the United States should reappraise its One China Policy by evaluating whether changes could be made to better suit the reality in Taiwan. Furthermore, the United States ought to abandon its reliance on strategic ambiguity and clarify its stance on Taiwan's international legal status. At the very least, the United States must clearly define what status quo it is defending. The United States should conduct a new Taiwan Policy Review to take into account the latest developments in the Taiwan Strait. Since its last review in 1994, Taiwan has completed democratic reforms, adopted a successful presidential electoral process, and achieved peaceful transfers of executive power in 2000 and 2008 respectively. Proponents of a second Taiwan Policy Review have made the numerous suggestions, insisting that these changes could "result in a more rational policy process and improve communications."[46] These include:

1) More transparent and open interactions with Taiwan at the working level, including visits between U.S. and Taiwan officials in official U.S. government buildings and invitations to Taiwan officials to attend special events such as swearing-in ceremonies;

2) Higher level U.S. government visits and exchanges with Taiwan counterparts;

3) Greater coordination within the U.S. government—including regular interdepartmental meetings involving the Departments of Commerce, Defense, State, and Treasury, among others—on policy and substantive issues involving Taiwan; and

4) More open and active support for Taiwan's participation in international organizations for which statehood is not a requirement, and greater support for observer status for Taiwan in organizations for which statehood is a requirement (such as the United Nations).[47]

The movement toward greater recognition for Taiwan is not limited to the United States. Lord Richard Faulkner, UK Parliament Minister and Baron of Worcester, called in 2012 for "Britain, other states in the European Union, and the

U.S. [to challenge] the so-called 'One China' policy, which has unfairly held back the Taiwanese people from establishing normal friendly relations with the rest of the world."[48] Notably, in 2015, the English government changed the name of its British Trade and Cultural Office in Taiwan to the more representative British Office. A statement from Taiwan's Ministry of Foreign Affairs suggested that the new name signaled potential future developments in the UK-Taiwan relationship.

VIII. Normalize Diplomatic Relations with Taiwan

The continuation of the One China Policy is at odds with the fact of Taiwan's evolution as an independent state. In 1978, when President Carter announced that the United States would derecognize the ROC government, many policymakers expected that the dispute between the PRC and the ROC would be swiftly resolved and that the PRC would emerge as the victorious party. Few could have anticipated the radical changes that would take place on the island or that Taiwan, despite lacking recognition as a *de jure* state, would undergo such tremendous economic and political development. Were it not for the PRC's claims over Taiwan, and the PRC's insistence on suppressing Taiwan's status through big power politics, Taiwan's status as an independent state would likely have been recognized years ago. The disparity between reality and the myth of One China is becoming more and more difficult to sustain. In light of this, the United States and other countries ought to reinstate diplomatic recognition of Taiwan.

The Obama administration has proven itself flexible in the foreign policy arena. In December 2014, President Obama made a surprise announcement that the United States would restore diplomatic relations with the Cuban government for the first time since 1961. Earlier that year, the administration coordinated with the European Union to adopt targeted sanctions against Russia as a result of Russian intervention in Crimea. In 2015, the United States joined a coalition of countries in negotiating a landmark agreement to curb Iran's nuclear development program. In the lead-up to the 2016 Taiwanese presidential elections many observers have noted that the United States appears to be adopting a more favorable stance toward the DPP than that of previous administrations. In June 2015, Tsai Ing-wen was invited to attend meetings at both the White House and the State Department, an honor that was not extended even to Ma Ying-jeou prior to his election. There are a multitude of steps the United States can take to assist Taiwan in its transition from *de facto* to *de jure* statehood. Paramount among these is restoring normalized relations with Taipei.

Normalization would not be an overnight process. The normalization of U.S.-Cuba relations offers a timely example. An announcement that the United States would establish formal diplomatic relations with Taiwan would likely be followed by a period of negotiations over various aspects of the relationship, as was witnessed following the announcement of the re-establishment of U.S.-Cuba relations. As was done with the PRC, the United States could permit the establishment of liaison offices for Taiwan in the United State prior to the establishment of an embassy. The Taipei Economic and Cultural Representative Office, which acts as the representative of Taiwan for conducting unofficial relations with the United States, could be elevated to serve this purpose. What is clear is that the United States cannot continue to treat Taiwan as an appendage of China. Taiwan is, in reality, an independent state which happens to be located in a dangerous part of the world. This is all the more reason to take a strong stance in support of the island nation. Otherwise, the United States risks losing influence in the region over time. Taiwan may eventually have no choice but to align itself with China to preserve its well-being and security, and the people of Taiwan will be in danger of losing their free and democratic society.

IX. Support an Internationally Supervised Plebiscite in Taiwan to Let the People of Taiwan Decide Taiwan's Future

The concluding chapter (Chapter 12) will provide a blueprint for a plebiscite on Taiwan's future. The idea of plebiscite for Taiwan gained a great deal of support in the years immediately after World War II. However, the outbreak of the Korean War and political realities in the Asia Pacific prevented its fruition. After seventy years since the end of World War II, the time has come to clarify definitively Taiwan's status under international law. A plebiscite would offer the people of Taiwan a powerful means for expressing their collective will in accordance with the fundamental principle of self-determination. Moreover, a plebiscite would over the long term benefit the shared interest of Taiwan, the United States, and China, as well as the world community as a whole. For the United States to support such a plebiscite would be the ideal, democratic way to fulfill the central mandate of the Taiwan Relations Act, which requires that the question of Taiwan's future be resolved in a peaceful manner.

From a larger and longer term perspective, the PRC may find a plebiscite as an acceptable alternative to resolving the Taiwan question for several reasons. First, this alternative directly addresses the intractable dispute that is at the heart of the triangular U.S.-Taiwan-China relationship. Second, it is in keeping with the purposes and principles of the UN Charter and international law. It will serve the common interest (common good) in maintaining minimum world order (international peace and security) and facilitating optimum world order (international cooperation in economic, social, cultural, humanitarian, human rights, and other related spheres). It will help move toward a world community of human dignity and human security. Third, supporting the proposal will help project a positive image for the PRC in full view of the world community and all humankind—transcending any concern about face-saving. It would be a good example for China to employ its soft and smart power to enhance its international image, prestige, and respect.

The cost of the alternative, military conquest, is too high, and the result would undermine regional and world order, causing disastrous consequences. The Taiwanese people are too accustomed to freedom and democracy. With the memory of the period of White Terror in mind, the Taiwanese people would not be content to be ruled by an authoritarian foreign power. Therefore, China, for its own sake, ought to renounce the use of force against Taiwan in compliance with the UN Charter. A confident power, let alone one of the permanent members of the Security Council, does not have to resort to coercion or violent tactics. The way to win the goodwill of the people of Taiwan is through the development of a peaceful relationship between neighbors built on mutual respect and mutual benefit.

Through the peaceful and democratic process of an internationally credible plebiscite in Taiwan—whatever the outcome—the future of the Taiwan-China relationship would likely be on a solid footing and with bright prospects. Such a peaceful and democratic experience would facilitate enduring friendship and good relations between Taiwan and China, given their shared cultural, ethnic, and historical backgrounds. When the free, democratic state of Taiwan is affirmed and solidified by the plebiscite, it would mean Taiwan's path toward enhanced democracy, freedom, and human rights protection could continue to grow and flourish without the constant threat of coercion from its giant neighbor. Taiwan's shining democratic example in protecting and fulfilling universal freedoms and human rights would be a huge contribution not only to the Asia Pacific but also to the world community as a whole. Finally, as an immediate neighbor of Taiwan, the Chinese people could be, and should be, the first to benefit from Taiwan's democratic and human rights experience. As China continues to rise, its people sooner or later will realize and demand that China's greatness must not stop at military might and economic wealth. The glory of a "great China" should move in the mainstream of the twenty-first-century human community—bringing the universal values of democracy, freedom, and human rights to the Chinese people. When such a great China becomes a reality, the Chinese people, the author is sure, will take great pride in being Chinese. Many of the overseas Chinese wish and hope that day will come soon.

Notes

1. *See* Joshua Meltzer, *Taiwan's Economic Opportunities and Challenges and the Importance of the Trans-Pacific Partnership*, BROOKINGS INSTITUTION (Jan. 2014), *available at* http://www.brookings.edu/research/papers/2013/09/30-taiwan-trans-pacific-partnership-meltzer.

2. *Id.*

3. Media Release: Taiwan-NZ Pact Attributed to Increase in Mutual Trade, New Zealand Trade and Enterprise, Dec. 5, 2014, *available at* https://www.nzte.govt.nz/en/news-and-media/taiwan-new-zealand-pact-attributed-to-increase-in-mutual-trade/.

4. Su Yung-yao, *ECFA Benefiting Wealthy: Report*, TAIPEI TIMES, Mar. 27, 2011, *available at* http://www.taipeitimes.com/News/front/archives/2011/03/27/2003499218.

5. Mo Yan-chih, *Cross-Strait Service Trade Pact Signed*, TAIPEI TIMES, June 22, 2013, *available at* http://www.taipeitimes.com/News/front/archives/2013/06/22/2003565371.

6. William Wan, *Taiwan's President, Ma Ying-jeou, Plans to Expand Relations with China*, WASH. POST, Oct. 24, 2013, *available at* http://www.washingtonpost.com/world/taiwans-president-ma-ying-jeou-plans-to-expand-relations-with-china/2013/10/24/0e38bb7e-3cbd-11e3-b6a9-da62c264f40e_story.html.

7. Jenny W. Hsu, *Taiwan Moves to Lift Ban on Some U.S. Beef Imports*, WALL ST. J., July 25, 2012, *available at* http://www.wsj.com/articles/SB10000872396390443343704577548543721324470.

8. Republic of China Ministry of Economic Affairs, Current Status of Taiwan's efforts in joining the Trans-Pacific Partnership (TPP), Mar. 25, 2013, *available at* http://www.moea.gov.tw/Mns/otn_e/content/wHandMenuFile.ashx?menu_id=8698.

9. John Liu, *US Cabinet-level Official to Meet Ma*, CHINA POST, Apr. 14, 2014, *available at* http://www.chinapost.com.tw/taiwan/intl-community/2014/04/14/405279/US-Cabinet-level.htm.

10. UN General Assembly, Resolution 2758, A/RES/2758 (XXVI), Oct. 25, 1971.

11. Ben Blanchard, *Taiwan Leader Says Protest-hit China Trade Pact Vital*, REUTERS, Mar. 23, 2014, *available at* http://www.reuters.com/article/2014/03/23/us-taiwan-protests-idUSBREA2M03220140323.

12. *Ma Calls for Early Passage of Services Pact Despite Wang's Pledge*, FOCUS TAIWAN, Apr. 4, 2014, *available at* http://focustaiwan.tw/news/aipl/201404060009.aspx.

13. Stacy Hsu & Rich Chang, *Separate Polls Put Ma's Approval Rate Under 18 Percent*, TAIPEI TIMES, May 14, 2014, *available at* http://www.taipeitimes.com/News/front/archives/2014/05/14/2003590295.

14. Crystal Hsu, *Trade Pact Siege: Majority Opposes Trade Agreement: Poll*, TAIPEI TIMES, Mar. 27, 2014, *available at* http://www.taipeitimes.com/News/taiwan/archives/2014/03/27/2003586647.

15. DEFENSE INTELLIGENCE AGENCY, TAIWAN AIR DEFENSE STATUS ASSESSMENT, DIA-02-1001-028 (2010).

16. *See* Taiwan Policy Act of 2011, H.R. Con. Res. 39, 112th Cong. (2011).

17. RONALD O'ROURKE, CHINA NAVAL MODERNIZATION: IMPLICATIONS FOR U.S. NAVY CAPABILITIES—BACKGROUND AND ISSUES FOR CONGRESS, CONGRESSIONAL RESEARCH SERVICE, at 24 (2014), *available at* https://www.fas.org/sgp/crs/row/RL33153.pdf.

18. Rich Chang, *MND Report Highlights Threat of PRC*, Taipei Times, July 20, 2011, *available at* http://www.taipeitimes.com/News/front/archives/2011/07/20/2003508663.

19. *See, e.g.*, Craig Murray, Taiwan's Declining Defense Spending Could Jeopardize Military Preparedness, U.S.-China Economic and Security Review Commission, Staff Research Background (June 11, 2013), *available at* http://www.uscc.gov/sites/default/files/Research/Taiwan%E2%80%99s%20Declining%20Defense%20Spending%20Could%20Jeopardize%20Military%20Preparedness_Staff%20Research%20Backgrounder.pdf.

20. Shirley A. Kan, China/Taiwan: Evolution of the "One China Policy"—Key Statements from Washington, Beijing, and Taipei, Congressional Research Service, at 40–41 (2014), *available at* http://www.fas.org/sgp/crs/row/RL30341.pdf.

21. H.R. Con. Res. 39, 112th Cong. (2011).

22. *Id.*

23. *Id.*

24. Press Release: Menendez Urges President Obama to Expedite Sale of Military Aircraft to Taiwan, Senator Bob Menendez, May 27, 2011, *available at* http://www.menendez.senate.gov/news-and-events/press/menendez-urges-president-obama-to-expedite-sale-of-military-aircraft-to-taiwan.

25. *Id.*

26. William Lowther, *Weapons Sales to Taiwan Likely on US-China Agenda*, Taipei Times, Sept. 6, 2014, *available at* http://www.taipeitimes.com/News/taiwan/archives/2014/09/06/2003599132.

27. Taiwan Security Enhancement Act (TSEA), H.R. 1838, 106th Cong. (2000).

28. *Id.*

29. *Id.* §3-5.

30. H.R. 3707, 106th Cong. (2000).

31. *Id.* §2-3.

32. H.R. Con. Res. 18, 111th Cong. (2009).

33. H.R. Con. Res. 55, 111th Cong. (2009).

34. Shu-Ling Ko & Hsiu-Chuan Shih, *DPP Unhappy with Obama Comments*, Taipei Times, Nov. 18, 2009, *available at* http://www.taipeitimes.com/News/front/archives/2009/11/18/2003458788.

35. Joint Press Statement by President Obama and President Hu of China, Nov. 17, 2009, http://www.whitehouse.gov/the-press-office/joint-press-statement-president-obama-and-president-hu-china.

36. *See, e.g.*, John Hung, *Uncle Sam Hasn't Abandoned Taiwan*, China Post, Nov. 18, 2009, *available at* http://www.chinapost.com.tw/commentary/the-china-post/joe-hung/2009/11/18/233200/Uncle-Sam.htm.

37. Peter Brookes, *O's China Kowtow: Punting on Security, Trade*, N.Y. Post, Nov. 19, 2009, *available at* http://www.nypost.com/p/news/opinion/opedcolumnists/china_kowtow_JpkM6Xk8ocogXfEFsDvEUO.

38. *Taiwan Expected to Honor Beef Trade Pact*, China Post, Nov. 24, 2009, *available at* http://www.chinapost.com.tw/taiwan/2009/11/24/233930/Taiwan%2Dexpected.htm.

39. Kan, *supra* note 20, at 66.

40. *Id.*, at 71.

41. *Id.* at 73.

42. *Id.* at 75 n.184.

43. *Id.* at 76.

44. *Id.* at 77.

45. H.R. Con. Res. 98, 109th Cong. (2005).

46. Kerry Dumbaugh, Taiwan-U.S. Relations: Developments and Policy Implications, Congressional Research Service, at 18, Nov. 2, 2009, *available at* https://www.fas.org/sgp/crs/row/R40493.pdf.

47. *Id.*

48. Lord Richard Faulkner, *Time for a Fresh Start with Taiwan*, The Diplomat, Apr. 27, 2012, *available at* http://thediplomat.com/2012/04/time-for-a-fresh-start-with-taiwan/2/.

12 Let the People of Taiwan Decide Taiwan's Future

TAIWAN HAS EXISTED in a state of legal limbo since 1952. Neither a territory of another state, nor widely recognized as an independent state of its own, Taiwan has for more than sixty years faced uncertainty about its long-term outlook and its position in the world community. The purpose of this concluding chapter is to recapture and clarify the common interests identified in the preceding chapters and to propose a solution to the Taiwan problem that is consistent with contemporary international law and the objectives of human dignity and human security. At its core, this solution recognizes that the Taiwanese people must be given a voice to express their wishes about the island's future development. This means undertaking a plebiscite on the island's status.

The idea of a Taiwanese plebiscite is not a new one. In the years immediately after World War II, before the Republic of China's (ROC) exile from China, it was widely expected that a plebiscite would take place on the island. The Taiwanese people would have been given the opportunity to decide their own fate in accordance with the principle of self-determination. George Kerr in his book *Formosa Betrayed* wrote of the hundreds of thousands of leaflets that were dropped by Allied aircraft over Taiwan during the last years of the Japanese occupation. The leaflets urged the Taiwanese people to resist the Japanese and, quoting the UN Charter, promised liberation after the war. Before the Kuomintang (KMT) military occupation that began in 1945, many urged the Allied Powers to establish a trusteeship under the auspices of the United Nations that would lead to an eventual plebiscite on the island's status.

These proposals were put on hold, first by the KMT military occupation, then by the outbreak of the Korean War, and more recently by the People's Republic of China's (PRC) persistent efforts to suppress Taiwan's international political identity. As articulated in earlier chapters, the PRC's claim that Taiwan is a part of China is baseless as a matter of both historical fact and international law. Chinese claims over the island should be recognized for what they are: naked territorial ambitions dressed up in the guise of a historical mission. Chinese leaders have never renounced the use of force as a means of resolving the Taiwan question. PRC leaders have maintained for decades that Taiwan is a renegade province and that it may use any means necessary to settle what it asserts is an internal affair. The People's Liberation Army, growing and strengthening its forces, maintains more than sixteen hundred missiles targeting Taiwan. Chinese leaders have longed used the specter of military conflict as a tool for intimidating the Taiwanese people. This tendency was put on display vividly during the Third Taiwan Strait Crisis in 1995 and 1996—on the eve of the first direct presidential election in Taiwan's history. Simultaneously, the PRC has deployed—enabled and encouraged by the KMT—its diplomatic, ideological, and economic resources to soften Taiwanese resistance to the idea of annexation by China and to block Taiwan's participation in international organizations. This strategy is having its desired effect. Threats of military force have cut off the island's move toward independence, while economic policies adopted under the Ma administration have ensured Taiwan's increasing dependence on China. Taiwan is unjustly excluded from the international community, not because its claim to statehood is weak, but because the PRC, enabled, condoned, or acquiesced by other states, has prevented Taiwan from conducting itself as a normalized state. If the present trend continues, forcible annexation in the name of unification may be inevitable, causing irreparable disasters and destruction to regional and global order.

Taiwan is not a piece of property to be bargained over. It is not a chip to be played in a game of power politics between more powerful nations. Its problems are not to be solved by a handful of local political elite without regard for the majority's opinions. Taiwan is the home of 23 million people who possess the preemptory right to self-determination and have thus chosen to live freely and democratically. Taiwan is a peace-loving and economically advanced state. Its people have contributed remarkably to the world community and global culture. Yet the effects of its continued political isolation are manifold and dangerous in a world of increasing globalization and interdependence. Taiwan has been marginalized in the international community while the promises and the purposes of the UN Charter and human rights treaties have gone unfulfilled. In 2009, the U.S. Court of Appeals for the District of Columbia, in its opinion in *Lin v. United States*, had this to say:

> America and China's tumultuous relationship over the past sixty years has trapped the inhabitants of Taiwan in political purgatory. During this time the people on Taiwan have lived without any uniformly recognized government. In practical terms, this means they have uncertain status in the world community which affects the population's day-to-day lives.[1]

The political, economic, and social costs of this trend will only compile over time. The moment has come to disrupt the course of Taiwan's history for the better. A plebiscite offers the ideal means to resolve a long-standing controversy in full view of the world community and all humankind.

I. Plebiscites under International Law

The standard of authority of any government recognized by international law is that it is based on the "will of the people," as enunciated in Article 21[3] of the Universal Declaration of Human Rights. A government cannot claim legitimacy if it fails to consult the wishes of its people in one way or another. The basic postulate that the people's consent provides a basis for sovereignty can be traced back to ancient concepts of natural law, and is a pillar of contemporary international law. The exact procedures for devising the people's will are nowhere prescribed. International law recognizes the legitimacy of a range of political systems, not all of which are representative in nature. In practice the level of consultation required for any decision may vary, depending on the magnitude of the change and other circumstances. A plebiscite may address questions occurring at the level of statutes and other policies or may take on more serious matters at the level of a polity's constitutional structure and processes. At the third and highest level, a plebiscite may address the very existence and survival of a sovereign nation state. A plebiscite of this sort, which concerns the fundamental status of a territory and all of its people, transcends all constitutional and statutory limitations.

A. HISTORICAL DEVELOPMENT

Plebiscites have been used as a means to clarify relationships with other states, endorse governmental changes, or in some cases declare independence. Historically, the use of plebiscites has "marked the curve of general demands for democracy in recent history."[2] The use of plebiscites grew after the French Revolution, but waned during the era of Napoleon and the Congress of Vienna. Plebiscites returned with the resurgence of nationalism and democracy in the late 1840s and, by the mid-1860s, had gained customary authority under international law. Plebiscites before World War I manifested varying features, from the rather informal procedures of the French Revolution and the Italian Unification of 1848–70 to more formal arrangements based upon agreements among interested parties and states. Early examples of plebiscites were in most instances executed by military authorities after having seized a new territory. In some cases the procedures were controlled by the state which stood to gain from a cession of territory. In other cases, particularly where a plebiscite was carried out under a formal agreement, the parties controlling a territory shaped the processes significantly. The conduct and effectiveness of plebiscites improved after World War I with the advent of more refined procedures, most of which were prescribed in the peace treaties following the war. Unlike plebiscites in the pre–World War I era, all postwar plebiscites were conducted under international administration and by secret ballot.

Chapter 4 discussed the authoritative status of the peace treaty under international law and the importance of peace treaties in the disposition of territories in the relative calm following a conflict. Indeed, the establishment of the United Nations has not altered the traditional significance of peace treaties as an authoritative expression of shared policy following hostilities. But the UN Charter did inject a new community policy into territorial changes: the principle of self-determination. Even in the nineteenth century, plebiscites were used to mitigate deprivations imposed on inhabitants in cases of cession. At a minimum, voting allowed concerned populations to express their preferences. In certain cases, treaties mandated that the cession of a territory be premised on the consent of the inhabitants. However, prior to the establishment of the United Nations, the principle of self-determination had yet to become an international guiding star.

The practice of the United Nations to date has made it clear that respect for the genuine aspirations of the people concerned is the ultimate guide for effecting territorial change, and the plebiscite has become a preferred device for determining the future status of territories. In the postcolonial context, Article 76(b) of the UN Charter provided that the progressive development of the inhabitants of the trust territories was to be guided by the "freely expressed wishes of the peoples concerned." Though the provision is not specific on how these wishes are to be ascertained, the plebiscite proved to be a particularly useful modality. In other situations, the United Nations has lent indirect assistance in ascertaining the wishes of a people in a disputed territory. Examples include elections held in South Korea in 1948 after World War II. In Malaysia (1963) and in Bahrain (1970), UN representatives consulted with leaders of the community and organized political groups. The United Nations supervised the elections held in the Cook Islands (1965) and Equatorial Guinea (1968). In July 1962, a bilateral agreement between the French government and Algeria led to a plebiscite on Algeria's future, a subject that was often before the United Nations during the country's war for independence. The United Nations also conducted a plebiscite of sorts in West New Guinea (West Irian) in 1961, though the General Assembly condemned it for procedural weakness. Plebiscites leading to independence in Togoland (1956 and 1968), Western Samoa (1961), Namibia (1989), and East Timor (Timor-Leste) (2002) were conducted under the supervisions of UN missions.

International plebiscites have also been conducted without UN supervision. A particularly interesting case concerning China was the plebiscite held in Outer Mongolia in October 1945. Both the Soviet Union and China were parties to this plebiscite and adhered to the wishes of the Mongolian people, who voted 100 percent in favor of independence from China. The outcomes and effectiveness of plebiscites can vary, but in general plebiscites have proved to be useful as a means for ascertaining the wishes of a population and for the establishment of title in contemporary international law. The essential challenge in each case is to ensure that the political desires of the people concerned are freely expressed.

B. RECENT EXAMPLES

The plebiscite is alive and well. The past several decades have seen a multitude of plebiscites carried out to resolve long-standing questions concerning the status of peoples in practically every part of the world. Plebiscites in recent history have been carried out in a variety of contexts and for various purposes: to settle territorial claims following armed conflict, to affirm or disavow a territory's membership in a political body, and to express the territorial aspirations of subgroups within a polity. The following examples will illustrate the versatility of the plebiscite as a tool of self-determination. The list is not exhaustive, as it is not possible to describe each and every recent plebiscite in detail in these pages.

1. Québec, Canada

The Canadian province of Québec has held two major referendums on the question of sovereignty, in 1980 and 1995. The majority of Québec's people are francophone, and the province, founded in 1867, is home to a vibrant secessionist movement. The movement's members have long advocated for Québec to declare independence from the rest of English-speaking Canada. In 1976, the Parti Québécois obtained control over the provincial government and began preparing for a vote on Québec sovereignty. In 1980, the Québécois people were asked to vote on the following lengthy question:

> The Government of Quebec has made public its proposal to negotiate a new agreement with the rest of Canada, based on the equality of nations; this agreement would enable Quebec to acquire the exclusive power to make its laws, levy its taxes and establish relations abroad—in other words, sovereignty—and at the same time to maintain with Canada an economic association including a common currency; any change in political status resulting from these negotiations will only be implemented with popular approval through another referendum; on these terms, do you give the Government of Quebec the mandate to negotiate the proposed agreement between Quebec and Canada?

The plebiscite's organizers contemplated that a second referendum could be held following negotiations with the Canadian government to permit the Québécois people to ratify the details of independence. Approximately 3.7 million people took part in the 1980 referendum. The measure failed, with 59.56 percent of voters answering "no" to the question. The Parti Québécois attempted a second referendum on October 30, 1995, offering a simpler question, which read: "Do you agree that Quebec should become sovereign after having made a formal offer to Canada for a new economic and political partnership within the scope of the bill respecting the future of Quebec and of the agreement signed on June 12, 1995?" The bill in question, known as the "Sovereignty Bill," would have given the Québec National Assembly the authority to declare Québec a sovereign state and to act as its primary legislative body. More than 4.75 million people, roughly 93.5 percent of eligible voters, turned out for the second referendum. Although the voters once again rejected the proposal, they did so with a razor-thin margin of 49.42 percent in favor and 50.58 percent against.

The 1995 Québec referendum led to an important decision by the Supreme Court of Canada in 1998 on the issue of whether international law permitted Québec to secede from Canada. The court found that international law did not afford Québec a right to unilaterally secede under the circumstances. The court emphasized the tension between territorial integrity and the right of self-determination:

> [I]nternational law expects that the right of self-determination will be exercised by peoples within the framework of existing sovereign states and consistently with the maintenance of the territorial integrity of those states. Where this is not possible, in [certain] exceptional circumstances . . . , a right of secession may arise.

The court described the narrow circumstances under which international law recognizes a right of secession may arise: (1) where a people has been colonized, and (2) where a people is otherwise subject to alien domination outside of the colonial context. The court also recognized, without deciding the issue, that there is debate as to whether international law recognizes a third circumstance that may give rise to a right of secession, that is, where a people is denied a meaningful right to internal self-determination, a right of secession may arise as a last resort. The common denominator among these two or three bases of the right of secession, the court recognized, is the frustration of a people to exercise its right to internal self-determination within the framework of an existing state.

The court went on to apply these standards to determine whether Québec had a proper basis to assert its claim to external self-determination and quickly rejected all three possible grounds. With regard to the third possible basis of a right to secede, the denial of any meaningful form of internal self-determination, the court pointed to the Québécois' access to participation in a democratic political process, their representation in all branches of government, and their ability to pursue economic, social, and cultural advancements. Having found that the Québécois have a meaningful ability and opportunity to participate in domestic political processes, the court concluded that, under the circumstances, a right for Québec to effect unilateral secession would not arise under international law.

2. Kosovo

The example of Kosovo is illustrative of the difficulties of attaining political recognition for a people despite numerous attempts at declaring independence over the course of many decades. Kosovo, a largely autonomous region in southern Serbia, is populated largely by ethnic Albanians. During the dissolution of the Socialist Federal Republic of Yugoslavia in the late 1980s and early 1990s, Serbia, under the leadership of President Slobodan Milosevic, increasingly attempted to exert control over Kosovo. In 1990, Serbia enacted a new constitution and dissolved the Kosovo Assembly, which led the Albanian members of the Assembly to declare Kosovo an independent state. In September 1991, a referendum was held in which 99.98 percent of voters endorsed the declaration of independence and to establish the Republic of Kosovo. However, only one country, neighboring Albania, recognized the outcome of the vote. Tensions intensified between 1991 and 1999 as Serbian and Yugoslav forces occupied the region and oppressed the ethnic Albanian population. The Kosovo Liberation Army began an armed struggle to liberate Kosovo beginning in 1996, which culminated in the NATO bombing campaign against Yugoslavia in 1999. In June 1999, Milosevic agreed to a ceasefire, and Kosovo was placed under the control of the UN Interim Administration Mission in Kosovo, established under UN Security Council Resolution 1244. Subsequent negotiations over Kosovo's status failed to reach an agreement, and on February 17, 2008, the Kosovo Assembly, having been reassembled by the UN Interim Administration, once again declared Kosovo's independence from Serbia. The Republic of Serbia denounced the move, and its National Assembly voted to reject the declaration. As of 2015, more than one hundred UN member states have recognized Kosovo as an independent state, including a majority of European Union (EU) members. Kosovo is currently on the path to becoming an EU member.

At the request of the UN General Assembly, the International Court of Justice rendered an advisory opinion on Kosovo's declaration in July 2010. The court emphasized the narrowness of the scope of the question posed to it by the General Assembly: "Is the unilateral declaration of independence by the Provisional Institutions of Self-Government of Kosovo in accordance with international law?" The court was careful to point out issues that were outside the scope of the query:

> It does not ask about the legal consequences of that declaration. In particular, it does not ask whether or not Kosovo has achieved statehood. Nor does it ask about the validity or legal effects of the recognition of Kosovo by those states which have recognized it as an independent state.

The court was also careful to contrast the narrowness of the question before it, the legality of Kosovo's declaration of independence, with the much broader question considered by the Supreme Court of Canada in the Québec case, the right of Québec to unilaterally secede from Canada, by pointing out that "it is entirely possible for a particular act—such as a unilateral declaration of independence—not to be in violation of international law without necessarily constituting the exercise of a right conferred by it." What the court did hold in its opinion on the legality of Kosovo's declaration of independence was that the practice of states, taken as a whole, has never suggested that the mere act of declaring independence is contrary to international law. Although the court recognized several instances in which the UN Security Council condemned specific declarations of independence, such condemnations were made in reference to the specific factual contexts of each case and did not reflect a general condemnation on unilateral declarations of independence. Perhaps the most significant aspect of the court's opinion was its rejection of the argument that the right of territorial integrity implies a prohibition on declarations of independence. The right of a sovereign state to control its territory does not include the right to prevent a people from expressing their desire for political independence. The court rejected this proposition, finding that state practice over the course of centuries provided no basis for outlawing such declarations.

3. East Timor (Timor-Leste)

The Democratic Republic of Timor-Leste, commonly known as East Timor, is a former Portuguese colony in Southeast Asia. In 1975, the territory gained its independence from Portugal, only to be invaded by Indonesia later that year. From 1976 until 1999, East Timor was governed as a province of Indonesia, although the United Nations continued to recognize it as a non-self-governing territory of Portugal. The people of East Timor faced brutal oppression under Indonesian President Suharto, and more than 102,000 civilians are estimated to have been killed during this period. In 1998, Suharto was forced to resign the presidency in the wake of the Asian financial crisis. Soon after, the Indonesian government entered negotiations with the United Nations and Portugal over the conditions of a plebiscite for East Timor. In May 1999, the parties adopted the Agreement between the Republic of Indonesia and the Portuguese Republic on the Question of East Timor, which outlined the details of the plebiscite to be held in August of 1999.

Voting took place on August 30, 1999. The referendum presented voters with the option of East Timor continuing as a Special Autonomous Region within Indonesia or declaring independence. The options were phrased with two questions:

Do you accept the proposed special autonomy for East Timor within the unitary state of the Republic of Indonesia?

Do you reject the proposed special autonomy for East Timor, leading to East Timor's separation from Indonesia?

More than 98 percent of the territory's approximately 451,000 eligible voters took part in the referendum, with 78.5 percent voting in favor of independence. Paramilitary groups who opposed the referendum responded with violence with the support of the Indonesian military. Thousands were killed, and hundreds of thousands of civilians were forced into UN refugee camps across the border in West Timor. The bloodshed led to an international outcry. On September 15, 1999, the UN Security Council approved Resolution 1264, authorizing a multinational effort to restore order to East Timor. The Australian-led International Force for East Timor was successful in driving out Indonesian soldiers, allowing for the establishment of the UN Transitional Administration in East Timor. The peacekeeping mission oversaw the administration of East Timor from October 1999 until its declaration of independence on May 20, 2002. On September 27, 2002, East Timor became the 191st member state of the United Nations.

4. South Sudan

South Sudan, one of the world's newest states, came into being following a successful plebiscite in 2011 held under the terms of a 2005 agreement between the government of Sudan and the Sudan People's Liberation Army (SPLA). The SPLA, then based in the Sudan's southern region, had been fighting the northern Sudanese government since 1983. In 2005, following a twenty-two-year civil war, the two sides signed the Naivasha Agreement (also known as the Comprehensive Peace Agreement), which ended the conflict and set a timetable for a plebiscite on the independence of Sudan's southern region.

The plebiscite was held from January 9 to 15, 2011. The voting ballot illustrated the importance of tailoring procedures to the needs of the voting population. The ballot featured two simple options—separation or unity—which were given in English and Arabic. Beneath the words were visual representations of the concepts for nonliterate voters, an open hand for separation and two clasped hands for unity. Following a period of public campaigning and education, more than 3.85 million people took part in the plebiscite, with 98.83 percent voting in favor of independence. The entire process was overseen by international monitors including a delegation from the Carter Center that consisted of former President Jimmy Carter, former UN Secretary-General Kofi Annan, and former Tanzanian Prime Minister Joseph Warioba. The United Nations convened a special UN Secretary-General's Panel on the Referenda in the Sudan to help oversee the voting. Other observers were provided by the African Union, European Union, League of Arab States, and other regional and international organizations. The nation of South Sudan was formally established on July 9, 2011, six and a half years after the signing of the Naivasha Agreement. Unfortunately, in recent years, South Sudan has been wracked by violence between government forces and rebel groups resulting in extensive casualties and continued suffering for civilians, especially women and girls. The example, like East Timor, underscores the need for continued vigilance and support from the international community to maintain peace and stability after the undertaking of a plebiscite.

5. The Falkland Islands

A highly relevant example to Taiwan is the case of the Falkland Islands. In March 2013, the citizens of the Falkland Islands participated in a plebiscite concerning their relationship with the United Kingdom. The islands, which are located in the Atlantic Ocean near the coast of Argentina, have been subject to a long-running territorial dispute between the British and Argentinian governments and have been under British rule since 1833. In 1982, the United Kingdom and Argentina fought a brief war over the islands when Argentinian forces attempted to seize them. The British were victorious in the war, and the islanders were made British citizens in 1983, but Argentina continues to maintain its claim to the islands.

The plebiscite was initiated by the Falkland Islands government in response to a request by Argentina to engage in negotiations over the islands' status some three decades after the Falkland Islands War. The islands, which are self-governing, have a constitution whose first chapter affirms the people's right to self-determination. The question posed to voters was: "Do you wish the Falkland Islands to retain their current political status as an Overseas Territory of the United Kingdom?" Voters affirmed the 2013 question with 98.9 percent in favor, with only three "no" votes out of 1,517 total ballots. Argentinian officials rejected the results and urged the United Nations to host talks to resolve the dispute. It may come as no surprise that the PRC has backed Argentina in the dispute. In June 2014, the PRC, during a meeting of the G77 in Bolivia, issued a statement supporting Argentina's demands for continued negotiations over the Falkland Islands.

6. Scotland, United Kingdom

Much of the English-speaking world was held in suspense during the referendum on Scottish independence from the United Kingdom in September 2014. Scotland has been a part of Great Britain since 1707. Since its founding in the 1930s, the Scottish National Party (SNP) has advocated for greater autonomy for the former kingdom. The issue gained prominence in the 1970s, and by the 1990s, the majority of voters supported giving more power to the Scottish Parliament, culminating in the Scotland Act of 1998. The movement for Scottish independence intensified in 2007, with the election of an SNP administration that circulated the draft Referendum (Scotland) Bill and a series of white papers outlining possible scenarios for a plebiscite. In 2012, the United Kingdom and Scotland signed the Edinburgh Agreement, which established the terms for an independence referendum. The Scottish Parliament passed the Scottish Independence Referendum (Franchise) Act on June 27, 2013, with the referendum scheduled for September 18, 2014.

After some deliberation on the proper wording for the plebiscite, the Scottish people were asked to vote on a simple proposal: "Should Scotland be an independent country?" The UK government had agreed that it would enter negotiations for an independent Scotland if a majority voted in favor of the question. However, if the plebiscite failed, then Scotland would remain a part of the United Kingdom, albeit with an enlarged role for the Scottish Parliament. After intense public debates on almost every aspect of the relationship between Scotland and the United Kingdom, including Scotland's role in the North Atlantic Treaty Organization (NATO) and the European Union, more than 3.6 million cast their votes, with 55.3 percent of the electorate answering "no" to the referendum question.

7. Crimea and Sevastopol, Ukraine

The Crimea region of Ukraine offers an example of a plebiscite that failed to gain international recognition due to the circumstances surrounding the vote. Crimea, and locally governed Sevastopol, had been a part of Ukraine since 1954, many years prior to the dissolution of the Soviet Union. More than half of Crimea's population is ethnically Russian, with ethnic Ukrainians accounting for roughly one-fourth of the population. In 1991, following the collapse of the Soviet Union, Crimea held a referendum to re-establish the Crimean Autonomous Soviet Socialist Republic of 1945. The measure was approved with 94 percent of voters in favor. In 1995, Ukraine voided Crimea's constitution. A new constitution was adopted three years later, which gave the Ukrainian parliament a veto over legislation passed by the Crimean legislature. In late 2013, the Euromaidan protests in Kiev rocked the Ukrainian government, leading to the overthrow of President Viktor Yanukovych, who fled the country on February 22, 2014. Meanwhile, armed troops, later revealed to be Russian, moved into the Crimean peninsula and Sevastopol. On February 27, the Supreme Council of Crimea announced plans to hold a referendum on Crimean independence in May of that year. As events intensified, the date of the referendum was moved to March 30, and then to March 16. A simultaneous vote was to be held in self-governing Sevastopol. Voters were given two choices, which were revealed just ten days prior to the referendum day:

> Do you support the reunification of Crimea with Russia with all the rights of a federal subject of the Russian Federation?
> Do you support the restoration of the Constitution of the Republic of Crimea in 1992 and the status of the Crimea as part of Ukraine?

In Crimea, 97.47 percent voted in favor of the first option. In Sevastopol, 96.59 percent voted in favor. On March 17, Russian President Vladimir Putin recognized Crimea as an independent state. On March 18, Russia, Crimea, and Sevastopol signed an agreement to integrate Crimea into the Russian Federation. International condemnation was swift. The United States, European Union, and many other nations declared that the referendum violated Ukrainian sovereignty and was procedurally defective for reasons that included the rapidity of the voting and the presence of Russian troops in Crimea. The UN Security Council voted 13 to 1 in favor of a draft resolution condemning the referendum. China abstained, and Russia vetoed the draft. The General Assembly, however, approved a resolution with support from one hundred members finding the referendum illegal under international law. The United States and the European Union imposed economic sanctions against Russia and the newly declared Republic of Crimea as a result of the events.

The aforementioned examples are only a few of the plebiscites held around the world in recent decades. Other notable examples include Gibraltar (2002), Montenegro (2006), South Ossetia (2006), North Kosovo (2012), Catalonia (2014), and Iraqi Kurdistan (postponed since 2014). It is likely that the use of plebiscites will continue to grow as more of the world's citizens express their political demands, empowered by the dissemination of communications technology amid rising expectations for democratic participation globally.

II. Blueprint for a Taiwan Plebiscite

In 1972, Professor Michael Reisman and I published an article in the *Yale Law Journal* entitled "Who Owns Taiwan: A Search for International Title."[3] In it, we described Taiwan as a type of non-self-governing territory and called for an immediate plebiscite under the auspices of the United Nations to ascertain the wishes of its then 15 million people regarding the island's status. One year prior, in 1971, the ROC was expelled from the General Assembly under Resolution 2758. The United States still maintained diplomatic relations with the ROC, but President Nixon was well on his way to establishing closer ties with the PRC—indeed, 1972 was the year of Nixon's historic state visit to the PRC. The ROC was still a regime in exile carrying out an illegal military occupation, and the Taiwanese people were living under a state of martial law that would remain in place for another sixteen years. The Taiwan Relations Act would not come into existence for seven years. At that time we wrote:

> The Taiwan title dispute has resulted in a rare opportunity for international law, for the lawful solution is plain and its realization is unusually feasible. . . . The primary and most urgent task of the world community is to guard against any unilateral or bilateral attempt to change the status of Taiwan before the wishes of the Taiwanese people have been fully and effectively expressed.[4]

The article described what we believed were the appropriate procedures for a fair and open plebiscite to be held in Taiwan, including the conditions for international supervision and steps to be taken to regulate political speech prior to the taking of a vote. Our proposal took into account the authoritarian milieu of the early 1970s pervading in Taiwan. It also was made at a time when the ROC still had a significant presence in the international community. Although it had lost its seat in the United Nations the year prior, most nations had yet to switch diplomatic relations away from the ROC. The PRC was for the most part an international pariah, still reeling internally from the disaster of Mao's Cultural Revolution. Nevertheless, by 1972, the writing was on the wall for the Chiangs' exiled regime. With the United States shifting course, most nations would soon begin normalizing relations with the PRC. We emphasized that a plebiscite, and a move toward greater democracy, would help repair the image of the delegitimized Chiang regime in the eyes of the world community during this critical transition period.

Conditions today are vastly different from what they were in 1972, and yet, many of our conclusions still ring true today. More than forty years ago, few could have predicted that Taiwan would undergo such a remarkable transformation, from the authoritarianism of Chiang Kai-shek and his son, Chiang Ching-kuo, to a full-fledged democracy on the verge of its sixth open presidential election in 2016. In March 2009, Taiwan's Legislative Yuan ratified both the International Covenant on Civil and Political Rights and the International Covenant on Economic, Social and Cultural Rights—more than forty years after the ROC first became a signatory to the documents. In ratifying the two covenants, the Legislative Yuan made them a part of the nation's laws. Both instruments declare self-determination as a fundamental right for all the world's peoples. The first article of both covenants declares: "All peoples have the right of self-determination. By virtue of that right they freely determine their political status and freely pursue their economic, social and cultural development." These are no uncertain terms. The people of Taiwan possess the right to freely determine their own destiny.

It must be borne in mind that the Taiwanese people are distinct from the ROC exiled regime. During the reign of Chiang Kai-shek and Chiang Ching-kuo this distinction was impossible to ignore. The KMT, through the ROC government, systematically imposed martial law to oppress the local population, denying them equal representation and dampening unpopular opinion through terror and other forms of political persecution. The situation improved rapidly during the presidency of Lee Teng-hui, who opened the government to the Taiwanese and ushered in a host of democratic reforms. By this time, however, Taiwan was already an isolated nation, the ROC having lost its seat in the United Nations, and suffered derecognition by most of its allies. The Taiwanese people have achieved representation in their domestic political system, but they have never been able to express themselves as a political unit in the eyes of the international community. A plebiscite on the island's political status would make Taiwan's democratic evolution more complete.

The recommendations that follow are made in the spirit of the proposals that Professor Reisman and I first offered in 1972, taking into account the evolution of Taiwan statehood since that time amid changing global conditions. These recommendations are tentative in nature and are not iron clad. They are meant as a guide for thinking about some of the issues likely to face a Taiwan plebiscite, taking into account the practices of other countries and with reference to the unique political conditions in Taiwan. A successful plebiscite for Taiwan will require the sharing of wisdom, knowledge, and expertise among all concerned parties.

A. INITIATING THE PLEBISCITE

As illustrated in the examples above, there are various modalities for initiating a plebiscite. Traditionally, plebiscites were provided for in treaties as a means of assessing the wishes of the inhabitants of a territory following a conflict. Later, in the post–World War II era, many plebiscites were established and carried out under the auspices of the United Nations, especially during the period of de-colonization. However, as stated, not all plebiscites need take place with the involvement of the United Nations. Recent examples have seen plebiscites initiated by national or local governments as a way to settle historical grievances or clarify relations with other political bodies. Referendums may even be propelled by grassroots efforts led by private citizens who commit their own resources to the cause of independence.

In the case of Taiwan, there are numerous conceivable options for initiating a plebiscite, two of which are considered here. First, the United Nations could initiate a plebiscite under a General Assembly resolution, ensuring that the process would be carried out with the full support of, and in full view of, the international community. Second, the government of Taiwan could establish a Plebiscite Commission charged with formulating and implementing the plebiscite. The Commission would have responsibility for drafting procedures covering every phase of the plebiscite process, subject to the oversight of a mixed tribunal consisting of Taiwanese and international representatives. Of the two options, the second is the most likely to achieve the desired result and will therefore be sketched out in more detail in the sections that follow.

The first proposal, to seek a UN-sponsored plebiscite, has many political advantages but is the least feasible under current conditions. A plebiscite carried out under the supervision of the United Nations would most likely be initiated by a General Assembly resolution, which, in order to pass, would necessarily enjoy the support of a majority of the world's countries. The participation of UN experts would help ensure that the plebiscite would be carried out according to international standards. The outcome of the plebiscite would be inoculated against many political attacks concerning its legitimacy. However, attaining the support of the United Nations for such an endeavor would be unlikely. With no seat of its own, Taiwan would need to rely on a small group of allies in the General Assembly to lobby on its behalf. It could count on strong, organized resistance from the PRC and possibly even the United States or other permanent members of the Security Council. In the unlikely event that it were to achieve a majority in favor of a plebiscite, there is no guarantee that the PRC or other powers would adhere to the outcome of the vote. The political costs to the United Nations of supporting such a measure would be enormous. The United Nations in its present condition is not the most likely forum from which a proposal for a Taiwan plebiscite would emerge, although the United Nations is likely to play a supporting role in any scenario.

The second proposal involves the creation of a special Plebiscite Commission, an independent body responsible for establishing the plebiscite procedures and monitoring every phase of the plebiscite process. As a locally incorporated entity, the Commission would ensure that the formulation of the plebiscite questions, the voting procedures, and the disclosure of the results would best conform to the interests of the Taiwanese people. It would ensure that implementation of the plebiscite is fair and transparent, and it would operate with the cooperation of international participants representing a wide range of perspectives. To be certain, the outcomes of a national plebiscite may not be readily endorsed by the PRC or the United States, and the results may face challenges domestically and internationally. However it would be the most feasible and the most likely to reach a result in conformity with the wishes of the Taiwanese people.

In recent years Taiwan has broached the topic of popular voting on fundamental political issues. Under Article 17 of the current constitution the people "have the rights of election, recall, initiative, and referendum." In 2003, President Chen Shui-bian proposed a national referendum on a range of topics, including the adoption of a new constitution and Taiwan's membership in the World Health Organization. On November 27, 2003, the Legislative Yuan adopted the Referendum Act outlining the procedures for initiating and conducting national referendums. The Act provides that referendums may be held on one of four topics: the repeal of laws, the adoption of national legislation with a specific purpose, changing major policies of the national government, and ratifying amendments to the constitution. Additionally, Article 31 of the Act states that "the president is empowered to initiate national referendums in the event of external intimidation that poses a threat to the nation's sovereignty." There are topics on which referendums may not be held. The Act defines these as "budgets, taxes, investments, wages, or government personnel affairs." The Act requires that more than half of all eligible voters participate in a given referendum and that a proposal receive a majority of ballots cast—a standard that has yet to be reached in any referendum since the law's inception. Furthermore, the law precludes voting on subjects such as the adoption of a new constitution or official country name. It also requires proposals to be reviewed by a committee whose seats are apportioned according to legislative representation. Because of these limitations, the Act is sometimes referred to as the "birdcage" law. Critics charge that the law was designed to restrict the application of direct democracy. The Act was first put into use during the 2004 presidential elections when President Chen Shui-bian proposed the following two questions:

> The People of Taiwan demand that the Taiwan Strait issue be resolved through peaceful means. Should Communist China refuse to withdraw the missiles it has targeted at Taiwan and to openly renounce the use of force against us, would you agree that the Government should acquire more advanced anti-missile weapons to strengthen Taiwan's self-defense capabilities?
>
> Would you agree that our Government should engage in negotiation with Communist China on the establishment of a "peace and stability" framework for cross-strait interactions in order to build consensus and for the welfare of the peoples on both sides?

In total, approximately 7 million people, approximately 45 percent of the country's 16.5 million eligible voters, participated. This was despite efforts by the Kuomintang (KMT) and other members of the Pan-Blue camp to intimidate and discourage voters from taking part. The public affirmed the first question with 91.8 percent of participants voting in favor, while the second question received 92.05 percent. However, both measures failed since the referendum failed to attract at least 50 percent of all eligible voters.

The Act was invoked again in 2008 when both the Democratic Progressive Party (DPP) and the KMT proposed referendum questions on Taiwan's participation in the United Nations. The DPP-proposed question asked:

> In 1971, the People's Republic of China joined the United Nations, replacing the Republic of China and causing Taiwan to become an orphan in the world. To strongly express the will of the people of Taiwan to enhance Taiwan's international status and participation in international affairs: Do you agree that the government should apply for UN membership under the name "Taiwan"?

The question proposed by the KMT asked:

> Do you agree that our nation should apply to return to the United Nations and join other international organizations based on pragmatic, flexible strategies with respect to the name [under which we apply to and participate in them]?

That is: Do you approve of applying to return to the United Nations and to join other international organizations under the name "Republic of China", or "Taiwan", or other name that is conducive to success and preserves our nation's dignity?

Both questions received the support of a majority of referendum participants, with the first question receiving 94.01 percent in favor, and the second question receiving 87.27 percent in favor. However, fewer than 36 percent of the country's 17.3 million eligible voters took part in the voting.

A plebiscite on the question of Taiwan's status as a normalized state would transcend the existing birdcage Referendum Act because it concerns an extraordinary subject that exceeds the bounds of a national statute. The Act is simply inadequate for addressing fundamental questions about the country's future under international law. Given the need for highly specialized procedures, and, as explained below, the establishment of a special Plebiscite Commission, a plebiscite on Taiwan's status would most likely arise under legislation adopted especially for this purpose. The following sections outline the basic requirements and key considerations for a Taiwan plebiscite.

B. ESTABLISHING A PLEBISCITE COMMISSION

A plebiscite on the status of Taiwan would be a major milestone in the island's evolution as a normalized state. Given the complex internal and external factors that must be managed to successfully undertake a plebiscite in Taiwan, it is recommended that a special Plebiscite Commission be established with responsibility for overseeing every phase of the plebiscite process with the aim of ensuring its fairness, transparency, and procedural legitimacy and integrity. Although the ultimate structure and operating model of the commission may be flexible, certain fixed features are desirable to promote its efficacy and to shield it from undue political influence. The commission will be independent from any existing government agency, and decisions adopted by a vote of the plebiscite commissioners should not be subject to further review or modification through ordinary domestic political procedures. The commission should receive sufficient financial resources, staff, and facilities to ensure its independence and free it from the need to seek additional appropriations. The commission's tenure should be of sufficient length to permit it to carry out its duties—up to and including reporting on and forming recommendations for implementing the outcome of the plebiscite vote.

The selection of the commission's membership is a critical task. The commission should include both voting members, consisting of Taiwanese citizens representing diverse social and professional backgrounds and political perspectives, and non-voting members, consisting of foreign experts from other Asian and non-Asian countries. The commission would be supported by a professional staff including administrators and legal experts on domestic and international law. Non-Taiwanese members, who should not be active members of foreign governments, would represent the perspectives of international governmental and civil society groups and should be permitted to deliberate on every aspect of the commission's proposals, although they would not be granted a vote. All members would be permitted to speak publically both in Taiwan and abroad on the commission's work, including offering reasonable appraisals of its activities. The commission would be subject to the oversight of a plebiscite tribunal consisting of a Taiwanese chairperson and an equal number of respected figures from both Taiwan and abroad, respectively. These could include well-known political and civic leaders, retired governmental officials, and jurists, both international and national, whose expertise and prestige would facilitate acceptance of the outcomes of the plebiscite. The tribunal's responsibilities would include rendering opinions on controversies surrounding the plebiscite and ensuring the commission and other parties adhere to the highest standards of fairness and integrity in the eyes of the international community.

Following an information gathering and public comment period, the commission's members would formulate and vote on procedures for implementing the plebiscite. The procedures, once finalized, should be adopted and implemented expeditiously under the supervision of the appropriate governmental body. Key questions for the Plebiscite Commission would include:

How much time will be needed to prepare for the plebiscite?

What questions will be put to the voters?

Who will be eligible to take part in the plebiscite vote?

What provisions will be made for educating voters and for protecting the right to speech and assembly leading up to the vote?

How will the plebiscite process be monitored to ensure domestic and international transparency?

How will the outcomes of the plebiscite vote be announced, and what will be the Commission's role in recommending steps to implement the outcomes?

1. Formulating the Questions

The Plebiscite Commission would be charged with formulating the options made available to the people of Taiwan through the plebiscite. The questions should be of sufficient breadth to give expression to a wide range of perspectives embracing a comprehensive set of potential outcomes and paths of future development. For example, the following yes-or-no question, which takes account of the evolution of Taiwan statehood over the past three decades, would be suitable for a Taiwan plebiscite:

> Are you in favor of Taiwan remaining a *de facto* country that is free and independent from the People's Republic of China?

The formulation of choices must take account not only of the aspirations of a majority of Taiwanese but also the political interests of outside states, especially those that may wish to challenge the legitimacy of the plebiscite itself. Voters may be asked whether Taiwan should seek closer ties with China. By giving expression to such a possibility, it will become somewhat more difficult for the PRC to denounce the plebiscite. Indeed, it may wish to become an active proponent of one or more of the outcomes, subject to appropriate restrictions on political speech and campaign spending during the pre-plebiscite period.

2. Eligibility for Voting

The commission will be responsible for elaborating voting requirements for those who will take part in the plebiscite. The requirements should be drafted in order to assemble a broad and representative electorate that encompasses all of the Taiwanese people who desire a say in their island's future. The commission may limit the plebiscite to all registered voters or to all ordinary residents of Taiwan. It may declare that all Taiwanese citizens of a certain age are automatically eligible to participate. Provision will need to be made for Taiwanese living overseas. For example, the criteria applied during presidential elections for identifying eligible voters, which include residency requirements for citizens with dual nationalities, may be utilized for the plebiscite. The PRC may insist that "Chinese on both sides of the Taiwan Strait" be allowed to take part in the plebiscite vote. This would include more than a million Taiwanese who live and do business in China, but also roughly 1.34 billion Chinese in China, most of whom have never traveled to Taiwan and have no connections with Taiwan. If this were allowed, what is to keep China from calling for a plebiscite on annexation in any country around the world where large numbers of Chinese people are found? The outcome of a vote under such absurd conditions would do no good in ascertaining the wishes of Taiwan's people. As the purpose of a plebiscite is to gauge the genuine desires of a people, any arrangement that undermines this objective should be rejected.

The commission may find reasons to exclude some populations from the plebiscite. For instance, will the inhabitants of Quemoy and Matsu be eligible to participate, even though the territories are legitimately claimed by the PRC? There are reasons for including these populations. After all, the inhabitants of Quemoy and Matsu do hold Taiwanese passports. On the other hand, the commission may find that the smaller islands would be better served through a separate plebiscite, given their unique geographic and political conditions. Should the plebiscite be open to the 1.34 billion Chinese people living on mainland China in addition to the Taiwanese themselves, as some have suggested? Of course not! If the Chinese leadership would like to have a plebiscite for China's 1.34 billion people, they should start by asking whether the population wishes to continue living under the Chinese Communist Party's authoritarian one-party rule. The plebiscite envisioned in this book is about the future of Taiwan.

3. Public Information

In 1972, Professor Reisman and I concluded that the greatest obstacle to a plebiscite in Taiwan was the risk that the population would not feel empowered to vote according to their genuine desires. We recommended that, after years of oppression and political conditioning, the announcement of a plebiscite, made by and through the government, would be taken as only one more signal to "go and dutifully vote the government line." Therefore, we proposed the establishment of a regulated pre-plebiscite period during which the people could openly discuss their alternative choices and their political inhibitions could be dispelled.

The world has changed significantly since 1972. Taiwan today is home to a vibrant democratic society. The political process is enlivened by the presence of numerous political parties representing a wide range of perspectives and demands. The Taiwanese people enjoy open access to information accessible through a variety of popular media, political talk shows, and personal communication devices. The people are generally well-educated, well-informed, and politically sophisticated. Vigorous debate on matters big and small, from the construction of new stadium in Taipei to the future of cross-strait relations, is a part of everyday life in Taiwan. The danger, as in any democratic society, is that certain parties may attempt to distort information through tactics of monopolization, misinformation, or coercion. Therefore, the commission must establish basic guidelines for conduct leading up to and during the plebiscite, including the means for the dissemination of views and information.

The commission may wish to establish a subcommittee responsible for regulating plebiscite campaigns. To what extent will national media, both public and private, be available for the promotion of viewpoints concerning the plebiscite? Persuasion is to be favored over coercion. The commission must consider methods for ensuring the public receives unbiased information from a variety of sources representing a range of perspectives. The people must feel free and secure to make their genuine choices. Interested nations including the PRC, the United States, and perhaps Japan, as the former colonial power, should be given opportunities to bring their cases to the Taiwanese people, although foreign spending on campaigns should be tightly regulated.

The supervised pre-plebiscite period would continue for a defined period of time, subject to extension by the commission if it should conclude that the purpose of the period—the dissemination of information relevant to the choices and the establishment of a political environment comparatively free from intimidation—has not been achieved. The commission may also wish to limit campaigning for a defined period of time prior to the plebiscite vote or restrict campaign activities in the proximity of polling stations or government buildings.

The Plebiscite Commission, in cooperation with the oversight tribunal, would monitor for harassment or intimidation that might obstruct the freedom of choice. In cases where any party is found to be acting in a way incompatible with the principles of the plebiscite, the commission should report a censure and broadcast it fully in all available media. If the free expression of the people's will is being obstructed, the plebiscite should be deferred or the controversy referred to the commission or oversight tribunal for further appraisal and recommendations. Members of either the Plebiscite Commission or the oversight tribunal should be free to speak on any matter perceived as damaging to the integrity of the plebiscite. The participation and appraisal of civic organizations and other international observer bodies would also be welcome. International media outlets would surely provide extensive coverage of important developments for eager audiences worldwide.

A closely related issue is campaign financing. The commission would be responsible for regulating the use of funds in the pre-plebiscite period. Key questions include the permissible sources of funds used in plebiscite campaigns, the use of taxpayer money, and reporting to ensure the transparency of spending. Considering the vast wealth held and controlled by the KMT, and the even larger resources available from foreign sources, campaign spending must be tightly restricted, supervised, and reported. No party should be permitted to spend unlimited funds in promoting or opposing any of the options. The commission's handling of the issue of campaign spending will likely be of utmost importance in ensuring the integrity of the process, given the large role played by private wealth in Taiwan's electoral scene, as with many democracies.

4. Adopting the Outcomes

A plebiscite should be conducted under international supervision and monitoring within a secure, fair, and free environment. The whole world should be a witness to the proceedings. The commission should invite the participation of regional and international organizations, including nongovernmental organizations focused on human rights. International observers should have broad access to every aspect of the plebiscite process and should be invited to audit and certify the results of voting. The United Nations, which generally does not oversee elections, may wish to establish a special committee to monitor the Taiwan plebiscite, as it did in South Sudan in 2011. The reports and findings of international organizations would help evidence the legitimacy of the plebiscite and would provide useful source materials for proponents of future plebiscites elsewhere.

The outcomes of the Taiwan plebiscite must be communicated freely and openly both internally and externally without undue delay following the vote. A plebiscite in Taiwan would have an immediate and profound impact both domestically and internationally. The most immediate effect would be on the domestic political system. Taiwanese elites, including its political parties and politicians, would be put on notice of the people's fundamental demands and expectations concerning the island's future. The political establishment would have no choice but to heed the demands of the people. A handful of politicians would no longer be able to claim to speak on behalf of Taiwan's population or to evade fundamental questions with expedient appeals to economic or other interests.

III. International Support for a Taiwan Plebiscite

The Taiwanese people are not new to the nation-building experience, unlike the inhabitants of some recently born states. Taiwan is a modern nation home to many valuable physical and human resources. Its population of 23 million people is significant in terms of size and in terms of educational and social development. Over the course of many years the Taiwanese people have been engaged in a process of effective self-determination. While they may not have China's military might, they do have international law and the UN Charter on their side. In an ideal world, where the principles of freedom and human rights always prevailed over naked power, China would not stand as an obstacle to Taiwan's continued evolution. In such a world, Taiwan would engage in normalized relations with diplomatic partners of its choosing. Its citizens and leaders would enjoy the benefits of unfettered trade and open travel. Taiwan would be a member of the United Nations and other international organizations. It would advocate for its own interests on the international stage while supporting others in the development of a more prosperous, safe, and just world. It would continue to serve as a beacon of democracy and human rights in Asia. As demonstrated by the Sunflower Movement, the Taiwanese people are determined to save their country through their own efforts. However, to be successful, they will need international support. Together with others—nation states, intergovernmental organizations, private associations, and individuals—Taiwan can realize the goal of self-determination in furtherance of the ultimate values of human dignity and human security for all. This is not a matter to be left to future generations. After seventy years since the end of World War II, the time has come to break the impasse that has prevented Taiwan from achieving its potential as a member of the world community of nations.

There should be no illusions about the likely impact of a plebiscite on Taiwan's relations with other states. Some nations may not recognize the outcome of the plebiscite or may even seek to undermine the implementation of new policies. Others will show their support directly or through a vote of the UN General Assembly. International jurists may be called upon to deliberate over the effect of a plebiscite on Taiwan's legal status under international law. What cannot be denied is that the outcome of a plebiscite, whatever it may be, would open a new chapter in Taiwan's struggle for continued development as a normalized *de jure* state. At this time, friendly nations must come to the defense of the purposes and principles of the UN Charter and international law. Taiwan's supporters should not be dissuaded from following their legal and moral conscience by expedient calculations or effective power considerations. They should seek to rally the decent opinion of humankind to their cause. In the words of Pope Francis, "Humanity has the ability to work together in building our common home."[5]

China, also, has a role to play. The PRC is often cast as the supreme obstacle in Taiwan's struggle for greater recognition. But as stated in Chapter 11, in reality, the PRC has much to gain by supporting a plebiscite in Taiwan. It is a fact that Taiwan cannot and will not live without China. Taiwan will certainly always remain within the PRC's zone of influence. It will always be vulnerable to pressure from its larger neighbor. But like all other states in the contemporary Asia Pacific—each of which relies on China in myriad ways—Taiwan must have the ability to stand up for itself and to engage its neighbors on an equal footing. This is the meaning of normalized statehood. China, whose leaders are endeavoring to develop their nation's smart and soft power, ought to nurture Taiwan's development as a means of positive engagement from which both the Chinese and Taiwanese peoples will benefit. China's greatness must not stop at military might and economic wealth. Its cultivation of soft power and smart power must be held in equal regard. This is a fact with which China's leaders are only beginning to grapple. The fostering of peaceful cross-strait relations built on the principles of mutual respect and mutual benefit would surely enhance China's prestige in the long term.

IV. Conclusion: Let the People of Taiwan Decide Taiwan's Future

The Taiwanese people exemplify the saying: "God helps those who help themselves." Their island nation's strategic location in the Asia Pacific has been both a blessing and a curse. Taiwan has been a focal point for geopolitical conflicts for centuries. One foreign power after another has tried to exploit the island for strategic gains. Yet it is the Taiwanese people who have emerged as the ultimate victors in their struggle for self-determination, overcoming adverse historical circumstances time and again. In the aftermath of World War II, it seemed that the Chinese Communist forces would launch an imminent attack on Taiwan, while the United States was waiting to "let the dust settle." But the outbreak of the Korean War changed all of that, and President Truman proclaimed the neutralization of the Taiwan Strait. The 228 Incident and the White Terror that followed decimated a generation of Taiwanese leaders. While Chiang Kai-shek and his son's exile regime imposed an unlawful military occupation, the Taiwanese engaged without ceasing in their struggle for self-determination and independence, many working underground or through expatriate communities abroad—especially in the United States, Canada, Japan, Europe, Australia, Brazil, and South Africa. President Carter announced the derecognition of the ROC in 1978, and it seemed that Taiwan would be left adrift and friendless. Then, members of the U.S. Congress acted decisively to defend the shared interests of the United States and the people of Taiwan. The Taiwan Relations Act (TRA) of 1979 declared resolutely that cross-strait relations should be continued peacefully and that the United States would provide Taiwan with defensive weapons to ensure its security. During the twelve years of leadership under President Lee Teng-hui, Taiwan embarked on a transformative process of democratization and Taiwanization. Through their perseverance and solidarity, and thanks to U.S. support under the TRA, the Taiwanese people achieved a remarkable democratic transformation, culminating in the election of DPP's Chen Shui-bian as president in 2000. The KMT lost power after fifty-five years of ruling Taiwan. Remarkably, many of the new leaders were the KMT's former political prisoners who were associated with the Kaohsiung Incident of 1979.

Those who survived the era of authoritarian rule sacrificed much to further the cause of self-determination and independence for Taiwan both at home and abroad. Yet it took many years for a new generation of Taiwanese to become active on the local political scene. Under President Chen, the DPP administration continued to intensify the process of democratic transformation, stressing Taiwan's existence as a free, democratic country separate from the PRC. Chen himself emphasized this by remarking in both Taiwanese and Chinese: "Taiwan, China, one side, one country." This straightforward declaration is often rendered in English as "one country on each side of the Taiwan Strait." President Chen campaigned for Taiwan's membership in the United Nations and to move Taiwan in the direction of normalized statehood.

Progress came to a sudden halt with the election of Ma Ying-jeou in 2008 and his re-election in 2012. During his presidential campaigns, Ma liked to call himself a "new Taiwanese." However, immediately after the election, and especially after his re-election in 2012, he acted in favor of China, effectively betraying his promise of Three Noes—no independence, no unification, and no use of force—by promoting Taiwan's economic dependence on China and calling for a diplomatic truce that would have extinguished any hope of Taiwan's realization of its sovereignty. According to Ma, who has perpetuated the myth of the 1992 Consensus, Taiwan and China have an "area-to-area relationship," rather than a state-to-state relationship, conceding to China's One China Principle, in stark contrast to his predecessors. Indeed, some have charged the Ma administration with beginning a process of Finlandization, aligning Taiwan more closely with China to the exclusion of the United States and other countries. This was most apparent in the adoption of the Economic Cooperation Framework Agreement (ECFA) in 2010 and the hasty push for the Cross-Strait Service Trade Agreement (CSSTA) in 2014. Ma's version of globalization has focused almost entirely on China.

To many in the older generations, the era of Ma Ying-jeou seemed to put an end to the vision of a free and independent Taiwan that had grown under Presidents Lee and Chen. There seemed to be no stopping the trend toward ultimate unification. But the KMT's attempts to force the passage of the CSSTA through opaque "black-box" procedures was a wake-up call for the Taiwanese people. Students, many of whom lacked political experience, realized the danger to their futures and, fearing the prospect of unemployment, began to protest under the banner of the Sunflower Movement. They adopted mottos: "We are Taiwanese, not Chinese," "Taiwan is our country," and "We must save our country through our own efforts." This was a critical moment and a turning point for the island nation. There is no telling how far the Ma administration would have gone had the people not intervened. The movement against the KMT's dangerous policies was sustained through the nine-in-one island-wide elections in November 2014, in which opposition candidates swept to victory throughout the middle and lower levels of government. In January 2016, the people of Taiwan will undertake the first national presidential and legislative elections since the emergence of the Sunflower Movement. For the first time, the Pan-Green camp may have a majority in the Legislative Yuan.

Taiwan still faces formidable challenges. Though at last, the nation's young people are awakened to the importance of politics. Today's younger generations are the most globally aware, well-educated, and technologically savvy of any before them. Their demands for greater democratic participation and self-determination will not go unheeded, a fact vividly demonstrated by the events of the past two years. As stressed throughout this book, Taiwan has evolved from a militarily occupied territory with an undetermined legal status to a state, both sovereign and independent. But more should be done to normalize its status and to enlarge its presence on the global stage. Should Taiwan become a member of the United Nations it would be larger than three-fourths of the other members in terms of population. Its economy would be among the largest in terms of gross domestic product. And its political system would be counted among the most free and democratic. Its participation would enrich the UN system, from the great hall of the General Assembly to the offices of the United Nations' specialized agencies. Taiwan has the resources, human capital, and willingness to contribute greatly to the objectives of global peacekeeping, public health, economic and technological development, and disaster relief. The full potentialities of Taiwan's people should be expressed and put into action for the common good of the world community. Indeed, Taiwan needs the United Nations, and the United Nations needs Taiwan.

The solution to the Taiwan question cannot be based only in pure theory or pure politics. The two need to be conjoined in a workable reality. This is a distinctive feature of the New Haven School of international law. The larger global context of the economy and political scene are brought to bear on every problem. The outcomes and effects are appraised in terms of minimum and optimum world order. Human security and human dignity are the paramount goals. Ultimately, the Taiwanese people should be the masters of their own destiny. In the final analysis what is good for Taiwan should be, and is in fact, good for the Asia Pacific and for the international community as a whole. It is time for all concerned citizens to take a principled stand in favor of freedom and self-determination. Allowing the Taiwanese people to freely and openly determine their destiny would fulfill the promises of the UN Charter and the international human rights covenants. It would bring us closer to a world order based on human dignity and human security. It would acknowledge the reality of Taiwan's evolution as a state.

What will be the future of Taiwan?

Let the people of Taiwan decide.

Notes

1. Roger C.S. Lin, et al. v. United States, 561 F.3d 502 (D.C. Cir. 2009), *cert. denied*, 130 S. Ct. 202 (2009).

2. Lung-chu Chen & W. Michael Reisman, *Who Owns Taiwan: A Search for International Title*, 81 YALE L. J. 599–671, 661 (1972).

3. *Id.* at 599–671.

4. *Id.* at 669.

5. Remarks by President Obama and His Holiness Pope Francis at Arrival Ceremony, Sept. 23, 2015, *available at* https://www.whitehouse.gov/the-press-office/2015/09/23/remarks-president-obama-and-his-holiness-pope-francis-arrival-ceremony.

Suggested Readings in English

American Law Institute. *Restatement of Law (Third): The Foreign Relations Law of the United States*. 2 vols. St. Paul., Minn.: American Law Institute, 1987.

American Society of International Law. *International Law in the Twentieth Century*. Edited by Leo Gross. New York: Appelton-Century-Crofts, 1969.

Anand, R. P., ed. *Asian States and the Development of Universal International Law*. New Delhi: Vikas, 1972.

Ando, Nisuke. "The Recognition of Governments Reconsidered." *Japanese Annual of International Law* 28 (1985): 29–46.

Andrade, Tonio. *How Taiwan Became Chinese: Dutch, Spanish, and Han Colonization in the Seventeenth Century*. New York: Columbia University Press, 2008.

Arsanjani, Mahnoush H., Jacob Katz Cogan, Robert D. Sloane, and Siegfried Wiessner, eds. *Looking to the Future: Essays on International Law in Honor of W. Michael Reisman*. Leiden/Boston: Martinus Nijhoff, 2010.

Bader, Jeffrey A. *Obama and China's Rise: An Insider's Account of America's Asia Strategy*. Washington, D.C.: Brookings Institution Press, 2012.

Bayefsky, Anne. *Self-Determination in International Law: Quebec and Lessons Learned*. The Hague/London/Boston: Kluwer Law International, 2000.

Beato, Andrew M. "Newly Independent and Separating States' Succession to Treaties: Considerations on the Hybrid Dependency of the Republics of the Former Soviet Union." *American University Journal of Law and Policy* 9 (1994): 525.

Blundell, David, ed. *Austronesian Taiwan: Linguistics, History, Ethnology, Prehistory*. Taipei: Shung Ye Museum of Formosan Aborigines, 2009.

Blust, Robert A. *The Austronesian Languages*. Canberra, Australia: Pacific Linguistics, 2009.

Bremmer, Ian. *Superpower: Three Choices for America's Role in the World*. New York: Portfolio/ Penguin, 2015.

Brown, Melissa J. *Is Taiwan Chinese? The Impact of Culture, Power, and Migration on Changing Identities*. Berkeley, Calif.: University of California Press, 2004.

Brzezinski, Zbigniew. *Strategic Vision: America and the Crisis of Global Power*. New York: Basic Books, 2013.

_____. *The Grand Chessboard: American Primacy and Its Geostrategic Imperatives*. New York: Basic Books, 1997.

Buchheit, Lee C. *Secession: The Legitimacy of Self-Determination*. New Haven, Conn.: Yale University Press, 1978.

Bühler, Konrad G. *State Succession and Membership in International Organizations: Legal Theories versus Political Pragmatism*. The Hague/London/Boston: Kluwer Law International, 2001.

Bush, Richard C. *At Cross Purposes: U.S.-Taiwan Relations Since 1942*. London and New York: Routledge, 2015.

_____. *The Perils of Proximity: China-Japan Security Relations*. Washington, D.C.: Brookings Institution Press, 2010.

_____. *Uncharted Strait: The Future of China-Taiwan Relations*. Washington, D.C.: Brookings Institution Press, 2013.

_____. *Untying the Knot: Making Peace in the Taiwan Strait*. Washington, D.C.: Brookings Institution Press, 2005.

Bush, Richard C., and Michael E. O'Hanlon. *A War Like No Other: The Truth About China's Challenge to America*. Hoboken, N.J.: John Wiley & Sons, Inc., 2007.

Cabestan, Jean-Pierre, and Jacques deLisle, eds. *Political Changes in Taiwan under Ma Ying-jeou: Partisan Conflict, Policy Choices, External Constraints and Security Challenges*. London and New York: Routledge, 2014.

Callick, Rowan. *The Party Forever: Inside China's Modern Communist Elite*. New York: St. Martin's Press, 2013.

Cass, Deborah Z., Brett G. Williams, and George Barker. *China and the World Trading System: Entering the New Millennium*. Cambridge, UK: Cambridge University Press, 2003.

Cassese, Antonio. *Self-Determination of Peoples: A Legal Reappraisal*. Cambridge, UK, and New York: Cambridge University Press, 1995.

Castellino, Joshua, and Steve Allen. *Title to Territory in International Law: A Temporal Analysis*. London: Ashgate, 2003.

Chang, Gordon G. *The Coming Collapse of China*. New York: Random House, 2001.

Charney, Jonathan I., and J. R. V. Prescott, "Resolving Cross-Strait Relations between China and Taiwan." *American Journal of International Law* 94 (2000): 453–77.

Charnovitz, Steve. "Two Centuries of Participation: NGOs and International Governance." *Michigan Law Journal* 18 (1997): 183.

Chemerinsky, Erwin. *Constitutional Law: Principles and Policies*, 4th Ed. New York: Aspen Publishers, 2006.

Chen, Lung-chu. *An Introduction to Contemporary International Law: A Policy-Oriented Perspective*, 3d Ed. New York: Oxford University Press, 2015.

_____. "Constitutional Law and International Law in the United States of America." *American Journal of Comparative Law*, Supplement 42 (1994): 453.

_____, ed. *Membership for Taiwan in the United Nations: Achieving Justice and Universality*. New York: New Century Institute Press, 2007.

_____. "Self-Determination as a Human Right." In *Toward World Order and Human Dignity*. Edited by W. Michael Reisman and Burns Weston. New York: Free Press, 1976: 198–261.

Chen, Lung-chu, and Harold D. Lasswell. *Formosa, China, and the United Nations: Formosa in the World Community*. New York: St. Martin's Press, 1967.

Chen, Lung-chu, and W. Michael Reisman. "Who Owns Taiwan: A Search for International Title." *Yale Law Journal* 81 (1972): 599.

Chen, Lung-Fong. *State Succession Relating to Unequal Treaties*. Hamden, Conn.: The Shoe String Press, Inc., 1974.

Chiang, Y. Frank. "State, Sovereignty, and Taiwan." *Fordham International Law Journal* 23 (2000): 959.

Chinkin, Christine, and Alan Boyle. *The Making of International Law*. New York: Oxford University Press, 2007.

Christensen, Thomas J. *The China Challenge: Shaping the Choices of a Rising Power*. New York: W.W. Norton & Company, 2015.

Clark, Paul. "Taking Self-Determination Seriously: When Can Cultural and Political Minorities Control Their Own Fate?" *Chicago Journal of International Law* 5 (2005): 737.

Cohen, Marc J., and Emma Teng, eds. *Let Taiwan Be Taiwan: Documentation on the International Status of Taiwan*. Washington, D.C.: Center for Taiwan International Relations, 1990.

Cohen, Warren I. *America's Response to China: A History of Sino-American Relations*, 5th Ed. New York: Columbia University Press, 2010.

Copper, John F. *Taiwan: Nation-State or Province?* Boulder, Colorado: Westview Press, 2013.

Coppieters, Bruno, and Richard Sakwa. *Contextualizing Secession: Normative Studies in Comparative Perspective*. New York: Oxford University Press, 2003.

Craven, Matthew. *The Decolonization of International Law: State Succession and the Law of Treaties*. New York: Oxford University Press, 2007.

Crawford, James. *The Creation of States in International Law*, 2d Ed. New York: Oxford University Press, 2006.

_____, ed. *The International Law Commission's Articles on State Responsibility: Introduction, Text and Commentaries*. Cambridge, UK: Cambridge University Press, 2002.

Dean, David. *Unofficial Diplomacy: The American Institute in Taiwan: A Memoir*. United States: Mary Dean Trust, 2014.

deLisle, Jacques. "China's Approach to International Law: A Historical Perspective." *American Society of International Law Proceedings* 94 (2000): 267.

_____. "Eroding the 'One China' Policy: A Tripartite Legal-Political Strategy for Taiwan." In *Reshaping the Taiwan Strait*. Edited by John Tkacik. Philadelphia: University of Pennsylvania Press, 2007.

_____. "Law and Democracy in China: A Complicated Relationship." In *Democratization in China, Korea, and Southeast Asia?: Local and National Perspectives*. Edited by Shelley Rigger, Lynn White, and Kate Zhou. London and New York: Routledge, 2014: 126–40.

_____. "Legislating the Cross-Strait Status Quo?: China's Anti-Secession Law, Taiwan's Constitutional Reform, and the United States' Taiwan Relations Act." In *Economic Integration, Democratization and National Security in East Asia: Shifting Paradigms in US, China, and*

Taiwan Relations. Edited by Peter C. Y. Chow. United Kingdom: Edward Elgar Publishing, 2007: 101–39.

———. "Soft Power in a Hard Place: China, Taiwan, Cross-Strait Competition and U.S. Policy." *Orbis* 54 (2010): 493.

———. "Vicious Cycles and Virtuous Circles: International Contexts, Taiwanese Democracy and Cross-Strait Relations." In *Cross-Strait at the Turning Point: Institution, Identity, and Democracy*. Edited by I. Yuan. Taipei: Institute of International Relations, 2009: 373.

deLisle, Jacques, and Avery Goldstein, eds. *China's Challenges*. Philadelphia: University of Pennsylvania Press, 2015.

Dreyer, June Teufel. *China's Political System: Modernization and Tradition*, 9th Ed. New York: Routledge, 2015.

Dumberry, Patrick. *State Succession to International Responsibility*. Leiden/Boston: Martinus Nijhoff, 2007.

Dyer, Geoff A. *The Contest of the Century: The New Era of Competition with China—And How America Can Win*. New York: Alfred A. Knopf, 2014.

Fan, Hua. "The Missing Link Between Self-Determination and Democracy: The Case of East Timor." *Northwestern Journal of International Human Rights* 6 (2008): 176.

Fox, Gregory H., and Brad R. Roth, eds. *Democratic Governance and International Law*. Cambridge: Cambridge University Press, 2000.

Franck, Thomas M. "The Emerging Right to Democratic Governance." *American Journal of International Law* 86 (1992): 46.

Friedberg, Aaron L. *A Contest for Supremacy: China, America, and the Struggle for Mastery in Asia*. New York/London: W.W. Norton & Company, 2011.

Friedman, Thomas L., and Michael Mandelbaum. *That Used to Be Us: How America Fell Behind in the World It Invented and How We Can Come Back*. New York: Picador, 2011.

Galloway, L. Thomas. *Recognizing Foreign Governments: The Practice of the United States*. Washington, D.C.: American Enterprise Institute for Public Policy Research, 1978.

Gong, Gerrit W. *The Standard of "Civilization" in International Society*. Oxford: Clarendon Press, 1984.

Gorman, Robert F. *Great Debates at the United Nations: An Encyclopedia of Fifty Key Issues, 1945–2000*. Westport, Conn.: Greenwood Press, 2001.

Grant, Thomas D. *Admission to the United Nations: Charter Article 4 and the Rise of Universal Organization*. Leiden/Boston: Martinus Nijhoff, 2009.

———. "Defining Statehood: The Montevideo Convention and Its Discontents." *Columbia Journal of Transnational Law* 37 (1999): 403.

Hachigian, Nina, ed. *Debating China: The U.S.-China Relationship in Ten Conversations*. New York: Oxford University Press, 2014.

Halper, Stefan. *The Beijing Consensus: How China's Authoritarian Model Will Dominate the Twenty-First Century*. New York: Basic Books, 2010.

Hannum, Hurst. *Autonomy, Sovereignty, and Self-Determination: The Accommodation of Conflicting Rights*. Rev. Ed. Philadelphia: University of Pennsylvania Press, 1996.

Harding, Harry. *A Fragile Relationship: The United States and China Since 1972*. Washington, D.C.: Brookings Institution, 1992.

Henckaerts, Jean-Marie, ed. *The International Status of Taiwan in the New World Order: Legal and Political Considerations*. London: Kluwer Law International, 1997.

Henkin, Louis. *Foreign Affairs and the United States Constitution*, 2d Ed. New York: Oxford University Press, 1996.

Higgins, Rosalyn. *Problems and Process: International Law and How We Use It*. New York: Oxford University Press, 1979.

Hoffmann, Fritz Leo, and Olga Mingo Hoffman. *Sovereignty in Dispute: The Falklands/Malvinas, 1493–1982*. Boulder, Colo.: Westview, 1984.

Holdridge, John H. *Crossing the Divide: An Insider's Account of Normalization of U.S.-China Relations*. Lanham, Maryland: Rowman & Littlefield, 1997.

Holsag, Jonathan. *China's Coming War with Asia*. Cambridge, UK/Malden, Mass.: Polity Press, 2015.

Hsieh, Pasha L. "An Unrecognized State in Foreign and International Courts: The Case of the Republic of China on Taiwan." *Michigan Journal of International Law* 28 (2007): 765.

Huang, Eric Tin-lun, "The Modern Concept of Sovereignty, Statehood and Recognition: A Case Study of Taiwan." *New York International Law Review* 16 (2003): 99

Jacques, Martin. *When China Rules the World: The End of the Western World and the Birth of a New Global Order*. New York: Penguin Press, 2009.

Jennings, R. Y. *The Acquisition of Territory in International Law*. Manchester: Manchester University Press; Dobbs Ferry, N.Y.: Oceana, 1963.

Kang, David C. *China Rising: Peace, Power, and Order in East Asia*. New York: Columbia University Press, 2010.

Kerr, George H. *Formosa Betrayed*. Boston: Houghton Mifflin, 1965. *Formosa Betrayed*, 2d Ed. Upland, Calif: Taiwan Publishing Co., 1992.

Kissinger, Henry. *On China*. New York: Penguin Books, 2012.

_____. *World Order: Reflections on the Character of Nations and the Course of History*. New York: Penguin Books, 2014.

Knoll, Bernhard. *The Legal Status of Territories Subject to Administration by International Organisations*. Cambridge, UK: Cambridge University Press, 2008.

Knop, Karen. *Diversity and Self-Determination in International Law*. Cambridge, UK: Cambridge University Press, 2002.

Koeck, Heribert Franz, Daniela Horn, and Franz Leidenmühler. *From Protectorate to Statehood: Self-Determination v. Territorial Integrity in the Case of Kosovo and the Position of the European Union*. Cambridge, UK: Intersentia, 2009.

Kohen, Marcelo G., ed. *Secession: International Law Perspectives*. Cambridge, UK: Cambridge University Press, 2006.

Kritz, Neil J., ed. *Transitional Justice: How Emerging Democracies Reckon with Former Regimes*. 3 vols. Washington, D.C.: United States Institute of Peace Press, 1995.

Lai, Zehan, Ramon H. Myers, and Wei Hou. *A Tragic Beginning: The Taiwan Uprising of February 28, 1947*. Stanford, Calif.: Stanford University Press, 1991.

Lampton, David M. *Same Bed, Different Dreams: Managing U.S.-China Relations, 1989–2000*. Stanford, Calif.: University of California Press, 2001.

_____. *The Three Faces of Chinese Power: Might, Money, and Minds*. Stanford, Calif.: University of California Press, 2008.

Lasswell, Harold D., and Myres S. McDougal. *Jurisprudence for a Free Society: Studies in Law, Science, and Policy*. 2 vols. New Haven, Conn.: New Haven Press; Dordrecht: Martinus Nijhoff, 1992.

Lauterpacht, Hersch. *International Law and Human Rights*. Hamden, Conn.: Archon Books, 1968.

———. *Recognition in International Law*. Cambridge, UK: Cambridge University Press, 1947.

Lee, David Tawei. *The Making of the Taiwan Relations Act: Twenty Years in Retrospect*. New York: Oxford University Press, 2000.

Lee, Shyu-tu, and Jack F. Williams, eds. *Taiwan's Struggle: Voices of the Taiwanese*. Lanham, Maryland: Rowman & Littlefield, 2014.

Lee, Teng-hui. "Understanding Taiwan: Bridging the Perception Gap." *Foreign Affairs* (Nov./Dec. 1999): 9–14.

Lemos, Gerard. *The End of the Chinese Dream: Why Chinese People Fear the Future*. New Haven and London: Yale University Press, 2013.

Li, Thian-hok. *America's Security and Taiwan's Freedom: Speeches and Essays by Li Thian-hok*. Bloomington, Ind.: Xlibris, 2010.

Lilley, James R., with Jeffrey Lilley. *China Hands: Nine Decades of Adventure, Espionage, and Diplomacy in Asia*. New York: Public Affairs, 2004.

Lin, Chia-lung, Ming-juinn Li, and Chih-cheng Lo, eds. *Unlocking the Secret of Taiwan's Sovereignty*. Taiwan: Taiwan Thinktank, 2008.

Lin, Tsung-yi, ed. *An Introduction to 2-28 Tragedy in Taiwan: For World Citizens*. Taipei: Renaissance Foundation Press, 1998.

Liu, Mingfu. *The China Dream: Great Power Thinking and Strategic Posture in the Post-American Era*. New York: CN Times Books, 2015.

Macedo, Stephen, and Allen Buchanan, eds. *Secession and Self-Determination*. New York: New York University Press, 2003.

McDougal, Myres S., Harold D. Lasswell, and Lung-chu Chen. *Human Rights and World Public Order: The Basic Policies of an International Law of Human Dignity*. New Haven, Conn.: Yale University Press, 1980.

McDougal, Myres S., and W. Michael Reisman. *International Law Essays: A Supplement to International Law in Contemporary Perspective*. Mineola, N.Y.: Foundation Press, 1981.

McDougal, Myres S., Harold D. Lasswell, and James C. Miller. *The Interpretation of Agreements and World Public Order: Principles of Content and Procedure*. New Haven: Yale University Press, 1967.

Mearsheimer, John J. *The Tragedy of Great Power Politics*, Updated Ed. New York/London: W. W. Norton & Company, 2014.

Musgrave, Thomas D. *Self-Determination and National Minorities*. New York: Oxford University Press, 2000.

Myers, Ramon H., ed. *A Unique Relationship: The United States and the Republic of China under the Taiwan Relations Act*. Stanford, Calif: Hoover Institution Press, 1989.

Nathan, Andrew J. *Chinese Democracy*. New York: Knopf, 1985.

Nathan, Andrew J., and Andrew Scobell. *China's Search for Security*. New York: Columbia University Press, 2012.

Nathan, Andrew J., Larry Diamond, and Marc F. Plattner, eds. *Will China Democratize?* Baltimore: Johns Hopkins University Press, 2013.

Noyes, John E., Laura A. Dickinson, and Mark W. Janis. *International Law Stories*. New York: Foundation Press, 2007.

Nye, Joseph S., Jr. *Is the American Century Over?* Cambridge, UK; Malden, Mass.: Polity, 2015.

_____. *Soft Power: The Means to Success in World Politics.* Cambridge, Mass.: Perseus, 2004.

Oppenheimer, Stephen. *Eden in the East: The Drowned Continent of Southeast Asia.* London: Orion Publishing, 1999.

Osnos, Evan. *Age of Ambition: Chasing Fortune, Truth, and Faith in the New China.* New York: Farrar, Straus and Giroux, 2014.

Oxman, Bernard. "Does the International Tribunal for the Law of the Sea Have Jurisdiction over Disputes with Taiwan?" *Taiwan International Law Quarterly* 2 (2005): 205.

Paulson, Henry M., Jr. *Dealing with China: An Insider Unmasks the New Economic Superpower.* New York/Boston: Twelve, 2015.

Paust, Jordan J. "UN Principles in Theory and Practice: Time for Taiwanese Self-Determination to Ripen into More Widely Recognized Statehood Status and Membership in the UN and the Prohibition of Armed Force Against Taiwan." In *Membership for Taiwan in the United Nations: Achieving Justice and Universality.* Edited by Lung-chu Chen. New York: New Century Institute Press, 2007: 3–18.

Paust, Jordan J., Jon M. Van Dyke, and Linda A. Malone. *International Law and Litigation in the U.S.,* 3d Ed. St. Paul, Minn.: West, 2009.

Peng, Ming-min. *A Taste of Freedom: Memoirs of a Formosan Independence Leader.* New York: Holt, Rinehart and Winston, 1972.

Peterson, M. J. *Recognition of Governments: Legal Doctrine and State Practice, 1815–1995.* New York: Palgrave Macmillan, 1997.

Pillsbury, Michael. *The Hundred-Year Marathon: China's Secret Strategy to Replace America as the Global Superpower.* New York: Henry Holt & Company, 2015.

Quigley, John. *The Statehood of Palestine: International Law in the Middle East Conflict.* New York: Cambridge University Press, 2010.

Ratner, Steven R. "Drawing a Better Line: UTI Possidetis and the Borders of New States." *American Journal of International Law* 90 (1996): 590.

Reisman, W. Michael. *Toward World Order and Human Dignity: Essays in Honor of Myres S. McDougal* (co-edited with Burns Weston). New York: Free Press, 1976.

_____. *International Law Essays* (co-edited with Myres S. McDougal). New York: Foundation Press, 1981.

_____. *Jurisprudence: Understanding and Shaping Law* (with Aaron M. Schreiber). New Haven, Conn.: New Haven Press, 1987.

_____. *International Law in Contemporary Perspective,* 2d Ed. (with Mahnoush H. Arsanjani, Siegfried Wiessner, and Gayl S. Westerman). New York: Foundation Press, 2004.

_____. "Sovereignty and Human Rights in Contemporary International Law." *American Journal of International Law* 84 (1990): 866.

_____. *The Quest for World Order and Human Dignity in the Twenty-First Century: Constitutive Process and Individual Commitment (General Course on Public International Law).* Leiden/Boston: Martinus Nijhoff, 2012.

Rigger, Shelley. *From Opposition to Power: Taiwan's Democratic Progressive Party.* Boulder, Colo.: Lynne Rienner Publishers, 2001.

_____. "Maintaining the Status Quo: What It Means, and Why the Taiwanese Prefer It." *Cambridge Review of International Affairs* 14 (2001): 103–14.

_____. "Party Politics and Taiwan's External Relations." *Orbis* (2005): 413–28.

_____. *Politics in Taiwan: Voting for Reform.* London and New York: Routledge, 1999.

_____. "Taiwan's Best-Case Democratization." *Orbis* 48 (2004): 285–92.

_____. *Taiwan's Rising Rationalism: Generations, Politics, and "Taiwanese Nationalism."* Washington, D.C.: East-West Center in Washington, 2006.

_____. *Why Taiwan Matters: Small Island, Global Powerhouse*, Updated Ed. Lanham, Maryland: Rowman & Littlefield, 2013.

Rogoff, Martin A. "The Interpretation of International Agreements by Domestic Courts and the Politics of International Treaty Relations: Reflections on Some Recent Decisions of the U.S. Supreme Court." *American University Journal of International Law & Policy* 11 (1996): 559.

Roth, Brad R. *Governmental Illegitimacy in International Law*. New York: Oxford University Press, 2000.

Roy, Denny. *Return of the Dragon: Rising China and Regional Security*. New York: Columbia University Press, 2013.

_____. *Taiwan: A Political History*. Ithaca and London: Cornell University Press, 2003.

Rubinstein, Murray A., ed. *Taiwan: A New History*. London and New York: Routledge, 2015.

Sanchez-Mazas, Alicia, Roger Blench, Malcolm D. Ross, Illia Peiros, and Marie Lin, eds. *Past Human Migrations in East Asia: Matching Archaeology, Linguistics and Genetics*. London and New York: Routledge, 2008.

Schachter, Oscar. "The Decline of the Nation-State and Its Implications for International Law." *Columbia Journal of Transnational Law* 36 (1997): 7.

Schell, Orville. *Virtual Tibet: Searching for Shangri-La from the Himalayas to Hollywood*. New York: Henry Holt and Company, 2000.

Schell, Orville, and John Delury. *Wealth and Power: China's Long March to the 21st Century*. New York: Random House Trade Paperbacks, 2013.

Schou, August, and Arne Olav Brundtland, eds. *Small States in International Relations*. Stockholm: Almqvist & Wiksell; New York: John Wiley & Sons, 1971.

Shambaugh, David. *China Goes Global: The Partial Power*. New York: Oxford University Press, 2013.

Shaw, Malcolm N. *The International Law of Territory*. New York: Oxford University Press, 2009.

Sloss, David L., Michael D. Ramsey, and William S. Dodge, eds. *International Law in the U.S. Supreme Court: Continuity and Change*. New York: Cambridge University Press, 2011.

Shirk, Susan L. *China: Fragile Superpower*. New York: Oxford University Press, 2008.

Simpson, Gerry. *Great Powers and Outlaw States: Unequal Sovereigns in the International Legal Order*. Cambridge, UK: Cambridge University Press, 2004.

Sinclair, Sir Ian. *The Vienna Convention on the Law of Treaties*, 2d. Ed. Manchester: Manchester University Press, 1984.

Song, Yann-huei. "China's Missile Tests in the Taiwan Strait: Relevant International Law Questions." *Marine Policy* 23 (1999): 81.

_____. "Managing Potential Conflicts in the South China Sea: Taiwan's Perspective." EAI Occasional Paper No. 14. East Asian Institute, National University of Singapore, Singapore University Press, 1999.

Steinberg, James, and Michael E. O'Hanlon. *Strategic Reassurance and Resolve: U.S.-China Relations in the Twenty-First Century*. Princeton and Oxford: Princeton University Press, 2014.

Sutter, Robert G. *Chinese Foreign Relations: Power and Policy Since the Cold War*, 3d Ed. Lanham, Maryland: Rowman & Littlefield, 2012.

_____. *U.S.-China Relations: Perilous Past, Pragmatic Present*, 2d Ed. Lanham, Maryland: Rowman & Littlefield Publishers, 2013.

Suzuki, Eisuke. "Self-Determination and World Public Order: Community Response to Territorial Separation." *Virginia Journal of International Law* 16 (1976): 779.

Swaine, Michael D. *America's Challenge: Engaging a Rising China in the Twenty-First Century.* Washington, D.C.: Carnegie Endowment for International Peace, 2011.

Syatauw, J. J. G. *Some Newly Established States and the Development of International Law.* The Hague: Martinus Nijhoff, 1961.

Talmon, Stefan. *Recognition of Governments in International Law: With Particular Reference to Governments in Exile.* New York: Oxford University Press, 1998.

Teng, Emma Jinhua. *Taiwan's Imagined Geography: Chinese Colonial Travel Writing and Pictures 1683–1895.* Cambridge, Mass.: Harvard University Press, 2004.

Tien, Hung-mao. *The Great Transition: Political and Social Change in the Republic of China.* Stanford, Calif.: Hoover Institute Press, 1989.

Tkacik, John J., Jr., ed. *Reshaping the Taiwan Strait.* Washington, D.C.: Heritage Foundation, 2007.

Tomuschat, Christian, ed. *Kosovo and the International Community: A Legal Assessment.* New York: Kluwer Law International, 2001.

_____, ed. *Modern Law of Self-Determination.* Dordrecht: Martinus Nijhoff, 1993.

Tucker, Nancy Bernkopf. *Strait Talk: United States–Taiwan Relations and the Crisis with China.* Cambridge, Mass.: Harvard University Press, 2009.

_____. *The China Threat: Memories, Myths, and Realities in the 1950s.* New York: Columbia University Press, 2012.

Umozurike, Oji. *Self-Determination in International Law.* Hamden, Conn.: Archon Books, 1972.

Vagts, Detlev F. "The United States and Its Treaties: Observance and Breach." *American Journal of International Law* 95 (2001): 277.

Waldron, Arthur. *From War to Nationalism: China's Turning Point, 1924–1925.* Cambridge, UK: Cambridge University Press, 1995.

_____. *The Great Wall of China: From History to Myth.* Cambridge, UK: Cambridge University Press, 1990.

Waters, Timothy William. "Contemplating Failure and Creating Alternatives in the Balkans: Bosnia's Peoples, Democracy." *Yale Journal of International Law* 29 (2004): 423.

Weller, Marc. *Contested Statehood: Kosovo's Struggle for Independence.* New York: Oxford University Press, 2009.

Xanthaki, Alexandra. *Indigenous Rights and United Nations Standards: Self-Determination, Culture and Land.* Cambridge, UK: Cambridge University Press, 2010.

Xi, Jinping. *The Governance of China.* Beijing: Foreign Languages Press, 2014.

Yang, Chi-chuan, and Cheng-Feng Shih, eds. *The Taiwan Relations Act at Twenty.* Taipei: International Interchange Foundation, 1999.

Yen, Sophia Su-Fei. *Taiwan in China's Foreign Relations, 1836–1894.* Brooklyn, N.Y.: Shoe String Press, Inc., 1965.

Zakaria, Fareed. *The Post-American World: Release 2.0.* New York/London: W. W. Norton & Company, 2012.

Zhang, Liang, comp., Andrew J. Nathan and Perry Link, eds. *The Tiananmen Papers: The Chinese Leadership's Decision to Use Force Against Their Own People—In Their Own Words.* New York: Public Affairs, 2001.

Zhou, Kate Xiao, Shelley Rigger, and Lynn T. White III, eds. *Democratization in China, Korea, and Southeast Asia?: Local and National Perspectives.* London and New York: Routledge, 2014.

Suggested Readings in Chinese

I. TAIWAN'S INTERNATIONAL LEGAL STATUS IN GENERAL

Chen, Lih-Torng (陳荔彤). *On the Subject of Taiwan* (台灣主體論). Taipei: Lih-Torng Chen, 2002.

Chen, Lung-chu (陳隆志). *The Independence and Nation-Building of Taiwan* (台灣的獨立與建國). New Haven, Conn.: Yale Law School, 1971.

———. *The Independence and Nation-Building of Taiwan* (台灣的獨立與建國). Taipei: Yuedan Publishing, 1993.

Chen, Lung-Fong (陳隆豐). *Taiwan and International Organizations* (台灣與國際組織). Taipei: San Ming Book, 2011.

Chen, Yi-shen (陳儀深), Hua-yuan Hsueh (薛化元), Ming-juinn Li (李明峻), and Ching-shan Hu (胡慶山), eds. *The History and Theory of Taiwan's National Identity* (台灣國家定位的歷史與理論). Taipei: Yushan Publishing, 2004.

Chiang, Huang-chih (姜皇池). *International Law and Taiwan—Historic Retrospect and Legal Reappraisal* (國際法與台灣：歷史考察與法律評估). Taipei: Sharing, 2000.

Chuang, Wan-shou (莊萬壽), ed. *The Theory and History of Taiwan Independence* (台灣獨立的理論與歷史). Taipei: Avanguard Publishing House, 2002.

Committee on Collective Writings of Taiwan Sovereignty Discourse (台灣主權論述論文集編輯小組), ed. *Collective Writings of Taiwan Sovereignty Discourse I* (台灣主權論述論文集-上). Sintian City, Taipei County, Taiwan: Academia Historica, 2001.

———. ed. *Collective Writings of Taiwan Sovereignty Discourse II* (台灣主權論述論文集-下). Sintian City, Taipei County, Taiwan: Academia Historica, 2001.

Committee on Selective Documentary Collection on Taiwan Sovereignty Discourse (台灣主權論述資料選編編輯小組), ed. *Selective Documentary Collection on Taiwan Sovereignty Discourse I* (台灣主權論述資料選編-上). Sintian City, Taipei County, Taiwan: 2001.

_____. ed. *Selective Documentary Collection on Taiwan Sovereignty Discourse II* (台灣主權論述資料選編-下). Sintian City, Taipei County, Taiwan: Academia Historica, 2001.

Committee on Taiwan Sovereignty and One China Discourse (台灣主權與一個中國論述大事記編輯小組編), ed. *A Chronology of Relevant Events of Taiwan Sovereignty and One China Discourse 1943–2001* (台灣主權與一個中國論述大事記). Sintian City, Taipei County, Taiwan: Academia Historica, 2002.

Dai, Tian-zhao (戴天昭). Ming-juinn Li (李明峻), trans. *Historical Review of the Legal Status of Taiwan* (台灣法律地位的歷史考察). Taipei: Avanguard Publishing House, 2010.

_____. *Taiwan's International Political History* (台灣國際政治史). Taipei: Avanguard Publishing House, 2002.

Hsueh, Hua-yuan (薛化元), Pao-tsum Tai (戴寶村), and Mei-li Chou (周美里), eds. *Taiwan Is Not Part of China—History of Taiwanese Nationals* (台灣不是中國的—台灣國民的歷史). Tanshui Town, Taipei County, Taiwan: Taiwan Advocates, 2005.

Huang, Jau-yuan (黃昭元), ed. *The Theory of Two States and Taiwan's National Identity* (兩國論與台灣國家定位). Taipei: Sharing, 2000.

Li, Ming-juinn (李明峻). "Divided Nations under International Law (分裂國家與國際法)." *Taiwan International Law Quarterly*, vol. 10, no. 4 (2013): 41–67.

Lin, Chia-lung (林佳龍), Ming-juinn Li (李明峻), and Chih-cheng Lo (羅致政), eds. *Unlocking the Secret of Taiwan's Sovereignty* (解開台灣主權密碼). Taipei: Taiwan Thinktank, 2008.

Oda, Shigeru (小田滋). "Taiwan as a Sovereign Independent State—Taiwan's Status in International Law (主權獨立國家的「台灣」—「台灣」在國際法上的地位)." *Taiwan International Law Quarterly*, vol. 4, no. 2 (2007): 295–322.

Peng, Ming-min (彭明敏), Chiau-tong Ng (黃昭堂). Chiou-shiung Tsai (蔡秋雄), trans. *Taiwan's Status in International Law* (台灣在國際法上的地位). Taipei: Yushan Publishing, 1995.

Taiwan Association of University Professors (台灣教授協會), ed. *Forum on Taiwan's National Status* (台灣國家定位論壇). Taipei: Avanguard Publishing House, 2009.

_____. ed. *The Republic of China Exiled in Taiwan for Six Decades and Taiwan's International Situation after World War II* (中華民國流亡台灣六十年暨戰後台灣國際處境). Taipei: Avanguard Publishing House, 2010.

Wang, Jing-hung (王景弘). *Big Power Politics and Taiwan: From Cairo Conference to San Francisco Peace Treaty* (強權政治與台灣：從開羅會議到舊金山和約). Taipei: Yushan Publishing, 2008.

II. DIFFERING VIEWPOINTS REGARDING TAIWAN'S INTERNATIONAL
LEGAL STATUS

A. Taiwan's International Legal Status Was Determined a Long Time Ago;
Taiwan Belongs to China

1. KMT's Viewpoint

Chiu, Hung-dah (丘宏達). *Collected Essays Concerning Chinese Territories under International Law.* Rev. Ed. (關於中國領土的國際法問題論集—修訂本). Taipei: Commericial Press, 2004.

Lin, Man-houng (林滿紅). *Witch-hunt, Soul Searching, and the Identity Crisis: A New Theory on Taiwan's Status* (獵巫、叫魂與認同危機—台灣定位新論). Taipei: Li Ming Cultural, 2008.

Ministry of Foreign Affairs, Republic of China (中華民國外交部). *Position Paper on Taiwan's International Status* (「台灣的國際地位」說帖). (Mar. 2010), http://www.mofa.gov.tw/webapp/ct.asp?xItem=40272&ctNod e=1810&mp=1.

2. CCP's Viewpoint

The Taiwan Affairs Office of the State Council PRC (中華人民共和國國務院台灣事務辦公室). *White Paper on the Taiwan Question and Reunification of China* (台灣問題與中國統一白皮書). (Jan. 1993), http://www.gwytb.gov.cn/en/Special/WhitePapers/201103/t20110316_1789216.htm.

_____. *White Paper on the One-China Principle and the Taiwan Issue* (一個中國 原則與台灣問題白皮書). (Feb. 2000), http://www.gwytb.gov.cn/en/Special/WhitePapers/201103/t20110316_1789217.htm.

Zhang, Chunying (張春英), ed. *History of Cross-Strait Relations,* 4 vols. (海峽兩岸關係史 第一卷～第四卷). Taipei: Hai Xia Xue Shu Chu Ban She, 2008.

3. Taiwan Is a Renegade Province of China, Pending a Declaration of Independence

Hsu, Ching-hsiung (許慶雄). "The Legal Status of the Republic of China—Discuss Also the Controversy of Taiwan's Unification or Independence (中華民國之法地位—兼論台灣之統獨爭議)." *Forum on Taiwan's National Status* (台灣國家定位論壇). 210–43. Edited by Taiwan Association of University Professors (台灣教授協會). Taipei: Avanguard Publishing House, 2009.

_____. *Theoretical Foundation of Taiwan Statehood* (台灣建國的 理論基礎). Taipei: Avanguard Publishing House, 2000.

Huang, Chu-Cheng (黃居正). "What Exactly Does Taiwan Claim to Be (台灣主張了甚麼)?" *Taiwan International Law Quarterly*, vol. 2, no. 4 (2005): 241–43.

B. Taiwan's International Legal Status Was Undetermined in the Past;
It Remains Undetermined

1. Taiwan's Sovereignty Belongs to the People of Taiwan

Chiang, Chi-chen (江啟臣). "'One China Policy' and the Legal Position of the Republic of China (「一個中國」與中華民國的法律地位)." *Taiwan International Law Quarterly*, vol. 3, no. 3 (2006): 133–60.

Shen, Jian-de (沈建德). "Taiwan Really Belongs to the Taiwanese People (台灣的確是台灣人的)." *Forum on Taiwan's National Status* (台灣國家定位論壇). 327–34. Edited by Taiwan Association of University Professors (台灣教授協會). Taipei: Avanguard Publishing House, 2009.

2. Taiwan's Sovereignty Belongs to the United States

Hartzell, Richard W. (何瑞元), ed. *Get Out the Chinese Pressure Cooker, and Find Your Own Way to Live with Freedom* (擺脫中國人打壓，走上自己的自由路). (Sept. 2015), http://www.taiwanadvice.com/notify22.htm.

Lin, Roger C. S. (林志昇) *A Key Report on Taiwan-U.S. Relations: Let Taiwan's Status Return to History's Original Point* (台美關係關鍵報告：讓台灣定位回到歷史原點). Taipei: Roger C. S. Lin, 2005.

Lin, Roger C. S. (林志昇) and Richard W. Hartzell (何瑞元). *Taiwan Under the U.S. Military Occupation: Total Repudiation of the Erroneous Controversy about Taiwan's Sovereignty* (美國軍事佔領下的台灣：徹底踢爆謬誤的台灣主權爭議). Taipei: Roger C. S. Lin, 2005.

3. Other

Wang, Yung-cheng (王雲程). "Taiwan's Status and Movement Integration Under the Model of 'Occupation and Exile' (「佔領與流亡」模型下台灣地位與運動整合)." *Forum on Taiwan's National Status* (台灣國家定位論壇). 249–56, 264–65. Edited by Taiwan Association of University Professors (台灣教授協會). Taipei: Avanguard Publishing House, 2009.

C. Taiwan's International Legal Status Was Undetermined in the Past, But Now Is Determined: Taiwan Is a Sovereign Independent State

1. The Theory of Taiwan's Evolution as a State

Chen, Lung-chu (陳隆志), ed. *Plebiscites and Taiwan's Future* (公民投票與台灣前途). Taipei: Avanguard Publishing House, 1999.

_____. "The Road to Taiwan's Constitutional Reform (台灣憲改之路)." *Liberty Times, The Sunday Featured Article*, p. 3 (July 30, 2005).

_____. "Taiwan Marching toward the United Nations (台灣入聯進行曲)." *Liberty Times, The Sunday Featured Article*, p. A4 (Nov. 4, 2007).

_____. "Taiwan's International Legal Status (台灣的國際法律地位)." *Law Forum* 17 (1996): 216–31.

_____. "The UN Principle of Self-Determination of Peoples—The Case of Taiwan (聯合國的人民自決原則—台灣的個案)." *New Century Think Tank Forum* 22 (June 2003): 4–6.

_____. *The Evolution and Regression of the Status of Island Nation Taiwan—Forty Years After the San Francisco Peace Treaty* (島國台灣地位的進化與退化—舊金山和約四十年後). Taipei: Plebiscites Publishing House, 1991.

_____. "Appraising UN General Assembly Resolution 2758 and Taiwan's Sovereignty (檢視聯大第2758號決議與台灣主權)." *Liberty Times, The Sunday Featured Article*, p. A8 (Oct. 23, 2011).

Chen, Lung-Fong (陳隆豐). "Identification of Taiwan's Statehood (台灣的國家認定)." *New Century Think Tank Forum* 40 (2009): 87–106.

Taiwan New Century Foundation (台灣新世紀文教基金會). "Important Statement on 'Rectification of Taiwan's Name: A Fundamental Right of the Taiwanese People' (「台灣正名:台灣人民的基本權利」重要聲明)." *New Century Think Tank Forum* 16 (2001): 4–6.

2. Taiwan as a Newborn State

Koh, Se-kai (許世楷) and Cheng-hwi Lo (盧千惠). Chiu, Sheng (邱慎) and Ching-hui Chen (陳靜慧), trans. *Taiwan, A Newborn State* (台灣新生的國家). Taipei: Yushan Publishing, 2011.

Koh, Se-kai (許世楷). "Promoting the Theory of a Newborn State (「新生國家理論」的提倡)." *The Theory and History of Taiwan Independence* (台灣獨立的理論與歷史). Edited by Chuang, Wan-shou (莊萬壽). Taipei: Avanguard Publishing House, 2009: 90–100.

_____. "The Theory of a Newborn State (新生國家理論)." *Forum on Taiwan's National Status* (台灣國家定位論壇). Edited by Taiwan Association of University Professors (台灣教授協會). Taipei: Avanguard Publishing House, 2009: 302–05.

3. Taiwan Is a *De Facto* State, But Not Yet a *De Jure* State

Ng, Chiau-tong (黃昭堂). *Establish Taiwan's National Sovereignty: From A De Facto State to A De Jure State* (確立台灣的國家主權: 由事實上的國家到法理上的國家). Taipei: Modern Cultural Foundation, 2008.

III. PROBABLE FUTURE DEVELOPMENTS FOR TAIWAN

A. Normalized Statehood

Chen, Lung-chu (陳隆志). "The Road to Taiwan as a Normalized State (台灣國家正常化之道)." *Liberty Times, The Sunday Featured Article*, p. A4 (Oct. 13, 2005).

_____. "Making Taiwan a Normalized State Is a Huge Task Requiring Continuous Efforts (台灣國家正常化是要持續打拚的大工事)." *Liberty Times, The Sunday Featured Article*, p. A4 (Apr. 1, 2007).

_____. "The March of the Taiwan Nation (台灣國家進行曲)." *Liberty Times, The Sunday Featured Article*, p. A4 (July 29, 2007).

_____. "Appraising Different Viewpoints Regarding the Evolution of Taiwan Statehood (剖析台灣國家進化異言堂)." *Liberty Times, The Sunday Featured Article*, p. A4 (Aug. 5, 2007).

Chen, Wen-hsien (陳文賢). "Taiwan's Application for U.N. Membership and Referendum on U.N. Membership in the Name of Taiwan: A View from International Politics (台灣申請加入聯合國及公投入聯: 國際政治的觀點)." *Taiwan International Law Quarterly*, vol. 4, no. 3 (2007): 5–33.

Joint Statement of Taiwan Club, Taiwan North, Central, South, and East Clubs (台灣社、台灣北中南東社等團體連署). "Action Platform for 'Normalization of Taiwan Statehood' (「台灣國家正常化」行動綱領)." *Liberty Times* (Aug. 21, 2007), http://news.ltn.com.tw/news/opinion/paper/149216/.

Li, Ming-juinn (李明峻). "On the International Law Issues in Taiwan's Application for UN Membership (以台灣名義申請入聯的國際法問題)." *Taiwan International Law Quarterly*, vol. 4, no. 3 (2007): 135–66.

Wang, Szu-wei (王思為). "A Brief Analysis of Foreign Countries' Reactions to Taiwan's Referendum on the U.N. (淺析外國對台灣入聯公投之反應)." *Taiwan International Law Quarterly*, vol. 4, no. 3 (2007): 167–92.

B. Neutrality of Taiwan

Akira, Mayama (真山全). Cheng-yi Hung (洪政儀), trans. "Speech: Neutralization of Taiwan and the Laws of Armed Conflict and Neutrality—Some Legal Considerations on Taiwan's National Security (演講: 台灣中立化與武力紛爭法·中立法— 從確保台灣之安全保障觀點之法的檢討)." *Taiwan International Law Quarterly*, vol. 10, no. 1 (2013): 215–30.

Fan, Lloyd Sheng-pao (范盛保). "Neutrality Under International Relations Theory: Ireland's Choice (國際關係理論下的中立性—愛爾蘭的選擇)." *Taiwan International Studies Quarterly*, vol. 11, no. 3 (2015): 63–84.

Hsiao, Hsiu-an (蕭琇安). "The Status of 'Neutrality' in the Changing International Order (轉變國際秩序下「中立」概念的地位)." *Issues & Studies*, vol. 47, no. 1 (2008): 29–54.

Lin, Iong-Sheng (林雍昇). "Austria as a Neutral State—Review on Its International Background (奧地利成為中立國的國際背景)." *Taiwan International Law Quarterly*, vol. 10, no. 1 (2013): 29–52.

Masahiko, Asada (淺田正彥). Ming-hao Yang (楊名豪), trans. "Speech: The Permanent Neutrality and International Law (演講: 永久中立與國際法)." *Taiwan International Law Quarterly*, vol. 10, no. 1 (2013): 189–96.

Peace and Neutrality for Taiwan Alliance (台灣和平中立大同盟). "Position Paper on 'Peace and Neutrality' (「和平中立」說帖)." (Aug. 2014), http://www.pntw.org.

Shih, Cheng-feng (施正鋒), ed. *Understand the Neutral State* (認識中立國). Taipei: Institute for National Development Foundation, 2015.

Shih, Cheng-feng (施正鋒). "The Concept, Theories, and Practices of Neutral States (中立國的概念、理論與實務)." *Taiwan International Law Quarterly*, vol. 11, no. 3 (2015): 1–22.

Wang, Szu-wei (王思為). "Review of the Permanent Neutrality Status of Switzerland from Its Historical Background (瑞士成為永久中立國之國際背景)." *Taiwan International Law Quarterly*, vol. 10, no. 1 (2013): 53–67.

Wu, Chih-chung (吳志中). "Review of Belgian Experience as a Permanently Neutral State (比利時的永久中立國經驗)." *Taiwan International Law Quarterly*, vol. 10, no. 1 (2013): 7–27.

C. Finlandization of Taiwan

Fan, Lloyd Sheng-pao (范盛保). "The Historical Analysis of Finland's Adaptive Politics: Before Finlandization (芬蘭適應政治的歷史分析—在「芬蘭化」以前)." *Taiwan International Studies Quarterly*, vol. 5, no. 4 (2009): 49–67.

Lee, Jyun-yi (李俊毅). "Political Community, Identity, and Foreign Policy: 'Finlandization' Revisited (政治社群、認同與外交政策: 「芬蘭化」概念的再思考)." *Issues & Studies*, vol. 53, no. 1 (2014): 35–67.

Lin, Chong-pin (林中斌). "Has Taiwan Been Findlandized? (台灣芬蘭化了嗎?)." *Wealth Magazine* 338 (2010): 66–67.

Su, Hsiu-fa (蘇秀法). *Europe under the Shadow of Findlandization and Denmarkization* (「芬蘭化」和「丹麥化」陰影下的歐洲). Taipei: Cheng Chung Bookstore, 1987.

Wei, Bai-ku (魏百谷). "A Small Country with Its Powerful Neighbor: Finland-Russia Relations (小國與強鄰相處之道—以芬蘭與俄羅斯關係為例)." *Taiwan International Studies Quarterly*, vol. 6, no. 1 (2013): 95–116.

Wu, Yu-shan (吳玉山). *Balancing or Bandwagoning: Cross-Straits Relations Revisited* (抗衡或扈從：兩岸關係新詮). Taipei: Cheng Chung Bookstore, 1997.

Yen, Chen-shen (嚴震生). "A Comparative Study of the Historical Experience of Finlandization and Cross-Strait Relations between Taiwan and Mainland China (「芬蘭化」的歷史經驗與兩岸關係發展之比較)." *Issues & Studies*, vol. 34, no. 12 (1995): 73–83.

Chang, Ya-chung (張亞中). *The Rise of a Small Country: The Key Decisions on the Turning Point* (小國崛起：轉捩點上的關鍵抉擇). Taipei: Linking Publishing, 2008.

D. Taiwan as a Part of the United States

Hsieh, Wen-hua (謝文華). "The Case of Roger Lin v. United States Has Been Dismissed (林志昇控美案遭駁回)." *Liberty Times* (Oct. 9, 2009), http://news.ltn.com.tw/news/politics/paper/340712.

Lin, Roger C. S. (林志昇). "Statement of the Taiwan Civil Government Concerning Taiwan's Status (台灣民政府對台灣地位的聲明)." *Taiwan Civil Government Web* (May 12, 2004), http://usmgtcg.ning.com/forum/topics/2014-5-12.

E. Unification with China

1. Armed Liberation of Taiwan

Standing Committee of the National People's Congress of the People's Republic of China (中國人大常務委員會). "National Security Law of the People's Republic of China (中華人民共和國國家安全法)" (July 1, 2015), http://www.lawinfochina.com, http://en.pkulaw.cn/display.aspx?cgid=250527&lib=law.

The National People's Congress of the People's Republic of China (中華人民共和國全國人民代表大會). "Anti-Secession Law (反分裂國家法)." *Taiwan Affairs Office of the State Council PRC* (Mar. 14, 2005), http://www.gwytb.gov.cn/en/Special/OneChinaPrinciple/201103/t20110317_1790121.htm.

2. Peaceful Liberation of Taiwan

Deng, Xaio-ping (鄧小平). "Six Conceptions for the Peaceful Reunification (中國大陸和台灣和平統一設想—鄧六條)." Taiwan Affairs Office of the State Council PRC (June 26, 1983), http://www.gwytb.gov.cn/en/Special/OneChinaPrinciple/201103/t20110317_1790064.htm.

Hu, Jin-tao (胡錦濤). "Let Us Join Hands to Promote the Peaceful Development of Cross-Straits Relations and Strive with a United Resolve for the Great Rejuvenation of the Chinese Nation (攜手推動兩岸關係和平發展同心實現中華民族偉大復興—胡六點)." Taiwan Affairs Office of the State Council PRC (Dec. 31, 2008), http://www.gwytb.gov.cn/en/Special/Hu/201103/t20110322_1794707.htm.

Jiang, Ze-min (江澤民). "Continuing to Strive Toward the Reunification of China (為促進祖國統一大業的完成繼續奮鬥—江八點)." Taiwan Affairs Office of the State Council PRC (Jan. 30, 1995), http://www.gwytb.gov.cn/en/Special/Jiang/201103/t20110316_1789198.htm.

Standing Committee of the National People's Congress of the People's Republic of China (中國人大常務委員會), "Message to Compatriots in Taiwan (告台灣同胞書)." China.org.cn (Jan. 1, 1979).

The Editorial Department of the Journalist (新新聞編輯部). "Full Text of Remarks by Two Leaders on Both Sides of the Strait (「馬習會」兩岸領導人致辭全文)." *The Journalist* 1497 (2015): 26–27.

The Taiwan Affairs Office of the State Council PRC (中華人民共和國國務院台灣事務辦公室). "*White Paper on the One-China Principle and the Taiwan Issue* (一個中國原則與台灣問題白皮書)." (Feb. 2000), http://www.gwytb.gov.cn/en/Special/WhitePapers/201103/t20110316_1789217.htm.

Ye, Jian-ying (葉劍英). "Ye Jian-ying on Taiwan's Return to Motherland and Peaceful Reunification (對台灣同胞的講話—葉九條)." Taiwan Affairs Office of the State Council PRC (Sept. 30, 1981), http://www.gwytb.gov.cn/en/Special/OneChinaPrinciple/201103/t20110317_1790062.htm.

3. One Country, Two Systems (Hong Kong Model)

Lee, Ming-hsuan (李明軒). "What Has Happened to Hong Kong's Reversion?—The Cost of 'One Country, Two Systems' (香港回歸為何變調?—一國兩制的代價)." *CommonWealth* 557 (2014): 66–76.

Leung, Man-to (梁文韜). "The Rise and Fall of Hong Kong, the Pearl of the East (香港東方之珠的興衰)." *Taiwan People News*, 2 (2014): 14–7.

The Government of the Hong Kong Special Administrative Region (香港特別行政區政府). "The Basic Law (基本法)." *The Government of the Hong Kong Special Administrative Region* (Apr. 4, 1990), http://www.basiclaw.gov.hk/en/facts/index.html.

_____. "Joint Declaration of the Government of the United Kingdom of Great Britain and Northern Ireland and the Government of the People's Republic of China on the Question of Hong Kong (中英聯合聲明)." (Dec. 19, 1984), http://www.cmab.gov.hk/tc/issues/jd2.htm.

The State Council of the PRC (中國國務院), *White Paper on the Practice of the "One Country, Two Systems" Policy in the Hong Kong Special Administrative Region* (《「一國兩制」在香港特別行政區的實踐》白皮書). English.gov.cn (June 10, 2014), http://english.gov.cn/archive.white_paper/2014/08/23/content_281474982986578.htm.

4. A Great China Structure

Chang, Ya-chung (張亞中), ed. *One China with Joint Expressions or One China with Separate Interpretations: An Account of the Debate Between the Cross-Strait Unification Association and the United Daily News* (一中同表或一中各表: 記兩岸統合學會與聯合報的辯論). Taipei: Sheng-Chih Book, 2010.

Chang, Ya-chung (張亞中). *Cross-Straits Integration Theory* (兩岸統合論). Taipei: Sheng-Chih Book, 2000.

Su, Chi (蘇起) and An-kao Cheng (鄭安國), eds. *"One China, with Respective Interpretations"*— *A Historical Account of the Consensus of 1992* (「一個中國，各自表述」共識的史實). Taipei: National Policy Foundation, 2002.

Su, Chi (蘇起). *An Account of the Ups and Downs of the Twenty-year Cross-Strait Relations* (兩岸波濤二十年紀實). Taipei: Global Views, 2014.

_____. *On the Brink of Danger: From the Two-State Theory to One Side One Country* (危險邊緣：從兩國論到一邊一國). Taipei: Commonwealth Publishing, 2003.

5. KMT-CCP Peace Agreement; Political Transaction; Buy Taiwan with Money

Chang, Ya-chung (張亞中). "The 'Cross-Taiwan Strait Basic Agreement' and the Future of Taiwan and Mainland China (兩岸未來：有關簽署《兩岸基礎協定》的思考)." *Issues and Studies*, vol. 38, no. 9 (1999): 1–29.

Lo, Chih-cheng (羅致政). "The Analysis of the International Laws and Politics of Cross-Strait Peace Agreement (兩岸和平協定的國際法政研析)." *Taiwan International Law Quarterly*, vol. 5, no. 4 (2008): 25–62.

National Policy Foundation (國家政策研究基金會). "Lien-Hu Joint Announcement (連胡會新聞公報)." (Apr. 29, 2005), http://old.npf.org.tw/Symposium/s94/940615-3-NS.htm.

F. Perpetuation of the Status Quo

Chen, Lung-chu (陳隆志). "What Does 'Status Quo' Stand For? (維持獨立於中國之外的現狀)." *Taipei Times*, p. 8 (Oct. 2, 2015).

Hsiao, Hsin-huang (蕭新煌). "Anti-Unification Means the Maintenance of the Status Quo (反統一就是維持現狀)." *Liberty Times*, p. A14 (Aug. 10, 2015).

_____. "Don't Distort the True Meaning of Maintaining the Status Quo (不容扭曲「維持現狀」的真諦)." *Liberty Times*, p. A14 (Mar. 2, 2015).

Keng, Shu (耿曙), Jia-wei Liu (劉嘉薇), and Lu-hui Chen (陳陸輝). "Between Principle and Pragmatism: The Unification-Independence Choice of the Taiwanese People (打破維持現狀的迷思：台灣民眾統獨抉擇中理念與務實的兩難)." *Taiwan Political Science Review*, vol. 13, no. 2 (2009): 3–56.

Leung, Man-to (梁文韜). "Defining the Dynamic 'Status Quo' (美、中博奕下難以維持的現狀)." *Taipei Times*, p. 8 (July 8, 2015).

Soong, Hseik-Wen (宋學文). "Elaborating the Meaning of 'Maintaining the Status Quo' and Its Implications towards Taiwan's Future: A Muddling-through Approach of Dynamic Equilibrium (闡述「維持現狀」對台灣前途之意涵—動態平衡的模糊過渡途徑)." *Taiwan Democracy Quarterly*, vol. 1, no. 2 (2004): 167–91.

Tsai, Ing-wen (蔡英文). "DPP China Affairs Committee: Maintain Cross-Strait Status Quo (民主進步黨中國事務委員會第二次會議新聞稿)." Democratic Progressive Party (Apr. 10, 2015), http://english.dpp.org.tw/dpp-china-affairs-committee/.

Text of Selected Documents

Selections from key documents cited throughout the book are provided here for the reader's convenience and ease of reference. Full versions of each document are widely available on the Internet at the citations provided here or through popular search tools and electronic libraries.

Taiwan Relations Act
(H.R. 2479; Public Law 96-8 98th Congress) (Excerpt)
January 1, 1979[1]

AN ACT

To help maintain peace, security, and stability in the Western Pacific and to promote the foreign policy of the United States by authorizing the continuation of commercial, cultural, and other relations between the people of the United States and the people on Taiwan, and for other purposes.

Be it enacted by the Senate and House of Representatives of the United States of America in Congress assembled,

SHORT TITLE

Section 1. This Act may be cited as the "Taiwan Relations Act".

FINDINGS AND DECLARATION OF POLICY

Section. 2.

    a. The President-having terminated governmental relations between the United States and the governing authorities on Taiwan recognized by the United States as the Republic of China prior to January 1, 1979, the Congress finds that the enactment of this Act is necessary—

1. to help maintain peace, security, and stability in the Western Pacific; and
2. to promote the foreign policy of the United States by authorizing the continuation of commercial, cultural, and other relations between the people of the United States and the people on Taiwan.

b. It is the policy of the United States—

1. to preserve and promote extensive, close, and friendly commercial, cultural, and other relations between the people of the United States and the people on Taiwan, as well as the people on the China mainland and all other peoples of the Western Pacific area;
2. to declare that peace and stability in the area are in the political, security, and economic interests of the United States, and are matters of international concern;
3. to make clear that the United States decision to establish diplomatic relations with the People's Republic of China rests upon the expectation that the future of Taiwan will be determined by peaceful means;
4. to consider any effort to determine the future of Taiwan by other than peaceful means, including by boycotts or embargoes, a threat to the peace and security of the Western Pacific area and of grave concern to the United States;
5. to provide Taiwan with arms of a defensive character; and
6. to maintain the capacity of the United States to resist any resort to force or other forms of coercion that would jeopardize the security, or the social or economic system, of the people on Taiwan.

c. Nothing contained in this Act shall contravene the interest of the United States in human rights, especially with respect to the human rights of all the approximately eighteen million inhabitants of Taiwan. The preservation and enhancement of the human rights of all the people on Taiwan are hereby reaffirmed as objectives of the United States.

IMPLEMENTATION OF UNITED STATES POLICY WITH REGARD TO TAIWAN

Section. 3.

a. In furtherance of the policy set forth in section 2 of this Act, the United States will make available to Taiwan such defense articles and defense services in such quantity as may be necessary to enable Taiwan to maintain a sufficient self-defense capability.
b. The President and the Congress shall determine the nature and quantity of such defense articles and services based solely upon their judgment of the needs of Taiwan, in accordance with procedures established by law. Such determination of Taiwan's defense needs shall include review by United States military authorities in connection with recommendations to the President and the Congress.
c. The President is directed to inform the Congress promptly of any threat to the security or the social or economic system of the people on Taiwan and any danger to the interests of the United States arising therefrom. The President and the Congress shall determine, in accordance with constitutional processes, appropriate action by the United States in response to any such danger.

APPLICATION OF LAWS; INTERNATIONAL AGREEMENTS

Section. 4.

a. The absence of diplomatic relations or recognition shall not affect the application of the laws of the United States with respect to Taiwan, and the laws of the United States shall apply with respect to Taiwan in the manner that the laws of the United States applied with respect to Taiwan prior to January 1, 1979.

b. The application of subsection (a) of this section shall include, but shall not be limited to, the following:

   1. Whenever the laws of the United States refer or relate to foreign countries, nations, states, governments, or similar entities, such terms shall include and such laws shall apply with such respect to Taiwan.

   2. Whenever authorized by or pursuant to the laws of the United States to conduct or carry out programs, transactions, or other relations with respect to foreign countries, nations, states, governments, or similar entities, the President or any agency of the United States Government is authorized to conduct and carry out, in accordance with section 6 of this Act, such programs, transactions, and other relations with respect to Taiwan (including, but not limited to, the performance of services for the United States through contracts with commercial entities on Taiwan), in accordance with the applicable laws of the United States.

   3.

      A. The absence of diplomatic relations and recognition with respect to Taiwan shall not abrogate, infringe, modify, deny, or otherwise affect in any way any rights or obligations (including but not limited to those involving contracts, debts, or property interests of any kind) under the laws of the United States heretofore or hereafter acquired by or with respect to Taiwan.

      B. For all purposes under the laws of the United States, including actions in any court in the United States, recognition of the People's Republic of China shall not affect in any way the ownership of or other rights or interests in properties, tangible and intangible, and other things of value, owned or held on or prior to December 31, 1978, or thereafter acquired or earned by the governing authorities on Taiwan.

   4. Whenever the application of the laws of the United States depends upon the law that is or was applicable on Taiwan or compliance therewith, the law applied by the people on Taiwan shall be considered the applicable law for that purpose.

   5. Nothing in this Act, nor the facts of the President's action in extending diplomatic recognition to the People's Republic of China, the absence of diplomatic relations between the people on Taiwan and the United States, or the lack of recognition by the United States, and attendant circumstances thereto, shall be construed in any administrative or judicial proceeding as a basis for any United States Government agency, commission, or department to make a finding of fact or determination of law, under the Atomic Energy Act of 1954 and the Nuclear Non-Proliferation Act of 1978, to deny an export license application or to revoke an existing export license for nuclear exports to Taiwan.

   6. For purposes of the Immigration and Nationality Act, Taiwan may be treated in the manner specified in the first sentence of section 202(b) of that Act.

7. The capacity of Taiwan to sue and be sued in courts in the United States, in accordance with the laws of the United States, shall not be abrogated, infringed, modified, denied, or otherwise affected in any way by the absence of diplomatic relations or recognition.

8. No requirement, whether expressed or implied, under the laws of the United States with respect to maintenance of diplomatic relations or recognition shall be applicable with respect to Taiwan.

c. For all purposes, including actions in any court in the United States, the Congress approves the continuation in force of all treaties and other international agreements, including multilateral conventions, entered into by the United States and the governing authorities on Taiwan recognized by the United States as the Republic of China prior to January 1, 1979, and in force between them on December 31, 1978, unless and until terminated in accordance with law.

d. Nothing in this Act may be construed as a basis for supporting the exclusion or expulsion of Taiwan from continued membership in any international financial institution or any other international organization.

[Section 5 omitted.]

THE AMERICAN INSTITUTE OF TAIWAN

Section. 6.

a. Programs, transactions, and other relations conducted or carried out by the President or any agency of the United States Government with respect to Taiwan shall, in the manner and to the extent directed by the President, be conducted and carried out by or through—
   1. The American Institute in Taiwan, a nonprofit corporation incorporated under the laws of the District of Columbia, or
   2. such comparable successor nongovermental entity as the President may designate, (hereafter in this Act referred to as the "Institute").

b. Whenever the President or any agency of the United States Government is authorized or required by or pursuant to the laws of the United States to enter into, perform, enforce, or have in force an agreement or transaction relative to Taiwan, such agreement or transaction shall be entered into, performed, and enforced, in the manner and to the extent directed by the President, by or through the Institute.

c. To the extent that any law, rule, regulation, or ordinance of the District of Columbia, or of any State or political subdivision thereof in which the Institute is incorporated or doing business, impedes or otherwise interferes with the performance of the functions of the Institute pursuant to this Act; such law, rule, regulation, or ordinance shall be deemed to be preempted by this Act.

SERVICES BY THE INSTITUTE TO UNITED STATES CITIZENS ON TAIWAN

Section. 7.

a. The Institute may authorize any of its employees on Taiwan—
   1. to administer to or take from any person an oath, affirmation, affidavit, or deposition, and to perform any notarial act which any notary public is required or authorized by law to perform within the United States;

2. To act as provisional conservator of the personal estates of deceased United States citizens; and

3. to assist and protect the interests of United States persons by performing other acts such as are authorized to be performed outside the United States for consular purposes by such laws of the United States as the President may specify.

b. Acts performed by authorized employees of the Institute under this section shall be valid, and of like force and effect within the United States, as if performed by any other person authorized under the laws of the United States to perform such acts.

[Sections 8 and 9 omitted.]

TAIWAN INSTRUMENTALITY

Section. 10.

a. Whenever the President or any agency of the United States Government is authorized or required by or pursuant to the laws of the United States to render or provide to or to receive or accept from Taiwan, any performance, communication, assurance, undertaking, or other action, such action shall, in the manner and to the. extent directed by the President, be rendered or provided to, or received or accepted from, an instrumentality established by Taiwan which the President determines has the necessary authority under the laws applied by the people on Taiwan to provide assurances and take other actions on behalf of Taiwan in accordance with this Act.

b. The President is requested to extend to the instrumentality established by Taiwan the same number of offices and complement of personnel as were previously operated in the United States by the governing authorities on Taiwan recognized as the Republic of China prior to January 1, 1979.

c. Upon the granting by Taiwan of comparable privileges and immunities with respect to the Institute and its appropriate personnel, the President is authorized to extend with respect to the Taiwan instrumentality and its appropriate; personnel, such privileges and immunities (subject to appropriate conditions and obligations) as may be necessary for the effective performance of their functions.

SEPARATION OF GOVERNMENT PERSONNEL FOR EMPLOYMENT WITH THE INSTITUTE

Section. 11.

a.

1. Under such terms and conditions as the President may direct, any agency of the United States Government may separate from Government service for a specified period any officer or employee of that agency who accepts employment with the Institute.

[Text omitted.]

REPORTING REQUIREMENT

Section. 12.

a. The Secretary of State shall transmit to the Congress the text of any agreement to which the Institute is a party. However, any such agreement the immediate public disclosure of which would, in the opinion of the President, be prejudicial to the national security of the United States shall not be so transmitted to the Congress but shall be transmitted to the Committee on Foreign Relations of the Senate and the Committee on Foreign Affairs of the House of Representatives under an appropriate injunction of secrecy to be removed only upon due notice from the President.

b. For purposes of subsection (a), the term "agreement" includes—
   1. any agreement entered into between the Institute and the governing authorities on Taiwan or the instrumentality established by Taiwan; and
   2. any agreement entered into between the Institute and an agency of the United States Government.

c. Agreements and transactions made or to be made by or through the Institute shall be subject to the same congressional notification, review, and approval requirements and procedures as if such agreements and transactions were made by or through the agency of the United States Government on behalf of which the Institute is acting.

d. During the two-year period beginning on the effective date of this Act, the Secretary of State shall transmit to the Speaker of the House and Senate House of Representatives and the Committee on Foreign Relations of Foreign Relations the Senate, every six months, a report describing and reviewing economic relations between the United States and Taiwan, noting any interference with normal commercial relations.

RULES AND REGULATIONS

Section. 13.

The President is authorized to prescribe such rules and regulations as he may deem appropriate to carry out the purposes of this Act. During the three-year period beginning on the effective date speaker of this Act, such rules and regulations shall be transmitted promptly to the Speaker of the House of Representatives and to the Committee on Foreign Relations of the Senate. Such action shall not, however, relieve the Institute of the responsibilities placed upon it by this Act.

CONGRESSIONAL OVERSIGHT

Section. 14.

a. The Committee on Foreign Affairs of the House of Representatives, the Committee on Foreign Relations of the Senate, and other appropriate committees of the Congress shall monitor—
   1. the implementation of the provisions of this Act;
   2. the operation and procedures of the Institute;
   3. the legal and technical aspects of the continuing relationship between the United States and Taiwan; and
   4. the implementation of the policies of the United States concerning security and cooperation in East Asia.

b. Such committees shall report, as appropriate, to their respective Houses on the results of their monitoring.

DEFINITIONS

Section. 15. For purposes of this Act—

1. the term "laws of the United States" includes any statute, rule, regulation, ordinance, order, or judicial rule of decision of the United States or any political subdivision thereof; and

2. the term "Taiwan" includes, as the context may require, the islands of Taiwan and the Pescadores, the people on those islands, corporations and other entities and associations created or organized under the laws applied on those islands, and the governing authorities on Taiwan recognized by the United States as the Republic of China prior to January 1, 1979, and any successor governing authorities (including political subdivisions, agencies, and instrumentalities thereof).

[Sections 16 and 17 omitted.]

EFFECTIVE DATE

Section. 18.
This Act shall be effective as of January 1, 1979. Approved April 10, 1979.

Joint Communiqué of the United States of America
and the People's Republic of China
(The Shanghai Communiqué)
February 27, 1972[2]

President Richard Nixon of the United States of America visited the People's Republic of China at the invitation of Premier Chou Enlai of the People's Republic of China from February 21 to February 28, 1972. Accompanying the President were Mrs. Nixon, U.S. Secretary of State William Rogers, Assistant to the President Dr. Henry Kissinger, and other American officials.

President Nixon met with Chairman Mao Tse-tung of the Communist Party of China on February 21. The two leaders had a serious and frank exchange of views on Sino-U.S. relations and world affairs.

During the visit, extensive, earnest, and frank discussions were held between President Nixon and Premier Chou En-lai on the normalization of relations between the United States of America and the People's Republic of China, as well as on other matters of interest to both sides. In addition, Secretary of State William Rogers and Foreign Minister Chi P'eng-fei held talks in the same spirit.

President Nixon and his party visited Peking and viewed cultural, industrial and agricultural sites, and they also toured Hangchow and Shanghai where, continuing discussions with Chinese leaders, they viewed similar places of interest.

The leaders of the People's Republic of China and the United States of America found it beneficial to have this opportunity, after so many years without contact, to present candidly to one another their views on a variety of issues. They reviewed the international situation in which important changes and great upheavals are taking place and expounded their respective positions and attitudes.

The U.S. side stated: Peace in Asia and peace in the world requires efforts both to reduce immediate tensions and to eliminate the basic causes of conflict. The United States will work for a just and secure peace: just, because it fulfills the aspirations of peoples and nations for freedom and progress; secure, because it removes the danger of foreign aggression. The United States supports individual freedom and social progress for all the peoples of the world, free of outside pressure or intervention. The United States believes that the effort to reduce tensions is served by improving communication between countries that have different ideologies so as to lessen the risks of confrontation through accident, miscalculation or misunderstanding. Countries should treat each other with mutual respect and be willing to compete peacefully, letting performance be the ultimate judge. No country should claim infallibility and each country should be prepared to re-examine its own attitudes for the common good. The United States stressed that the peoples of Indochina should be allowed to determine their destiny without outside intervention; its constant primary objective has been a negotiated solution; the eight-point proposal put forward by the Republic of Vietnam and the United States on January 27, 1972 represents a basis for the attainment of that objective; in the absence of a negotiated settlement the United States envisages the ultimate withdrawal of all U.S. forces from the region consistent with the aim of self-determination for each country of Indochina. The United States will maintain its close ties with and support for the Republic of Korea; the United States will support efforts of the Republic of Korea to seek a relaxation of tension and increased communication in the Korean peninsula. The United States places the highest value on its friendly relations with Japan; it will continue to develop the existing close bonds. Consistent with the United Nations Security Council Resolution of December 21, 1971, the United States favors the continuation of the ceasefire between India and Pakistan and the withdrawal of all military forces to within their own territories and to their own sides of the ceasefire line in Jammu and Kashmir; the United States supports the right of the peoples of South Asia to shape their own future in peace, free of military threat, and without having the area become the subject of great power rivalry.

The Chinese side stated: Wherever there is oppression, there is resistance. Countries want independence, nations want liberation and the people want revolution—this has become the irresistible trend of history. All nations, big or small, should be equal; big nations should not bully the small and strong nations should not bully the weak. China will never be a superpower and it opposes hegemony and power politics of any kind. The Chinese side stated that it firmly supports the struggles of all the oppressed people and nations for freedom and liberation and that the people of all countries have the right to choose their social systems according to their own wishes and the right to safeguard the independence, sovereignty and territorial integrity of their own countries and oppose foreign aggression, interference, control and subversion. All foreign troops should be withdrawn to their own countries.

The Chinese side expressed its firm support to the peoples of Vietnam, Laos, and Cambodia in their efforts for the attainment of their goal and its firm support to the seven-point proposal of the Provisional Revolutionary Government of the Republic of South Vietnam and the elaboration of February this year on the two key problems in the proposal, and to the Joint Declaration of the Summit Conference of the Indochinese Peoples. It firmly supports the eight-point program for the peaceful unification of Korea put forward by the Government of the Democratic People's Republic of Korea on April 12, 1971, and the stand for the abolition of the "U.N. Commission for the Unification and Rehabilitation of Korea." It firmly opposes the revival and outward expansion of Japanese militarism and firmly supports the Japanese people's desire to build an independent, democratic, peaceful and neutral Japan. It firmly maintains that India and Pakistan should, in accordance with the United Nations resolutions on the India-Pakistan question, immediately withdraw all their forces to their respective territories and to their own sides of the ceasefire line in Jammu and Kashmir and firmly supports the Pakistan Government and people in their struggle to preserve their independence and sovereignty and the people of Jammu and Kashmir in their struggle for the right of self-determination.

There are essential differences between China and the United States in their social systems and foreign policies. However, the two sides agreed that countries, regardless of their social systems, should conduct their relations on the principles of respect for the sovereignty and territorial integrity of all states, nonaggression against other states, noninterference in the internal affairs of other states, equality and mutual benefit, and peaceful coexistence. International disputes should be settled on this basis, without resorting to the use or threat of force. The United States and the People's Republic of China are prepared to apply these principles to their mutual relations.

With these principles of international relations in mind the two sides stated that:

- progress toward the normalization of relations between China and the United States is in the interests of all countries;
- both wish to reduce the danger of international military conflict;
- neither should seek hegemony in the Asia–Pacific region and each is opposed to efforts by any other country or group of countries to establish such hegemony; and
- neither is prepared to negotiate on behalf of any third party or to enter into agreements or understandings with the other directed at other states.

Both sides are of the view that it would be against the interests of the peoples of the world for any major country to collude with another against other countries, or for major countries to divide up the world into spheres of interest.

The two sides reviewed the long-standing serious disputes between China and the United States. The Chinese side reaffirmed its position: The Taiwan question is the crucial question obstructing the normalization of relations between China and the United States; the Government of the People's Republic of China is the sole legal government of China; Taiwan is a province of China which has long been returned to the motherland; the liberation of Taiwan is China's internal affair in which no other country has the right to interfere; and all U.S. forces and military installations must be withdrawn from Taiwan. The Chinese Government firmly opposes any activities which aim at the creation of "one China, one Taiwan," "one China, two governments," "two Chinas," and "independent Taiwan" or advocate that "the status of Taiwan remains to be determined."

The U.S. side declared: The United States acknowledges that all Chinese on either side of the Taiwan Strait maintain there is but one China and that Taiwan is a part of China. The United States Government does not challenge that position. It reaffirms its interest in a peaceful settlement of the Taiwan question by the Chinese themselves. With this prospect in mind, it affirms the ultimate objective of the withdrawal of all U.S. forces and military installations from Taiwan. In the meantime, it will progressively reduce its forces and military installations on Taiwan as the tension in the area diminishes.

The two sides agreed that it is desirable to broaden the understanding between the two peoples. To this end, they discussed specific areas in such fields as science, technology, culture, sports and journalism, in which people-to-people contacts and exchanges would be mutually beneficial. Each side undertakes to facilitate the further development of such contacts and exchanges.

Both sides view bilateral trade as another area from which mutual benefit can be derived, and agreed that economic relations based on equality and mutual benefit are in the interest of the people of the two countries. They agree to facilitate the progressive development of trade between their two countries.

The two sides agreed that they will stay in contact through various channels, including the sending of a senior U.S. representative to Peking from time to time for concrete consultations to further the normalization of relations between the two countries and continue to exchange views on issues of common interest.

The two sides expressed the hope that the gains achieved during this visit would open up new prospects for the relations between the two countries. They believe that the normalization of relations between the two countries is not only in the interest of the Chinese and American peoples but also contributes to the relaxation of tension in Asia and the world.

President Nixon, Mrs. Nixon and the American party expressed their appreciation for the gracious hospitality shown them by the Government and people of the People's Republic of China.

Joint Communiqué of the United States of America
and the People's Republic of China
on the Establishment of Diplomatic Relations
(The Second Communiqué)
January 1, 1979[3]

The United States of America and the People's Republic of China have agreed to recognize each other and to establish diplomatic relations as of January 1, 1979.

The United States of America recognizes the Government of the People's Republic of China as the sole legal Government of China. Within this context, the people of the United States will maintain cultural, commercial, and other unofficial relations with the people of Taiwan.

The United States of America and the People's Republic of China reaffirm the principles agreed on by the two sides in the Shanghai Communiqué and emphasize once again that:

- Both wish to reduce the danger of international military conflict.
- Neither should seek hegemony in the Asia-Pacific region or in any other region of the world and each is opposed to efforts by any other country or group of countries to establish such hegemony.
- Neither is prepared to negotiate on behalf of any third party or to enter into agreements or understandings with the other directed at other states.
- The Government of the United States of America acknowledges the Chinese position that there is but one China and Taiwan is part of China.
- Both believe that normalization of Sino-American relations is not only in the interest of the Chinese and American peoples but also contributes to the cause of peace in Asia and the world.

The United States of America and the People's Republic of China will exchange Ambassadors and establish Embassies on March 1, 1979.

Joint Communiqué of the United States of America and the People's Republic of China
(The Third Communiqué)
August 17, 1982[4]

In the Joint Communiqué on the Establishment of Diplomatic Relations on January 1, 1979, issued by the Government of the United States of America and the People's Republic of China, the United States of America recognized the Government of the People's Republic of China as the sole legal Government of China, and it acknowledged the Chinese position that there is but one China and Taiwan is part of China. Within that context, the two sides agreed that the people of the United States would continue to maintain cultural, commercial, and other unofficial relations with the people of Taiwan. On this basis, relations between the United States and China were normalized.

The question of United States arms sales to Taiwan was not settled in the course of negotiations between the two countries on establishing diplomatic relations. The two sides held differing positions, and the Chinese side stated that it would raise the issue again following normalization. Recognizing that this issue would seriously hamper the development of United States–China relations, they have held further discussions on it, during and since the meetings between President Ronald Reagan and Premier Zhao Ziyang and between Secretary of State Alexander M. Haig, Jr. and Vice Premier and Foreign Minister Huang Hua in October 1981.

Respect for each other's sovereignty and territorial integrity and non-interference in each other's internal affairs constitute the fundamental principles guiding United States China relations. These principles were confirmed in the Shanghai Communiqué of February 28, 1972 and reaffirmed in the Joint Communiqué on the Establishment of Diplomatic Relations which came into effect on January 1, 1979. Both sides emphatically state that these principles continue to govern all aspects of their relations.

The Chinese Government reiterates that the question of Taiwan is China's internal affair. The Message to Compatriots in Taiwan issued by China on January 1, 1979 promulgated a fundamental policy of striving for peaceful reunification of the motherland. The Nine-Point Proposal put forward by China on September 30, 1981 represented a further major effort under this fundamental policy to strive for a peaceful solution to the Taiwan question.

The United States Government attaches great importance to its relations with China, and reiterates that it has no intention of infringing on Chinese sovereignty and territorial integrity, or interfering in China's internal affairs, or pursuing a policy of "two Chinas" or "one China, one Taiwan." The United States Government understands and appreciates the Chinese policy of striving for a peaceful resolution of the Taiwan question as indicated in China's Message to Compatriots in Taiwan issued on January 1, 1979 and the Nine-Point Proposal put forward by China on September 30, 1981. The new situation which has emerged with regard to the Taiwan question also provides favorable conditions for the settlement of United States–China differences over United States arms sales to Taiwan.

Having in mind the foregoing statements of both sides, the United States Government states that it does not seek to carry out a long-term policy of arms sales to Taiwan, that its arms sales to Taiwan will not exceed, either in qualitative or in quantitative terms, the level of those supplied in recent years since the establishment of diplomatic relations between the United States and China, and that it intends gradually to reduce its sale of arms to Taiwan, leading, over a period of time, to a final resolution. In so stating, the United States acknowledges China's consistent position regarding the thorough settlement of this issue.

In order to bring about, over a period of time, a final settlement of the question of United States arms sales to Taiwan, which is an issue rooted in history, the two Governments will make every effort to adopt measures and create conditions conducive to the thorough settlement of this issue.

The development of United States–China relations is not only in the interests of the two peoples but also conducive to peace and stability in the world. The two sides are determined, on the principle of equality and mutual benefit, to strengthen their ties in the economic, cultural, educational, scientific, technological and other fields and make strong, joint efforts for the continued development of relations between the Governments and peoples of the United States and China.

In order to bring about the healthy development of United States–China relations, maintain world peace and oppose aggression and expansion, the two Governments reaffirm the principles agreed on by the two sides in the Shanghai Communiqué and the Joint Communiqué on the Establishment of Diplomatic Relations. The two sides will maintain contact and hold appropriate consultations on bilateral and international issues of common interest.

President Reagan's "Six Assurances" to Taiwan
July 14, 1982[5]

In negotiating the third Joint Communiqué with the PRC, the United States:

1. has not agreed to set a date for ending arms sales to Taiwan;
2. has not agreed to hold prior consultations with the PRC on arms sales to Taiwan;
3. will not play any mediation role between Taipei and Beijing;
4. has not agreed to revise the Taiwan Relations Act;
5. has not altered its position regarding sovereignty over Taiwan;
6. will not exert pressure on Taiwan to negotiate with the PRC.

President Reagan's Secret Memorandum on the
1982 Communiqué
August 17, 1982[6]

The U.S. willingness to reduce its arms sales to Taiwan is conditioned absolutely upon the continued commitment of China to the peaceful solution of the Taiwan-PRC differences. It should be clearly understood that the linkage between these two matters is a permanent imperative of U.S. foreign policy. In addition, it is essential that the quantity and quality of the arms provided Taiwan be conditioned entirely on the threat posed by the PRC. Both in quantitative and qualitative terms, Taiwan's defense capability relative to that of the PRC will be maintained.

Democratic Progressive Party (DPP) 1999 Resolution
Regarding Taiwan's Future (Excerpt)
December 2, 1999[7]

I. PREFACE

Through years of hardship and struggle, the Democratic Progressive Party (DPP) and the people of Taiwan have compelled the Kuomintang (KMT) to accept democratic reforms by lifting Martial Law and terminating one-party authoritarian rule. Following the 1992 general elections of the national legislature, the 1996 direct presidential elections, and constitutional reform to abolish the provincial government, Taiwan has become a democratic and independent country.

In order to face the new environment and to create a vision for the future based on past accomplishments, the DPP continues to push for structural reforms in the state institutions while taking further steps to define Taiwan's status and the direction in which the nation is headed. This proclamation unequivocally clarifies the outlook of the DPP regarding Taiwan's future at this juncture in time. Our past experiences and achievements can be used as a foundation to face the challenges of the next century.

II. PROCLAMATION

1) Taiwan is a sovereign and independent country. Any change in the independent status quo must be decided by all the residents of Taiwan by means of plebiscite.

2) Taiwan is not a part of the People's Republic of China. China's unilateral advocacy of the "One China Principle" and "One Country Two Systems" is fundamentally inappropriate for Taiwan.

3) Taiwan should expand its role in the international community, seek international recognition, and pursue the goal of entry into the United Nations and other international organizations.

4) Taiwan should renounce the "One China" position to avoid international confusion and to prevent the position's use by China as a pretext for forceful annexation.

5) Taiwan should promptly complete the task of incorporating plebiscite into law in order to realize the people's rights. In time of need, it can be relied on to establish consensus of purpose, and allow the people to express their will.

6) Taiwan's government and opposition forces must establish bi-partisan consensus on foreign policy, integrating limited resources, to face China's aggression and ambition.

7) Taiwan and China should engage in comprehensive dialogue to seek mutual understanding and economic cooperation. Both sides should build a framework for long-term stability and peace.

[SECTION III OMITTED.]

National People's Congress of the People's Republic of China Anti-Secession Law
March 14, 2005[8]

Article 1: This Law is formulated, in accordance with the Constitution, for the purpose of opposing and checking Taiwan's secession from China by secessionists in the name of "Taiwan independence", promoting peaceful national reunification, maintaining peace and stability in the Taiwan Straits, preserving China's sovereignty and territorial integrity, and safeguarding the fundamental interests of the Chinese nation.

Article 2: There is only one China in the world. Both the mainland and Taiwan belong to one China. China's sovereignty and territorial integrity brook no division. Safeguarding China's sovereignty and territorial integrity is the common obligation of all Chinese people, the Taiwan compatriots included. Taiwan is part of China. The state shall never allow the "Taiwan independence" secessionist forces to make Taiwan secede from China under any name or by any means.

Article 3: The Taiwan question is one that is left over from China's civil war of the late 1940s. Solving the Taiwan question and achieving national reunification is China's internal affair, subject to no interference by any outside forces.

Article 4: Accomplishing the great task of reunifying the motherland is the sacred duty of all Chinese people, the Taiwan compatriots included.

Article 5: Upholding the principle of one China is the basis of peaceful reunification of the country. To reunify the country through peaceful means best serves the fundamental interests of the compatriots on both sides of the Taiwan Straits. The state shall do its utmost with maximum sincerity to achieve a peaceful reunification. After the country is reunified peacefully, Taiwan may practice systems different from those on the mainland and enjoy a high degree of autonomy.

Article 6: The state shall take the following measures to maintain peace and stability in the Taiwan Straits and promote cross-Straits relations:

(1) to encourage and facilitate personnel exchanges across the Straits for greater mutual understanding and mutual trust;

(2) to encourage and facilitate economic exchanges and cooperation, realize direct links of trade, mail and air and shipping services, and bring about closer economic ties between the two sides of the Straits to their mutual benefit;

(3) to encourage and facilitate cross-Straits exchanges in education, science, technology, culture, health and sports, and work together to carry forward the proud Chinese cultural traditions;

(4) to encourage and facilitate cross-Straits cooperation in combating crimes; and

(5) to encourage and facilitate other activities that are conducive to peace and stability in the Taiwan Straits and stronger cross-Straits relations.

The state protects the rights and interests of the Taiwan compatriots in accordance with law.

Article 7: The state stands for the achievement of peaceful reunification through consultations and negotiations on an equal footing between the two sides of the Taiwan Straits. These consultations and negotiations may be conducted in steps and phases and with flexible and varied modalities. The two sides of the Taiwan Straits may consult and negotiate on the following matters:

(1) officially ending the state of hostility between the two sides;
(2) mapping out the development of cross-Straits relations;
(3) steps and arrangements for peaceful national reunification;
(4) the political status of the Taiwan authorities;
(5) the Taiwan region's room of international operation that is compatible with its status; and
(6) other matters concerning the achievement of peaceful national reunification.

Article 8: In the event that the "Taiwan independence" secessionist forces should act under any name or by any means to cause the fact of Taiwan's secession from China, or that major incidents entailing Taiwan's secession from China should occur, or that possibilities for a peaceful re-unification should be completely exhausted, the state shall employ non-peaceful means and other necessary measures to protect China's sovereignty and territorial integrity.

The State Council and the Central Military Commission shall decide on and execute the non-peaceful means and other necessary measures as provided for in the preceding paragraph and shall promptly report to the Standing Committee of the National People's Congress.

Article 9: In the event of employing and executing non-peaceful means and other necessary measures as provided for in this Law, the state shall exert its utmost to protect the lives, property and other legitimate rights and interests of Taiwan civilians and foreign nationals in Taiwan, and to minimize losses. At the same time, the state shall protect the rights and interests of the Taiwan compatriots in other parts of China in accordance with law.

Article 10: This Law shall come into force on the day of its promulgation.

Peace Treaty between Japan and China
(The Treaty of Shimonoseki) (Excerpt)
April 17, 1895[9]

TREATY OF PEACE

His Majesty the Emperor of Japan and His Majesty the Emperor of China, desiring to restore the blessings of peace to their countries and subjects and to remove all cause for future complications, have named as their Plenipotentiaries for the purpose of concluding a Treaty of Peace. . . .

Who, after having exchanged their full powers, which were found to be in good and proper form, have agreed to the following Articles:

Article 1

China recognises definitively the full and complete independence and autonomy of Korea, and, in consequence, the payment of tribute and the performance of ceremonies and formalities by Korea to China, in derogation of such independence and autonomy, shall wholly cease for the future.

Article 2

China cedes to Japan in perpetuity and full sovereignty the following territories, together with all fortifications, arsenals, and public property thereon:

(a) The southern portion of the province of Fêngtien [Fengtian] within the following boundaries [Liaodong agreement in November 1895 deleted this and replaced it with an indemnity of 30 million taels of silver to be paid Japan]. . . .
(b) The island of Formosa, together with all islands appertaining or belonging to the said island of Formosa.
(c) The Pescadores Group, that is to say, all islands lying between the 119th and 120th degrees of longitude east of Greenwich and the 23rd and 24th degrees of north latitude.

[Articles 3 and 4 omitted.]

Article 5

The inhabitants of the territories ceded to Japan who wish to take up their residence outside the ceded districts shall be at liberty to sell their real property and retire. For this purpose a period of two years from the date of the exchange of ratifications of the present Act shall be granted. At the expiration of that period those of the inhabitants who shall not have left such territories shall, at the option of Japan, be deemed to be Japanese subjects.

Each of the two Governments shall, immediately upon the exchange of the ratifications of the present Act, send one or more Commissioners to Formosa to effect a final transfer of that province, and within the space of two months after the exchange of the ratifications of this Act such transfer shall be completed.

Article 6

All Treaties between Japan and China having come to an end as a consequence of war, China engages, immediately upon the exchange of the ratifications of this Act, to appoint Plenipotentiaries to conclude with the Japanese Plenipotentiaries, a Treaty of Commerce and Navigation and a Convention to regulate Frontier Intercourse and Trade. The Treaties, Conventions, and Regulations now subsisting between China and the European Powers shall serve as a basis for the said Treaty and Convention between Japan and China. From the date of the exchange of ratifications of this Act until the said Treaty and Convention are brought into actual operation, the Japanese Governments, its officials, commerce, navigation, frontier intercourse and trade, industries, ships, and subjects, shall in every respect be accorded by China most favoured nation treatment.

[Text omitted.]

[Articles 7 to 9 omitted.]

Article 10

All offensive military operations shall cease upon the exchange of the ratifications of this Act.

Article 11

The present Act shall be ratified by their Majesties the Emperor of Japan and the Emperor of China, and the ratifications shall be exchanged at Chefoo on the 8th day of the 5th month of the 28th year of MEIJI, corresponding to the 14th day of the 4th month of the 21st year of KUANG HSÜ [Guangxu].

In witness whereof the respective Plenipotentiaries have signed the same and affixed thereto the seal of their arms.

Done in Shimonoseki, in duplicate, this 17th day of the fourth month of the 28th year of MEIJI, corresponding to the 23rd day of the 3rd month of the 21st year of KUANG HSÜ [Guangxu].

The Cairo Declaration
November 27, 1943[10]

President Roosevelt, Generalissimo Chiang Kai-shek and Prime Minister Churchill, together with their respective military and diplomatic advisers, have completed a conference in North Africa.

The following general statement was issued:

The several military missions have agreed upon future military operations against Japan. The Three Great Allies expressed their resolve to bring unrelenting pressure against their brutal enemies by sea, land, and air. This pressure is already rising.

The Three Great Allies are fighting this war to restrain and punish the aggression of Japan. They covet no gain for themselves and have no thought of territorial expansion. It is their purpose that Japan shall be stripped of all the islands in the Pacific which she has seized or occupied since the beginning of the first World War in 1914, and that all the territories Japan has stolen from the Chinese, such as Manchuria, Formosa, and The Pescadores, shall be restored to the Republic of China. Japan will also be expelled from all other territories which she has taken by violence and greed. The aforesaid three great powers, mindful of the enslavement of the people of Korea, are determined that in due course Korea shall become free and independent.

With these objects in view the three Allies, in harmony with those of the United Nations at war with Japan, will continue to persevere in the serious and prolonged operations necessary to procure the unconditional surrender of Japan.

Proclamation Defining Terms for Japanese Surrender
(The Potsdam Declaration)
July 26, 1945[11]

We—the President of the United States, the President of the National Government of the Republic of China, and the Prime Minister of Great Britain, representing the hundreds of millions of our countrymen, have conferred and agree that Japan shall be given an opportunity to end this war.

The prodigious land, sea and air forces of the United States, the British Empire and of China, many times reinforced by their armies and air fleets from the west, are poised to strike the final blows upon Japan. This military power is sustained and inspired by the determination of all the Allied Nations to prosecute the war against Japan until she ceases to resist.

The result of the futile and senseless German resistance to the might of the aroused free peoples of the world stands forth in awful clarity as an example to the people of Japan. The might that now converges on Japan is immeasurably greater than that which, when applied to the resisting Nazis, necessarily laid waste to the lands, the industry and the method of life of the whole German people. The full application of our military power, backed by our resolve, will mean the inevitable and complete destruction of the Japanese armed forces and just as inevitably the utter devastation of the Japanese homeland.

The time has come for Japan to decide whether she will continue to be controlled by those self-willed militaristic advisers whose unintelligent calculations have brought the Empire of Japan to the threshold of annihilation, or whether she will follow the path of reason.

Following are our terms. We will not deviate from them. There are no alternatives. We shall brook no delay.

- There must be eliminated for all time the authority and influence of those who have deceived and misled the people of Japan into embarking on world conquest, for we insist that a new order of peace, security and justice will be impossible until irresponsible militarism is driven from the world.
- Until such a new order is established and until there is convincing proof that Japan's war-making power is destroyed, points in Japanese territory to be designated by the Allies shall be occupied to secure the achievement of the basic objectives we are here setting forth.
- The terms of the Cairo Declaration shall be carried out and Japanese sovereignty shall be limited to the islands of Honshu, Hokkaido, Kyushu, Shikoku and such minor islands as we determine.
- The Japanese military forces, after being completely disarmed, shall be permitted to return to their homes with the opportunity to lead peaceful and productive lives.
- We do not intend that the Japanese shall be enslaved as a race or destroyed as a nation, but stern justice shall be meted out to all war criminals, including those who have visited cruelties upon our prisoners. The Japanese Government shall remove all obstacles to the revival and strengthening of democratic tendencies among the Japanese people. Freedom of speech, of religion, and of thought, as well as respect for the fundamental human rights shall be established.

- Japan shall be permitted to maintain such industries as will sustain her economy and permit the exaction of just reparations in kind, but not those which would enable her to re-arm for war. To this end, access to, as distinguished from control of, raw materials shall be permitted. Eventual Japanese participation in world trade relations shall be permitted.

- The occupying forces of the Allies shall be withdrawn from Japan as soon as these objectives have been accomplished and there has been established in accordance with the freely expressed will of the Japanese people a peacefully inclined and responsible government.

- We call upon the government of Japan to proclaim now the unconditional surrender of all Japanese armed forces, and to provide proper and adequate assurances of their good faith in such action. The alternative for Japan is prompt and utter destruction.

Treaty of Peace with Japan
(The San Francisco Peace Treaty) (Excerpt)
September 8, 1951[12]

Whereas the Allied Powers and Japan are resolved that henceforth their relations shall be those of nations which, as sovereign equals, cooperate in friendly association to promote their common welfare and to maintain international peace and security, and are therefore desirous of concluding a Treaty of Peace which will settle questions still outstanding as a result of the existence of a state of war between them;

Whereas Japan for its part declares its intention to apply for membership in the United Nations and in all circumstances to conform to the principles of the Charter of the United Nations; to strive to realize the objectives of the Universal Declaration of Human Rights; to seek to create within Japan conditions of stability and well-being as defined in Articles 55 and 56 of the Charter of the United Nations and already initiated by post-surrender Japanese legislation; and in public and private trade and commerce to conform to internationally accepted fair practices;

Whereas the Allied Powers welcome the intentions of Japan set out in the foregoing paragraph;

The Allied Powers and Japan have therefore determined to conclude the present Treaty of Peace, and have accordingly appointed the undersigned Plenipotentiaries, who, after presentation of their full powers, found in good and due form, have agreed on the following provisions:

CHAPTER I

PEACE

Article 1

    (a)   The state of war between Japan and each of the Allied Powers is terminated as from the date on which the present Treaty comes into force between Japan and the Allied Power concerned as provided for in Article 23.

    (b)   The Allied Powers recognize the full sovereignty of the Japanese people over Japan and its territorial waters.

CHAPTER II

TERRITORY

Article 2

    (a)   Japan, recognizing the independence of Korea, renounces all right, title, and claim to Korea, including the islands of Quelpart, Port Hamilton and Dagelet.

    (b)   Japan renounces all right, title and claim to Formosa and the Pescadores.

    (c)   . . . .

    (d)   . . . .

    (e)   . . . .

    (f)   Japan renounces all right, title and claim to the Spratly Islands and to the Paracel Islands.

[Articles 3 and 4 omitted.]

CHAPTER III

SECURITY

Article 5

(a) Japan accepts the obligations set forth in Article 2 of the Charter of the United Nations, and in particular the obligations.

    (i) to settle its international disputes by peaceful means in such a manner that international peace and security, and justice, are not endangered;

    (ii) to refrain in its international relations from the threat or use of force against the territorial integrity or political independence of any State or in any other manner inconsistent with the Purposes of the United Nations;

    (iii) to give the United Nations every assistance in any action it takes in accordance with the Charter and to refrain from giving assistance to any State against which the United Nations may take preventive or enforcement action.

(b) The Allied Powers confirm that they will be guided by the principles of Article 2 of the Charter of the United Nations in their relations with Japan.

(c) The Allied Powers for their part recognize that Japan as a sovereign nation possesses the inherent right of individual or collective self-defense referred to in Article 51 of the Charter of the United Nations and that Japan may voluntarily enter into collective security arrangements.

[Article 6 omitted.]

CHAPTER IV

POLITICAL AND ECONOMIC CLAUSES

[Article 7 omitted.]

Article 8

(a) Japan will recognize the full force of all treaties now or hereafter concluded by the Allied Powers for terminating the state of war initiated on September 1, 1939, as well as other arrangements by the Allied Powers or in connection with the restoration of peace. Japan also accepts the arrangements made for terminating the former League of Nations and Permanent Court of International Justice.

[Text omitted.]

[Article 9 omitted.]

Article 10

Japan renounces all special rights and interests in China, including all benefits and privileges resulting from the provisions of the final Protocol signed at Peking on September 7, 1901, and all annexes, notes and documents supplementary thereto, and agrees to the abrogation in respect to Japan of the said protocol, annexes, notes and documents.

Article 11

Japan accepts the judgments of the International Military Tribunal for the Far East and of other Allied War Crimes Courts both within and outside Japan, and will carry out the sentences imposed thereby upon Japanese nationals imprisoned in Japan. The power to grant clemency, to reduce sentences and to parole with respect to such prisoners may not be exercised except on the decision of the Government or Governments which imposed the sentence in each instance, and on the recommendation of Japan. In the case of persons sentenced by the International Military Tribunal for the Far East, such power may not be exercised except on the decision of a majority of the Governments represented on the Tribunal, and on the recommendation of Japan.

[Articles 12 and 13 omitted.]

CHAPTER V
CLAIMS AND PROPERTY

[Articles 14 to 21 omitted.]

CHAPTER VI
SETTLEMENT OF DISPUTES
Article 22

If in the opinion of any Party to the present Treaty there has arisen a dispute concerning the interpretation or execution of the Treaty, which is not settled by reference to a special claims tribunal or by other agreed means, the dispute shall, at the request of any party thereto, be referred for decision to the International Court of Justice. Japan and those Allied Powers which are not already parties to the Statute of the International Court of Justice will deposit with the Registrar of the Court, at the time of their respective ratifications of the present Treaty, and in conformity with the resolution of the United Nations Security Council, dated October 15, 1946, a general declaration accepting the jurisdiction, without special agreement, of the Court generally in respect to all disputes of the character referred to in this Article.

CHAPTER VII
FINAL CLAUSES

[Articles 23 to 25 omitted.]

Article 26

Japan will be prepared to conclude with any State which signed or adhered to the United Nations Declaration of January 1, 1942, and which is at war with Japan, or with any State which previously formed a part of the territory of a State named in Article 23, which is not a signatory of the present Treaty, a bilateral Treaty of Peace on the same or substantially the same terms as are provided for in the present Treaty, but this obligation on the part of Japan will expire three years after the first coming into force of the present Treaty. Should Japan make a peace settlement or war claims settlement with any State granting that State greater advantages than those provided by the present Treaty, those same advantages shall be extended to the parties to the present Treaty.

Article 27

The present Treaty shall be deposited in the archives of the Government of the United States of America which shall furnish each signatory State with a certified copy thereof.

IN FAITH WHEREOF the undersigned Plenipoterntiaires have signed the present Treaty.

DONE at the city of San Francisco this eighth day of September, 1951, in the English, French and Spanish languages, all being equally authentic, and in the Japanese language.

Treaty of Peace between Japan and the Republic of China
(The Treaty of Taipei) (Excerpt)
April 28, 1952[13]

Japan and the Republic of China,

Considering their mutual desire for good neighborliness in view of their historical and cultural ties and geographical proximity;

Realizing the importance of their close cooperation to the promotion of their common welfare and to the maintenance of international peace and security; Recognizing the need of a settlement of problems that have arisen as a result of the existence of a state of war between them;

Have resolved to conclude a Treaty of Peace and have accordingly appointed as their Plenipotentiaries. . . .

Who, having communicated to each other their full powers found to be in good and due form, have agreed upon the following articles:

ARTICLE I

The state of war between Japan and the Republic of China is terminated as from the date on which the present Treaty enters into force.

ARTICLE II

It is recognized that under Article 2 of the Treaty of Peace with Japan signed at the city of San Francisco in the United States of America on September 8, 1951 (hereinafter referred to as the San Francisco Treaty), Japan has renounced all right, title and claim to Taiwan (Formosa) and Penghu (the Pescadores) as well as the Spratly Islands and the Paracel Islands.

ARTICLE III

The disposition of property of Japan and of its nationals in Taiwan (Formosa) and Penghu (the Pescadores), and their claims, including debts, against the authorities of the Republic of China in Taiwan (Formosa) and Penghu (the Pescadores) and the residents thereof, and the disposition in Japan of property of such authorities and residents and their claims, including debts, against Japan and its nationals, shall be the subject of special arrangements between the Government of Japan and the Government of the Republic of China. The terms nationals and residents whenever used in the present Treaty include juridical persons.

ARTICLE IV

It is recognized that all treaties, conventions and agreements concluded before December 9, 1941, between Japan and China have become null and void as a consequence of the war.

[ARTICLE V OMITTED.]

ARTICLE VI

(a) Japan and the Republic of China will be guided by the principles of Article 2 of the Charter of the United Nations in their mutual relations.

(b)   Japan and the Republic of China will cooperate in accordance with the principles of the Charter of the United Nations and, in particular, will promote their common welfare through friendly cooperation in the economic field.

ARTICLE VII

Japan and the Republic of China will endeavor to conclude, as soon as possible, a treaty or agreement to place their trading, maritime and other commercial relations on a stable and friendly basis.

ARTICLE VIII

Japan and the Republic of China will endeavor to conclude, as soon as possible, an agreement relating to civil air transport.

ARTICLE IX

Japan and the Republic of China will endeavor to conclude, as soon as possible, an agreement providing for the regulation or limitation of fishing and the conservation and development of fisheries on the high seas.

ARTICLE X

For the purposes of the present Treaty, nationals of the Republic of China shall be deemed to include all the inhabitants and former inhabitants of Taiwan (Formosa) and Penghu (the Pescadores) and their descendants who are of the Chinese nationality in accordance with the laws and regulations which have been or may hereafter be enforced by the Republic of China in Taiwan (Formosa) and Penghu (the Pescadores); and juridical persons of the Republic of China shall be deemed to include all those registered under the laws and regulations which have been or may hereafter be enforced by the Republic of China in Taiwan (Formosa) and Penghu (the Pescadores).

ARTICLE XI

Unless otherwise provided for in the present Treaty and the documents supplementary thereto, any problem arising between Japan and the Republic of China as a result of the existence of a state of war shall be settled in accordance with the relevant provisions of the San Francisco Treaty.

ARTICLE XII

Any dispute that may arise out of the interpretation or application of the present Treaty shall be settled by negotiation or by other pacific means.

ARTICLE XIII

The present Treaty shall be ratified and the instruments of ratification shall be exchanged at Taipei as soon as possible. The present Treaty shall enter into force as from the date on which such instruments of ratification are exchanged.

ARTICLE XIV

The present Treaty shall be in the Japanese, Chinese and English languages. In case of any divergence of interpretation, the English text shall prevail.

IN WITNESS WHEREOF, the respective Plenipotentiaries have signed the present Treaty and have affixed thereto their seals.

DONE in duplicate at Taipei, this Twenty Eighth day of the Fourth month of the Twenty Seventh year of Showa of Japan corresponding to the Twenty Eighth day of the Fourth month of the Forty First year of the Republic of China and to the Twenty Eighth day of April in the year One Thousand Nine Hundred and Fifty Two.

Mutual Defense Treaty Between the United States
and the Republic of China (Excerpt)
December 2, 1954[14]

The Parties to this Treaty,

Reaffirming their faith in the purposes and principles of the Charter of the United Nations and their desire to live in peace with all peoples and all Governments, and desiring to strengthen the fabric of peace in the West Pacific Area,

Recalling with mutual pride the relationship which brought their two peoples together in a common bond of sympathy and mutual ideals to fight side by side against imperialist aggression during the last war,

Desiring to declare publicly and formally their sense of unity and their common determination to defend themselves against external armed attack, so that no potential aggressor could be under the illusion that either of them stands alone in the West Pacific Area, and

Desiring further to strengthen their present efforts for collective defense for the preservation of peace and security pending the development of a more comprehensive system of regional security in the West Pacific Area,

Have agreed as follows:

ARTICLE I

The Parties undertake, as set forth in the Charter of the United Nations, to settle any international dispute in which they may be involved by peaceful means in such a manner that international peace, security and justice are not endangered and to refrain in their international relations from the threat or use of force in any manner inconsistent with the purposes of the United Nations.

ARTICLE II

In order more effectively to achieve the objective of this Treaty, the Parties separately and jointly by self-help and mutual aid will maintain and develop their individual and collective capacity to resist armed attack and communist subversive activities directed from without against their territorial integrity and political stability.

ARTICLE III

The Parties undertake to strengthen their free institutions and to cooperate with each other in the development of economic progress and social well-being and to further their individual and collective efforts toward these ends.

[ARTICLE IV OMITTED.]

ARTICLE V

Each Party recognizes that an armed attack in the West Pacific Area directed against the territories of either of the Parties would be dangerous to its own peace and safety and declares that it would act to meet the common danger in accordance with its constitutional processes.

Any such armed attack and all measures taken as a result thereof shall be immediately reported to the Security Council of the United Nations. Such measures shall be terminated when the Security Council has taken the measures necessary to restore and maintain international peace and security.

ARTICLE VI

For the purposes of Articles II and V, the terms "territorial" and "territories" shall mean in respect of the Republic of China, Taiwan and the Pescadores; and in respect of the United States of America, the island territories in the West Pacific under its jurisdiction. The provisions of Articles II and V will be applicable to such other territories as may be determined by mutual agreement.

[ARTICLES VII TO IX OMITTED.]

ARTICLE X

This Treaty shall remain in force indefinitely. Either Party may terminate it one year after notice has been given to the other Party.

IN WITNESS WHEREOF the undersigned Plenipotentiaries have signed this Treaty.

DONE in duplicate, in the English and Chinese languages, at Washington on this second day of December of the Year One Thousand Nine Hundred and Fifty-four, corresponding to the second day of the twelfth month of the Forty-third year of the Republic of China.

United Nations General Assembly Resolution 2758 (XXVI)
October 25, 1971[15]

THE GENERAL ASSEMBLY,

Recalling the principles of the Charter of the United Nations,

Considering the restoration of the lawful rights of the People's Republic of China is essential both for the protection of the Charter of the United Nations and for the cause that the United Nations must serve under the Charter.

Recognizing that the representatives of the Government of the People's Republic of China are the only lawful representatives of China to the United Nations and that the People's Republic of China is one of the five permanent members of the Security Council,

Decides to restore all its rights to the People's Republic of China and to recognize the representatives of its Government as the only legitimate representatives of China to the United Nations, and to expel forthwith the representatives of Chiang Kai-shek from the place which they unlawfully occupy at the United Nations and in all the organizations related to it.

1967th plenary meeting

25 October 1971

Notes

1. *Available at* http://www.ait.org.tw/en/taiwan-relations-act.html.

2. *Available at* http://www.ait.org.tw/en/us-joint-communique-1972.html.

3. *Available at* http://www.ait.org.tw/en/us-joint-communique-1979.html.

4. *Available at* http://www.ait.org.tw/en/us-joint-communique-1982.html.

5. *Available at* http://www.taiwandocuments.org/assurances.htm.

6. SHIRLEY A. KAN, CHINA/TAIWAN: EVOLUTION OF THE "ONE CHINA POLICY"—KEY STATEMENTS FROM WASHINGTON, BEIJING, AND TAIPEI, CONGRESSIONAL RESEARCH SERVICE, at 46 (2014), *available at* http://www.fas.org/sgp/crs/row/RL30341.pdf.

7. *Available at* http://english.dpp.org.tw/1999-resolution-regarding-taiwans-future/.

8. SHIRLEY A. KAN, CHINA/TAIWAN: EVOLUTION OF THE "ONE CHINA POLICY"—KEY STATEMENTS FROM WASHINGTON, BEIJING, AND TAIPEI, CONGRESSIONAL RESEARCH SERVICE, at 79–80 (2014), *available at* http://www.fas.org/sgp/crs/row/RL30341.pdf.

9. *Available at* http://www.taiwandocuments.org/shimonoseki01.htm.

10. *Available at* http://avalon.law.yale.edu/wwii/cairo.asp.

11. *Available at* http://www.ndl.go.jp/constitution/e/etc/c06.html.

12. *Available at* https://treaties.un.org/doc/Publication/UNTS/Volume%20136/volume-136-I-1832-English.pdf.

13. UN Treaty Series, vol. 138, no. 1858, at 3, *available at* https://treaties.un.org/doc/Publication/UNTS/Volume%20136/volume-136-I-1832-English.pdf.

14. *Available at* http://avalon.law.yale.edu/20th_century/chin001.asp.

15. *Available at* http://daccess-dds-ny.un.org/doc/RESOLUTION/GEN/NR0/327/74/IMG/NR032774.pdf.

Index

Tables are indicated by "t" following the page numbers.